Peter S. Perry

The Rhetoric of Digressions

Revelation 7:1–17 and 10:1–11:13 and Ancient Communication

WIPF & STOCK · Eugene, Oregon

RHETORIC OF DIGRESSIONS
Revelation7:1–17 and 10:1—11:13 and Ancient Communication

Original work published by Mohr GmbH & Co. KG Tübingen, 2014. Published by permission.

Wipf & Stock
An imprint of Wipf and Stock Publishers
199 W. 8th Avenue, Suite 3
Eugene OR, 97401
www.wipfandstock.com

ISBN 13: 978-1-4982-0056-1

Manufactured in the U.S.A.

Preface

This monograph is a slightly revised version of my Ph.D. dissertation submitted to the faculty of the Lutheran School of Theology at Chicago in October 2008. The project began at Our Savior's Lutheran Church in Mesa, Arizona in 1999 when members of the congregation approached me with questions and concerns about the book of Revelation. I am grateful to the people of Our Savior's who attended the classes I taught and read the book of Revelation with me. They supported our decision to begin doctoral studies in 2004, and invited me back to perform the book of Revelation in January 2007.

I am deeply grateful to my advisor, Prof. Barbara Rossing, who read numerous drafts and gave substantive comments, and to my dissertation committee, Profs. Hans-Josef Klauck, Edgar Krentz, and David Rhoads. Profs. Craig Koester and Margaret Mitchell gave me incisive feedback at critical moments in formulating the dissertation proposal. After the dissertation colloquy, Prof. Klaus-Peter Adam helped me clarify the relationship of a rhetorical perspective with redaction history.

Writing a dissertation can be a socially, spiritually, and scholastically isolating experience. The dissertation writing group at the Lutheran School of Theology at Chicago helped me to overcome that isolation. Over the years, this group has included Bonnie Flessen, Jin Yang Kim, Stephen Kimondo, Stephen Knapp, May May Latt, Britt Leslie, Michael Macchia, Paul Moonu, Cheryl Pero, Josh Rice, Wiriya Tipvarakankoon, and Ji Woon Yoo. I am grateful that they discussed ideas, read drafts, made suggestions, and supported me as I researched and wrote.

My wife, Dana, and daughters, Ruth and Esther, have been my primary supporters and cheerleaders. This book would not have been written without their love and patience.

"Victory belongs to our God, the One Who is Sitting on the Throne, and to the Lamb!" (Rev 7:10).

Chicago, June 20, 2009 Peter S. Perry

Table of Contents

List of Tables

Introduction

Experiencing Rev 7:1–17 and 10:1–11:13

The thesis of this book is that first century audiences could identify Rev 7:1–17 and 10:1–11:13 with other experiences of παρέκβασις (digression) heard in contemporary speeches and literature and described by Greco-Roman rhetoricians. Revelation 7:1–17 interrupts the series of seven seals before the seventh seal is opened and Rev 10:1–11:13 interrupts the series of seven trumpets before the seventh trumpet is blown. As with other examples of παρέκβασις, these passages become more important for understanding the rhetorical goals and strategy of the whole book because they require additional effort to understand the connection with what precedes and follows, they develop the ethos of the author and audience, and they excite the emotions of the audience. These passages characterize John and the people of God in worship and witness. They evoke confidence in God's protection and promises in the midst of the fear of the seals and trumpets, like islands of mercy in a sea of destruction. Analyzing Rev 7:1–17 and 10:1–11:13 as digressions reveals how these passages are a critical part of the strategy to persuade an audience to witness even when it may result in death.

One approach to describe the experience of Rev 7 and 10–11 is to imagine an audience listening to Revelation read aloud. As the visions unfold, how do members of the audience relate each vision? What emotions do they feel?

The members of our imagined audience first hear the description of the glorified Jesus and his messages to seven assemblies in Asia Minor (Rev 1–3). They hear the description of the heavenly throne room, resplendent with glowing colors, fantastic living creatures, and white-robed elders (Rev 4). There is a scroll in God's hand that is sealed with seven seals. A Lamb takes the scroll and the cosmos erupt in praise. The living creatures, elders, angels, and creatures in heaven, earth, underworld, and sea are swept up in a wave of praise of God and the Lamb (Rev 5).

The audience hears how the Lamb breaks the seals one by one. Each seal seems to be a harbinger of suffering and death (Rev 6). After each of the first four seals is opened, a living creature calls out a rider who bears destruction to people on earth. After the Lamb breaks the fifth seal, the audience hears about the souls of people killed because they witnessed to the word of God. The sixth seal brings the most terrifying vision: the sky rolling up, the sun darkening, the moon turning red like blood, the stars falling like fruit on fig trees, and a great earthquake. The kings of the earth, the magnates and generals, the rich and powerful, everyone – even slave and freed persons – they all cry out and hide from God and the Lamb. The sixth seal climaxes with the question, *"Who is able to stand?"* (Rev 6:17). If everyone is hiding, who indeed is able to stand?

The audience knows that there are seven seals on the scroll. After each of the first six seals, a brief event was described. By that pattern, the seventh seal should be opened following the climactic question, "Who is able to stand?" The audience waits for that question to be answered, for fear to be relieved or realized by the seventh seal.

Instead of the expected seventh seal, the audience hears a new vision begin with the words "After this…." Four angels restrain destructive winds while another angel seals God's slaves, who are identified with 144,000 from the tribes of Israel (7:1–8). A second vision shows a great multitude around God's throne, dressed in white, praising God and the Lamb (7:9–17). One of the elders explains the vision to John. Finally, the Lamb opens the seventh seal, which is followed by a half-hour of silence in heaven (8:1).

How do members of our imagined audience experience the visions that interrupt progress towards the seventh seal? How do they relate the visions to the seals? What impact does this have on their experience of the whole book?

After the seventh seal, seven angels with seven trumpets are introduced (Rev 8). As each blows their trumpet, disaster strikes the world. The first four trumpets bring destruction to the earth, sea, waters, and sky. Then, an eagle announces that three woes are coming. The demonic locusts following the fifth trumpet are identified as the first woe. After the sixth trumpet, demonic cavalry kills one-third of humanity by plagues. This catastrophe climaxes with John's summary that "*the rest of humankind, who were not killed by these plagues, did not repent...*" (Rev 9:20).

The audience has to wait to experience the seventh trumpet. "Another mighty angel" makes an announcement and gives a scroll to John (Rev 10:1–11). Then, two witnesses are killed by the beast and left shamefully unburied on the street of a Great City before they are raised from the dead to ascend to heaven. A great earthquake punctuates their ascension, killing seven thousand people in the Great City while the rest give glory to God (11:1–13). These visions conclude with the announcement that the second woe has passed, which recalls the similar declaration following the fifth trumpet. Finally, the seventh trumpet is blown, announcing the Reign of the Lord.

How do members of the audience experience these visions before the seventh trumpet? How would they relate these visions to the trumpets? What connections would they make with the two visions in Rev 7? How would these experiences shape their interpretation of the book of Revelation?

These questions assume that 'audience' is the proper term for the recipients of the book of Revelation. The text can be read silently, of course, and in the age of iPods and multimedia, one can experience Revelation in a variety of ways. 'Audience' is not a generic term for recipients of the text but implies a particular reception scenario: a group of people in a specific time and place gathered to hear someone speak the text aloud. The audience has gathered, at least in part, to hear a letter from John.

Biblical scholars assume the author intended the book to be read aloud before an audience. For example, Adela Yarbro Collins concludes, "it is better to speak of the first 'hearers' of Revelation, rather than the 'readers.'"[1] This conclusion is in large part based upon the explicit blessing on reader and audience in Rev 1:3: "Blessed is the one who reads aloud the words of the prophecy, and blessed are those who hear and who keep what is written in it." The author, John, wrote Revelation to be read by another person to an audience and pronounced blessings on these participants in his work. Further, John expects audiences to keep what is written. The communication is meant to transform the audience, shaping their beliefs, attitudes, and actions.

The assumption of a listening audience is also based on the awareness that communication in the ancient world was dominated by speaking.[2]

---

[1] A. Y. Collins, *Crisis and Catharsis: The Power of the Apocalypse* (Philadelphia: Westminster, 1984), 144. Others who draw a similar conclusion include R. H. Charles, *The Revelation of St. John* (2 vols; ICC; Edinburgh: T & T Clark, 1920), 1:6; D. Barr, "The Apocalypse as Oral Enactment," *Interpretation* 40.2 (1984): 243–256; R. H. Mounce, *The Book of Revelation* (2nd Ed; Grand Rapids, Michigan: Eerdmans, 1998); D. Aune, *Revelation* (3 vols; WBC; Waco, Texas: Word, 1997–1998), 1:20–21; R. Bauckham, *Climax and Prophecy: Studies on the Book of Revelation* (London: T & T Clark, 1993), 1–2; S. Pattemore, *The People of God in the Apocalypse: Discourse, structure and exegesis* (Cambridge: Cambridge University, 2004), 53.

[2] This thesis is now commonplace, although its implications for Biblical studies are not. For a description of what "primarily oral cultures" means in the Greco-Roman world see the brief discussion in G. Kennedy, *The Art of Persuasion in Greece* (Princeton: Princeton University, 1963), 3–8; and more substantially E. A. Havelock, *The Muse Learns to Write: Reflections on Orality and Literacy from Antiquity to the Present* (New Haven, Conn.: Yale University Press, 1986). For specifically biblical texts, see H. Y. Gamble, *Books and Readers in the Early Church: A History of Early Christian Texts* (New Haven, Conn.: Yale University Press, 1995). W. Ong (*Orality and Literacy: The Technologizing of the Word* [London: Methuen, 1982]) and W. Kelber (*The Oral and the Written Gospel* [Philadelphia: Fortress, 1983]) have been very influential in emphasizing

Writers of letters, history, and prose recorded their words with ink and parchment so they could be read aloud. As one example, consider a book by Dionysius of Halicarnassus in the 1st c. BCE called περὶ συνθέσεως ὀνομάτων (often translated "On Literary Composition"). By such a title, one may think he will instruct readers on how to compose a pleasing essay, but his discussion of vowels and sounds is quite uninteresting and irrelevant for modern writing. He describes how to compose art with words, but his focus is on how the words sound not how they look on a page. For Dionysius, writing serves the spoken event that an audience experiences. Most modern readers experience Revelation individually while looking silently at characters on a page. For us to understand how the book of Revelation was originally received, we need a conceptual shift. Revelation can and should be conceived primarily as sound in oral communication, not as ink for silent readers.

'Experience' is the proper way to describe an audience's relationship with Revelation. 'Understanding' limits the audience to intellectual engagement with Revelation. Members of the audience not only think but also feel. They are moved by emotions evoked by hearing the visions read aloud. Even 'hearing' is insufficient because an audience looks at the reader and observes gestures, posture, and tone. 'Experience' best captures the full sensory experience and the full humanity of an audience that thinks and feels. "Experiencing Rev 7:1–17 and 10:1–11:13" therefore refers to how an audience hears, sees, and responds intellectually and emotionally to those passages while someone reads the whole book of Revelation aloud.

To understand the experience of Rev 7 and 10–11, one could assemble an audience to hear the book of Revelation read aloud. Even with a modern audience it would be an interesting and helpful conversation about how structure affects the experience of a performed text. Yet, this modern audience could never stand in for the original audiences that heard Revelation. In my social location, an audience would hear the work in English, in the twenty-first century, in the United States, within a particular faith community, within almost two thousand years of interpretation tradition, and within contemporary controversies over the use and meaning of the book of Revelation. This social location is important because it informs me and this book, but it does not help us understand how the first audiences heard

---

the features of oral cultures. Although there may be a tendency to dichotomize and oversimplify the relationship of writing to orality, their basic insight has withstood scrutiny: Mediterranean cultures in the first century were predominantly oral and this fact impacts the production and experience of texts. For nuance, especially see J. M. Foley, *How to Read an Oral Poem* (Urbana: University of Illinois, 2002) and J. Wise, *Dionysius Writes: The Invention of Theatre in Ancient Greece* (Ithaca: Cornell University, 1998).

Revelation in Greek, in the late 1st century, in western Asia Minor within the Roman Empire, within a faith emerging from Judaism in a Greco-Roman context, within the interpretations and controversies of that time and place. If we better understand how people in John's time communicated, we may better explain how the book of Revelation is structured and better answer the driving questions of this investigation: How would a first century audience experience Rev 7 and 10–11? How would this experience shape their understanding of the whole?

1. Methodology

Barring a visionary experience, the only way to access the first audiences of Revelation is to focus on the patterns of communication in the first century CE and reflected in the text. We can develop greater sensitivity to the communication dynamics of that time and place by immersing ourselves into (1) discussions of effective communication contemporary with Revelation (e.g. Greco-Roman rhetoricians), (2) other texts that audiences may have heard that reflect communication patterns and expectations and (3) the text of Revelation itself and its assumptions for communication. Since I am trying to understand how the first audiences of Revelation interpreted the arrangement of the visions, I am especially interested in theoretical discussions about effective arrangement and in texts that exhibit similar phenomena as observed in Revelation.

This methodology is based on the work of Margaret M. Mitchell, Bruce Longenecker, and Stephen Pattemore. I examine each of these scholars' methods in detail below and summarize their influence briefly here. Mitchell argues for a historical rhetorical criticism that interprets a text in light of contemporary Greco-Roman rhetorical handbooks and actual speeches. Longenecker's analysis of the chain-link transition, especially in Revelation, is consistent with Mitchell's method and provides a model for this investigation. Pattemore uses Relevance Theory to analyze the structure of Revelation. For the present investigation, Relevance Theory provides the conceptual framework that explains why Mitchell and Longenecker's method is appropriate for interpreting ancient texts. These three methods in different ways advocate the same principle: interpreting a text as communication within a particular context.[3] Each makes a specific contribution to this principle: Relevance Theory (as applied by Pattemore) provides the cognitive framework for understanding communication;

[3] For a recent introductory hermeneutics text founded on this principle, see J. K. Brown, *Scripture as Communication: Introducing Biblical Hermeneutics* (Grand Rapids, Mich.: Baker, 2007).

Mitchell points to specific resources relevant for 1st century Greco-Roman communication; Longenecker gives a specific example of identifying a structural feature in Revelation using Greco-Roman handbooks and contemporary speeches and literature.

a) Margaret M. Mitchell and Historical Rhetorical Criticism

When rhetorical critics were focusing almost exclusively on rhetorical handbooks or modern philosophy of rhetoric, Mitchell issued a call for immersion in ancient speeches to broaden and deepen analysis.[4] In *Paul and the Rhetoric of Reconciliation*, she lays out mandates for what she calls "historical rhetorical criticism."[5] These mandates can be summarized by two concerns. First, Mitchell is concerned that analysis should be situated in history, consulting actual speeches, handbooks, and texts from the same historical period. This concern rejects modern philosophical approaches to rhetoric, on one hand, and rejects a mechanistic approach of applying rhetorical handbooks without actual speeches on the other. Second, she argues that the focus of analysis should be identifying the genre of the text and demonstrating evidence for that genre in both form and content. Her concern for the coherence of genre with form and content arises out of too facile designations of a text as epideictic, deliberative, or forensic without showing that the topics and arrangement are consistent with other examples of the genre. Mitchell responds to these concerns by explicitly following in the tradition of Hans Dieter Betz (and his seminal study of Galatians) and drawing on a huge range of ancient speeches, handbooks and texts. She analyzes the conventions of invention and arrangement of argumentation in these texts and compares them to Biblical texts.

In her later reflections in the *Oxford Handbook of Biblical Studies*, she moderates the importance of identifying and rigorously demonstrating genre to focus on immersion in contemporary literature.[6] She more generally argues that the student of the Greek New Testament who is interested in historical rhetorical criticism should develop a sensibility about how people communicated in those times and places. Rather than emphasizing detection and demonstration of genre, she proposes a more flexible and dynamic understanding of historical rhetorical Criticism.

---

[4] M. M. Mitchell, *Paul and the Rhetoric of Reconciliation* (Louisville, Kentucky: Westminster/John Knox Press, 1991).

[5] Mitchell, *Paul,* 6–17.

[6] M. M. Mitchell, "Rhetorical and New Literary Criticism," in *Oxford Handbook of Biblical Studies* (eds. J. W. Rogerson and J. M. Lieu; Oxford: Oxford University, 2006), 615–33.

> Historical rhetorical criticism as I am defining it here (also Mitchell 1991: 6–17, which sketches five 'mandates' for such study) requires equal contextualization on both sides of the comparison; it is not just a procedure, but an awareness about ancient literary culture that one brings to the reading of any individual piece. It is an attempt to meet ancient *paideia* with modern *paideia*.[7]

Mitchell's primary insight is at the core of the methodology for this investigation. In order to understand ancient texts – and more generally, ancient communication – we should be engaged in education (*paideia*) that produces an awareness of ancient literary culture. We need to be immersed in ancient literature, speeches, and rhetorical handbooks.

Immersion in first-century communication builds on the work of many scholars who have interpreted the book of Revelation in light of Greco-Roman rhetoric.[8] A brief summary identifies some of the key contributors. Elisabeth Schüssler Fiorenza blazed the trail by analyzing the visionary rhetoric that John uses to construct a "symbolic universe" (1985, 1991).[9] This investigation builds on her insights into how the structure of Revelation furthers the Seer's rhetorical goals. Adela Yarbro Collins (1984) investigated how the Seer uses emotion, a crucial topic of this investigation. Her analysis depends largely on modern psychology with some reference to Aristotle's *Poetica* to show how the Seer encourages a perceived crisis and provides catharsis.[10] Using Aristotle's *Rhetorica*, John Kirby (1988) analyzed the ethos, pathos, genre, and rhetorical situation as expressed in Rev 1–3.[11] Robert Royalty (1997, 1998) described how the Seer uses the rhetoric of wealth and such figures as *ekphrasis* (vivid description) and

---

[7] Mitchell, "Rhetorical and New Literary Criticism," 623.

[8] For a fine summary of rhetorical criticism of Revelation from 1980 to 2005, see D. A. DeSilva, "What has Athens to Do with Patmos? Rhetorical Criticism of the Revelation of John (1980–2005)," *Currents in Biblical Research* 6.2 (2008): 256–289. A. K. W. Siew (*The War Between the Two Beasts and the Two Witnesses: A Chiastic Reading of Revelation 11.1–14.5* [London: T & T Clark, 2005], 279) suggests that Greco-Roman rhetorical categories are not suitable for study of Revelation. He argues that "Hebrew rhetorical devices" (e.g., p. 22) explain the structure. With Longenecker (discussed below), I will argue that some techniques (such as the chain-link transition and digressions) can be observed in both Hebrew and Greek literature, but theoretical discussions are in Greek.

[9] E. Schüssler Fiorenza, "The Followers of the Lamb: Visionary Rhetoric and Social-Political Situation," in *Discipleship in the New Testament* (ed. F. Segovia; Philadelphia: Fortress, 1985) republished in *The Book of Revelation: Justice and Judgment* (2nd ed; Minneapolis: Fortress, 1998), 181–204; *Revelation: Vision of a Just World* (Minneapolis: Fortress, 1991).

[10] A. Y. Collins, *Crisis and Catharsis: The Power of the Apocalypse* (Philadelphia: Westminster, 1984).

[11] J. T. Kirby, "The rhetorical situations of Revelation 1–3," *NTS* 34.2 (1988): 197–207.

synkrisis (comparison) to change the audience's perception of the world.[12] Barbara Rossing illustrated how Revelation draws on a common "Two Women" *topos* to present a choice between two cities.[13] Royalty and Rossing draw on both rhetorical handbooks and actual speeches consistent with Mitchell's method. David deSilva (1998, 2008) complements handbooks with the socio-rhetorical criticism pioneered by Vernon Robbins to discover John's persuasive strategies, especially with respect to honor discourse and the *topoi* of deliberative rhetoric.[14] Greg Carey (1999) augments ancient rhetorical theory with post-colonial theory to study John's construction of his ethos.[15] Paul Duff (2001) argues that John uses indirect accusation that is consistent with Quintilian's advice on how to malign opponents.[16] Konstantin Nikolakopoulos (2001) argues that John carefully uses rhetorical figures of speech and thought such as hyperbole, oxymoron, paradox, and rhetorical questions.[17] Each in their own way illuminates Revelation using Greco-Roman rhetorical conventions, although none of these scholars quite reach Mitchell's ideal of immersion in contemporary literature and none of them look to rhetorical conventions to explain the structure of Rev 7:1–17 and 10:1–11:13. Schüssler Fiorenza and Yarbro Collins offer specific contributions to understand Rev 7:1–17 and 10:1–11:13 that will be discussed in later chapters. Bruce Longenecker, dis-

---

[12] R. Royalty, "The rhetoric of Revelation," *Society of Biblical Literature Seminar Papers* 36 (1997): 596–617; *The Streets of Heaven: The Ideology of Wealth in the Apocalypse of John* (Macon, Ga.: Mercer University Press, 1998).

[13] B. R. Rossing, *The Choice Between Two Cities: Whore, Bride, and Empire in the Apocalypse* (Harrisburg, Pennsylvania: Trinity Press International, 1999).

[14] D. A. deSilva, "Honor Discourse and the Rhetorical Strategy of the Apocalypse of John," *JSNT* 71 (1998): 79–110; "The persuasive strategy of the Apocalypse: a socio-rhetorical investigation of Revelation 14:6–13," *Society of Biblical Literature Seminar Papers* 37.2 (1998): 785–806. Most recently, deSilva has been investigating logos and pathos in Rev 1–3. See "The Strategic Arousal of Emotions in the Apocalypse of John: A Rhetorical-Critical Investigation of the Oracles to the Seven Churches," *NTS* 54 (2008): 90–114; "Out of our Minds? Appeals to Reason (Logos) in the Seven Oracles of Revelation 2–3," *JSNT* 31.2 (2008): 123–155; and the helpful summary of scholarship, "What has Athens to Do with Patmos? Rhetorical Criticism of the Revelation of John (1980–2005)," *Currents in Biblical Research* 6.2 (2008): 256–289.

[15] G. Carey, *Elusive Apocalypse: Reading Authority in the Revelation to John* (Studies in American Biblical Hermeneutics 15; Macon, GA: Mercer University Press, 1999).

[16] P. B. Duff, *Who Rides the Beast? Prophetic Rivalry and the Rhetoric of Crisis in the Churches of the Apocalypse* (New York: Oxford, 2001).

[17] K. Nikolakopoulos, "Rhetorische Auslegungsaspekte der Theologie in der Johannesoffenbarung," in "*...Was ihr auf dem Weg verhandelt habt": Beiträge zur Exegese und Theologie des neuen Testaments: Festschrift für Ferdinand Hahn zum 75. Geburtstag* (eds. P. Müller, C. Gerber, T. Knöppler and P. Muller; Neukirchen-Vluyn: Neukirchener Verlag, 2001), 166–180.

cussed in detail below, provides the best example of an investigation into structure that is consistent with Mitchell's methodology.

b) Bruce Longenecker and Chain-Link Transitions

Although he does not explicitly follow Mitchell's method, Bruce Longenecker's analysis of the chain-link transition is congruent with historical rhetorical criticism as she proposes it.[18] His analysis is the primary model for this investigation. Similar to our quest to understand the structure of Revelation 7:1–17 and 10:1–11:13, he sought to explain the odd structure of Revelation 22:6–9 which seems to belong both to the previous vision of the New Jerusalem and at the same time to the concluding visions. To approach this problem, he triangulated (1) rhetorician's recommendations, (2) sources prior or contemporary to the New Testament, and (3) the New Testament texts.[19] Consistent with Mitchell's method, he analyzes a text in light of rhetorical conventions expressed in both handbooks and contemporary texts.

From a few brief passages in Quintilian and Lucian of Samosata, Longenecker identifies a technique he calls a "chain-link transition" that he discovers in the ancient literature, including the Hebrew Bible and the New Testament.[20] Lucian advises

> [T]hough all parts must be independently perfected, when the first is complete the second will be brought into essential connection with it, and *attached like one link of a chain to another* (ἁλύσεως τρόπον συνηρμοσμένον); there must be no possibility of separating them; no mere bundle of parallel threads; the first is not simply to be next to the second, but part of it, their extremities intermingling.[21]

If an orator wants to join units A and B together in way that gives it "continuity of motion and connection of style" (as Quintilian says), the orator will take the end of A and overlap it with the beginning of B, so that the

---

[18] B. Longenecker, *Rhetoric at the Boundaries: The Art and Theology of the New Testament Chain-Link Transitions* (Waco, Texas: Baylor University, 2005).

[19] Longenecker, 9.

[20] The chain-link transitions he finds include Plutarch's *Quomodo adul. (How to Tell a Flatterer from a Friend, Moralia* 51D–55E and 66E); Philo of Alexandria, *De Vita Mosis* 1.334–2.1; Josephus, *Contra Apionem* 1.320–2.2; 4 Ezra 5:14–22; 6:30–35; 13:56–14:1; Isaiah 48:16b–22; 53:2b–6; John 12:20–50; 1 Cor 8:7–8; Rom 7:25; 10:16–17; 12:15–16; 13:13–14.

[21] Lucian, *Hist. conscr.* 55: ἀπόλυτα γὰρ καὶ ἐντελῆ πάντα ποιήσει, καὶ τὸ πρῶτον ἐξεργασάμενος ἐπάξει τὸ δεύτερον ἐχόμενον αὐτοῦ καὶ ἁλύσεως τρόπον συνηρμοσμένον ὡς μὴ διακεκόφθαι μηδὲ διηγήσεις πολλὰς εἶναι ἀλλήλαις παρακειμένας, ἀλλ᾽ ἀεὶ τῷ πρώτῳ τὸ δεύτερον μὴ γειτνιᾶν μόνον, ἀλλὰ καὶ κοινωνεῖν καὶ ἀνακεκρᾶσθαι κατὰ τὰ ἄκρα. Translation from Longenecker, 12. My emphasis.

final structure is A-b-a-B.[22] This technique for transitioning between two units makes sense when heard, but looks out of place to the modern eye.[23] By better understanding this technique, Longenecker argues, we can better understand how a first century audience heard the text.

For example, Rev 22:6–9 has long stymied interpreters.[24]

22:6a And he said to me, "These words are trustworthy and true,
22:6b for the Lord, the God of the spirits of the prophets, has sent his angel to show his servants what must soon take place."
22:7a "See, I am coming soon!
22:7b Blessed is the one who keeps the words of the prophecy of this book."
22:8 I, John, am the one who heard and saw these things. And when I heard and saw them, I fell down to worship at the feet of the angel who showed them to me;
22:9 but he said to me, "You must not do that! I am a fellow servant with you and your comrades the prophets, and with those who keep the words of this book. Worship God!"

Rev 22:6a is almost a word-for-word repetition of Rev 19:9, and Rev 22:8–9 a repetition of Rev 19:10. This repetition closes the vision of Rev 21:9–22:9, mirroring the function of Rev 19:9–10 for 17:1–19:10.[25] On the other hand, Rev 22:6b–7 repeats wording from Rev 1:1–3 and anticipates 22:10–21. By recalling the opening words, Rev 22:6b–7 initiates the conclusion of the book. Longenecker writes, "22:6–9 seems to have been constructed in a back-and-forth manner, with 22:6–7 largely introducing later material, and 22:8–9 largely concluding earlier material."[26] The structure of these units is

A (21:9–22:5/9) - b (22:6–7a) - a (22:7b–9) - B (22:6/10–21).

He concludes that this is a chain-link construction described by Quintilian and Lucian. Longenecker finds four cases of the chain-link transitions in

---

[22] Longenecker, 18–20. Quintilian, *Inst.* IX.4.129: "a certain continuity of motion and connection of style. All its members are to be closely linked together, while the fluidity of its style gives it great variety of movement; we may compare its motion to that of people who link hands to steady their steps, and lend each other mutual support." (Historia non tam finitos numeros quam orbem quendam contextumque desiderat. Namque omnia eius membra connexa sunt et, quoniam lubrica est, hac atque illac fluit, ut homines, qui manibus invicem apprehensis gradum firmant, continent et continentur. Translation from Longenecker, 13.)

[23] Longenecker, 51.

[24] Longenecker, 106, categorizes scholars as follows: Some suggest that 19:10 is an redactional insertion duplicating 22:8–9 (e.g. Charles) while others suggest 22:8–9 duplicates 19:10 (e.g. Kraft, Aune). See discussion about the complexity of these verses in Bauckham, *Climax of Prophecy*, 18–21.

[25] Longenecker, 105.

[26] Longenecker, 108.

Revelation (3:21–22; 8:2–5; 15:1–4; 22:6–9), each of which occurs at a major division of the text.[27]

Longenecker's work is significant for the present study of Rev 7:1–17 and 10:1–11:13 because it illustrates Mitchell's method and illuminates a structural technique described by rhetoricians and used in a variety of contemporary literature. Longenecker makes the case that these four transitions are "calculated" expressions of the chain-link technique, demonstrating that the Seer deployed a convention of speech described by Greco-Roman rhetoricians and used by various orators and authors.[28] He does not claim that the Seer studied rhetorical handbooks, but that this convention was freely accessible, even expressed in the Hebrew Bible.[29] The working assumption for the present investigation is that conventions found in Greco-Roman handbooks and speeches may explain the structure of Rev 7:1–17 and 10:1–11:13 within the series of seals and trumpets. Longenecker only had scant passages from Quintilian and Lucian to interpret the chain-link technique, but there is abundant theoretical reflection and practical use of digressions in speeches and literature. In chapter 4, I provide examples in both Greek and Hebrew sources that demonstrate widespread use and familiarity with digressions.

The distinction between 'articulated' and 'unarticulated' rhetorical techniques is another of Longenecker's contributions to the present investigation.[30] An articulated chain-link explicitly identifies that a transition is being made, while an unarticulated one does not. He gives examples of articulated transitions in Josephus.[31] This distinction explains why this technique has not been detected in the New Testament before now. Longenecker explains, "most of the examples of chain-link construction in the New Testament are precisely of this unarticulated kind."[32] I also apply this distinction to digressions and discover that while Josephus uses some articulated digressions, those in the New Testament are unarticulated.

---

[27] Longenecker, 112–116.

[28] Longenecker, 103. Consider Nikolakopoulos' similar conclusion with respect to figures of thought: "Die Untersuchung der Rhetorik hat jedoch gezeigt, dass die Anwendung rhetorischer Gedankenfiguren nicht zufällig, sondern bewusst mit (bedeutendem) inhaltlichem Sinn und Zweck erfolgt." (The investigation of the rhetoric showed that the application of rhetorical figures of thought does not take place coincidentally, but consciously with (important) sense and purpose in respect to content. "Rhetorische Auslegungsaspekte," 179.)

[29] Longenecker, 69–79, identifies Isaiah 48:16b–22, 53:2b–6 and Daniel 7 as chain-link transitions in the Hebrew Bible.

[30] Longenecker, 45.

[31] *Contra Apionem* 1.320 and 2.1–2. Longenecker, 65–66.

[32] Longenecker, 46.

Longenecker goes beyond identifying this structural technique to reflect on its theological implications. Structure impacts meaning; he shows how the chain-link affects the meaning of the text. He argues that the use of chain-link transitions in Revelation simultaneously demarcates and unites the units, hybridizes the epistolary and apocalyptic genres, and democratizes the visions. By use of chain-link construction in Rev 8:2–5, the seven seals "hands off" the narrative to the seven trumpets. John creates an epistolary-apocalyptic hybrid by fusing the epistolary framework and apocalyptic visions with chain-links in Rev 3:21–22 and 22:6–9. This new hybrid democratizes the visions, revealing them to both the worthy and unworthy, a break from other Jewish apocalyptic (e.g. 4 Ezra) directed only to a select group. Longenecker draws this conclusion from the Seer's use of the chain-link technique:

> By means of chain-link interlock, the author not only links apocalyptic and epistolary genres together, but does so precisely in order that the visionary scenarios of suprahuman phenomena might be seen as relevant to the ordinary lives of those who would seek to follow the Lamb.[33]

In summary, Longenecker helps us to identify a transition technique described by Greco-Roman rhetoricians and used in contemporary literature. He provides the terminology of 'articulated' and 'unarticulated.' He explores its impact on the meaning of a text. In these ways, his analysis provides a model that I employ for identifying and understanding the structural features observed in Rev 7:1–17 and 10:1–11:13.

c) Stephen Pattemore and Relevance Theory

Stephen Pattemore's use of Relevance Theory is a third contributor to the methodology of this investigation.[34] Developed from the linguistic study of pragmatics by Dan Sperber and Deirdre Wilson, Relevance Theory is a theory of communication that, in part, provides a framework for explaining how people understand utterances and decide between things that are more or less relevant in a particular context.[35] Since an audience cannot explore every possible implication of an utterance, they must go through some kind of process of limiting and selecting relevant implications. This cognitive

---

[33] Longenecker, 119; cf. 7–8.

[34] S. Pattemore, *Souls under the Altar: Relevance Theory and the Discourse Structure of Revelation* (New York: United Bible Societies, 2003); *The People of God in the Apocalypse: Discourse, structure and exegesis* (Cambridge: Cambridge University, 2004).

[35] D. Sperber and D. Wilson, *Relevance: Communication and Cognition* (2nd ed; Oxford: Blackwell, 1995), 193–202. Pattemore (*People of God*, 11) proposes that Relevance Theory provides "a discriminatory hermeneutic criterion by which to evaluate the significance of proposed background information for the understanding of the text."

process is the chief insight of Relevance Theory: that an audience will choose the most meaningful connections to their environment that requires the least amount of effort. In the technical sense, the *relevance* of a particular expression or communication is based on these two factors, contextual effects and processing effort. *Contextual effects* are those meaningful connections with their environment, which include negating, strengthening, extending, or enriching existing assumptions.[36] *Processing effort* refers to the mental energy needed to bring about these contextual effects.[37] The previous paragraph is a good example of this trade-off. I have italicized technical terms in order to minimize the reader's effort to recognize them as technical words and to maximize the strength of the reader's assumptions about these terms.

The concept of *manifestness* is critical to understanding how speaker and audience relate, especially what modern interpreters can conclude about an audience's experience of an ancient text. A fact is *manifest* to an individual if that person can mentally represent it at a given time and accept that representation as true or probably true.[38] Fact is too strong a word, because Sperber and Wilson extend 'fact' to include all perceptions and awareness including assumptions and falsehoods that a person believes to be true.[39] That person's *cognitive environment* is the set of facts that are manifest at a given time. The set of facts that are manifest to both speaker and audience is called the *mutual cognitive environment*. This does not necessarily mean that they at all times and places do share this set, but that in a given time they are capable of sharing a set of facts.[40] This concept assists our analysis of how an audience understands an ancient text because it is extremely difficult (if not impossible) to demonstrate that a specific audience interpreted a text in a specific way. Using Relevance Theory, it is sufficient to present evidence that at that general time and place audiences were capable of understanding it in a specific way. I will show that the technique of digression (discussed under the technical term παρέκβασις) was a part of the *mutual cognitive environment*; therefore audiences *could* experience it in relationship to other experiences of digression.

[36] Sperber and Wilson, 108–9, define *contextual effects* as the contextualization of the union of old information and new information. For example, "new information may provide further evidence for, and therefore strengthen old assumptions; or it may provide evidence against, and perhaps lead to the abandonment of, old assumptions." Cf. Pattemore, *People of God*, 16.

[37] Sperber and Wilson, 124.

[38] Sperber and Wilson, *Relevance*, 39; Pattemore, *People of God*, 15.

[39] Sperber and Wilson, 39.

[40] Sperber and Wilson, 41.

In Relevance Theory, *communication* is therefore "the attempt to change the cognitive environment of another person, and thus enlarge the scope of what is mutually manifest to both communicator and audience."[41] Based on the mutually manifest cognitive environment, a communicator produces the stimulus that leads the audience to his or her intended meaning.[42] In these terms, John writes the book of Revelation in order to modify his audiences' cognitive environment, i.e. to transform their lives by transforming what they know to be true about God, the world, and themselves.

When someone exhibits behavior that makes it clear they want to communicate, Sperber and Wilson call this *ostensive*.[43] Clearing one's throat, for example, can be a signal that a person wants to communicate. This *ostensive* behavior therefore lays the foundation for successful communication because it suggests that the communication is worth the hearer's attention and effort. In terms of a written text, Relevance Theory assumes that the author intended optimal relevance and left clues that a reader can detect.[44] For the book of Revelation, the author is ostensive when he writes, "Blessed is the one who reads aloud the words of the prophecy, and blessed are those who hear and who keep what is written in it…" (1:3). The Seer believes that the audience can understand and keep what is communicated in this book, and pronounces a blessing on those who expend the energy to do so. With respect to this investigation, I am interested in discovering the possible *contextual effects* of the digressions between the sixth and seventh seals and trumpets that makes the increased *processing effort* worthwhile for the audience in a first century Asia Minor *cognitive environment*. In other words, how do the digressions maximize *relevance*?

This framework for understanding communication is congruent with Mitchell's proposal and Longenecker's implementation, although neither are using Relevance Theory. Both Mitchell and Longenecker implicitly assume that the author of a text uses techniques that are intelligible to the audience under optimal circumstances. Longenecker specifically asserts that the Seer intentionally uses the chain-link transition in Rev 22:6–9 saying, "it has been intentionally and extensively calculated and executed."[45]

---

[41] Pattemore, *People of God*, 15; cf. Sperber and Wilson, 61.

[42] Pattemore, *People of God*, 17.

[43] Sperber and Wilson, 49; Pattemore, *People of God*, 16.

[44] See the discussion of applying Relevance Theory to texts in Pattemore, *People of God*, 22–46, and his response to critics.

[45] Longenecker, 103. Pattemore (*People of God*, 22–23) addresses the "intentional fallacy" by arguing that it does not apply to Relevance Theory, since relevance theory does not consider intentions before the communication, but examines how communication indicates a mutual cognitive environment. For example, allusions to Daniel, Zechariah, and Exodus within the first eight verses of Revelation indicate that the Seer assumes they are a part of the set of "facts" shared by author and audience for optimal relevance. By

This calculation is based on the assumption that the chain-link transition will lead the audience to the intended meaning, i.e. that the chain-link transition is a part of the *mutual cognitive environment*. Relevance Theory provides the cognitive rationale for the assumption that the Seer used this technique expecting his audience to understand that it smoothly joins and fuses units together. Using a similar line of thought, I argue that digressions were a part of the mutual cognitive environment of the Seer and audiences in Asia Minor in the first century CE.

Greg Carey offers three criticisms of Pattemore's application of Relevance Theory.[46] First, he suggests that Pattemore emphasizes cognition over affect and, second, collaborative over conflicted communication. Last, he wonders if the same results could be reached without Relevance Theory. The first two objections are valid in part because neither Sperber and Wilson nor Pattemore discuss emotion or conflict but subsume these under the category of *cognitive environment*.[47] The emotional state of a hearer is one piece of the hearer's cognitive environment, which may be *manifest* if the hearer can represent it as true. It is *mutually manifest* if both speaker and hearer can represent it. The same is true of conflict.[48] Emotion or conflict may be features of the cognitive environment that the speaker is

---

alluding to these texts, he signals them as a part of the cognitive environment in which hearers should search for relevance. The hearer is then left to deduce the particular contextual effect. Hearers who do not have access to these texts, or have to expend too much processing effort to access them, will not reach optimal relevance.

[46] G. Carey, "The People of God in the Apocalypse (Review)," *Catholic Biblical Quarterly* 67.4 (Oct 2005): 722–3. For other responses to critics of Relevance Theory (esp. E. Wendland), see Pattemore, *People of God*, 35–36.

[47] E.g. Sperber and Wilson, 153: "A stimulus is a phenomena designed to achieve cognitive effects....Someone who wants to achieve a specific cognitive effect must therefore try to produce a stimulus which, when optimally processed, will achieve just the intended effect. This effect may be achieved at either the attentive or the sub-attentive level. When a child wants her parents to feel sorry for her, the best course might be to cry in a manifestly sincere way: the parents' attention will be pre-empted, and the most relevant assumption will be that the child is distressed." On emotion and conflict as parts of the cognitive environment, see *inter alia* elsewhere in *Relevance*.

[48] Carey may be reacting to the word "collaborative" to describe the communication, but in Relevance Theory this does not mean the absence of conflict or that a hearer cannot reject the speaker's inferences. As far as I can tell, Pattemore and Sperber and Wilson do not use "collaborative," but do modify Grice's "co-operative principle." They understand that conflict between speaker and hearer may mean that stimuli are not optimally processed, and misunderstanding is a result. The point, however, is that ostensive communication requires the audience's attention and will attempt to maximize relevance. For example, see Sperber and Wilson, 155: "Someone who asks you to behave in a certain way, either physically or cognitively, suggests that he has good reason to think it might be in your own interests, as well as his, to comply with his request. This suggestion may be ill founded or made in bad faith, but it cannot be wholly cancelled."

trying to change. (Recall that *communication* is the attempt to change the cognitive environment of another.) In this way, Relevance Theory more robustly incorporates both the fact and the awareness of emotion or conflict in the communication situation, and understands that the speaker may be communicating in order to alter the emotion or conflict. In this study, I address emotion explicitly because of its importance to digressions specifically and to rhetoric in general.

Carey also critiques Pattemore's application of Relevance Theory, suggesting that the same results can be reached by traditional methodologies. As discussed below, the payoff for Pattemore is a theoretical framework for deciding which allusions and sources are most relevant for understanding the text. Carey correctly notes that other scholars have reached similar conclusions about allusions; however, Relevance Theory offers a foundation for these conclusions based on a fully developed, cross-disciplinary communication theory. Conceiving biblical texts as communication in a specific context requires some kind of theory about how human beings communicate. Rather than accepting vague definitions of terms like "communication" and "context," Relevance Theory provides definitions for our analysis of a text grounded in a comprehensive cognitive framework.

More specifically in relationship to this project, the concepts of Relevance Theory help to explain why later interpreters may misinterpret structural techniques like the digression and the chain-link transition. To someone familiar with hearing chain-link transitions (i.e. part of their cognitive environment), the technique will be familiar and produce significant contextual effects. To someone reading the text and unfamiliar with its use, it may be awkward and lead to misunderstanding. The Seer uses this device because he assumes it will have significant effect on his audiences. I will show that digressions were commonly used in the first century and would be a part of many audiences' cognitive environments, but as composition became more mechanical and amplification took over many of the functions of digressions, the technique was no longer a part of audiences' cognitive environments.[49] As a result, I argue, Revelation 7:1–17 and 10:1–11:13 have been labeled with a wide variety of terms in order to explain the arrangement of visions.

Pattemore's application of Relevance Theory also provides a process for analyzing units of text. Similar to Hellholm and E. Müller's application of text linguistics and discourse analysis to Revelation, Pattemore breaks

---

[49] On the changing role of amplification see M. Poser, *Der abschweifende Erzähler: Rhetorische Tradition und deutscher Roman im achtzehnten Jahrhundert* (Berlin: Verlag Gehlen, 1969). Unarticulated chain-link transitions and unarticulated digressions seem especially prone to misinterpretation.

down the text into its smallest expressions and analyzes how these expressions are constructed.[50] He delimits units by words and phrases (such as μετὰ ταῦτα, καὶ ἰδού, etc.), personal references, change in communication axis, *dramatis personae*, spatial signals, or temporal signals. Then these units are examined to determine which environments are activated. As described above, *cognitive environment* is a broader and more specific term than simply 'context' because it includes the social and existential situation of the hearers (situational context), textually defined environments (intertext),[51] and the progressive processing of the text itself (co-text). On the last point, Relevance Theory emphasizes the need to study a text linearly just as the audience experiences it in a linear fashion.[52] Each utterance adds sequentially to the mutual cognitive environment, so that the audience refers back to previous utterances as potentially the most relevant. After determining what cognitive environments may have been triggered in the search for optimal relevance, the interpreter prioritizes which environments yield the most positive contextual effects (meaningful connections to the audience's environment) for the least amount of processing effort.[53]

The main payoff for using Relevance Theory is a framework for deciding which elements of a cognitive environment are most relevant. For example, Pattemore excludes Ezekiel 9 (an angel makes a mark on people in Jerusalem to protect them from destruction) as a necessary cognitive environment for understanding the sealing in Rev 7 because it would "require significant processing effort, computing differences in general tenor, in circumstances, and in detail, before John's audience could extract positive cognitive effects."[54] In contrast, the description of the two witnesses as "two olive trees and two lampstands" (Rev 11:4) is not optimally relevant unless the audience recognizes the allusion to Zechariah 4 which describes

[50] D. Hellholm, "The Problem of Apocalyptic Genre and the Apocalypse of John," *Semeia* 36 (1986): 13–64; E. Müller, *A Microstructural Analysis of Revelation 4–11* (Berrien Springs, Michigan: Andrews University Press, 1996).

[51] Pattemore, *People of God*, 39.

[52] Pattemore, *People of God*, 49. This does not rule out non-linear study of the text, but the initial and most common experience of the text is a sequential hearing. Bauckham, *Climax of Prophecy*, 2, makes a key distinction between three ways of experiencing the text: oral performance, attentive rereading and study, and assiduous study. Cf. E. F. Lupieri, *A Commentary on the Apocalypse of John* (trans. M. P. Johnson and A. Kamesar; Grand Rapids, Mich.: Eerdmans, 2006), 99–100.

[53] Pattemore, *Souls under the Altar*, 28. This is not to say that Relevance Theory assumes "easy listening." Co-text and contextual markers may indicate that a meaning obtained through minimum processing is not adequate, and that hearers must expend additional effort to obtain optimal relevance. See Pattemore, *People of God*, 26, 36 (responding to Wendland's critique of Relevance Theory).

[54] Pattemore, *People of God*, 131.

the high priest Joshua and the governor Zerubbabel in a similar way. If the audience makes the connection, they will receive the significant effect of being identified with the roles of priest and king, secure in God's presence.[55] Relevance Theory provides a cognitive framework for making decisions about allusions, sources, and their significance for understanding a text.

In addition to the application of Relevance Theory, Pattemore sharpens and confirms previous conclusions about ecclesiology in Revelation. He uses the phrase "the People of God" to refer to the addressees of the book (esp. in the epistolary framework, Rev 1:1–11; 22:10–21), the actual audience hearing the book recited (e.g. Rev 13:9 "Let anyone who has an ear listen"), and actors in the book.[56] Some are indirectly referenced in narration or discourse (e.g. their prayers offered as incense, Rev 5:8; 8:3). Other times they are in the chorus, singing with all creation (5:13) or a great crowd (19:1, 6). Finally, they sometimes are on center stage. In Rev 7:1–8, the People of God are referred to in the speeches about sealing the slaves of God and the 144,000. In Rev 7:9–17, the great multitude and John are both on center stage. In Rev 10:1–11, John again is an actor in his visions while the Two Witnesses are the focus of 11:3–13. Throughout this project, I will also use 'the people of God' in the general sense that overlaps author, audience, addressees, and actors.

Pattemore concludes that Rev 7:1–17 and 10:1–11:13 are essential to constructing the messianic and martyr ecclesiology for the people of God.[57] This conclusion is not new or unique to Pattemore,[58] but he underlines the point. The Seer communicates through Rev 7 that "in their identity and in their lives and actions the people of God are a messianic people, inseparable from their Messiah."[59] The analysis of Rev 10:1–11:13 in the present investigation further confirms Pattemore's conclusion that the Seer is trying to communicate through these units that "[f]aithful, uncompromising witness results in persecution and martyrdom for the people of God in the pattern of their Lord, but also leads to their resurrection and redemp-

---

[55] Pattemore, *People of God*, 162.

[56] Pattemore, *People of God*, 64–67.

[57] Pattemore, *People of God*, 125–159; 160–164.

[58] For example, see P. Minear, *I Saw a New Earth: An Introduction to the Visions of the Apocalypse* (Washington: Corpus, 1968), 74–76, 95; A. Y. Collins, *Crisis and Catharsis*, esp. 127, 153; R. Bauckham, *The Theology of the Book of Revelation* (Cambridge: Cambridge University, 1993), 76–88; B. K. Blount, *Can I Get A Witness: Reading Revelation through African American Culture* (Louisville, KY: Westminster, 2005), 55.

[59] Pattemore, *People of God*, 159.

tion for the world."[60] Rev 7:1–17 and 10:1–11:13 are essential to this message, but paradoxically the units can be omitted without any loss of narrative logic by skipping directly to the seventh seal or seventh trumpet. I investigate how this paradox (simultaneously essential and non-essential) may be explained.

Two problems in Pattemore's analysis illustrate the need for the present investigation. First, it is not clear what Pattemore's terms for Rev 7:1–17 and 10:1–11:13 mean in Relevance Theory. He calls Revelation 7 a 'hinge' because it juxtaposes two structures: the seven seals following each other in close parallel structure yet beginning a new structure at 7:9.[61] In his view, Rev 10:1–11:13 is not a hinge but a 'major interlude.'[62] (I will discuss these terms and others in chapter 1.) What kind of cognitive environment does it presume? What processing effort is required of an interlude? What are its possible contextual effects? These questions expose the need for appropriate terminology in first century Asia Minor cognitive environments.

The second problem is that the local cognitive environments of Asia Minor and the larger context of the Greco-Roman world play only a minor role in Pattemore's analysis.[63] This may simply reflect that optimal relevance is reached without accessing non-canonical texts or the general cognitive environment. This, however, is surprising given the level of tension (real or projected) between Christians and the larger culture, local and imperial. The text, after all, was read in Greek in first-century Asia Minor, in some of the largest cities in the Roman Empire. Pattemore should consider more extra-textual information from the local cognitive environment.

Consideration of the wider environment is the strength of augmenting Pattemore's analysis with Mitchell's historical rhetorical criticism and Longenecker's specific application. All three interpret the text as communication within a specific environment. Mitchell insists that interpreters immerse themselves in rhetorical handbooks and speeches of the time in order to understand the invention and arrangement of a text. Longenecker

[60] Pattemore, *People of God*, 164. These conclusions have been recognized generally for the book of Revelation for some time, see for example Schüssler Fiorenza, *Justice and Judgment*, 24: "Christians are the representatives of God's and Christ's eschatological power on earth and, at the same time, are still subject to the political powers of their time. Those rejecting the beast and its cult are excluded from the economic and social life of their time and have to expect captivity and death (13:10–15)."

[61] Pattemore, *Souls under the Altar*, 128–130.

[62] Pattemore, *Souls*, 140. In addition, he describes Rev 12:10–12 as an 'interlude' (*People of God*, 95).

[63] Pattemore explicitly acknowledges the Greco-Roman context in *People of God*, 57–58, but does not find that many local details are necessary to explain the structure of Revelation.

discerns the chain-link transition as a contemporary rhetorical device that the Seer uses to fuse the epistolary and apocalyptic genres and to 'democratize' visions to the unworthy as well as the worthy. In Relevance Theory terms, Mitchell is arguing that these texts illuminate the general cognitive environment. Longenecker's description of the chain-link shows that it is accessible and yields significant contextual effects.

2. The Cognitive Environment of the Seven Assemblies in Asia

Relevance Theory defines the *cognitive environment* as the set of facts (including assumptions) that a person can mentally represent as true or probably true at a given time. 'Cognitive environment' includes the broader social situation, the specific communication situation, the intertextual context, and the sequential experience of the text itself. The text is our most accessible entry into the cognitive environment of the author and audience, although it is only one facet. In order to be relevant (that is, maximize effect and minimize processing effort), the communicator must interact with the audience's broader environment. The modern interpreter of a text, therefore, needs to reconstruct a general cognitive environment from which ancient audiences could draw inferences. Yet, any reconstruction is limited by the fact that the interpreter only has insight into the cognitive environment as it is implicitly or explicitly signaled by the text.[64]

Scholars have written many books and articles discerning the social setting of Revelation, more than can be summarized here.[65] I adopt the modest assumptions used by Pattemore, augmented by Steven Friesen's analysis of the different social settings of the seven assemblies and by a discussion of persecution and deception.

---

[64] I am not arguing that Revelation should be taken as an objective or accurate description of Christian communities in the seven cities. Relevance Theory mitigates any claims to objectivity by focusing on the assumptions that the communicator holds to be true and his efforts to change the audience's assumptions.

[65] For example, W. M. Ramsay, *The Letters to the Seven Churches and their place in the plan of the Apocalypse* (ed. M. W. Wilson; Peabody, Mass.: Hendrickson, 1994 [1904]); C. J. Hemer, *The Letters to the Seven Churches of Asia in their Local Settings* (JSNTsup 11; Sheffield: JSOT, 1986); L. L. Thompson, *The Book of Revelation: Apocalypse and Empire* (New York: Oxford University Press, 1990); J. N. Kraybill, *Imperial Cult and Commerce in John's Apocalypse* (JSNTss 132; Sheffield: Sheffield Academic, 1996); S. J. Friesen, *Twice Neokoros: Ephesus, Asia and the Cult of the Flavian Imperial Family* (Leiden: Brill, 1993); *Imperial Cults and the Apocalypse of John* (New York: Oxford, 2001); P. R. Trebilco, *Jewish Communities in Asia Minor* (New York: Cambridge, 1991); *The Early Christians in Ephesus from Paul to Ignatius* (Tübingen: Mohr Siebeck, 2004).

Pattemore summarizes the cognitive environment of Revelation with a concise paragraph:

> The book of Revelation is the record of a communication from a prominent individual, John, intended to be read aloud to gatherings of mixed Jewish-Gentile Christian communities in Asia Minor in the last decade of the first century AD. The beliefs and loyalties of these communities brought them into conflict, both potential and real, with other religious and governmental groups.[66]

Some scholars may want to say more about John's identity, but it is sufficient to conclude he is unknown to us but known to his audiences.[67] With Pattemore and others, I conclude John is composing the final form late in the reign of Domitian, although some dispute the date of authorship.[68] Others may disagree about the extent of real or perceived conflict with the Roman Empire, but I argue below that John makes the most of Antipas' death in Pergamum and subtle social and economic pressure on Christians.[69] Despite these disagreements, many scholars would agree that Pattemore's paragraph is an uncontroversial summary of John's social situation.[70] For this investigation, the general date and location are significant for identifying contemporary literature. The most relevant sources will be those that are accessible in late first century Asia Minor, especially by Greek-speaking Jews and Gentiles living in the large cities of the time.

I also adopt Steven Friesen's conclusion that John is not addressing one rhetorical situation but many. Both internal and external pressures are at

---

[66] Pattemore, *People of God*, 51–52. I have left out Pattemore's last sentence, "[t]he book was positively received and accorded a status which led to its preservation and eventual inclusion in the canon of the NT," because it glosses over Revelation's complex reception.

[67] Kirby, 199; Aune, *Revelation* 1:xlvii–lvi; Trebilco, *Early Christians in Ephesus*, 295. S. S. Smalley (*The Revelation to John* [Downers Grove, Illinois: InterVarsity Press, 2005]) holds a traditional position that John is the Son of Zebedee.

[68] Most recently Smalley argues for Nero's reign, van Kooten for Otho/Vitellius', Witulski for Hadrian's. G. H. van Kooten, "The Year of the Four Emperors and the Revelation of John: The 'pro-Neronian' Emperors Otho and Vitellius and the images and colossus of Nero in Rome," *JSNT* 30.2 (2007): 205–248. T. Witulski, *Die Johannesoffenbarung und Kaiser Hadrian: Studien zur Datierung der neutestamentlichen Apokalypse* (Göttingen: Vandenhoeck & Ruprecht, 2007).

[69] E.g. Yarbro Collins argues for perceived conflict, van Kooten for real Roman persecution. For a summary of arguments about conflict, see P. Duff, *Who Rides the Beast? Prophetic Rivalry and the Rhetoric of Crisis in the Churches of the Apocalypse* (New York: Oxford, 2001), 3–14.

[70] See a similar summary by M. E. Boring, *Revelation* (Louisville: John Knox Press, 1989), 1; cf. G. Caird, *The Revelation of St. John the Divine* (New York: Harper & Row, 1966), 1–7.

play in differing degrees, and Friesen argues that we cannot assume one set of problems.[71]

> I argue that Revelation had several social settings, not one; that these settings were characterized by distinct problems having mostly to do with relations to outsiders; that the assemblies agreed with John about abstention from imperial cults; and that John used their agreement about imperial cults as a rhetorical tool in order to link their settings together within the framework of the rejection of mainstream Roman imperial society.[72]

Friesen concludes that John links issues specific to each assembly into a broader analysis of religion, economy, and imperialism. Both John and his audiences agreed that emperor worship was idolatrous. Some disagreed (especially other Christian prophets) about topics such as eating sacrificial meat, imperial commerce, and whether or not the Roman Empire intends violence towards Christians.[73] Friesen argues that by linking these local issues with emperor worship, John creates a broad critique of imperial society. John urges his audience to disassociate from the Empire and from Christian leaders who encourage integration and accommodation.

Friesen's last point about the Empire's violent intentions is the most salient to the investigation of Rev 7 and 10–11. In Rev 7:14, the elder tells John that the great crowd is coming "out of the great persecution" (ἐκ τῆς θλίψεως τῆς μεγάλης) and washing their clothes in the blood of the Lamb. In Rev 11:7, the beast from the abyss kills the two witnesses. John sees violent persecution of Christians in their future.

Recent scholarship has shown that there may have been sporadic and localized but not systematic persecution of Christians by the Roman Empire during Domitian's reign.[74] Pliny's correspondence with Trajan (*Ep.*

---

[71] S. J. Friesen, "Satan's Throne, Imperial Cults and the Social Settings of Revelation," *JSNT* 27.3 (2005): 351–373. Duff makes an argument for three different scenarios based on the Seer's relationship: (1) those with whom the Seer had a strong relationship and influence (Smyrna and Philadelphia), (2) weak relationship and little influence (Sardis and Laodicea), and (3) a faction of loyalists in Ephesus, Pergamum, and Thyatira (*Who Rides the Beast?*, 127, cf. 31–47).

[72] Friesen, "Satan's Throne," 352.

[73] On John's disagreement with other prophets on accommodation to imperial society, see esp. Duff, *Who Rides the Beast?*; Schüssler Fiorenza, *Justice and Judgment*, 24, cf. 115–117; Yarbro Collins, *Crisis and Catharsis*, 111; H.-J. Klauck, "Das Sendschreiben nach Pergamon und der Kaiserkult in der Johannesoffenbarung," *Biblica* 73 (1992): 153–182; cf. Lohmeyer, 31; Caird, 38–41. Witulski, 111–112, argues that this inner-Christian conflict is precipitated externally, "concretely by developments of the cultic-religious admiration of the emperor in the Roman province of *Asia*." (konkret durch Entwicklungen in der kultisch-religiösen Kaiserverehrung in der römischen Provinz *Asia* ausgelöst worden ist.)

[74] L. L. Thompson, *Book of Revelation*, 97–101; also A.Y. Collins, *Crisis and Catharsis*, 69–73; Schüssler Fiorenza, *Revelation*, 124–9; Duff, *Who Rides the Beast?*, 3–14;

X.96–97, ca. 112 CE) is often used to suggest that there was some kind of pressure in the 90's CE to reject Christ.[75] Some Christians were likely killed at that time just as Pliny executed a few Christians who refused to make libations to the Emperor's image and reject Christ. John is able to name only one Christian, Antipas, who has been killed, a fact which confirms that violent persecution was very limited. Yet, he makes the most of Antipas by linking his identity as "my faithful witness" (ὁ μάρτυς μου ὁ πιστός μου, 2:13) to Jesus' identity as "faithful witness" (1:5) and, by implication, to Jesus' death. By naming Antipas in this prominent way, John uses him as an example of anticipated violent persecution. He predicts more killing: the souls under the altar (6:9–11; cf. 20:4), the two witnesses killed by the beast (11:7), those who do not worship the beast (13:15), and those whose blood is shed by Babylon (17:6; cf. 16:6; 18:24). When John imagines future persecution, he anticipates more Christians killed for their witness.[76]

John suggests that these communities were already undergoing subtle and systemic pressure to conform to imperial society. In Ephesus, Christians had born up for the sake of Jesus' name (2:3).[77] Some Christians in Smyrna had been slandered (βλασφημία, 2:9) and some thrown in prison (2:10). Others in Pergamum and Philadelphia had not denied Jesus (2:13; 3:8). These past events suggest subtle but real pressure to publicly reject Christ and conform to social norms.[78] John anticipates social pressure from peoples, tribes, languages, and nations who are tormented by the two witnesses and rejoice when they are killed (11:9–10). He forsees economic pressure to accept the mark of the beast in order to buy or sell (13:16–17) and to enjoy the profits gained from trading with Babylon (18:11–19).[79] As

---

Boring, 17; Koester, *Revelation and the End,* 63; Aune, *Revelation*, lxvii; Pattemore, *People of God*, 58.

[75] A critical line in Pliny's letter is, "Others, whose names were given to me by an informer, first admitted the charge and then denied it; they said that they had ceased to be Christians two or more years previously, and some of them even twenty years ago" (X.96.6 [Radice, LCL]). The question is whether those who gave up Christianity twenty years ago (i.e. in the reign of Domitian) renounced their faith as the result of persecution or some other cause. Caird (*Revelation*, 20), Schüssler Fiorenza (*Justice and Judgement*, 193), Boring (*Revelation*, 18), Kraybill (*Imperial Cult*, 52), and Koester (*Revelation and the End,* 65), argues their apostasy was a result of some kind of persecution. Royalty (*Streets of Heaven*, 35) suggests that the events twenty years prior are not clear in Pliny's correspondence. Cf. Thompson, 130–132.

[76] Rev 18:24 suggests non-Christians are also killed by Babylon.

[77] Aune, *Revelation*, 1:146; Trebilco, *Early Christians in Ephesus*, 303.

[78] Aune, *Revelation*, 1:184, 237.

[79] John's critique of the violence and excessive consumption of the Roman Empire is similar to the complaint of his contemporary, Dio of Prusa. See P. S. Perry, "Critiquing

in the case of violence against Christians, there is evidence for unorganized and sporadic social and economic pressure on Christians. John uses past experiences as a basis to predict extreme future oppression.

If some Christians were benefiting from participation in the imperial society and economy, one can imagine how they could dismiss Antipas' death as exceptional and believe the Empire did not intend harm. Some believers in Ephesus, Pergamum, and Thyatira participated in social meals where idol meat was consumed (2:6, 14, 20).[80] The assembly at Laodicea was prosperous enough for Jesus to exhort them to trade in their gold, fine clothes, and ointments.[81] Merchants, shipmasters, and sailors had become rich from Rome (18:11–19). There was much to gain from participating in imperial society. John has a difficult case to convince his audiences not to participate.

In this cognitive environment, John's challenges his audiences to recognize that the Empire was deceiving them about its intentions and that some Christians promoted imperial idolatry. Using forms of the verb πλανάω (deceive) and of the stem *ψευδ– (lie), John connects rival prophets to idolatry to the imperial cult to imperial commerce and finally to Satan. Ephesus has found false apostles to be liars (ψευδεῖς, 2:2). John accused Jezebel of deceiving (πλανᾷ) Christians to practice fornication (i.e. idolatry) and eat idol meat (2:20). The beast from the earth deceives (πλανᾷ) the people of the earth into making an image of the first beast to worship (13:14). The merchants and magnates were deceived (ἐπλανήθησαν) by Babylon's sorcery (18:23). The false prophet (ψευδοπροφήτης, 16:13; 19:20; 20:10) deceived (ἐπλάνησεν) people into receiving the mark of the beast (19:20). John unveils Satan as the ultimate source of deception practiced by the imperial beast (12:9; 20:3, 8, 10).

The fact that John focuses on deception suggests that many Christians are not aware that the empire has violent intentions and that participation in the imperial economy and social meals are problematic.[82] The assembly in Pergamum tolerates those who follow the teachings of the Nicolaitans (2:14–15). John divides Christians in Thyatira into those who know "the deep things of Satan" and those that do not, but there is no evidence of

---

the Excess of Empire: A *Synkrisis* of John of Patmos and Dio of Prusa," *JSNT* 29.4 (2007): 473–496.

[80] See Kraybill's discussion of upward mobility for Jews and Christians (*Imperial Cult*, 86–101) and Trebilco's discussion of the Nicolaitans' position (*Early Christians in Ephesus*, 319–22).

[81] See Royalty, *Streets of Heaven*, 164–176.

[82] Cf. Collins, *Crisis and Catharsis*, 77; also Friesen ("Satan's Throne," 352–6) demonstrates that five of the seven assemblies receive strong praise for most members, and overall John approves of what most members of the congregations are doing. John exposes the complex deception to well-meaning Christians.

conflict between members of the assembly (2:24). The Laodiceans are content with being Christian and participating in the imperial economy, which John mocks (3:17). Only in Ephesus have they rejected the Nicolaitans (2:6). Most assemblies seem unaware of any conflict between their Christian identity and participation in imperial society. That Christians may be killed for their witness is a difficult thesis in this cognitive environment.

John exhorts audiences to "come out" of participation in the Empire (18:4). By gradually revealing the connections between Antipas' death and the Empire, its economy, its cult, its meals, its violence, and the cooperation of some Christian teachers, John brushes aside the web of deception in order that his audiences can let go of their attachment to imperial society, recognize Rome's violent intentions, and witness to Jesus even if it means facing death. I argue in the following chapters that his use of digressions between the sixth and seventh seals and trumpets is a key strategy towards these goals. In Rev 7:1–17 and 10:1–11:13, John gradually reveals his conviction that all Christians who witness face the threat of violence. He discloses this in digressions that overcome fear of persecution and evoke confidence in God's promised vindication.

3. Outline of the Argument

In Chapter 1 (On Structure and Terminology), I situate this investigation in the general trends of Revelation scholarship and in the diverse terminology for Rev 7:1–17 and 10:1–11:13. Interpreters use a variety of terms (interlude, intercalation, parenthesis, etc.) to describe some units of Revelation, which I initially call 'deviations' as a general term for units that have received special terminology. Since Charles, Schüssler Fiorenza, Beale, and Pattemore agree that Rev 7:1–17 and 10:1–11:13 are deviations in this general sense, I focus on these two units. A broader survey of interpreters illuminates the nuances of terms used for Rev 7:1–17 and 10:1–11:13 and especially how terms are used to imply continuity and discontinuity with the seals and trumpets. One set of terms emphasizes discontinuity between these two passages and the series in which they are embedded. Another set of terms emphasizes continuity. These various terms express a paradox: Rev 7:1–17 and 10:1–11:13 simultaneously seem unessential to the seal and trumpet series, and yet are essential to the message and impact of the whole book.

In Chapter 2 (Discontinuity and Continuity in Revelation 7 and 10–11), I use Pattemore's criteria for delimiting texts to describe continuity and discontinuity between Rev 7:1–17 and the series of seven seals and Rev 10:1–11:13 and the series of seven trumpets. These criteria include delimiting markers, shifts in personal references, communication axis,

iting markers, shifts in personal references, communication axis, *dramatis personae*, spatial signals, temporal signals, and thematic vocabulary. The majority of signals indicate discontinuity between Rev 7:1–17 and the seal series and Rev 10:1–11:13 and the trumpet series. These two passages can be omitted without loss of narrative logic, but omitting them highlights the significant role they play in developing the identity of the Seer and his audience. How would a first century audience explain these signals?

Chapter 3 (Digressions in Theory) describes the technique of παρέκβασις, or digression, discussed by rhetoricians from the 2nd c. BCE to the 1st c. BCE. Hermagoras, Cicero, and Quintilian define this technique and discuss its appropriate function, length, location, relevance, transitions, and topics in a speech. The technique and term 'digression' was as problematic for ancient interpreters as for modern ones, since how can a section of a speech be both appropriate and off subject? Modern literary critics explain that authors used digressions to manage disorder (either in the material or the audience), and the audience has to determine the relevance of the digression. Interpreters replicate this attempt to impose order on a text by labeling and rationalizing the structure. Some ancient rhetoricians (e.g. Aristotle, the author of *Rhetorica ad Herennium*, and Anonymous Seguerianus) manage disorder by rejecting or limiting the technique. These debates show that digressions were a part of those cognitive environments. There was agreement that their main purpose was to evoke the audience's emotion, often focusing directly on the orator and/or the audience. For this reason, digressions could be more memorable than other parts of a speech. Digressions were often used immediately before a conclusion in order to influence the audience's perception of the whole speech. Since emotion is a primary motivation for using digressions, I conclude with a discussion of emotions (τὰ πάθη) based on Aristotle's analysis in *Rhetorica* book 2 and how an analysis of emotion illuminates the rhetorical effect of digressions.

Following Mitchell's advice to immerse ourselves in contemporary literature (i.e. clues to the cognitive environment), Chapter 4 (Digressions in Practice) elaborates how authors and orators used digressions. Rhetoricians did not describe every facet of the use of digressions in their theoretical discussions. In practice, digressions were used either simply or systematically, terms I use to describe the relationships between multiple digressions in a text. A 'simple' digression has little or no relationship with other digressions. A 'systematic' digression builds on the topics of previous digressions. Following Longenecker's terminology for chain-link transitions, I call a digression 'articulated' if an author acknowledges the digression and 'unarticulated' if not.

Unarticulated and articulated, simple and systematic digressions can be observed in Jewish literature and literature relevant to 1st century Asia Minor. Josephus uses the technical term παρέκβασις in *Contra Apionem* and *Vita* and unarticulated digressions in all his works. Digressions in *Aristeas ad Philocrates* and 2 Maccabees demonstrate their use by other Greek-speaking Jews. Dio of Prusa spoke in first century Asia Minor and throughout the Mediterranean and used digressions in his oratory. Homer's impact on communication patterns continues to be evident in the first century, and his digressions in the *Iliad* and *Odyssey* provide a model for Pliny the Younger and Dio of Prusa. In the New Testament, Craig Koester has shown how the author of Hebrews has used digressions. They also occur in Jewish apocalyptic and the Hebrew Bible, most importantly in *Sibylline Oracles* I/II, *Jubilees* 23, Exodus 12, and Zechariah 2. These last four may have familiarized John with their use. Moreover, Exod 12:1–28 (the Passover narrative) is uniquely relevant. Like Rev 7:1–17 and 10:1–11:13, Exod 12:1–28 also interrupts a series of plagues caused by divine agents before the last element of the series, it describes a sign that protects God's people from the effects of the destruction, and it leads to the liberation and vindication of God's people.

In Chapter 5 (Rev 7:1–17 and 10:1–11:13 as digressions), I interpret Rev 7 and 10–11 in light of digressions in theory and practice. Given the cognitive environment illuminated in chapter 3 and 4, audiences would likely experience Rev 7:1–17 and 10:1–11:13 as παρέκβασις, specifically unarticulated, systematic digressions. These two units systematically develop the difficult thesis that witnesses to Jesus must be prepared to suffer and even be killed. In order to help the audience accept this difficult thesis, John makes an emotional argument in the digressions. I propose that these digressions are a crucial part of John's rhetorical strategy to persuade audiences to let go of their fear of persecution and instead witness confidently. The use of digressions has profound implications for the theology of the book of Revelation, especially in regards to the relationship of God's grace and God's wrath, judgment and repentance, and ecclesiology.

In Chapter 6 (Conclusions and Trajectories) I summarize the contributions of this study and pose questions for future research. Experiencing Rev 7:1–17 and 10:1–11:13 as digressions reveals how they challenge the claim that God's wrath and judgment are inexorable. God's promise and protection delay judgment and provide opportunities for witness and repentance. God's people are not whisked away from the trials of the world, but are exhorted to witness even in the Great City. Furthermore, they are urged to leave behind passivity for active witness and worship, to leave behind ignorance for knowledge of God, and to leave behind powerlessness in the face of ungodly powers to embrace authority as God's agents.

Chapter 1

On Structure and Terminology

Interpreters of Revelation have used a variety of methods to analyze the structure of Revelation and have applied many terms to units that did not fit their conception of the structure. In this chapter, first I will summarize how four modern scholars (R. H. Charles, Elisabeth Schüssler Fiorenza, Greg Beale, and Stephen Pattemore) identify and explain what I will generally call 'deviations' in the structure of whole book of Revelation. Next, I will narrow the focus to Rev 7:1–17 and 10:1–11:13 and broaden the number of interpreters to examine the various terms they use, teasing out their specific nuances. Some interpreters emphasize continuity between Rev 7:1–17 and the seal series and 10:1–11:13 and the trumpet series while others highlight discontinuity with the surrounding units and more significant connections elsewhere in Revelation.

The problem of finding a term for deviations in Revelation is not new. Before turning to modern scholars, an ancient scholar offers some initial examples.

1. Oecumenius: An initial approach

Oecumenius commented on the book of Revelation in the 6th century CE[1] and used two terms that reveal an early experience of the text.

---

[1] Oecumenius is either the 6th century correspondent of Severus (John Suggit's position), a 7th century bishop of Tricca (Hoskier followed by de Groote), or the 10th century bishop of Tricca (the traditional position before Hoskier). Andreas of Caesarea's commentary in the early seventh century is dependent on Oecumenius, and suggests the *terminus ante quem*. A problem is that Oecumenius places himself five hundred years "since this was said" (1.3.6). If this vague statement is dated to the time when the Seer spoke during the reign of Domitian (1.21), this would place the commentary at the end of the sixth century. However, Oecumenius interprets the Apocalypse as written about the events of the incarnation of our Lord (7.3.1), which suggests 500 years from the birth of Christ, thus in the early sixth century. Further evidence may be suggested by the fact that Oecumenius speaks approvingly of Evagrius (6.3.12) who was condemned with Origen at the second council of Constantinople in 553 CE. See the thorough discussion in *Oecumenius: Commentary on the Apocalypse* (trans. J. N. Suggit; Washington D. C.: Catholic University of America, 2006), 4–6, and M. de Groote, *Oecumenii commentarius in*

The first term is παρέξοδος, which may be translated 'side-way' or 'aside.'[2] Oecumenius uses this word to describe how the seven trumpets, the "matter in hand," are interrupted. When introducing his commentary on the seventh trumpet, he writes that,

> [a]fter narrating in an aside (παρεξόδῳ) the account of the two witnesses, or prophets, and going over everything concerning them, the vision comes to the matter in hand also from where it had started.[3]

A couple observations are salient. First, the term παρέξοδος is used to describe the unit relating to the two witnesses (11:3–13). He writes that the παρέξοδος is "the account of the two witnesses, or prophets," and "everything concerning them." Second, the seventh trumpet is referred to as a resumption of a narrative that had been interrupted, "the matter in hand also from where it had started."

We can make three inferences from these observations: First, Oecumenius experiences the structure of the trumpet series as A-B-A': "the matter in hand" refers to the trumpet series (A) which resumes with the seventh trumpet (A') but is interrupted by the story of the two witnesses (B). Second, the story of the two witnesses can be omitted without loss of narrative logic, since the seventh trumpet resumes "also from where it started." Third, Oecumenius seems to include 10:1–11:2 in this category since he suggests that the trumpets and their plagues are the primary subject matter and not John's encounter with the mighty angel in Rev 10.

Thus, Oecumenius understood Rev 11:3–13 (and likely 10:1–11:13) as a unit of text that required a special term, παρέξοδος, which suggests an 'off-road' excursion (παρα–ἐξ–ὁδος). In this context, Oecumenius uses it to describe a unit of text that interrupts a continuous narrative. It returns "to the matter in hand also from where it had started." In other words, the παρέξοδος can be removed from the narrative, and the surrounding units retain their narrative logic and flow.

The second term, ἐκδρομή ('digression'), is used not to describe Rev 11 but to introduce Rev 13:11–18 (the Beast from the Earth). "After many digressions (ἐκδρομάς) and after reverting from these beginnings to

---

Apocalypsin (Leuven: Peeters, 1999), 2–3. Cf. H. C. Hoskier, *The Complete Commentary of Oecumenius on the Apocalypse* (Ann Arbor, Michigan: University of Michigan, 1928). I date Oecumenius with Suggit to the 6th century.

[2] *LSJ*, s.v. "παρέξοδος," 1336, gives 'side-way' as the first translation. Suggit translates παρέξοδος as 'aside.'

[3] *Oec.* 6.17.1. Ὡς ἐν παρεξόδῳ τὰ κατὰ τοὺς δύο μάρτυρας ἤτοι προφήτας διηγησαμένη ἡ ὀπτασία και πάντα τὰ περὶ αὐτῶν ἐπεξελθοῦσα, ἐπι τὸ προκείμενον καὶ ὅθεν ἐξελήλυθεν ἔρχεται. Greek text from de Groote, 168. All translations are my own unless noted.

previous beginnings, he came to the serious matter."[4] The "serious matter" was explaining the Antichrist, but our interest is that he describes previous units as ἐκδρομαί, which John Suggit translates as "digressions."[5] Oecumenius is most immediately referring to Rev 13:9–10, in which the Seer directly addresses the audience ("If anyone has an ear…") in contrast to the narration about the Beast from the Sea (Rev 13:1–8). However, ἐκδρομάς is plural and so it implies that other unspecified units prior to this one are digressions.

In summary, as we approach the problem of the structure and terminology of Rev 7:1–17 and 10:1–13, the 6th century interpreter Oecumenius offers two terms to describe the experience. He uses the term παρέξοδος to refer to Rev 11:3–13 and describes 13:9–10 and other unspecified units before 13:11 as ἐκδρομαί. Both terms give the sense of deviating off a path.

2. 'Digression' and 'Deviation'

The thesis proposed in this book is that first century audiences in Asia Minor would have been familiar with digressions in speeches, histories, poems, and prose and could find them more significant than the surrounding material in which they were embedded. When ancient rhetoricians discussed this phenomenon, they used the term παρέκβασις (digression), although in practice other terms were also used, as we have seen in Oecumenius' use of παρέξοδος and ἐκδρομή.[6] I argue that audiences paid more attention to Rev 7:1–17 and 10:1–11:13 than the surrounding material because of other experiences of digressions. Digressions required the hearer to work harder to understand the relationship with the surrounding material, which highlighted their significance but at the same time opened the possibility for the hearer to interpret the unit in multiple, even divergent, ways. Understanding these two units as digressions helps to explain the variety of terms and interpretations given by the modern scholars surveyed below.

---

[4] *Oec.* 8.1.1. Πολλὰς ἐκδρομὰς καὶ ἐκ τῶνδε τῶν ἀρχῶν εἰς προγενεστέρας ἀρχὰς ἐπαναβάς, ἔφθασεν εἰς τὸ σπουδαζόμενον·. Arethas of Caesarea (10th century) repeats this phrase, only changing Oecumenius' ἐπαναβὰς to ἀναβάς. (PG 106.677). Andreas does not use this phrase.

[5] Suggit, 123. *LSJ*, s.v. "ἐκδρομή," 505.

[6] παρέκβασις is the technical term used by Hermagoras, Cicero, Quintilian, and Anonymous Seguerianus but, as observed in Oecumenius, a wide variety of other terms are used in practice, including παρέξοδος, ἐκβάσις, ἐκδρομάς, ἐκτροπή. These rhetoricians are discussed further in chapter 3, and the variety of terms in practice are discussed in chapter 4.

In this chapter, I use 'deviation' as a general term, broadly defined as some unit of text for which interpreters have used special terminology (such as interlude, expansion, aside, etc.) to explain its relationship to the material preceding and following the unit. This designation can apply to many more texts than Rev 7:1–17 and 10:1–13, as I will show. For example, the chain-link transition analyzed by Longenecker in Rev 22:6–9 can be classified a deviation by this definition. Such units are deviants in the sense that the hearer/reader has to expend effort to normalize the unit in the overall structure.[7] By using a general umbrella term like 'deviation,' I hope to situate the analysis of Rev 7 and 10–11 within the larger group of units that have required more processing effort to understand. Although I will argue in chapter 5 that παρέκβασις (digression) is the most appropriate term for the ancient experience of Rev 7:1–17 and 10:1–11:13, there are many other texts that have received special terms and deserve their own analysis.[8] These are listed in Table 1 below as loci for future study.

3. An Overview of Deviations in the Structure of Revelation

Although the structure of Revelation has long been an enigma to its hearers and readers, there is some agreement about a broad outline. Interpreters agree that the book has a prologue (1:1–3), an epistolary framework (1:4–8; 22:6*–21), an inaugural vision of Christ who dictates letters to the seven congregations (1:9–3:22) and the central body of visions (4:1–22:5*).[9] The

---

[7] Here I am following A. Härter (*Digressionen: Studien zum Verhältnis von Ordnung und Abweichung in Rhetorik und Poetik* [Verlag: Wilhem Fink, 2000]) who uses 'Abweichung' as the general term and 'Abschweifung' in relationship to Quintilian's *digressio* and *parekbasis* in ancient texts. Härter helpfully emphasizes how authors normalize deviations by using transitions, retrospectives, and other devices.

[8] For example, Rev 13:9–10 ("Let anyone who has an ear listen..."), 14:1–5 (The 144,000 on Mt. Zion), and 15:2–4 (Song of Moses and the Lamb).

[9] G. K. Beale recently made this assertion (*The Book of Revelation* [NIGTC; Grand Rapids, Mich: Eerdmans, 1999], 108), but this broad agreement can be traced back at least to Swete. As a brief sample, see H. B. Swete, *The Apocalypse of St. John* (2nd ed; New York: Macmillan, 1907), xxix–xli; J. Moffatt, *An Introduction to the Literature of the New Testament* (New York: Scribner, 1915), 485–487; R. H. Charles, *The Revelation of St. John* (Edinburgh: T & T Clark, 1985 [1920]), 1:xxiii–xxv; R. J. Loenertz, *The Apocalypse of Saint John* (trans. H. J. Carpenter; London: Sheed & Ward, 1947), ix–xiii; F. Hahn, "Zum Aufbau der Johannesoffenbarung," in *Kirche und Bibel: Festgabe für Bischof Eduard Schick* (Paderborn: Ferdinand Schöningh, 1979), 145–6; E. Schüssler Fiorenza, *Revelation: Vision of a Just World* (Minneapolis: Fortress, 1991), 35–36; R. Bauckham, *Climax of Prophecy: Studies in the Book of Revelation* (Edinburgh: T & T Clark, 1993), 3–4; P. Richard, *Apocalypse: A People's Commentary on the Book of Revelation* (trans. P. Berryman; Maryknoll, New York: Orbis, 1995), 33–35; D. Aune, *Reve-*

disagreement centers on how to outline and analyze the central visions. As David Barr says, "there are, unfortunately, nearly as many outlines of the Apocalypse as there are commentators on it."[10]

Since it is not my purpose to review and evaluate the history of interpreting the entire structure of Revelation, I will only briefly situate the present investigation within the trajectory of scholarship. Ugo Vanni provides the most comprehensive treatment of the history of scholarship in the second edition of *La Struttura Letteraria dell'Apocalisse* (1980).[11] A student of Revelation's structure also has Wilhelm Bousset's exhaustive treatment of 19th century scholarship (1896).[12] Adele Yarbro Collins (1976), Elisabeth Schüssler Fiorenza (1977), and David Aune (1997) also have made important contributions to understanding the history of scholarship on the structure of Revelation.[13]

Given this background on the structure of the whole book, it is heuristically useful to chart four different approaches to the structure of Revelation.[14]

---

lation (3 vols; WBC; Dallas, Texas: Word, 1997–8), 1:c; and most recently, J. F. T. Cuadrado, *Apocalipsis: Estética y Teología* (Rome: Editrice Pontificio Istituto Biblico, 2007), 72–3. The asterisks (*) by 22:5 and 22:6 denote that the boundary between the visions concluding in Rev 22:5 and the epistolary postscript has been a site of scholarly debate. As discussed in the introduction, Longenecker argues convincingly that this is an example of a chain-link transition. See B. Longenecker, "'Linked like a Chain': Rev 22:6–9 in Light of Ancient Transition Technique," *New Testament Studies* 47 (2001), 105–117, and the thorough treatment of the subject in *Rhetoric at the Boundaries* (Waco, Texas: Baylor, 2005).

[10] D. Barr, "The Apocalypse as a Symbolic Transformation of the World: A Literary Analysis," *Interpretation* 38 (1981): 43.

[11] See U. Vanni, *La Struttura Letteraria dell'Apocalisse* (2nd ed; Brescia: Morcelliana, 1980), 9–15, for a more thorough history of responses to the structure of the Apocalypse from its first interpreters to the 19th century.

[12] W. Bousset, *Die Offenbarung Johannis* (Göttingen: Vandenhoeck and Ruprecht, 1896), 108–118.

[13] A. Y. Collins, *The Combat Myth in the Book of Revelation* (Missoula, Mont.: Scholars, 1976), 1–13. Collins' summary is focused around the issue of a linear vs. recapitulative structure, an argument that continues today (cf. Steinmann, etc. below). E. Schüssler Fiorenza, "The Composition and Structure of Revelation," in *Justice and Judgment*, 159–180, originally published in *CBQ* 39 (1977): 344–66. Aune, 1:xci–xcix.

[14] The names are listed in rough chronological order. Some of these categories overlap (especially source and literary-rhetorical). For example, Russell Morton assigns Bousset and Kraft to a "linguistic/literary" category (*One Upon the Throne and the Lamb: A Tradition Historical/Theological Analysis of Revelation 4–5* [SBL 110; New York: Peter Lang, 2007]), 45–46. He uses "Source Critical Approaches," "Linguistic/Literary Analysis," "Recapitulation Theory," and "Chiastic Theory" as his categories, which seems to confuse methods and results. For further classification of Source Critical theories and other scholars not mentioned above, see Schüssler Fiorenza, *Justice and Judgment*, 160–164; Aune, *Revelation*, 1:cv–cxvii.

(1) A *Source Critical approach* for explaining structure is used by Bousset, Lohse, Kraft, Prigent, Gaechter, Ford, and Aune. I am using R. H. Charles to represent this stream.

(2) A *Literary–Rhetorical approach* to structure can be found in Swete, Loisy, Loenertz, Lohmeyer, Ladd, Minear, Collins, Lambrecht, Vanni, Bauckham, Boring, Richard, Giblin, Steinmann, Filho, and Tavo. I am using E. Schüssler Fiorenza to represent this approach

(3) *Allusions to the Hebrew Bible/Jewish Literature* provides insights into structure to Ulfgard, Hall, Smith, Siew, and Lupieri. I am using G. Beale to represent this approach.

(4) *Discourse Theory* is used by Hellholm and E. Müller. I am using Pattemore as representative of this approach.

Some scholars have worked on the structure of specific texts (e.g. Steinmann, Giblin), but Charles, Schüssler Fiorenza, Beale, and Pattemore treat the whole book and are representative of others using similar methodologies. R. H. Charles continues the 19th century trend of identifying sources and editors as the cause of deviations, even while insisting on the unity of the author's thought and style. Using literary-rhetorical criticism, E. Schüssler Fiorenza argues that the text is a literary whole within which deviations play a significant rhetorical function. G. Beale emphasizes the role of the Hebrew Bible, especially Daniel, in discerning the structure. S. Pattemore uses relevance theory to detect structural signals to the audience. In the section below, I summarize each of these four interpreters' responses to three questions: (1) which units are marked as deviations, (2) by what criteria those units are marked, and (3) how these deviations are explained.

(1) *Units marked as deviations.* The following table summarizes the units that Charles,[15] Schüssler Fiorenza,[16] Beale,[17] and Pattemore[18] identify as deviations, i.e. units that are labeled with special terminology to de-

---

[15] Charles, 1:lvi–lxv. Aune's list of 12 self-contained units roughly correspond to Charles' (Aune, *Revelation 1–5*, cxxxii). Rev 14:1–20, 19:11–16, 20:1–10, and 21:9–22:5 do not correspond between Aune and Charles' lists.

[16] Schüssler Fiorenza, *Justice and Judgment*, 171–3.

[17] Beale does not offer a detailed outline. For this list, see *Revelation*, 405, 454, 520–1, 657, 730.

[18] S. Pattemore, *Souls under the Altar: Relevance Theory and the Discourse Structure of Revelation* (UBS 9; New York: UBS, 2003), 128–130, 140, 152, 161; *The People of God in the Apocalypse: Discourse, Structure and Exegesis* (MSSNTS 128; Cambridge: Cambridge University Press, 2004), 63, 65, 95. He finds interludes more common in the first half, asides in the last half. Significantly, "The breaking of the unitary communication mode prepares the way for and leads into the finale, where the variation of voices may appear confusing. In fact, that variation is seen to be a deliberate structural device, used to bring the voice of God with immediate force to the audience, who themselves are far removed in time and space from the visionary experience" (*People of God*, 63).

scribe their relationship to the surrounding material. The term used for each unit is given in parentheses, except for Charles who uses the following terms: interpolations, dislocations, lacunae, dittographs, and sourced material. Dislocations are marked with a plus sign (+), with Charles' suggested location marked after a slash. Lacunae are marked with a minus sign (–). Dittographs are marked with an ampersand (&). Material believed to be from a Greek or Hebrew source is marked with an asterisk (*).

Table 1. Units identified as deviations

Charles	*Schüssler Fiorenza*	*Beale*	*Pattemore*
1:4c			
2:5, 22			
+2:26b / 27c			
+3:8a / 8bc			
4:5, 6, 8		4:8–10 (hymn)	
5:8d, 11		5:6–14 (hymn)	
6:8b			
**7:1–8*	*7:1–17 (interlude)*	*7:1–17 (parenthesis)*	*7:1–8 (second part of seal)*
+7:5c / 6			
**7:9–17*			*7:9–17 (hinge)*
8:2			
+8:2 / 5	8:2–5 (intercalation)	8:2–5 (interlock)	
9:5c, 11c, 16b–17a, 19b			
**10:1–11:13*	*10:1–11:13 (intercalation)*	*10:1–11:13 (parenthesis)*	*10:1–11:13 (interlude)*
11:5b			
+11:18b / h, 18g / c	11:15–19 (interlude and intercalation)		
*12:1–17	12:10 (interlude)	12:10–12 (hymn)	12:10–12 (interlude)
*13:1–18			
+13:5b / 6b			13:9–10, 18 (aside)
&13:3c, 8 = 17:8			
14:3–4	14:1–5 (interlude)	14:2–5 (hymn)	
14:12–13 / 13:18			14:12 (aside)
14:15–17, 18, 19			
15:1			
15:2–4	15:2–4 (intercalation)	15:3–4 (hymn)	15:2–4 (interlude)
*15:5–8	15:5–8 (intercalation)		
–16:10			
+16:15 / 3:3b		16:15 (parenthesis)	16:15 (aside)
*17:1–18; 18:1–24	17:1–19:10 (intercalation)		

Charles	*Schüssler Fiorenza*	*Beale*	*Pattemore*
+16:15 / 3:3b		16:15 (parenthesis)	16:15 (aside)
*17:1–18; 18:1–24	17:1–19:10 (intercalation)		
+17:14–17 / 17:17, 16, 14			
17:9b, 15, 17		17:7–18 (hymn)	17:9a (aside)
18:2–23a–e			
18:13			
+18:14–23			
–18:22a			
19:8b, 12c, 16	19:1–9 (interlude)		19:8b (aside)
–19:9a			
&19:9b = 21:5c = 22:6a			
&19:10 = 22:8b, 9			
20:4–6	20:4–6 (interlude)		20:5b–6 (aside)
20:12, 13, 14b			
&20:14b = 21:8e			
21:6a, 25			
22:11, 12, 18b–19			22:7 (aside)

The most significant result from this table is that there is agreement that Rev 7:1–17 and 10:1–11:13 require special explanation. For this reason I examine these two units as a test case for future analysis of other deviations. With less agreement on the extent of the deviation, these four scholars agree also on Rev 12:10–12 (Song of victory over the Dragon) and 15:2–4 (Song of Moses and the Lamb). Three out of four identify 8:2–5 (Seven angels and the Angel at the altar), 14:1–5 (144,000 with the Lamb on Mt. Zion), 16:15 ("See, I am coming like a thief"), 17:9 ("This calls for a mind that has wisdom"), 19:8b (the bride's fine linen), and 20:4–6 (the millennium) as deviations. In addition, Charles identifies more texts as needing special terminology and explanation, while later interpreters seem more likely to attribute many of these features to the author's style.

(2) *Criteria for identifying units as deviations.* Charles identifies his list of deviations based on variation in idiom, diction, and thought.[19] Schüssler Fiorenza's criteria are less clear but seem based on the content of the unit expressing eschatological protection and salvation, although this is not the true for 8:2–5 (Seven angels and the Angel before the altar), 12:10–12 (Song of victory over the dragon), or 16:15 ("See, I am coming like a thief").[20] Beale, like Schüssler Fiorenza, does not give explicit criteria for detecting deviations, but emphasizes the use of repetition and allusion as

[19] Charles, 1:lxii–lxii, cf. 194, 299–300; cf. Bousset, 122, cf. 279–280.

[20] Schüssler Fiorenza, *Justice and Judgment*, 171.

structural markers.[21] Pattemore distinguishes units by delimiting words or phrases with a change in personal references, communication axis, dramatis personae, spatial signals, or temporal signals.[22] Although Pattemore does not define what he means by 'interlude' (10:1–11:13; 12:10–12),[23] his criteria are helpful in illustrating the relationships among units and will be used in chapter 2 to analyze Rev 7 and 10–11.

(3) *Explaining units.* Each scholar explains Rev 7:1–17 and 10:1–11:13 in different ways. Charles interprets these units as either 'proleptic visions' of a future reality (for example, the great multitude in Rev 7 anticipates the multitude in heaven in the eschaton) or as evidence of sloppy editing.[24] Schüssler Fiorenza sees them as essential to the design of Revelation, interrupting and delaying the septets, relating the present situation of the audience to the eschatological future, and commenting on the apocalyptic action.[25] She explains these units as interludes or intercalations.[26] Beale agrees with Schüssler Fiorenza that Rev 7:1–17 and 10:1–11:13 delay the narrative, relate the audience's situation to the future, and comment on the previous units, but calls these units 'parentheses,' 'hymns' or 'interlocking units.'[27] Pattemore explains these deviations with sensitivity to the oral context, labeling short units as 'asides' to the audience and the longer units of 12:10–12 and 10:1–11:13 as 'interludes.'[28] He argues that the juxtaposition of structures in 7:1–17 and 10:1–11:13 creates tension and puts the people of God on center stage.[29]

Overall, there are three important shifts illustrated by these four interpreters that prepare the ground for this investigation. First, scholars have shifted away from attributing deviations to sources and editing (Charles) instead describing them as part of the Seer's literary and rhetorical strategy (Schüssler Fiorenza, Beale, Pattemore). Scholars have become increasingly

---

[21] Beale, *Revelation*, 140–141.

[22] Pattemore, *Souls*, 100–101.

[23] E.g. Pattemore, *Souls*, 134–135.

[24] Charles, 1:xxv, lv. P. Gaechter ("The Role of Memory in the Making of the Apocalypse," *Theological Studies* 9 [1948]: 419–452) agrees that a follower of the Seer is the source of the confusion, but argues that the Seer's disciple has a poor memory. Gaechter lists 7:1–17, 10:1–11:13, 12:10–12, 14:1–5, 14:6–20, 16:5–7, and 19:1–8 as "weak spots" that caused the amanuensis disciple to insert material.

[25] Schüssler Fiorenza, *Revelation*, 65, cf. 68–69.

[26] Schüssler Fiorenza, *Revelation*, 73, and *Justice and Judgment*, 172.

[27] Beale, *Revelation*, 109.

[28] Pattemore, *Souls*, 140, 152; *People of God*, 95 (interludes) and Pattemore, *People of God*, 63 (asides).

[29] Pattemore, *People of God*, 66. Despite partitioning Rev 7:1–8 with the sixth seal, he nonetheless notes links between 7:1–8 and 11:1–2. Both describe the protection of the people of God (*People of God*, 161). On the phrase "People of God," see p. 18 above.

aware of stylistic or contextual reasons why the Seer may have deviated.[30] These possibilities should be considered before concluding that a different source explains the deviation. The hypothesis of this book is that first century audiences expected deviations in speeches and other literature and interpreted them in ways consistent with these other examples.

Second, these scholars have shifted from viewing the text as a compilation of parts to viewing the text as a whole, especially its impact on the audience. The shift was already at work when Charles asserted the overall unity of Revelation, even as he championed sources and editors to explain deviations.[31] Most scholars now accept the probability that Revelation draws on sources and that it was presented to audiences as an integrated whole and therefore should be studied as a unity.[32] The unity of the text *in performance* to first century audiences is a starting point for this investigation. For this reason, it is important to analyze deviations together. Therefore, I will investigate Rev 7:1–17 and 10:1–11:13 together as suggested by Schüssler Fiorenza and Beale.[33]

Third, there is a shift among these four interpreters from analyzing the whole of Revelation in its entirety to recognizing that audiences would initially experience it sequentially and cumulatively. Schüssler Fiorenza and Beale suggest a sequential reading when they observe that progressive repetition intensifies the theme of judgment (e.g. of water turning to blood after the second trumpet and second bowl plagues).[34] Yet, elsewhere Charles, Schüssler Fiorenza, and Beale interpret the text as if the audience

---

[30] See especially Longenecker's analysis of the chain-link technique discussed in the introduction, D. Lee's analysis of narrative asides (*The Narrative Asides in the Book of Revelation* [Lanham, Maryland: University Press of America, 2002]), and K. Nikolakopoulos' analysis of rhetorical figures of thought ("Rhetorische Auslegungsaspekte der Theologie in der Johannesoffenbarung," in *"...Was ihr auf dem Weg verhandelt habt": Beiträge zur Exegese und Theologie des Neuen Testaments: Festschrift für Ferdinand Hahn zum 75. Geburtstag* [eds. P. Müller, C. Gerber, T. Knöppler; Neukirchen-Vluyn: Neukirchener Verlag, 2001], 166–180).

[31] Charles was following Bousset in this trend.

[32] Schüssler Fiorenza, Beale, Pattemore. For an insightful discussion of what is meant by the "unity" of the text see Aune, *Revelation*, 1:cvii–cix.

[33] Schüssler Fiorenza, *Justice and Judgment*, 171–172; Beale, *Revelation*, 520. The point is persuasively argued first by Loenertz, *Apocalypse*, xiv–xix, and independently, A. Steinmann, "The tripartite structure of the sixth seal, the sixth trumpet, and the sixth bowl of John's Apocalypse," *Journal of the Evangelical Theological Society* 35 (March 1992): 69–79; cf. Bauckham, *Climax*, 257; Richard, 77–86. Pattemore does not connect Rev 7:1–17 and 10:1–11:13, perhaps because he distinguishes them by different terms, 'hinge' for Rev 7 and 'major interlude' for Rev 10–11. See discussion below.

[34] Schüssler Fiorenza, 176; Beale, *Revelation*, 145.

has simultaneous access to every part of it.[35] In part, this may be a reaction against interpreting Revelation in a "futuristic sequential scheme,"[36] but it obscures the sequential experience of the audience hearing the scroll read aloud. Like other interpreters who use communication models (e.g. Hellholm and E. Müller), Pattemore focuses on the sequential and cumulative nature of communication, analyzing how the audience may interpret each new utterance in light of previous statements.[37] The sequential and cumulative experience of the text is another key assumption behind this investigation. Deviations should be studied not only together, but also in order as they appear in the text noting how they build on and relate to one another.

4. Terms for the role of Rev 7:1–17 and 10:1–11:13 in the structure of Revelation

The overview in the previous section demonstrated consensus among four interpreters that Rev 7:1–17 and 10:1–11:13 require special terminology to describe their relationship with surrounding units. Whether 'interlude,' 'intercalation,' 'parentheses,' or 'hinge,' the proliferation and variety of these terms confirms that these are deviations in the general sense defined above.

The survey below lists terms used by a larger group of scholars to describe Rev 7:1–17 and 10:1–11:13. Whereas the last section examined four scholars, the current section focuses on terminology, with the goal being to understand what is at stake and why there has not been consensus. Some patterns begin to emerge. Each scholar's term and emphasis can be located on a spectrum of continuity. On one end of the spectrum, some interpreters use terms to emphasize discontinuity between Rev 7:1–17 and the seal series and Rev 10:1–11:13 and the trumpet series. On the other end, some choose terms that emphasize continuity, while yet others nuance terms to lie somewhere in between.

---

[35] For example, Schüssler Fiorenza (*Justice and Judgment*, 171) describes the narrative movement as a combination of "a cyclic form of repetition with the end-oriented movement of the whole book." Although it is a helpful visualization, it minimizes the cumulative progression experienced by an audience.

[36] Beale, *Revelation*, 144–145.

[37] Discourse theory assumes the sequential nature of communication, cf. D. Hellholm, "The Problem of Apocalyptic Genre and the Apocalypse of John," *Semeia* 36 (1986): 13–64; E. Müller, *A Microstructural Analysis of Revelation 4–11* (Berrien Springs, Michigan: Andrews University Press, 1996). Others outside of discourse theory also argue that the sequence of Revelation is critical, for example, Bauckham, *Climax of Prophecy*, 2; Boring, 127.

The following survey also shows that scholars agree that Rev 7:1–17 and 10:1–11:13 delay the narrative, although the significance of this delay is contested. For example, is the delay only in the experience of the audience whose perspective is enlarged by the vision of the 144,000 sealed? Or do these units retard the action in the world of the text? The issue of delay can also be expressed in terms of continuity and discontinuity. Interpreters who understand the delay only in terms of the audience's experience of the text emphasize continuity, for example, between Rev 7 and the seal series. Others emphasize discontinuity and delay in the narrated action.

Because definition of these terms has not been a concern for many scholars, the following survey is based often on my inferences. The list is in order of most common to least common. At times, especially with languages other than English, I have included multiple terms in one category. Some scholars use more than one term and appear in multiple categories.

a) *Interlude* (also interval, intermezzo, intermède, Zwischenspiel).[38] This is by far the most common label affixed to Rev 7:1–17 and 10:1–11:13. Schüssler Fiorenza goes the furthest in offering a definition of this term, suggesting that 'interludes' in Revelation are "visions or hymns of eschatological protection and salvation."[39] She argues that their literary function is to interrupt the linear and cyclic narrative pattern, their theological function is to relate the present reality of the audience to the eschatological future, and their narrative function is to comment on the apocalyptic action in a similar way that a Greek chorus comments during a tragic play. The word 'interlude' seems to be chosen to emphasize the musical and dramatic connotations that may have evoked the experience of Greek drama (this suggestion will be examined in chapter 4).[40]

Delay in both the audience's experience and the narrative action is central to most interpreters who use this term. For example, Schüssler Fiorenza concludes that the interruption of the narrative both "delays the opening of the last seal and keeps the reader in suspense."[41] R. H. Mounce writes that Rev 7 "serves as a dramatic interlude that delays for a brief moment the disclosure of that which is to take place when the seven and

[38] *Interlude*: Minear, Rissi, Laymon, Ladd, Schüssler Fiorenza, Boring, Mazzaferri, Mounce, Wendland, C. Koester, Osborne, Boxall. *Intermezzo*: Bousset, Moffatt. *Intermède*: Loisy. *Zwischenspiel*: Lohse and Kraft. Aune, Giblin, and Pattemore argue against calling Rev 7 an interlude but do call 10:1–11:13 an interlude, as discussed below. Prigent, *L'Apocalypse*, 149, is also more willing to call 10:1–11:14 an interlude (une intermède) but without defining the term.

[39] Fiorenza, *The Book of Revelation,* 171.

[40] Swete, xli, also makes the connection between drama and the term 'interlude.' See section 4.6.

[41] Schüssler Fiorenza, *Revelation*, 65. Similarly, see P. Minear, *I Saw a New Earth: An Introduction to the Visions of the Apocalypse* (Washington: Corpus, 1968), 75.

final seal is removed…."[42] For these, the term 'interlude' expresses delay that highlights discontinuity in the temporal progress of the story.

P. Minear uses 'extraneous' to modify his description of 10:1–11:13, which underlines the level of discontinuity he experienced.[43] He observes that 10:1–11:13 is unnecessary to the narrative logic and that there is marked contrast of intensity between the trumpet series and the interlude.

> Because of the rise in dramatic intensity in the description of blasts five and six, the reader's attention is drawn all the more strongly to the seemingly extraneous interlude of 10:1–11:13. If one deletes this section he can move without apparent loss from 9:21 to 11:14. Why should John insert so long a section at precisely this point?44

Minear concludes that John wanted to relate the mission of Christian prophecy to the trumpets by juxtaposing these units. To Minear, any continuity is a result of this juxtaposition.

Others who use this term explain that they do not mean that the interlude can be interpreted independently from the surrounding narrative.[45] In stressing the continuity with the seven seals, Boring also illuminates a cognitive process in the hearer who at first is surprised by Rev 7, but over time interprets it with Rev 6 and 8. "What seems at first to be a postponement or narrative digression turns out to be a skillfully constructed interlude, which pictures the church during the time of persecution and builds suspense before the final seal is broken."[46] Although Boring is commenting on the author's design, he also is describing how the hearer initially experiences the unit as a deviation but as the reader continues the hearer makes connections to understand the unit as a part of the structure of the whole book.[47]

Mathias Rissi seems to use the word 'interval' to emphasize continuity and discontinuity in a way consistent with 'interlude' as described above.[48] For Rissi, Rev 7 clarifies the sixth seal and begins something new. "That

---

[42] R. H. Mounce, *The Book of Revelation* (2nd ed; Grand Rapids, Michigan: Eerdmans, 1998), 154.

[43] Minear, 95; cf. 75 for a milder assessment of Rev 7.

[44] Minear, 95.

[45] E.g. Schüssler Fiorenza, *Justice and Judgment*, 172; G. R. Osborne, *Revelation* (BECNT; Grand Rapids Michigan: Baker, 2002), 301.

[46] M. E. Boring, *Revelation* (Interpretation; Louisville, Kentucky: John Knox Press, 1989), 127.

[47] Boring emphasizes the oral/aural culture on p. 33.

[48] M. Rissi, *Time and History: A Study on the Revelation* (trans. G. C. Winsor; Richmond, Virginia: John Knox, 1966), 43. Rissi does use the word 'interlude' on p. 7, but also describes Rev 7 as an 'insertion' on p. 3. S. S. Smalley, *The Revelation to John* (Downers Grove, Illinois: InterVarsity Press, 2005), 21, calls 4:1–5:14, 7:1–17, and 10:1–11:19 'intervals,' which he uses in a dramatic sense similar to Schüssler Fiorenza, and for that reason I have included it under 'interlude' (a term Smalley uses on p. 177).

7:1ff. not only brings out more clearly the event of the sixth seal but also introduces something new is made evident by the introductory formula *meta touto*."[49] The sealing is new, and the destructive winds do not relate to the sixth seal but anticipate the trumpet visions.[50]

Some, such as David Aune and Stephen Pattemore, explicitly argue that the term 'interlude' is inappropriate. Aune argues that 'interludes' is not an accurate description of Rev 7:1–17 and 10:1–11:13 because these are the "focal set pieces" that the author wrote first and around which the author created the larger narrative structure.[51] From his source-critical perspective, these are not interludes from the main action, but in fact the focus of the narrative surrounding them.[52] Aune is not consistent, however, in this perspective. When he analyzes Rev 7 in detail, he concludes that it has been inserted after the sixth seal to answer the question asked in 6:17 (Who is able to stand?).[53] Again in analyzing Rev 10, he comments that "the author abruptly inserts two episodes (10:1–11; 11:1–13) that function to delay the sounding of the seventh trumpet...."[54] Despite his initial conclusion that these two units are focal set pieces, Aune analyzes them as insertions into a main narrative.

Pattemore argues that Rev 7:1–8 is not an interlude because there is no change in scene and μετὰ τοῦτο ("After this") refers only to the sixth seal.[55] Revelation 7:9–17, on the other hand, shifts the scene back to heaven, recalling the throne room scene of 4:1–5:14. The result for Pattemore is that Rev 7 as a whole functions as a hinge between the seals and the trumpets. On the other hand, Pattemore suggests that Rev 10:1–11:13 is a 'Major Interlude' without discussion of the term.[56] He shows that Rev 10:1 is delimited by the phrase Καὶ εἶδον ἄλλον ἄγγελον ("and I saw another angel") and the shift of *dramatis personae* (from kings, magnates, etc. to John as a character). However, it is not clear why Rev 10:1–11:13 is a 'major interlude' to Pattemore whereas Rev 7:1–17 is a 'hinge.'

---

[49] Rissi, 44.

[50] Rissi, 44–45.

[51] Aune, *Revelation*, cxxiii.

[52] Aune ratifies this conclusion in the article on Revelation in the *Westminster Dictionary of Early Christian Literature and Rhetoric* (Louisville, Kentucky: Westminster/John Knox, 2003), 404: "Each of these texts [7:1–17; 10:1–11; 11:1–13; 12:1–17; 13:1–18; 14:1–20] appears to be more important to the author-editor than the heptads themselves and probably originated in another context before their incorporation in the final text of Revelation."

[53] Aune, *Revelation*, 479.

[54] Aune, *Revelation*, 555.

[55] Pattemore, *Souls*, 130. For a complete discussion, see chapter 2.2.

[56] Pattemore, *Souls,* 140.

b) *Intercalation* (also interposition, insertion, Zwischenstück, Einschaltung).[57] Other scholars prefer the term 'intercalation' that lacks the musical and dramatic connotations but do not explicitly define what an intercalation is. Lambrecht describes Rev 7:1–17; 10:1–11:13; and 12:1–14:20 as "so-called intercalations" that "break the pattern of continuous narrative."[58] Fiorenza uses 'intercalations' in two divergent ways: first, following R. Loenertz, to mean an overlapping technique A-B-A'-B' (e.g. Rev 8:2–5).[59] In other places, she uses 'intercalation' almost interchangeably with 'interlude.'[60] Lohse highlights the introduction of four angels and four winds in 7:1–3 as a key to seeing Rev 7 as a 'Zwischenstück.'[61] Although these scholars emphasize that Rev 7:1–17 and 10:1–11:13 are more closely related to the sixth seal and trumpet respectively,[62] this term emphasizes the foreignness of the material and suggests editorial insertion.[63]

Delay is a key effect of the intercalations. For example, Bauckham identifies both Rev 7:1–17 and 10:1–11:13 as intercalations that symbolize the delay of judgment for the sake of the people of God. For Bauckham, this is a primary element of discontinuity: the intercalations focus on the people of God while the seal and trumpet series are focused on judgment.

In the first intercalation (7:1–17), the delay is for the sake of protecting the people of God from the judgments, so that they might triumph in heaven, while in the second inter-

[57] *Intercalation*: Bauckham, A. Y. Collins, Lambrecht, Hellholm, C. R. Smith, Filho. *Interposition*: Caird. *Insertion*: Gaechter, A. Y. Collins. *Zwischenstück*: Lohse, Lohmeyer, Conzelmann, and Lindemann. *Einschaltung*: Kraft. H. Ulfgard (*Feast and Future: Revelation 7:9–17 and the Feast of Tabernacles* [Stockholm: Almqvist & Wiksell, 1989], 32–33) argues that the term "Zwischenstück" mistakenly implies that Rev 7, and especially 7:9–17, is a "proleptic vision of the final blessedness in heaven." He argues that the whole of Rev 7 refers back to the martyrs under the altar following the fifth unsealing (6:9–11).

[58] J. Lambrecht, "A Structuration of Revelation 4,1–22,5," in *L'Apocalypse johannique et l'Apocalyptique dans le Nouveau Testament* (ed. J. Lambrecht; Leuven: University Press, 1980), 95. Also, J. A. Filho, "The Apocalypse of John as an Account of a Visionary Experience: Notes on the Book's Structure," *JSNT* 25.2 (2002): 222–3.

[59] Schüssler Fiorenza, *Justice and Judgment*, 172; Loenertz, xviii–xix. A. Y. Collins (*Combat Myth*, 16–19) calls 8:2–5 an example of "interlocking" which Longennecker identifies as a chain-link transition.

[60] For example, Schüssler Fiorenza, *Revelation*, 34.

[61] E. Lohse, *Die Offenbarung des Johannes* (Göttingen: Vandenhoeck & Ruprecht, 1960), 50. Like Lohse, H. Conzelmann and A. Lindemann (*Arbeitsbuch zum Neuen Testament* [Tübingen: J. C. B. Mohr (Paul Siebeck), 1995], 388) also highlight the introduction of the 144,000 from the 12 tribes and the unnumbered multitude as decisive for identifying Rev 7 as a Zwischenstück.

[62] For example, Bauckham, *Climax*, 11–12.

[63] See s.v. "Intercalation," in Aune, *Westminster Dictionary*, 230–232.

calation (10:1–11:13) the delay is for the sake of the prophetic witness of the people of God.[64]

As with those who used 'interlude,' users of 'intercalation' and similar terms suggest that Rev 7:1–17 and 10:1–11:13 cause delay in audience experience and narrative action, discontinuous from the seal and trumpet series.

c) *Interruption* (also intrusion, episode, narrative apposition).[65] This seems like a more general term than either of the above, perhaps avoiding the musical and dramatic connotations of 'interlude' and the more technical 'intercalation.' Rowland does not define his terms, only saying that "the catalogue of destruction is suddenly interrupted in ch. 7" and "[t]here is an interruption in the sequence of trumpet blasts after 9:22...."[66] Maier calls Rev 7 a "narrative apposition," writing that, "John splices a rapid-fire recitation of the seals with a vision that slows narrative time to a crawl."[67] The primary effect is delay.

> The time of narration is lengthened at chapter 7, between the sixth and seventh seal, giving a heightened sense of drama to the opening of the seventh seal at 8:1...the introduction of yet another scroll at 10:1–11, together with a return to heaven (10:1; 11:1, 19), seems to rewind the narrative clock and to mark the beginning of still more Apocalypse.[68]

Scholars who use these terms also do not argue for continuity between the unit and its surrounding text, but highlight the discontinuity and emphasize the delay in both the action and the audience's experience.

d) *Parenthesis* (also parenthèse).[69] Beale, Mounce, Prigent, and Tenney use this term to emphasize that Rev 7 is not independent from Rev 6 or 8 but embedded in it, thus emphasizing continuity. Beale asserts that it is not a proleptic vision (*contra* Charles), but that it explains Rev 6 and describes

---

[64] Bauckham, *Climax*, 13; also H. Kraft, *Die Offenbarung des Johannes* (Tübingen: Mohr Siebeck, 1974), 123.

[65] *Interruption:* Rowland, *Revelation*; Kovacs and Rowland, *Revelation*; and Mazzaferri. *Narrative Apposition:* Maier. I have included Swete's term 'episode' here because he uses the term to highlight that the reader expects the seventh element but instead encounters an episode. He uses the term for 7:1–17, 10:1–11:14, and 14:1–20. Swete, xxxix, cf. 95, 126.

[66] C. Rowland, *Revelation* (London: Epworth Press, 1993), 89, 97.

[67] H. O. Maier, *Apocalypse Recalled: The Book of Revelation after Christendom* (Minneapolis: Fortress, 2002), 154. He also lists 11:15; 1:10; 15:2–4; and 16:4–7 as other examples of "narrative appositions" (p. 239 n.54).

[68] Maier, 158.

[69] Beale, *Revelation*, 406; Mounce, 154; M. C. Tenney, *Interpreting Revelation* (Grand Rapids, Michigan: Eerdmans, 1957), 40–41; Prigent, *L'Apocalypse de saint Jean* (Lausanne: Delachaux et Niestlé, 1981), 117; cf. 149.

a broader context for interpreting the seals.[70] Mounce uses 'parenthesis' as a more general category for understanding Rev 7, but prefers the term 'interlude' modified with the word 'dramatic.'[71] Prigent clarifies that although Rev 7 is parenthetical, it would be a mistake to see it as secondary. "It is not necessary to infer that it acts as a foreign element in the primitive plan, or even that it is an erratic secondary block introduced through a development with which it had nothing to do."[72] As a parenthesis, these interpreters stress that the interruption of the septets between the sixth and seventh indicates the recapitulative nature of the visions. The septets are not to be taken as a succession of literal events, but as a prophetic message presented in different aspects. The seventh element introduces the next series. Somewhat differently than those discussed above, Tenney uses the term 'parenthetical' with the stress on discontinuity, suggesting that the "parenthetical" material "apparently interrupts the logical process of the main action."[73] For these scholars 'parenthesis' connotes both discontinuity and continuity with surrounding units.

Delay remains an important effect of these parentheses, but interpreters who use 'parenthesis' focus on the audience's experience over delay in the narrative action. Beale concludes that Rev 7 and 10:1–11:13 do not represent "chronological delay" but "parenthetical literary delay."

> The literary parallel of delay between the sixth and seventh seals and between the sixth and seventh trumpets suggests a thematic parallel. Ch. 7 shows that Christians are sealed against the spiritually destructive harm of the six trumpet judgments. 11:1–13 reveals that Christians are sealed so as to bear an enduring and loyal witness to the gospel, which begins to lay a basis for the final judgment of those who reject their testimony.[74]

This conclusion is strikingly similar to Bauckham's in three respects. First, Rev 7:1–17 and 10:1–11:13 are linked together by their common position between sixth and seventh elements and by the theme of protection. Second, the purpose of the parenthesis is to portray delay for the sake of the people of God to be protected and then to witness. Third, the people of God are protected from the trumpet plagues and their witness is in view of the final judgment. These three aspects express discontinuity between Rev 7:1–17 and the seal series and 10:1–11:13 and the trumpet series. In short,

---

[70] Beale, *Revelation*, 406. Schüssler Fiorenza (*Justice and Judgment*, 172) also suggests that Rev 7 comments on the action of chapter 6.

[71] Mounce, 154.

[72] Prigent, *L'Apocalypse*, 117: "Il ne faut pourtant pas en inférer qu'il s'agit d'un element étranger au plan primitif, voire meme d'un bloc erratique secondairement introduit dans un développement avec lequel il n'avait rien à faire." Cf. 149.

[73] Tenney, 40.

[74] Beale, *Revelation*, 521. Cf. Prigent, 117.

Beale's use of 'parenthesis' connotes delay that emphasizes continuity but also implies discontinuity.

e) *Digression.* Interpreters who deploy this term emphasize discontinuity.[75] W. Bousset calls Rev 10:1–11:13 a 'digression' rather than a supplement (*Nachtrag*). Revelation 10:1–11:13 is "a digression in which the Apocalypse endeavors to give an account of the further process of its revelation, since the visions fill gradually, threatening to cause a certain disorder."[76] He does not explain why digression is an appropriate term, but emphasizes how Rev 10 anticipates Rev 12–18 and holds it together with the trumpet series.

Although Charles calls Rev 7:1–17 a 'proleptic vision' (discussed below), he followed Bousset to label 10:1–11 an introduction to the 'proleptic digression' of 11:1–13, emphasizing that

> [i]t is a *digression* because the author has turned aside for the moment from his main theme of the Antichrist as identified with Rome and its empire, in order to describe [the Antichrist's] appearance in Jerusalem. This task done, he can pursue without interruption to its close the struggle between Christ and the Antichrist as embodied in the Roman Empire.[77]

For Charles, the term 'digression' emphasizes the disruption of "subject, time and place" between the trumpet series and 10:1–11:13.[78] Aune also uses this term to describe 7:1–17 and 10:1–11:13 as emphasizing protection between the sixth and seventh elements.[79]

f) *Contrasting Unit.* L. Thompson emphasizes the contrast between the sealing of the 144,000 and the destruction on the earth in the opening of the six seals.[80] In order to understand the unity of Revelation, Thompson suggests, one must consider that the Seer has structured the central visions in binary, contrasting units.

g) *Interlock.* A. Y. Collins, followed by M. S. Hall, uses this term to examine how 10:1–11:13 links major units together with retrospective and

---

[75] *Digression:* Bousset, Charles, Aune. As noted above under 'Interlude,' Boring, 127, argues that Rev 7 may appear to be a digression at first, but later seems to be a "skillfully constructed interlude."

[76] "eine Digression, in welcher der Apok. sich Rechenschaft über den weiteren Verlauf seiner Offenbarung zu geben bemüht, da die Fülle der Gesichte allmählich eine gewisse Unordnung herbeizuführen droht" (Bousset, 315).

[77] Italics in original. Charles, 1:269; cf. 257.

[78] Charles, 1:257–8.

[79] Aune, *Revelation*, 2:605.

[80] L. L. Thompson, *The Book of Revelation: Apocalypse and Empire* (New York: Oxford University Press, 1990), 41. He further lists 11:15–19 as contrast to the trumpets (8:7–9:20) and Rev 13 in contrast to Rev 14. The marriage of the Lamb (19:9) is contrasted with the feast of the birds (19:17–18).

anticipatory elements.[81] She argues that 10:1–11:13 interrupts the series of seven trumpets to link the first series of visions (4:1–11:19) with the second series (12:1–22:6).[82] The anarthrous mention of the beast in 11:7 anticipates the prominence of beasts in Rev 13–20.[83] The Seer's commissioning in Rev 10 recalls the initial command to write in Rev 1. The little scroll in Rev 10 also recalls Rev 5. By using the term 'interlock,' Collins helpfully describes the complex relationship of Rev 10:1–11:13 to the whole book.

h) *Pause, Proleptic Vision.* Charles uses these two terms to describe 7:1–17 and 10:1–11:13. It is worth listing here because 'pause' highlights the temporal experience of hearing the text read in sequence. As noted above, other scholars comment how 7:1–17 and 10:1–11:13 delay or retard the expected seventh element of the series.[84]

Charles also argues that this pause is also a delay in the narrative action, referring to 7:1–17 and 10:1–13 as a "proleptic visions" and "proleptic digression."[85] Not all scholars agree that there is delay of the chronological sequence of events. When does chapter 7 take place? In the sequence of narration, chapter 7 occurs between the sixth seal and the seventh seal. In the sequence of story, is it a proleptic vision of final salvation (e.g. Bousset, Charles, Loisy) or a vision of events contemporaneous with the sixth seal (e.g. Ulfgard, Beale)? Charles' use of terms like 'pause' and 'proleptic vision' helps focus attention on this issue. However the question is settled, the debate illuminates how Rev 7:1–17 and 10:1–11:13 require additional processing effort to establish their relevance to the seals and trumpets and how there is ambiguity about their temporal relationships.

i) *Expansion* (also Enlargement and Unexpected prolongation). Farrer, Giblin, Steinmann, E. Müller, Ruiz, and Richard reject the above terms because they minimize the continuity between the unit and the preceding material. These scholars emphasize the continuity of Rev 7:1–8 and 7:9–17

---

[81] A. Y. Collins, *Combath Myth*, 26; M. S. Hall, "The Hook Interlocking Structure of Revelation," *Novum Testamentum* 44.3 (2002): 278–296.

[82] A. Y. Collins, *Combat Myth*, 26–27.

[83] A. K. W. Siew argues that 11:1–14:5 is a literary unity. His observations of a chiastic structure is, in part, based on some of the same evidence that Collins uses to argue that Rev 10:1–11:13 is an 'interlock.' Siew argues 10:11 is a "frame passage" for this chiasm, but otherwise it is not clear how he relates 11:1–13 to 10:1–11 or the trumpet series. He does not seem to engage the argument that 10:1–11:13 is an deviation or a unity. A. K. W. Siew, *The War between the Two Beasts and the Two Witnesses: A Chiastic Reading of Revelation 11:1–14:5* (London: T & T Clark, 2005).

[84] A. Loisy, *L'apocalypse de Jean* (Paris: Nourry, 1923), 155.

[85] Charles, 1: 257.

with the fifth and sixth seals.[86] They are consistent with R. Loenertz, who seems to be the earliest to suggest that Rev 7:1–17 represents the second and third scenes of the sixth seal and 10:1–11:13 represents the second and third scenes of the sixth trumpet.[87] He sees these "triptychs" as an important structuring device, but does not assign any other special terminology to them. Nonetheless, he cautions readers against finding symmetries, noting that there is a lack of continuity caused by this structure.

> The unequal length of the sections in the Apocalypse has misled more than one commentator and sets snares for readers enamoured of a merely material symmetry consisting of a more or less equal length of corresponding passages. ... The wide inequality of the sections is aggravated by dissimilarity in structure. Within some of them there is to be remarked the same lack of continuity as characterizes the sequence of the sections.[88]

For Loenertz, the key is to see the plan of the triptych that is subordinated to the septet.[89] Rev 7:1–17 and 10:1–11:13 must be taken with the sixth seal and sixth trumpet respectively.[90]

In a similar vein, Farrer suggests that the theme of the sixth seal is unbroken in Rev 7, but that the chapter is an "unexpected prolongation."[91] The great earthquake of Rev 6:12–17 is the prayed-for vindication of the martyrs under the altar, but is held back until the saints have been sealed in 7:1–8. The last scene of the sixth seal is 7:9–17, which shows the multitude that desired vindication in 6:9–11.

Giblin likewise argues that 7:1–17 and 10:1–11:14 do not interrupt or retard the progress of the action, but enlarge the perspective and scope of events.[92] Rev 6:12–7:17 is a *Visionsreihen*, a series of visions that help to explain one another. Following the great earthquake (6:12–17), God's people will be sealed to protect them from the terror that will come on sinners (7:1–8). Hearing a numbered Israel is equated with seeing an innumerable

---

[86] F. Hahn, "Zum Aufbau der Johannesoffenbarung," 150, suggests that 7:1–8 is a part of the sixth seal but that Rev 7:9–17 points ahead to 21:1–22:5. "Vor allem ist als sechste Siegel-Vision der ganze Abschnitt 6,12–7,8 zusammengefaßt, woran sich dann 7,9–17 als selbstaendige, auf 21,1–22,5 vorausweisende Einheit anschließt."

[87] Loenertz, xvi–xvii; cf. 66–69; 76.

[88] Loenertz, xvi.

[89] Loenertz, xvii.

[90] See also Richard, 71–75, who takes 6:12–7:8 as referring to "What Is Happening on Earth" and 7:9–17 as "What Is Happening in Heaven" in the same time period.

[91] A. Farrer, *The Revelation of St. John the Divine* (Oxford: Clarendon, 1964), 104–105.

[92] C. H. Giblin, *The Book of Revelation: The Open Book of Prophecy* (Collegeville, MN: Liturgical Press, 1991), 90, followed by J.–P. Ruiz, "Hearing and Seeing but Not Saying: A Rhetoric of Authority in Revelation 10:4 and 2 Corinthians 12:4," in *The Reality of Apocalypse: Rhetoric and Politics in the Book of Revelation* (ed. D. Barr; SBLss 39; Atlanta: SBL, 2006), 94 n. 13.

group from every nation, tribe, people, and tongue (7:9–17).[93] Analogously, 9:13–11:13 presents three visions. Rev 10:1–11 and 11:13 clarify the "salvific aspects of the frightening sixth, penultimate element in the septenary, to encourage John and his readers."[94] The sixth trumpet focuses on humanity's failure to repent, followed by assurance of the fulfillment of God's promise (10:1–7), the need for John's prophetic testimony (10:8–11), and the final triumph of prophetic testimony (11:1–13).

In a way reminiscent of Loenertz, Steinmann argues that Rev 7:1–8 and 7:9–17 are the second and third scenes of the sixth unsealing, analogous with Rev 10:1–11 and 11:1–13. According to Steinmann, the three scenes of the sixth seal express the preparations of the whole human race for the Lamb's final advent: expanding from unbelievers on earth (6:12–17) to saints on earth (7:1–8) and saints in heaven (7:9–17).[95] Likewise, the sixth trumpet is expanded to encompass 9:13–11:14, concluded by the announcement of the second woe (11:14). Witness is the theme of the sixth trumpet for Steinmann. Differently from others, he interprets the cavalry of the sixth trumpet as Christians who witness in the world, being able to kill the soul with the fire of their mouths (like the two witnesses).[96] The second scene (10:1–11) presents John as a type of every prophet who receives God's word. The third scene (11:1–14) depicts two witnesses as the activity of all Christian witnesses.[97]

E. Müller uses discourse theory to argue that 'expansion' is better than 'interlude' to describe Rev 7, but acknowledges that it is closer in vocabulary and themes to Rev 4–5 than 6.[98] "Rev 7 does not interrupt the flow of the seals and does not introduce totally unrelated material into this point of Revelation, although it is true that on the literary level, Rev 7 is closer to Rev 4–5 than it is to the seals."[99] He demonstrates that Rev 7:1–8 and 7:9–17 each have distinct vocabulary, confirming they are two sections.[100] He does not, however, argue that Rev 10:1–11:13 is an expansion of the sixth trumpet in the same way as Rev 7. Instead he notes that Rev 10:1–11 and 11:1–13 differ in regard to personnel and vocabulary and lack a transition. Despite these discontinuities, Müller argues that Rev 10:1–11:13 is an ex-

---

[93] Giblin, *Open Book*, 91–92.

[94] C. H. Giblin, "Revelation 11:1–13: Its form, function and Contextual Integration," *NTS* 30 (1984): 434. Cf. Loenertz, xvi–xvii, who describes Rev 6:12–7:17 and 9:13–11:14 as "triptychs."

[95] Steinmann, 72.

[96] Steinmann, 74.

[97] He also briefly argues that the septet of bowls also follows a tripartite pattern, with 16:15 as the interruption between in the sixth bowl. See Steinmann, 70–71.

[98] E. Müller, 250–251.

[99] E. Müller, 251.

[100] E. Müller, 254–256.

pansion of the sixth trumpet because they do share some common verbs and nouns.[101] For Müller, an 'expansion' seems to be defined by the continuity of vocabulary and themes.

5. Conclusions from Survey of Terms

From this survey of terms used to describe Rev 7:1–17 and 10:1–13, a number of conclusions may be drawn.

(1) The proliferation of terms highlights that these units need some special explanation of their relationship to the surrounding material and therefore are what I have called 'deviations.' Even the commentators who resist using any term still have to explain the abruptness of these units.[102] In terms of relevance theory, Rev 7:1–17 and 10:1–13 have required additional processing effort to understand their relevance to the seven seals and seven trumpets respectively.

(2) This survey demonstrates the need to investigate deviations within the cognitive environment of 1st century Asia Minor. None of the scholars surveyed has attempted to correlate terminology or criteria with contemporary ancient practice. Would John's audiences also have experienced these as deviations? By what criteria might they detect them as deviations? What term(s) would they have available to describe them? The term that we choose to use in modern scholarship should correlate with appropriate Greek terminology and usage to represent more accurately what impact it may have had on an audience. Within the context of the oral culture of 1st century Asia Minor, clear criteria for detecting and identifying deviations need to be developed. Longenecker has persuasively demonstrated how the chain-link transition explains the deviations of Rev 3:21–22, 8:2–5, 15:1–4, and 22:6–9 within the cognitive environment of 1st century Greco-

---

[101] E. Müller, 377–381.

[102] For example, Witherington tries to avoid focusing on the transition between 6:17 and 7:1, but admits that in 6:17, "John takes us to the brink of the end but does not go on to describe the end itself." Rather than an interruption, he concludes that Rev 10–11 is divine commentary on the action (as Schüssler Fiorenza and others). As with other scholars (e.g. Farrer, Giblin), Witherington is concerned that labeling these units 'interludes' or 'interruptions' minimizes their importance. He stresses that "[w]orship and adoration of God and the Lamb is one of the main goals of the rhetoric of this work, and so the worship scenes should not be seen as heavenly commercials or interruptions" (B. Witherington III, *Revelation* [NCBC; Cambridge: Cambridge University Press, 2003], 136, 155). W. J. Harrington (*Revelation* [SP; Collegeville, Minnesota: Liturgical Press, 1993], 97) does not try to explain the structure of Rev 7:1–17, only saying it is "a fresh vision of special importance."

Roman rhetoric. Is there a rhetorical technique that explains the deviations of 7:1–17 and 10:1–11:13?

(3) The term needs to emphasize both continuity and discontinuity between the septet and deviation that interrupts it between the sixth and seventh element. The disagreement over terms is in part about the degree of continuity or discontinuity. Some scholars use 'interruption' or 'intrusion' to emphasize discontinuity that is experienced when hearing or reading the text and expecting the seventh element. Some interpreters who use 'interlude' and 'intercalation' stress that this does not mean the unit is secondary or unrelated to the previous material. Those who reject the most common term, 'interlude,' do so because they feel it implies independence from the septet. Words like 'expansion' and 'enlargement' are used to connote continuity and relationship. If a more accurate term is to be found, it needs to express both discontinuity experienced and continuity of vocabulary and theme.

(4) There is agreement that these units cause some delay in the audience's experience but there is not agreement whether the units delay the progress of the action or expand the perspective of the action. This, of course, depends on how one defines "the action." For example, Steinmann unifies Rev 7 under the heading of "preparing for the Lamb's advent," and so naturally it is not a delay. Schüssler Fiorenza, on the other hand, sees the great earthquake as the beginning of judgment and the sealing of the 144,000 as the beginning of salvation. This question again revolves around the degree of discontinuity one perceives. If the contrast is experienced as great, then the unit delays the action. If there is a high degree of continuity, then the perspective is enlarged but not contrasted.

(5) The degree of continuity seems to reflect a cognitive process, moving from an initial experience of discontinuity to appropriation of the unit into a coherent structure. Boring demonstrated this by differentiating between an initial experience of delay or postponement to an understanding that the unit was a suspenseful portrait of the church.[103] Richard suggests that an initial reaction to these units is to identify them as interruptions or hiatus, but he argues that they are at the core of the message of the book.[104] Likewise, Aune suggested that these units are more important to the author than the surrounding material and Minear argues that Rev 7 is the climax of the seal visions.[105]

These comments demonstrate that at first Revelation 7:1–17 and 10:1–11:13 seem abrupt, but as these interpreters continue to experience the book sequentially and in multiple readings and hearings, they normalize

[103] Boring, 127.

[104] Richard, 87.

[105] Aune, *Westminster Dictionary*, 404; Minear, 75.

them into a coherent structure. This reader-oriented description focuses on the cognitive experience, but the difference between a sequential and holistic reading may illustrate the literary dimensions of the same phenomena. When compared with the units preceding and following, these units seem like deviations and, from this perspective, terms that emphasize discontinuity are appropriate. But when the text is experienced as a whole, the deviations seem to disappear because they are linked so thoroughly by idiom, diction, and thought to the whole text. In this case, interpreters choose terms that emphasize continuity.

Emphasis on continuity or discontinuity is therefore linked to interpreter's cognitive experience of the text and to what extent the unit is viewed from the perspective of its immediate literary context or the whole book. Some interpreters emphasize the position of these units within the seal and trumpet series, while others emphasize the connections with the rest of the book, while others lie in between. To better understand this spectrum, we need to better understand the text's signals that contribute to this ambiguity.

Chapter 2

Discontinuity and Continuity in Revelation 7 and 10–11

Revelation 7:1–17 is embedded in the seal series and Rev 10:1–11:13 in the trumpet series. In what ways do these passages signal continuity with the seal and trumpet series? In what ways do they indicate discontinuity? What are the implications of these signals?

In order to trace the signals that an audience could use to determine relevance, I use Pattemore's criteria to delimit and analyze the relationships between units. I place signals into four categories: (1) signals of continuity with the seal or trumpet series respectively, (2) signals that indicate discontinuity by recalling units before the seal or trumpet series, (3) signals that indicate discontinuity by anticipating future units that resolve ambiguity, and (4) ambiguous signals that are left unresolved. Analyzed in terms of these four categories, it becomes apparent that a few signals indicate continuity with the seal or trumpet series and reinforce the perception that Rev 7 is embedded in the seal series and Rev 10:1–11:13 in the trumpet series. However, many more signals are discontinuous or ambiguous at best. Since hearers receive signals of discontinuity and continuity, it becomes clear why interpreters have used diverse and divergent terms for these passages.

Discontinuous signals give the impression that Rev 7:1–17 and 10:1–11:13 sit awkwardly in the seal and trumpet series. The audience has to expend more effort to understand them, either to recall previous units (primarily Rev 1–3, 5, or 6:9–11) or to wait for the signals to be clarified in later visions. As a result of their length and the heightened effort to process them, I argue that Rev 7:1–17 and 10:1–11:13 take on increased significance for understanding the book.

In terms of content, these units also take on additional significance because of the characters they feature (analyzed below under 'personal references' and '*dramatis personae*'). Revelation 7:1–17 and 10:1–11:13 play a significant role in developing the perception of John and the people of God. In this chapter, I will show how these passages develop the themes of protection, separation, suffering and vindication of the people of God. John and the people of God are transformed from passivity to activity, from ignorance to knowledge, and from powerlessness to authorization. The audience that identifies with these characters likewise is invited to participate in their transformation.

1. Criteria for Delimiting Units

An audience discerns a change in scene based on a variety of signals, some overt (such as a transitional word or phrase like "after this, I saw...") and others more subtle (such as introduction of new characters). Some criteria are necessary to discern and describe the different signals that lead to the perception of continuity and discontinuity. In *Souls under the Altar*, Pattemore proposes six features that contribute to the perception of the limits of a unit (delimiting markers, personal references, communication axis, *dramatis personae*, spatial signals, and temporal signals), to which I add a seventh, thematic vocabulary, based on Ekkehardt Müller's *Microstructural Analysis of Revelation 4–11.*[1] I use these seven features to delimit units and describe the relationships between them. Except for thematic vocabulary, the following definitions are drawn from *Souls under the Altar*.[2]

(1) *Delimiters* are textual signals (lexical, syntactic, semantic, or formal) that delineate textual units. For example, the phrase καὶ εἶδον ὅτε ἤνοιξεν ("and I saw when it opened") marks the beginning of a new unit in the series of seals and signals the end of the previous unit. Because it repeats the delimiter of the previous seal, it signals continuity. A change in delimiter may signal discontinuity to the audience.

(2) The *communication axis* refers to a speaker and hearer in a communication situation within a textual unit. Levels of communication can be embedded in direct discourse, for example, a character reporting the direct speech of another character. When the communication axis changes either in level or speaker and hearer, this is a signal of discontinuity to the audience. For example, when the kings, magnates, rich and powerful cry out to the mountains and rocks (Rev 6:15–17), their direct speech signals discontinuity with the rest of the seal series lacking this communication axis.

(3) *Personal references* lists human, divine or spiritual beings named in the unit but who do not act in it. Shifts in non-acting characters suggest discontinuity to an audience, either when a non-acting character is introduced, is depicted in a way that recalls a previous event, is absent, or becomes an active character (i.e. *dramatis persona*). For example, the "slaves

[1] E. Müller, *A Microstructural Analysis of Revelation 4–11* (Berrien Springs, Mich.: Andrews University Press, 1996).

[2] S. Pattemore, *Souls under the Altar: Relevance Theory and the Discourse Structure of Revelation* (UBS 9; New York: UBS, 2003), 100–101.

of God" and the 144,000 are introduced in Rev 7:1–8, but are absent from Rev 6.

(4) *Dramatis personae* are participants who perform some action in the textual unit. As with the criterion of personal references, shifts in *dramatis personae* suggest discontinuity when new acting characters are introduced, repeated, disappear, or become non-acting (i.e. personal references). For example, in Rev 6:12–17 the Lamb acts to open the scroll. Kings, great ones, generals, rich, poor, slave, and free hide and shout. None of these characters act in Rev 7:1–8.

(5) *Spatial signals* identify locations in space or describe the space by direction of movement. Shifts in space suggest discontinuity. Revelation 6:12–17 gives a location viewing the earth and sky, stars falling to earth, and the movement of kings, etc. to caves and mountains. Revelation 7:1–3 depicts a space that includes the four corners of the earth.

(6) *Temporal signals* identify locations in time or describe movement in time. These signals can suggest temporal continuity or discontinuity between units. In Rev 6 the phrase "when the Lamb opened..." signals the temporal sequence of seals.

(7) A seventh feature, *thematic vocabulary*, identifies key words and phrases that recall previous units or foreshadow later ones. These signals form a 'map' of Revelation that reminds the audience of what it has heard and gives clues to what will come. Processing these signals requires the audience to expend additional effort to relate the signal to previous material or to cope with ambiguity that may be resolved later. The following analysis builds on Ekkehardt Müller's dissertation, *Microstructural Analysis of Revelation 4–11,* in which he analyzes the pattern of vocabulary in each unit.[3] In my analysis, thematic vocabulary includes words and phrases within the passage that also occur outside the unit either verbatim or within the same semantic field. For example, Rev 6:12–17 uses the following vocabulary that relate it to the rest of Revelation: seal; earthquake happened; sun, moon, stars; heaven; opened; scroll; kings; mountain; wrath of God and lamb; and stand.[4] Each of these words or phrases is part of the mental geography of the text relating textual units in order to optimize relevance.

---

[3] See Pattemore's critique that Müller does not adequately consider the function and context of repetition (*Souls*, 73–81).

[4] Cf. E. Müller, 253; Pattemore, *Souls*, 58. E. Müller lists a number of words that are repeated in Rev 6:12–17 but not significantly elsewhere, such as πέτραι and κρύπτω. πίπτω does occur 23 times, but most often in worship (8 times), followed by falling cities (6), falling heavenly bodies (5), reference to death (2) and sin (1). John does not seem to use πίπτω thematically.

2. Experiencing the Structure of Rev 7:1–17

Before applying the above criteria to Rev 7:1–17 it is useful to describe in greater detail the experience of the hearing the text read aloud. What do members of the audience experience when they hear Rev 6 followed by Rev 7? They expect that seven seals will be opened in order (5:1; 6:1). They hear brief events after the lamb opens each seal. The number of words in Greek to describe the opening and events of first four seals are relatively few (46, 40, 56, and 59 words respectively) and occur in a regular pattern and in quick succession.[5] The event following the fifth seal shifts focus from the living creatures and riders to souls under the altar and requires 82 words. The unit immediately following the sixth seal is the longest, 135 words, three times longer than the shortest seal. The length of the fifth and sixth events slows down the pace.

Compared to the first six seal openings, the audience has to wait an exceptional length of time for the seventh seal. Revelation 7 includes 400 words in Greek (161 in 7:1–8 and 239 in 7:9–17), ten times the shortest seal unit. If one includes the unit immediately following the sixth seal, the audience hears 535 words before the seventh seal is opened, more than the first five seals combined. This is almost twice the total number of words used to describe the first five seals (283 words). Revelation 7 (400 words) alone has almost as many words as Rev 6 (418 words). By sheer word count, it seems that John is emphasizing the events in Rev 7 over the opening of the seals.

The location of the visions before the seventh seal further emphasizes their impact on the audience. Following the sixth seal, the audience expects the conclusion of the seal openings. Instead the audience experiences the sealing of the 144,000 and the great crowd around the throne. If Rev 7 had occurred following the seven seals, it could have been experienced as a set of independent visions. In this location, it takes a penultimate place within the seal series in juxtaposition with the climax of the seals. The audience is faced with evaluating Rev 7's relationship to the series of seals.

a) Delimiting Markers: Signaling Ambiguity

I use Pattemore's criteria as a way to trace the signals that audiences use to determine the relevance of Rev 7:1–17 to prior and subsequent units. It is widely acknowledged that this passage is divide into two units, 7:1–8 and

---

[5] Counting words gives some basis for the time required to read the text and emphasizes the audiences' experience of the text. It is an imperfect measure since there is little indication of pauses or pace. For a similar conclusion, see R. Bauckham, *Climax of Prophecy* (London: T & T Clark, 1993), 12.

7:9–17, by the markers μετὰ τοῦτο εἶδον and μετὰ ταῦτα εἶδον, καὶ ἰδοὺ.[6] Revelation 7:1 begins a new vision with the phrase "After this, I saw four angels standing at the four corners of the earth..." (μετὰ τοῦτο εἶδον τέσσαρας ἀγγέλους ἑστῶτας ἐπὶ τὰς τέσσαρας γωνίας τῆς γῆς). Revelation 7:9 begins a distinct vision using the plural pronoun following μετά, "After these things, I saw, and behold, a great crowd..." (μετὰ ταῦτα εἶδον, καὶ ἰδοὺ ὄχλος πολὺς).

There is some question about how to interpret the difference between the singular and plural delimiting markers. The pronoun τοῦτο is singular in Rev 7:1 and plural (ταῦτα) in 7:9. The issue is not trivial. The significance one attaches to these markers impacts whether or not one discerns continuity or discontinuity. In the following discussion, I suggest that both of these markers are ambiguous. They allow the audience to hear both continuity and discontinuity with the sixth seal.

Interpreters vary on the significance of the singular pronoun in Rev 7:1. Does it refer to the sixth seal only or all the seals as a whole? Some interpreters minimize the difference between the singular and plural arguing that both simply introduce a new vision (e.g. Charles, Hellholm, Aune, Beale), while others argue that the singular signals a close relationship between the sixth seal and Rev 7:1–8 (e.g. Pattemore, E. Müller, Steinmann).[7]

Textual criticism of Rev 7:1 reinforces the conclusion that the singular pronoun signals ambiguity. The three variants for this verse suggest three different experiences of continuity and discontinuity.[8] The best witnesses, codices A and C, have the singular pronoun without parataxis (μετὰ τοῦτο) and maximum ambiguity is a result. The phrase indicates a new vision without clarifying the referent for the pronoun, which could refer to the events following the sixth seal or the first six seals as a whole. The audience is faced with additional processing effort to decide which makes the most sense. Codex Siniaticus, the Majority text traditions (excluding Andreas) and most Syriac mss. resolve some of the ambiguity through καί parataxis (καὶ μετὰ τοῦτο) that more clearly links 7:1–8 to the sixth seal. Andreas and Harkel's Syriac texts resolve the ambiguity in the other direction by changing the singular to the plural, bringing the phrase into

---

[6] E.g. R. H. Charles, *The Revelation of St. John* (2 Vols; ICC; Edinburgh: T & T Clark, 1920), 2:189–190; D. Aune, *Revelation* (3 vols; Waco, TX: Word, 1997–8), 2:434.

[7] D. Hellholm, "The Problem of Apocalyptic Genre and the Apocalypse of John," *Semeia* 36 (1986): 39. Cf. Charles, 1:cxxxiv; Pattemore, *Souls*, 104, cf. 130. Pattemore warns that μετὰ ταῦτα does not always function this way, but does here and in 4:1 and 15:5.

[8] Charles, *Revelation*, 2:278; Aune, *Revelation*, 2:426.

harmony with John's usage elsewhere and clearly separating it from the sixth seal.

Charles, Beale, Aune, and others take the position that the singular pronoun τοῦτο is equivalent to the plural, distinguishing Rev 7:1–8 from the sixth seal in the same way as other occurrences of the phrase μετὰ ταῦτα (4:1; 15:5; 18:1).[9] Beale takes the singular pronoun to refer to Rev 6:1–17, that is, the vision of the opening of the first six seals as a whole.[10] He emphasizes that the delimiting marker sets Rev 7:1–8 as an independent vision that John received following Rev 6:1–17. Overall, Beale's concern is to show recapitulation in Revelation and not a linear progression of end-time predictions. He interprets the plural in Rev 7:9 to be equivalent to the singular, only marking that the vision was received following the preceding one.[11] Aune likewise minimizes the difference between the singular and plural pronouns. The formula in both cases signals a change in subject and introduces a new unit.[12] Since John normally uses the plural, the difference may only indicate a different source for Rev 7:1–8.[13]

Pattemore discusses this issue more substantively and proposes what he calls a "hierarchy of discourse connectives" to distinguish the importance of each connective.[14] He suggests that the singular pronoun has "less scope" than the plural, but he does not define its scope.[15] He argues against equating each μετὰ ταῦτα, since the phrase has a variety of functions in Revelation (compare Rev 1:19; 9:12; 20:3). For Pattemore, the referent for the plural μετὰ ταῦτα will maximize cognitive effects and minimizing

[9] Charles, 1:cxxxiv; G. K. Beale, *Revelation The Book of Revelation* (NIGTC; Grand Rapids, Mich: Eerdmans), 406; Aune, *Revelation*, 2:450. Also A. Loisy, *L'apocalypse de Jean* (Paris: Nourry, 1923), 156. Taking this position without comment: H. B. Swete, *The Apocalypse of St. John* (2nd ed; New York: Macmillan, 1907), 95; E. Lohmeyer, *Die Offenbarung des Johannes* (Tübingen: Mohr Siebeck, 1953), 67; M. S. Hall, "The hook interlocking structure of Revelation," *Novum Testamentum* 44:3 (2002): 281.

[10] With A. Farrer, *The Revelation of St. John the Divine* (Oxford: Clarendon, 1964), 104; F. Hahn, "Zum Aufbau der Johannesoffenbarung," in *Kirche und Bibel. Festgabe für Bischof Eduard Schick* (München: Paderborn, 1979), 150; C. H. Giblin, *The Book of Revelation: The Open Book of Prophecy* (Collegeville, MN: Liturgical Press, 1991), 90; E. Müller, 254; A. E. Steinmann, "The tripartite structure of the sixth seal, the sixth trumpet, and the sixth bowl of John's Apocalypse," *Journal of the Evangelical Theological Society* 35 (Oct 1992): 71.

[11] Beale, *Revelation*, 426.

[12] Aune, *Revelation*, 2:450.

[13] With Charles, *Revelation*, 1:106, 203. Charles lists other apocalyptic literature that uses this as a formula to separate visions.

[14] Pattemore, *Souls*, 117.

[15] Pattemore, *Souls*, 115; cf. 104–5; *The People of God in the Apocalypse: Discourse, Structure and Exegesis* (MSSNTS 128; Cambridge: Cambridge University Press, 2004), 125.

processing effort in each context.[16] In Rev 7:9, the pronoun is plural and the phrase is joined with καὶ ἰδοὺ to begin a new unit (cf. 4:1; 15:5). He suggests that the singular μετὰ τοῦτο is the same level of connectives as καὶ... εἶδον and καὶ... ἤκουσα, which is the formula used to introduce each seal event.[17] However, he confuses matters by arguing that μετὰ τοῦτο in Rev 7:1 introduces a "major new segment or subsegment" as other markers do in Rev 4:1; 7:9; 12:1; 14:1, 14; 19:11. If μετὰ τοῦτο in Rev 7:1 functions like μετὰ ταῦτα in Rev 7:9 to introduce major new segments, then μετὰ τοῦτο must be at a higher level of connective than καὶ ... εἶδον that merely introduces each seal event.[18] Pattemore concedes that his hierarchy of connectives is approximate and that "the picture is much more complicated than this."[19]

Since the singular pronoun is most likely original to Rev 7:1, and its ambiguity was evident to early copyists, it seems best simply to note the ambiguity and the disruption to the flow of the seven seals. Although not delimiting Rev 7:1 as significantly as the higher order marker in Rev 7:9, the phrase μετὰ τοῦτο εἶδον signals either the whole of the first six seals or simply the sixth seal and delimits the beginning of a new vision. The ambiguous delimiting phrase allows audiences to decide if the new vision relates to the sixth seal or the whole seal series.

In contrast, Rev 7:9 is more sharply delimited by Μετὰ ταῦτα εἶδον, καὶ ἰδοὺ, which suggests a significant break and beginning of a new unit. Following Korner and Hellholm, Pattemore ranks this phrase as the highest level in the hierarchy of discourse connectives because it combines delimiters.[20] Since this phrase is used in Rev 4:1, Pattemore concludes that Rev 7:9 is "intended to be seen as a new beginning, almost on par with that of chapter 4."[21] The great multitude around the throne (Rev 7:9–17) introduces a new set of visions, just as the throne room vision of Rev 4 introduced the seal series. This is not so decisive, however, since the opening of the seventh seal is still anticipated and the audience waits for the completion of the previous series. For Pattemore, this indicates two structures superimposed. The throne room vision of Rev 7:9–17 introduces the trumpet series and overlaps with the conclusion of the seven seals.

Pattemore's solution minimizes the connections between Rev 7:1–8 and 7:9–17. Although he argues that Rev 7:9 begins a new vision akin to the

---

[16] Pattemore, *Souls*, 58.

[17] Pattemore, *Souls*, 117.

[18] Cf. Pattemore, *Souls*, 125–126.

[19] Pattemore, *Souls*, 117.

[20] Pattemore, *Souls*, 117; Hellholm, "Problem," 39; R. J. Korner, "'And I Saw…' An Apocalyptic Literary Convention for Structural Identification in the Apocalypse," *Novum Testamentum* 42 (2000): 162; cf. E. Müller.

[21] Pattemore, *Souls*, 130; *People of God*, 140.

throne-room scene of Rev 4, he also acknowledges the close connections between the two halves of Rev 7.[22] John contrasts the number and ethnicity of the 144,000 and the innumerable crowd and international origin.[23] Pattemore suggests that John provides clues for the audience to identify with both groups. He agrees with Bauckham who argues that 7:9–17 reinterprets 7:1–8, just as the vision of the slaughtered Lamb reinterpreted the audition of the Lion of Judah (5:5, 6).[24] In this way, the hope of restored Israel is reinterpreted as the salvation of all humanity.[25] Because of the juxtaposition of these two visions of the people of God, most interpreters take Rev 7 as a unity.[26]

Therefore, even the "high-level marker" μετὰ ταῦτα εἶδον, καὶ ἰδοὺ (7:9) is ambiguous. It clearly demarcates a new vision, summarizing previous visions by the plural pronoun. It also reminds the audience of the throne room scene in Rev 4–5 that was also introduced with this phrase (4:1). On the other hand, the content of Rev 7:9–17 juxtaposes another vision of the people of God with the 144,000 sealed in Rev 7:1–8. In short, the markers in Rev 7:1 and 7:9 both delimit units and create ambiguity for the audience.

b) Communication Axis: Discontinuity

The communication axis of Rev 7 distinguishes it from the surrounding units, signaling discontinuity to the audience.[27] The communication situation in Rev 6 is primarily between throne-room participants (living creatures, voices) and new participants (riders, those under the throne). This situation changes in the sixth seal, which features the kings of the earth,

---

[22] Pattemore, *Souls*, 130; *People of God*, 140.

[23] Bauckham, *Climax*, 224.

[24] Pattemore, *People of God*, 141. Bauckham, *Climax*, 215–216. Cf. D. Barr, "The Apocalypse as a Symbolic Transformation of the World: A Literary Analysis," *Interpretation* 38 (1981): 39–50; R. Bauckham, "The List of the Tribes in Revelation 7 Again," *JSNT* 42 (1991): 99–115.

[25] Pattemore, *People of God,* 142. He also finds weak implicatures with the promise to Abraham to multiply descendants and bless all nations and a similar expansion of God's promise in Isa 49:6.

[26] By 'unity,' I mean that 7:9–17 is interpreted as if essentially related to 7:1–8, a position held *inter alia* by W. Boussett, *Die Offenbarung Johannis* (Göttingen: Vandenhoeck and Ruprecht, 1896), 288–9; Charles, 1:189–190; Lohmeyer, 70; E. Schüssler Fiorenza, *The Book of Revelation: Justice and Judgment* (2nd ed; Minneapolis: Fortress, 1998), 67–68; Aune, 2:434; Beale, *Revelation*, 404–5. This does not mean that these interpreters agree that the 144,000 are equated with the multitude (as discussed below), but that Rev 7:1–8 and 7:9–17 are interpreted together. I suggest that the combination of delimiting signals makes the relationship between Rev 7:1–8 and 7:9–17 more ambiguous and allows variant interpretations.

[27] Pattemore, *Souls*, 102. Hellholm, "Problem," 49.

etc. speaking to the mountains and rocks. In contrast, Rev 7:1–8 shows new angelic characters speaking to one another, which only occurs here and Rev 14:18.[28] In Rev 7:1–8, an angel shouts to the four angels at the corners of the earth and a voice speaks the number of the sealed to an unknown target. John reports the number as if he is the target of the speech.

The communication situations in Rev 7:9–17 are reminiscent of Rev 4–5. Rev 7:10–12 feature communication between throne room participants (living creatures, elders, angels) and God. Revelation 7:13–17 also portrays a unique conversation between John and another character. The audience may recall in Rev 4–5 that characters communicated with the One on the throne and that John was directly addressed by an elder (5:5).

Judging by the communication axis, Rev 7:1–8 anticipates later communication of angel to angel and of unidentified voices to an unidentified audience, while Rev 7:9–17 recalls communication in Rev 4–5 between figures around the throne and between an elder and John. Neither Rev 7:1–8 nor 7:9–17 replicate the communication axes of the six seals in Rev 6. As a result, the two halves of Rev 7 are separated from one another and from the sixth seal by their distinct axes of communication.

c) Personal References: Discontinuity then Continuity

Personal references (meaning characters who are named but do not act in the unit) also change between the sixth seal and the two halves of Rev 7, which signal discontinuity to the audience. The first six seals and Rev 7:1–8 have different non-acting participants. In the event following the sixth seal, the Lamb and the one sitting on the throne are named but do not act. In contrast, the slaves of God and the 144,000 children of Israel are named in Rev 7:1–8. The reference to "slaves of God" reminds the audience of the way it was initially addressed, of John's identity (Rev 1:1; cf. 2:20), of the martyrs under the altar (Rev 6:11), and of the language of slave manumission used in the hymn to the Lamb (Rev 5:9).[29] Following Pattemore, I use the term 'people of God' as inclusive of the audience, the addressees of the seven letters, John, and characters in Revelation who are signified with similar language, including 'slaves of God,' 'witnesses,' 'saints,' etc. and more specific categories, such as 'prophets' and 'apostles.'[30]

The 144,000 children of the tribes of Israel are the dominant personal references in Rev 7:1–8. The audience may relate them to the list of those redeemed (5:9: "you ransomed for God saints from every tribe…") or to answer the question in Rev 6:17, "Who will stand?" (discussed more fully

[28] Cf. 16:1. Noted by Aune, *Revelation*, 2:455.

[29] Schüssler Fiorenza, *Revelation*, 61; Aune, *Revelation*, 1:361; Beale, *Revelation*, 411; Pattemore, *People of God*, 133. Cf. Richard, 67

[30] See p. 18.

under thematic vocabulary below). More closely, the 144,000 anticipate the messianic army who gather to follow the Lamb on Mt. Zion (14:1–5) and follow the Rider on the White Horse (19:14).[31] The signal of the 144,000 is discontinuous with the seal series and ambiguous until optimal relevance is reached in these later passages.

Revelation 7:9–17 has a different set of personal references, closer to the references following the fifth and sixth seal. Those clothed in white may remind the audience of the souls under the altar (Rev 6:9–11). Mention of God and the Lamb recall their wrath in the sixth seal (Rev 6:16–17).

Based on personal references, Rev 7:1–8 anticipates visions to come while Rev 7:9–17 has the greatest relevance to the fifth and six seals. By this measure, Rev 7:1–8 is anticipatory, and 7:9–17 is retrospective.

d) Dramatis Personae: *Discontinuity*

In contrast to characters who do not act (personal references), *dramatis personae* are characters who act in a unit. Revelation 7 introduces new *dramatis personae*: four angels standing at the four corners of the earth, another angel coming up from the direction of the rising sun (Rev 7:1–3), and a "great crowd" gathered around the throne (Rev 7:9). Do these new characters signal continuity with the seal series or discontinuity?

Some interpreters argue that these angels should be identified with the four horsemen introduced during the first four seals and, as a result, signal continuity to the audience. Others argue that the angels and horsemen are not related, and thus signal discontinuity. Because their winds target the earth, sea, and trees, I argue that the angels in Rev 7:1–3 signal discontinuity with the seal series and their identity is ambiguous until resolved by the trumpet plagues that affect earth, sea, and trees.

These angels are introduced anarthrously, which suggests that the audience is not expected to be familiar with these characters. Previously, the audience has experienced four living creatures and four horses and riders, and a voice of many angels around the throne (5:11), but this is the first time a smaller group of angels is identified. The lack of the definite article signals discontinuity in these *dramatis personae*.

Some interpreters argue that extra-textual allusions connect the characters in Rev 7:1–8 with the first four seals. Caird, Rissi, Kraft, Roloff, and

---

[31] Aune, *Revelation*, 2:447–448; Bauckham, *Climax*, 230–231; Pattemore, *People of God*, 184–193. Aune underlines the ambiguity created when the 144,000 are introduced without a definite article in 14:1. Does this group refer to the same one "heard" in 7:1–8? He concludes it is logical, but that the anaphoric reference leaves the audience wondering. See D. Aune, "Following the Lamb: Discipleship in the Apocalypse," in *Apocalypticism, Prophecy and Magic in Early Christianity* (Tübingen: Mohr Siebeck, 2006), 66–7.

Beale suggest Zechariah's visions of four horsemen are relevant (Zech 6:5–8).[32] They argue that Rev 7 should be identified with the four horsemen in Rev 6 since there are four horsemen and four winds in Zech 6:5–8.[33] If this were true, the four angels and four winds would signal continuity to the audience. However, Mounce, Witherington, and Pattemore point out that in Zech 6 these chariots are patrolling the earth not unleashing destruction and the winds are from heaven and not of earth as in Rev 7.[34] In his comprehensive analysis of Revelation's use of Zechariah, Marko Jauhiainen confirms this conclusion, arguing that Zech 6 is not relevant to understanding these angels or winds. "[A]n analysis of 7:1–3 suggests that the attempts to demonstrate the presence of an allusion to Zech 2:6; 6:5 tend to confuse and complicate the exegesis of the pericope, rather than clarifying and facilitating it."[35]

Caird, Rissi, Kraft, Roloff, and Beale also suggest that Daniel's vision of four winds over the Great Sea (Dan 7:2) may resolve the relevance of the winds in Rev 7.[36] Although there are four winds in Dan 7:2, the number and previous allusions to Daniel (e.g. Rev 1:7–8) are the only significant data.[37] In Dan 7:2 the four winds are directed at the sea, but there is no indication that they destroy or are controlled by angels.

Some interpreters argue that the depiction of four winds in the Synoptic Apocalypse (Matt 24:31; Mark 13:27) would lead the audience to relate the four winds to the destruction of the sixth seal.[38] In the Synoptic Apocalypse, destruction is followed by angels who blow trumpets before they gather the elect from the four winds. Yet, the Synoptic Apocalypse fails to explain these four angels and their role. The four angels of Rev 7:1–8 are not blowing trumpets nor gathering, but in control of destroying winds. A fifth angel in Rev 7 has a seal and does not fit the four winds paradigm in the Synoptic Apocalypse. The winds in the Synoptic Apocalypse only indicate the extent of the diaspora, not destructive forces. The angels of

---

[32] G. Caird, *The Revelation of St. John the Divine* (New York: Harper & Row, 1966), 94; M. Rissi, *Time and History: A Study on the Revelation* (trans. G. C. Winsor; Richmond, Virginia: John Knox, 1966), 44; H. Kraft, *Die Offenbarung des Johannes* (Tübingen: Mohr Siebeck), 124; J. Roloff, *The Revelation of John* (trans. J. E. Alsup; Minneapolis: Fortress, 1993), 96; Beale, 406–7.

[33] Beale, 406–407; Roloff, 96.

[34] Mounce, 155; Witherington, 136; Pattemore, *People of God*, 126–127.

[35] M. Jauhiainen, *The Use of Zechariah in Revelation* (WUNT 2.199; Tübingen: Mohr Siebeck, 2005), 71.

[36] See references in note 32.

[37] Pattemore, *People of God*, 127.

[38] Hahn, 149–150; Schüssler Fiorenza, *Revelation*, 65; cf. *Justice and Judgment*, 103–5; Pattemore, *People of God*, 126. Also suggested by Jauhiainen, 70 n. 40. The Synoptic Apocalypse seems to be most closely related to the sixth seal, cf. Matt 24:29–31.

Rev 7 control winds that will injure the earth, sea and trees.[39] When scrutinized, none of these extra-textual allusions provide a satisfactory connection between these angels and the first six seals.

Charles, Rissi, and Lupieri and others relate these destroying angels and winds to an apocalyptic topos, for example in 1 Enoch 76.[40] 1 Enoch 76 portrays four winds bringing plagues similar to the trumpet plagues. Charles argues that the sealing protects the people of God from the demonic powers released after the sixth trumpet, noting that 1 Enoch 76 describes the wind bringing locusts, an apocalyptic text modeled on the Exodus plague (Exod 10:13).[41] Locusts also would naturally be seen as the enemy of grass (9:4) and trees (7:1–3; 9:4).[42] Charles concludes that the angels and winds anticipate the events following the fifth and sixth trumpets, writing that 7:1–3 "serves in part to introduce the plague of demonic locusts."[43] If the audience recalls this topos, the angels and winds of Rev 7 anticipate the trumpet plagues and are discontinuous with the seal series.

Rissi concurs that the angels and winds anticipate the trumpet series, but he puts stress on the connection between Rev 7:1–3 and 9:4. "The inner homogeneity of the winds with the trumpet visions is even expressly mentioned in 9:4."[44] Both Rev 7:1–3 and 9:4 describe a command to destructive forces not to damage (ἀδικήσαι) trees. In Rev 9:4, these demonic figures are explicitly ordered to harm only those who do not have the seal of God on their foreheads (ἀνθρώπους οἵτινες οὐκ ἔχουσι τὴν σφραγῖδα τοῦ θεοῦ ἐπὶ τῶν μετώπων). This is clearly the first direct reference to the protection of the seal, but it does not satisfactorily resolve the identity

---

[39] Charles, 1:203, argues that "angels of the winds" are stock figures in the cosmology behind the Apocalypse, that includes angels of fire (14:18) and water (16:5) – set over the works of nature (cf. 1 Enoch 60:11–21; 65:8; 69:22; Jubilees 2:2).

[40] Charles, *Revelation*, 1:203; Lohse, 49; R. H. Mounce, *The Book of Revelation* (2nd ed; Grand Rapids, Mich.: Eerdmans, 1998), 155; Rissi, *Time and History*, 44; Aune, *Revelation*, 2:451–2; B. Witherington III, *Revelation* (NCBC; Cambridge: Cambridge University Press, 2003), 136; G. R. Osborne, *Revelation* (BECNT; Grand Rapids Mich.: Baker, 2002), 305; E. Lupieri, *A Commentary on the Apocalypse of John* (trans. M. P. Johnson and A. Kamesar; Grand Rapids, Mich.: Eerdmans, 2006), 148.

[41] Charles, 1:248–249.

[42] Locusts, especially their destruction of trees and grass, are also consequences of siege warfare. See J. C. Wright, "Warfare and Wanton Destruction: A Reexamination of Deuteronomy 20:19–20 in Relation to Ancient Siegecraft," *JBL* 127.3 (2008): 423–458.

[43] Charles, 1:204; cf. 196–197, 243, 248–249. Others include G. E. Ladd, *A Commentary on the Revelation of John* (Grand Rapids, Mich.: Eerdmans, 1972), 111; A. Y. Collins, *The Combat Myth in the Book of Revelation* (Missoula, Mont.: Scholars Press, 1976), 34; Witherington, 137.

[44] Rissi, *Time and History*, 44

of the four angels.[45] Neither Charles nor Rissi identify the four angels of Rev 7:1 with the four angels released following the sixth trumpet.

Lupieri, on the other hand, argues that these four angels are the same as the four released after the sixth trumpet blast (Rev 9:14–15).[46] He notes possibly relevant texts in 2 Bar 6:4–5 and 1 Enoch 66:1 that describes four punishing angels restrained by another. The association between Rev 7:1–3 and 9:14–15 is strengthened by the spatial signal of the East, usually associated with the Euphrates.[47]

In the final evaluation, the identity of the four angels remains ambiguous. Nonetheless, they are new characters who act and this fact differentiates Rev 7:1–8 from the sixth seal. The audience is presented with a challenge to identify them.[48] There are contextual effects if the audience accesses the Synoptic Apocalypse, but the *dramatis personae* of Rev 7:1–8 better anticipate the activity of destroying forces following the fifth and sixth trumpets. In short, the change in *dramatis personae* signals discontinuity with the seal series and anticipate the trumpet series.

The *dramatis personae* of Rev 7:9–17, on the other hand, are retrospective with one exception. The characters are not new but have been introduced through the throne room scene of Rev 4–5 (one sitting on throne, Lamb, living creatures, elders, angels) and those robed after the fifth seal (Rev 6:9–11). The one new group is the "great crowd" (Rev 7:9), which reappears in Rev 19:1, 6 to celebrate the fall of Babylon.[49] All of these characters are discontinuous from those presented in the sixth seal and even Rev 7:1–8, creating further ambiguity for the audience to resolve. The juxtaposition of the 144,000 and this multitude suggests to some that they are identical groups viewed from two points of view,[50] but the textual

---

[45] Indirect references to the seal on the forehead include 14:1; 22:4; cf. 3:12. Cf. Aune, *Revelation*, 2:452.

[46] Lupieri, 148.

[47] Beale, *Revelation*, 408.

[48] "Challenge to identification" is a term that Pattemore uses to indicate an audience will exert more processing effort (*People of God*, 93–94).

[49] Pattemore, *People of God*, 103; Mounce, 337; Caird, 232; M. E. Boring, *Revelation* (Interpretation; Louisville, Kent.: John Knox Press, 1989), 192. This Great Crowd is contrasted with the crowds ruled by the whore (17:15). Cf. Pattemore, *People of God*, 140.

[50] The position that 144,000 and the multitude are the same group (or are a subset) from two points of view is held by Swete, 99; Lohse, 53; Caird, 96; Boring, 129–132; Giblin, 91–92; Bauckham, *Climax*, 215–6; Aune, *Revelation*, 2:447; Beale, *Revelation*, 424–5; Witherington, 138; P. Prigent, *L'Apocalypse de saint Jean* (Lausanne: Delachaux et Niestlé, 1981), 121–123; H. Ulfgard, *Feast and Future: Revelation 7:9–17 and the Feast of Tabernacles* (Stockholm: Almqvist & Wiksell, 1989), 70–2; C. Koester, *Revelation and the End of All Things* (Grand Rapids, Mich.: Eerdmans, 2001), 90.

signals are ambiguous and allow the audience various interpretations that may or may not be resolved later.[51]

e) Spatial Signals: Discontinuity

Spatial signals focalize the events of Rev 7:1–8 in a different location than 6:12–17 and 7:9–17, a shift that signals discontinuity. The sixth seal ends with the kings, etc. in the caves and mountains. Revelation 7:1 offers a wider view of the four corners of the earth, where one may watch an angel rise from the east. The focus is no longer on caves and mountains, but on the whole earth, the sea, and specifically trees. Based on these signals, most interpreters conclude that Rev 7:1–8 shifts the scene from heaven to earth.[52]

Against this consensus, Aune and Pattemore argue that the point of view remains in heaven. Aune argues that the perspective of the author is fixed in heaven from Rev 4:1 to 6:17 and does not shift in 7:1–8.[53] Pattemore also suggests that there is no change in scene, because each seal inevitably involves earth.[54] It is true that both Rev 6:1–17 and 7:1–8 involve the earth, but their particular relationship to earth is different. John only hears about the four horsemen's effects on the earth. The events following the fifth seal focus on the altar in heaven. The events after the sixth seal opening begin in the sky before moving to a narrow view of caves and mountains. The shift to an encompassing view of the four corners of the earth is substantial, and cannot simply be equated with the same focalization of the first six seals.

The mention of trees (δένδρα) in Rev 7:1–3 also signals a different location than the seal series and anticipates the trumpet series. The Greek word δένδρον (tree) only occurs in Rev 7:1–3 and in the trumpet series (8:7; 9:4).[55] Pattemore argues that the audience would immediately think of the metaphor of the stars falling like fruit from a fig tree (συκῆ, Rev

---

[51] Bousset, 287, argues that two different groups are in view; also Lohmeyer, 70–71; Kraft, 126–8.

[52] Charles, *Revelation*, 1:199; Schüssler Fiorenza, *Revelation*, 67; Mounce, 161; Boring, 131; Osborne, 301. Lupieri, 148, argues that "John has the whole earth in mind, but nonetheless the context of 7:1–8 does suggest the scene takes place within the borders of Israel."

[53] Aune, *Revelation*, 2:450.

[54] Pattemore, *Souls*, 128.

[55] ξύλον is the word used for the tree of life (Rev 2:7; 22:4, 14, 19) which refers to cut wood in Rev 18:12. Lupieri, 117–118, 354, interprets ξύλον to refer to the cross of Jesus: the cross is the tree of life; the river of the water of life in the New Jerusalem is lined with crosses bearing fruit in an ironic reversal of Roman roads that might be lined with crosses.

6:13), but the fig tree is only weakly relevant.[56] The earth, sea, and trees are destroyed after the first and second trumpets (Rev 8:7–9). Therefore, when earth, sea, and trees are repeated as targets of destruction, the weak relevance between fig trees and trees is replaced.

It is more likely that Rev 7:1–8 positions audiences in a vantage point to observe the effects of the seven trumpets.[57] The location that includes earth, sea, and trees lexically and semantically prepares the audience for the first two trumpets. Pragmatically, a view of the four corners of the earth is ideal for observing the effects of the trumpet plagues on one third of the earth, sea, streams, and springs, as well as the sky

In contrast, Rev 7:9 shifts the scene back to the throne room as it was introduced in Rev 4:1.[58] This spatial signal is retrospective, turning the focus away from the space of the four angels of Rev 7:1–8 and mountains of Rev 6:12–17 to recall the view of the throne and attendants. A new location is also introduced in Rev 7:9–17. Revelation 7:15 introduces the temple of God as a location (recalling the promise of Rev 3:12), which foreshadows protection in the earthly temple (Rev 11:1–2) and the opening of the temple in Rev 11:19.[59] In summary, the spatial signals of Rev 7 signal discontinuity with the seal series, although each half of Rev 7 signals in a different direction. Rev 7:1–8 anticipates the trumpet series while 7:9–17 recalls the throne room scene and its attendants from Rev 4–5.

f) Temporal Signals: Discontinuity and Delay then Continuity

The two halves of Rev 7 give conflicting signals about their temporal relationship with the seal and trumpet series. Rev 7:1–8 prepares for the time

---

[56] Pattemore, *Souls*, 128. He grants that the connection with fig trees is tenuous, since it is only based on the semantic relationship. The view of Rev 6:13 is not the earth or sea but the sky and falling stars. The use of figs and a fig tree is metaphorical, and the focus is on the stars falling. The fig tree itself is incidental to this metaphor. Finally, there is no lexical connection between συκῆ and δένδρον. If Rev 6:13 is relevant to understanding the trees of Rev 7:1–3, it is only weakly relevant. In contrast, there is a direct lexical connection between the trees threatened in Rev 7:1, 3 and the event following the first trumpet: a third of the trees (τὸ τρίτον τῶν δένδρων) are burned.

[57] Charles, Rissi, and Lupieri argue that the sealing of the 144,000 anticipates the effects of the fifth and sixth trumpet.

[58] Charles, *Revelation*, 1:209; Schüssler Fiorenza, *Revelation*, 67; Mounce, 161; Boring, 131; Osborne, 316; Lupieri, 148.

[59] Cf. Charles, *Revelation*, 1:215; Tenney, 171–2. Beale, *Revelation*, 441, does not think that Rev 7:15 portrays a literal "temple" but the presence of God and the Lamb. This fails to consider the role of the temple in the seven messages (3:12) and its climactic opening in 11:19, both of which encourage the audience to picture a literal temple in addition to the presence of God.

of the trumpet series while Rev 7:9–17 recalls the hymns of Rev 5 and anticipates the New Jerusalem in Rev 21–22.

Specifically, Rev 7:1–8 gives two temporal signals. First, the delimiting marker μετὰ τοῦτο ("After this") is ambiguous. As discussed above, it can be taken to refer to the sixth seal or to the entire seal vision of Rev 6:1–17. It either refers to a new event temporally after the sixth seal or a new vision received after the seal vision.

The second signal is ἄχρι ("until," Rev 7:3), which signals a future event and, most importantly, delay.[60] The angel commands, "Do not damage the earth or the sea or the trees, until (ἄχρι) we have sealed the slaves of our God with a seal on their foreheads" (7:3). This damage has not yet taken place. When does the damage happen? Interpreters are divided on the answer, but they all suggest that this temporal signal communicates discontinuity to the audience.

On one hand, Caird, Beale, and Pattemore correlate this damage to the disasters of Rev 6:12–17 and argue that the sealing occurs chronologically before the sixth seal.[61] As a result, these interpreters note that the events of Rev 7:1–8 occur either contemporary with fifth seal or prior to the seals. In either case, there is temporal discontinuity between the sixth seal and the sealing of the 144,000.

On the other hand, Charles, Rissi, Bauckham, and others argue that some or all of the trumpet plagues should be understood as the disasters indicated by the winds.[62] As discussed under *dramatis personae* and spatial signals, the repetition of 'earth,' 'sea,' and 'trees' suggests that the sealing takes place before the entire trumpet series. ἄρχι signals temporal discontinuity with the seal series.

More importantly, this signal indicates delay for protection and separation. The damaging winds are delayed by protecting the slaves of God. The theme of delay began when the souls under the altar cried out, "How long will it be until you judge and vindicate our blood on the inhabitants of the earth?" (6:10). The signal "until we have sealed the slaves of God" indicates that the purpose of the delay is sealing, which means protection and separation (discussed below under thematic vocabulary).

Revelation 7:9–17, on the other hand, uses a mixture of past, present and future forms, and has caused controversy about its temporal relation-

---

[60] Rissi, *Time and History*, 45.

[61] Caird, 94; Beale, *Revelation*, 406; Pattemore, *People of God*, 128. Hahn, 150, also seems to hold this position *inter alia.*

[62] Charles, *Revelation*, 1:196–7; Rissi, *Time and History*, 44–5; Bauckham, *Climax*, 316; Lupieri, 148; Witherington, 137; Osborne, 306. Cf. Charles, *Revelation*, 1:204, who agrees but adds that the form changes: the trumpets are the disasters. Boring, 128, suggests that the disasters of these winds are forgotten about.

ship to the rest of Revelation. Two options are often presented. First, Charles, Hahn, and Beale interpret the whole scene as a prolepsis of Rev 21:1–22:5.[63] The repetition of language in Rev 7:15b–17 in 21:3–6 is clear. The phrases "the one sitting on the throne will dwell with them," "he will wipe away every tear from their eyes," and "springs of living water" are repeated verbatim in the final scene when the New Jerusalem descends out of heaven from God (ὁ καθήμενος ἐπὶ τοῦ θρόνου σκηνώσει ἐπ' αὐτους...ἐξαλείψει πᾶν δάκρυον ἐκ τῶν ὀφθαλμῶν αὐτῶν...ζωῆς πηγὰς ὑδάτων). Likewise, the service of God's slaves before the throne is repeated from Rev 7:15a in 22:3: "they serve him" (λατρεύουσιν αὐτῷ). The verbs of Rev 7:15b–17, however, are future, which suggests that this prediction is fulfilled in Rev 21–22 but is not identical with it. This conclusion is further strengthened by the presence of the temple in Rev 7:15 and its absence in 21:22.

The second option (held by Schüssler Fiorenza and Pattemore) takes the throne room scene of Rev 5 and the white robed figures under the altar (Rev 6:9–11) as more relevant to Rev 7:9–17. In Rev 7:9–15a, the primary temporal signals are the present verbs that emphasize the continuous aspect of the action: the great crowd *is crying* (κράζουσιν), those clothed in white robes *are coming* (οἱ ἐρχόμενοι) out of the great persecution, they *are* (εἰσιν) before the throne of God, and they *are serving* God (λατρεύουσιν αὐτῷ). In Rev 7:15b–17, the temporal signals are the future verbs that anticipate the fulfillment of God's promises of shelter, food, drink, and protection from the sun. When the present tense of Rev 7:9–15a is juxtaposed with the future of Rev 7:15b–17, it suggests that the action in Rev 7:9–17 occurs at an ambiguous time between the fifth seal and the fulfillment the promises in Rev 21.[64]

Combining the analysis of Rev 7:1–8 and 7:9–17 helps to explain why interpreters struggle to locate Rev 7 in time and are inclined to resolve the tension one way or the other. Rev 7:1–8 occurs narratively after the sixth seal but seems to anticipate the seven trumpets. Rev 7:9–17 on the other hand, refers back to the hymns of Rev 5 and the white-robed martyrs of the fifth seal, while announcing promises that will only be fulfilled in Rev 21–22. When Rev 7:1–8 and 7:9–17 are juxtaposed, the audience has to work harder to understand the relevance of these units. Both halves are further detached from the seal septet in time, which increases the likelihood that

---

[63] Charles, 1:201–202; Hahn, 150; Beale, *Revelation*, 443–445. Also Osborne, 326–329.

[64] Schüssler Fiorenza, *Revelation*, 68; Caird, 102–3; Pattemore, *Souls*, 130. Rissi, *Time and History*, 109: "They are not yet in the renewed world of the consummation, as it is portrayed in 21:1–22:5, and yet they already are serving before God's throne and have a share in the comforts of the future (7:15b–17)."

the audience will interpret Rev 7:1–8 and 7:9–17 together. This may be a reason for this arrangement, but our purpose is to merely note the temporal disruptions signal discontinuity to the audience.

g) Thematic Vocabulary: Ambiguous Standing and Seals

As discussed above, I have added "Thematic Vocabulary" as a criterion for delimiting units in order to expose the web of lexical and semantic connections between units that signal continuity or discontinuity.

Two key words, stand (ἵστημι) and seal (σφραγίς), suggest continuity between Rev 7 to the seal series. I argue below, first, that this continuity is ambiguous and, second, that the plague narrative in Exodus 7–12 is relevant to understanding the sealing in Rev 7. I devote special attention here to the relationship with Exodus because in chapter 4 I will argue that the plague narrative (and especially the Passover in Exod 12) may be a model for understanding a deviation before the last element of a series.

E. Müller (*A Microstructural Analysis of Revelation 4–11*) pays special attention to verbal repetition. He argues that the most important lexical connection for Rev 7 is the theme of standing (forms of ἵστημι).[65] This is one of the primary links between the sixth seal and Rev 7, one that leads Müller and other interpreters (e.g. Farrer, Giblin, Steinmann) to argue that Rev 7 (or at least 7:1–8, with Lohse and Pattemore) is an 'expansion' of the sixth seal. The event following the sixth seal ends with the dramatic cry of the kings, etc.: "the great day of their wrath has come and who is able to stand?" (6:17). Most interpreters take 7:1–8 to be the answer to this question: those who are sealed will be able to stand.[66] This is far from clear, however, as many have noted.[67] Pattemore observes that the first answer to this question is that the angels stand (ἑστῶτας) – at the four corners of the earth. This is an ambiguous answer. The angels are not targets of God's wrath, but are instead presented as instruments of God's judgment. They stand as God's agents.

It is weakly implied that the sealed 144,000 will be protected against God's wrath. These figures are not portrayed as standing and are not seen by John. Instead, he hears their number and their status as sealed. As argued above, they are sealed against the effects of the trumpets. Although the audience may initially relate the sealing to God's wrath, that initial

[65] E. Müller, 251–252.

[66] Lohse, 48; Caird, 93; Mounce, 154; Schüssler Fiorenza, *Revelation*, 65; Prigent, 117; Bauckham, *Climax,* 11; Aune, *Revelation*, 2:479; Pattemore, *People of God*, 125.

[67] Pattemore, *People of God*, 125–128. Charles, 1:183, Beale, *Revelation*, 405, and Richard, 73 also connect 7:9–17 to the question in 6:17, not 7:1–8. Aune, *Revelation*, 2:423, suggests that the question may be purely rhetorical. "The implied answer to this desperate question is obvious: no one can withstand the day of divine wrath."

relevance is overshadowed by more direct references during the trumpet series.

The stronger answer to the question "Who will stand?" is "the great crowd" (7:9). Charles, Beale, and Pattemore observe that the great crowd stands (ἑστῶτες) before the throne and the Lamb (Rev 7:9).[68] The dialogue between the elder and John (7:13–17) clarifies the identity of those who will stand: they are the ones who are coming out of the great persecution and wash their robes in the blood of the lamb. However, this answer is not free of difficulties. The white robes connect these figures with those under the throne, who were slaughtered by the inhabitants of the earth for their testimony (Rev 6:9–11), who were not protected from earthly persecution. Additionally, God's wrath is not relevant especially if these white robes also suggest ethical or spiritual purity.[69]

To conclude the discussion of ἵστημι, I suggest that Rev 7 only offers ambiguous answers to who will stand in the day of God's wrath. At best, Rev 7 offers a tentative but ambiguous and incomplete answer to the question. Revelation 7:1–8 suggests that angels will stand and weakly implies that those sealed will also. Revelation 7:9 more clearly shows a multitude who are standing. Perhaps more to the point, the question is no longer "Who will stand in the day of wrath" in the elder's dialogue with John (Rev 7:13–17) but "who will stand before God after the day of persecution?" The answer to this new question is that those who wash their robes and make them white in the blood of the Lamb will stand. I argue in chapter 5 that the transformation of the theme of "standing" is one of the key functions of Rev 7. It moves their attention from worrying about God's wrath to how to endure faithfully.

The second key word is σφραγίς ("seal") and the related verb σφραγίζω ("I seal") that superficially signals continuity with the series of seals. When an angel comes in Rev 7:2 with a seal of the living God (σφραγῖδα θεοῦ ζῶντος) and John hears that 144,000 have been sealed (ἐσφραγισμένοι) it may bring to mind the scroll that the Lamb takes and opens was sealed with seven seals (κατεσφραγισμένον σφραγῖσιν). Ownership and protection are a weak connection between the two kinds of

---

[68] Charles, 1:183; Beale, *Revelation*, 405; Pattemore, *People of God*, 143.

[69] Bauckham, *Climax*, 227–229, takes the white robe as a symbol of moral probity as faithful witnesses, demonstrated in martyrdom. Beale, *Revelation*, 436–438, argues the white robe refers to purity demonstrated by persevering faith. Pattemore, *People of God*, 143, stresses ethical purity citing Rev 3:4, 5 and 3:17 as most relevant. Charles, *Revelation*, 1:184–188, agrees that the symbol suggests ethical purity in this life, but goes further to argue that in 6:11 it specifically refers to "spiritual bodies given to the martyrs, but not to the rest of the faithful departed till after the Final Judgment" (1:184).

seals.[70] The seals on the scroll protect them from unauthorized opening and indicate they belong to God. The seal on the "slaves of God" (Rev 7:3) indicates that they are owned by God. Why a seal on the forehead implies protection is not clear without additional information.

The sealed scroll is not relevant to understanding the sealed people of God because the differences between the two kinds of seals signal discontinuity to the audience.[71] Pattemore argues that this contrast produces new cognitive effects,[72] but the contrast fails to explain how the seal is protection from the threat to earth, sea, and trees and how the seal indicates separation from the inhabitants of the world.[73] Without this information, the audience would search for additional relevance elsewhere, some other passage that describes the people of God being sealed as protection from destructive forces unleashed by divine agents against land, sea, and trees.

Many interpreters have found relevance for the sealing of God's people especially in the Passover narrative (Exodus 12) and the marking of the faithful few in Jerusalem (Ezekiel 9).[74] For example, Schüssler Fiorenza writes,

> The function of sealing could be compared to the marking of the door of the house with the blood of the paschal lamb designed to protect the Israelites from the Exodus plagues, which initiated the liberation of Israel. The symbolic act of sealing could also derive from Ezek 9:4–6, where God commanded an angel to mark those citizens of Jerusalem

---

[70] On the evidence of this lexical connection, Pattemore argues that the audience can infer the meaning of the sealing of the people of God by seals of the scroll with a common understanding of sealing as ownership and a Christian concept of being sealed by the Spirit (*People of God*, 132–3). Cf. Aune, *Revelation*, 2:456–459; Beale, *Revelation*, 410–11. See discussion about the sealing of the Spirit in Bousset, 287–288; Charles 1:195–6; Aune, *Revelation*, 2:456–9.

[71] Interestingly, Beale does not make any connection between the seals on the scroll and the seals on the forehead in his long discussion of the seal in Rev 7. See Beale, *Revelation*, 409–416. Likewise, Aune, *Revelation*, 2:434, notes that σφραγίς is a catchword connecting 6:1–17 and 7:1–8, but does not draw any implications for understanding the seal on the forehead. Many interpreters (e.g. Lohse, Caird, Mounce, Boring, and Richard) do not note any lexical connection but seem to assume that the scroll seals are not relevant to sealing in Rev 7. Ladd, 112, and Lupieri, 148, distinguish sealing as closing (as on the scroll and in response to the seven thunders) and an identifying mark.

[72] Pattemore, *People of God*, 132.

[73] Osborne, 306, makes similar observations as he argues that 7:1–3 anticipates "the use of God's creation for judgment, a theme that will carry through the trumpets and the book with the first four of each being disasters centering on nature."

[74] Charles, *Revelation*, 1:193–5; Ladd, 112; Schüssler Fiorenza, *Revelation*, 66; Caird, 96–7; Boring, 128; Bauckham, 216; Richard, 73; Beale, *Revelation*, 413; Harrington, 98. Bousset, 281, only discusses Ezek 9.

who rejected the city's abominations. Those marked would be protected during the judgment of the city.[75]

The location of the seal on the forehead may trigger an audience to think of Ezekiel 9, but with Pattemore I argue that it is not necessary for optimal relevance.[76] In Ezekiel 9, angels are instructed to mark faithful people on the forehead before killing the inhabitants of Jerusalem. The angels are then commanded, "Cut down old men, young men and young women, little children and women, but touch no one who has the mark (LXX: σημεῖον). And begin at my sanctuary" (Ezek 9:6). When listening to Rev 7, the audience may connect the location of the seal and deduce that, like Ezek 9, the plagues are the punishment for sin.[77] Ezekiel also confirms the seal as protection from divine agents of destruction and separation from other Jerusalemites, but the relevance of Ezek 9 ends there. Human beings are directly affected by the destroying angels, not indirectly as in Rev 7. Although it does yield some contextual effects, Ezekiel 9 is not necessary to make sense of the sealing.

The Exodus plague narrative (Exod 7–12), and especially the Passover narrative, assists audiences in making sense of the sealing in Rev 7.[78] Since Exodus themes run through Revelation, many interpreters suggest that the Passover narrative is relevant to understanding the angel's command to seal the slaves of God.[79] After the first nine plagues (Exod 7–11) the Passover narrative (Exod 12) describes the people of God protected from destruction by a divine agent. The angel of death strikes the first born in the land but passes over those whose houses have the sign (LXX: σημεῖον) of the blood of a lamb (Exod 12:3). Aune concludes that the protective function of the seal in Rev 7 is derived from the sign in Exod 12.

> The sealing…protects them against the plagues unleashed upon the unbelieving world as well as against those Romans and Anatolians who would kill them. This conception of immunity from the plagues is ultimately derived from the tradition that the plagues harmed Egyptians only, not Israelites.[80]

---

[75] Schüssler Fiorenza, *Revelation*, 66–67.

[76] Pattemore, *People of God*, 131.

[77] Pattemore, *People of God*, 131.

[78] Aune, *Revelation*, 2:456, Caird, 97, and Beale, 409, suggest that the Passover mark may be the relevant background to understand the mark in Ezek 9.

[79] Schüssler Fiorenza, *Revelation*, 66; A. Y. Collins, *Combat Myth*, 34; Ladd, 112; Caird, 97; Bauckham, *Climax*, 216 n.13; Beale, *Revelation*, 409; Aune, *Revelation*, 480; Harrington, 99. It is a common assumption that the trumpet plagues are modeled after the Exodus plagues, e.g. Lohmeyer, 72; Charles, 1:233–7; A. Y. Collins, *Combat Myth*, 35.

[80] Aune, *Revelation*, 479–80.

While Aune may go too far in suggesting the sealing protects believers against the Romans and Anatolians, his point about the relevance of the Exodus plagues is worth investigation.

When audiences hear Rev 7:1–3 they can relate it to the Exodus plagues because of the similar context of (1) destruction targeting land, sea, and trees, (2) protection from divine agents, and (3) separation from the surrounding population. Each of these points increases discontinuity with the seal series, while strengthening connections with Exodus and the themes of protection and separation.

(1) Both the sign of the lamb's blood in Exod 12 and the seal of Rev 7:1–8 occur within the context of plagues on the land, water, and trees. As argued above, the angels in Rev 7:1–3 anticipate the trumpet plagues by the combination of land, sea, and trees being affected. Like the Exodus plagues, the target of these plagues only indirectly affect humans but directly affect land, water and trees. The first Exodus plague turns water to blood, which as a consequence stank and could not be drank by the Egyptians (Exod 7:21). Another plague covered the whole land with frogs (Exod 8:6). During another plague, hail struck everything in the field and "shattered every tree in the field" (Exod 9:25). During the eighth plague, the wind blew locusts to devour everything left by the hail and "every tree of your that grows in the field" (Exod 10:5).[81] In short, "land, water, and trees" summarizes the primary targets of the plagues in Exodus.[82] Knowing the Exodus plagues (that did not affect the Israelites) and the protection of the sign of Lamb's blood, audiences can identify themselves with Israelites who were protected from the plagues.

(2) Both the seal of Rev 7 and the sign of Exod 12 mark the people of God for protection from divine agents of destruction.[83] In Revelation, the seals protect the slaves of God from the destroying winds controlled by angels. As argued above, the nature of the destruction is ambiguous until the angels blow the seven trumpets. The seal explicitly protects from the fifth trumpet plague, the locusts from the abyss (Rev 9:1–11). Like the locusts of the Exodus plague, they attack green grass, growth, and trees (Exod 10:15; Rev 9:4). The demonic locusts led by'Απολλύων (the Destroyer) (9:11) do not harm anyone with the mark on their foreheads. In Exodus 12, the destroying angel enters unmarked houses to strike down the Egyptians. Without Exodus 12, the audience can deduce that the sealing

[81] A. Y. Collins, *Combat Myth*, 35, and Osborne, 305, suggests this as relevant to understanding the four winds.

[82] This is especially evident in the seven-plague tradition reflected in Psalm 78:42–52 (LXX 77:43–53) and 105:27–36 (LXX 104:27–36). Consistent with what I argued above, trees are highlighted in these seven-plague traditions.

[83] Caird, 97; Ladd, 114.

means protection because the angel calls for the delay of damaging winds, but it is not clear how the seal can protect from angels controlling destroying winds. With Exod 12 and the whole plague narrative, audiences have precedent for understanding that a seal may protect from plagues and an angelic destroyer.

(3) Both the seal of Rev 7 and the sign of Exod 12 separate the people of God from the surrounding population.[84] In Rev 7, the seal distinguishes the slaves of God from those affected by the damage to land, sea and trees. When the sealed are numbered, this explicitly distinguishes them from the rest of the tribes of Israel (7:4–8). As discussed below, separation becomes the most important function of the seal in the rest of Revelation. In the Passover narrative, the sign of blood on the doorpost distinguishes the Egyptians and Israelites. There is implicitly the possibility that some Israelites may not observe the Passover with the implied threat they too could suffer the same consequences as the Egyptians. In this respect, the marked may be distinguished from the unobservant. The emphasis in Exodus, however, is on how the mark distinguishes Egyptian and Israelite. This focus on separation is repeated three times in Exod 12 (12:12–13, 23 and 27). The contrast is especially clear in Exod 12:23:

For the LORD will pass through to strike down the Egyptians; when he sees the blood on the lintel and on the two doorposts, the LORD will pass over that door and will not allow the destroyer to enter your houses to strike you down.

The blood marks the difference between an observant Israelite and an Egyptian household.

The theme of separation is not confined to the Passover narrative, but is a focus of throughout the plague narratives. Protection from the plagues is a sign that Israelites are separated from Egyptians. The LORD explicitly says regarding the plague of flies:

But on that day I will set apart the land of Goshen, where my people live, so that no swarms of flies shall be there, that you may know that I the LORD am in this land. Thus I will make a distinction between my people and your people (Exodus 8:22–23).[85]

In Rev 7:1–3, sealing protects from the predicted damage to land, sea and trees. Sealing as protection has the greatest relevance in light of the Exodus plagues, in which the plagues were directed at the land, water, trees and other agricultural resources of Egypt but distinguished between God's people and the Egyptians. In Rev 9:4, a similar contrast is made between

[84] Aune, *Revelation*, 480.

[85] The themes of separation and protection are also explicitly intertwined in the plague of diseased livestock (Exod 9:4, 6) and implied in the other plagues.

green grass, growth, and trees and people who do not have the seal of God.[86]

In Rev 12–22, the meaning of the seal shifts to emphasize ownership and separation, especially separation from people marked by the beast. After the trumpet series, references to the seal connote the elect status of the sealed and not protection from God's wrath. The 144,000 with marked foreheads stand with the Lamb on Mt. Zion as those who have been "redeemed from the earth" (14:1–5). God's slaves in the New Jerusalem have foreheads marked with God's name (22:4). In contrast, the mark of the beast designates people for punishment (14:9–11; 16:2; 19:20; 20:4).

This shift in the seal's meaning from protection in Rev 7–9 to separation in Rev 12–22 suggests that Rev 7:1–8 addresses the fear of believers that they will suffer the wrath of God along with the rest of humanity. This fear is alleviated, even if ambiguously, by the sealing of the 144,000 and the demonstration of protection from the effects of fifth trumpet. After this fear is assuaged, the seal then becomes a sign of election to stand on Mt. Zion with the Lamb and opposition to the mark of the Beast. The sign of election in Rev 7:9–17 foreshadows this new emphasis on election and separation: white robes. Those who stand before God wear these robes. Their separation came through suffering. They have come out of the "Great Persecution." (ἐκ τῆς θλίψεως τῆς μεγάλης, 7:14). In the face of persecution, they have been vindicated and now stand in white robes before God. In short, Rev 7:1–8 and 7:9–17 together transform fear of God's wrath into confidence in God's election.

To summarize the discussion of σφραγίς (seal): the seal in Rev 7:1–8 signals ownership in weak continuity with the sealed scroll. Discontinuous with the scroll, the sealing of the slaves of God indicates protection and separation when heard with the Exodus plague narrative. In Rev 12–22, the meaning of the seal emphasizes God's ownership and separation from humanity, especially people with the mark of the beast.

h) Summary of Analysis of Rev 7:1–17

In summary, Rev 7 sits awkwardly between Rev 6:17 and 8:1. The audience expected seven seals to be opened (Rev 6:1) and experienced the first six openings in regular succession, with a change of focus in the fifth seal and a slightly lengthier event following the sixth seal. Based on this pattern, the audience is led to expect the seventh seal to be opened after Rev 6:17.

---

[86] Some (from Oecumenius to Lupieri) have taken the grass, growth, and trees to be symbolic for God's people. In the context of the Exodus plagues, such allegorization requires greater processing effort.

Instead, two new visions are reported. These two units are clearly delimited, but have an ambiguous relationship to the surrounding units. The primary links between Rev 7:1–8 and the first six seals is the ambiguous marker μετὰ τοῦτο ("after this"), and the catchwords ἵστημι ("stand") and σφραγίς ("seal"). These are weak connections with the sixth seal. Otherwise, Rev 7:1–8 anticipates subsequent units (trumpet series; 144,000 on Mt. Zion; mark of the beast) by communication axis, personal references, *dramatis personae*, spatial and temporal references. In contrast, 7:9–17 refers back to the initial throne room scene (Rev 4–5) and the fifth seal and concludes by anticipating the fulfillment revealed in Rev 21–22. Given the complexity of the relationships between Rev 7 and the surrounding units, it is no wonder that interpreters label it with various and divergent terms.[87] The following table lists the elements of continuity and discontinuity in order to visualize how Rev 7:1–8 predominately anticipates future units and 7:9–17 recalls previous units.

Table 2. Continuity and Discontinuity in Rev 7:1–17

	Continuity with Seal series	*Discontinuity Recalling Previous Units*	*Discontinuity Anticipating Future Units*	*Ambiguous*
7:1–8	Standing (6:17; cf. 7:9) Slaves of God (6:11)	Slaves of God (1:1; 2:20; cf. 5:9)	Seal (9:4; 14:1–5; 22:4) Angel=>Angels (14:18) Four angel (9:14–15) Earth, sea, trees (8:7–9) 'until' (7:3) 144,000 (14:1–5) Army (19:14)	μετὰ τοῦτο Standing (6:17; 7:9) Sealing (Rev 5–6) Four corners of earth
7:9–17	God & Lamb (6:16) White robes (6:9–11)	μετὰ ταῦτα attendants=>God (Rev 4–5) God, Lamb, living creatures, angels (Rev 4–5) elder=>John (5:5) throne room (Rev 4–5) temple (3:12)	Great Crowd (19:1, 6) Temple (11:13, 19; 15:5) 'will dwell…' (21:3–6) service by God's slaves (22:3)	

[87] Wenland, 378, detects both the continuity and discontinuity. He calls 7:1–17 an interlude, but notes the significant continuity when he suggests that it is perhaps an "extension" of the scene.

Put another way, one could omit Rev 7 with no loss to the narrative cohesion. If one read Rev 6:17 and continued with 8:1, the audience would be satisfied by the opening of the seventh seal and the introduction of the trumpets. The only narrative loss would be the reference to the seal in Rev 9:4 that becomes ambiguous without the sealing in Rev 7. Otherwise the logic of the story is intact – although the seal series would lack these two visions of the people of God.

The effect of the seals, however, changes substantially because of Rev 7. Within the seal septet, Rev 7 plays a significant role in developing the people of God. Revelation 7:1–8 responds to the question "who will stand?" from a believer's point of view, even if it does not answer it unambiguously. It transforms the 'seal' by introducing the people of God as sealed. With assistance from the Exodus plague narrative, the seal implies protection from plagues unleashed by divine agents and anticipates that the elect are owned by God and separated from people marked by the beast. The second vision (Rev 7:9–17) specifically portrays the people of God among the other heavenly throne room attendants. It shifts the question from "Who will stand during God's wrath?" to "who will stand before the throne?" and concludes with a promise that will only be fulfilled in the end.

Revelation 7 has key connections with the fifth seal (Rev 6:9–11), amplifying four themes: delay, separation, suffering, and vindication and applying these themes to a broader group of characters. After the Lamb opened the fifth seal, John sees the souls of those slaughtered for the word of God and their witness (Rev 6:9). They have suffered because of their witness and they question the delay in vindication, "How long will it be before you judge and vindicate our blood on the inhabitants of the earth?" (Rev 6:10). They receive white robes and instructions to rest during the delay. After the fifth seal there is delay in vengeance and in Rev 7 there is delay in releasing the four winds. Those under the altar are separated from the inhabitants of the earth, and the sealed are separated from the unsealed. Those under the altar suffer but receive white robes (6:9–11) and those wearing white robes came out of great persecution (7:14). The souls under the altar are implicitly assured of future vindication, and those coming out of the Great Persecution are vindicated by standing before the throne of God. The fifth seal hints at these themes, and Rev 7 applies them to broader groups of the people of God: first the sealed and then the multitude clothed in white.

The broadening groups of the people of God anticipates my argument that Rev 7's vision becomes more significant to the audience than the rest of the seal series, in part, because of this unique focus on the people of God coupled with the penultimate position before the seventh seal. In Rev

6 the people of God only appear as slaughtered, and in Rev 8 prayers are the only evidence of their existence. In contrast, Revelation 7 deals directly with “slaves of God,” the primary way the audience is identified (Rev 1:1). Wenland notes that, “the contrast with what has gone before and that which follows after (*silence*) is indeed striking, and this seems to foreground the vision [of Rev 7] even more.”[88] Structure reinforces content so that the audience may naturally finds Rev 7 more personally relevant than the surrounding material.

3. Experiencing the Structure of Rev 10:1–11:13

As discussed in chapter 1, interpreters have labeled Rev 10:1–11:13 as a deviation between the sixth and seventh trumpet. Like the seal series, the number of events is announced (Rev 8:2, 6) and creates the expectation of the completion of the series. Like the seal series, the fifth event is longer than the first four, and there is a significant amount of material between blowing the sixth and seventh trumpets.[89] For these reasons, Loenertz, Farrer, Schüssler Fiorenza, Giblin, and Steinmann insist that the units between the sixth and seventh of each series should be analyzed together.[90] Schüssler Fiorenza concludes that Rev 10–11 “have the same structural function within Revelation as the interlude of chapter 7.”[91]

In addition, Rev 7:1–17 and 10:1–11:13 should be analyzed sequentially because the seals are more relevant for audiences hearing the trumpet series. Aune suggests this when he writes, “[s]ince the author has already interrupted the opening of the seventh seal, it comes as no great surprise that he interrupts the blowing of the seventh trumpet.”[92] As members of the audience hear the trumpets blown, they again experience a series of seven, four short events (on average 50 words), a much longer fifth event (257 words). After the sixth trumpet and an event (233 words), they experience two very long units (292 and 330 words) before the seventh trumpet. After the seal series, this will not be a surprise, and audiences would naturally compare and relate these two extra units. From Rev 7, the audience learns

[88] Wenland, 378.

[89] The length of each trumpet unit are respectively (in Greek): 34, 41, 54, 70 (including 8:13), 257 (including 9:12), and 233 (not including 10:1–11:13). Revelation 10:1–11 is 292 words and 11:1–13 is 330 words.

[90] Loenertz, 66–68; Farrer, 104; Steinmann; Hall; cf. Bauckham, *Climax*, 12. Bauckham suggests that there are no literary links between 7:1–17 and 10:1–11:13 but that their parallel structure relate them. Also, Ladd, 140.

[91] Schüssler Fiorenza, *Justice and Judgment,* 74.

[92] Aune, “Apocalypse Renewed,” 55.

that a delay may happen before the last element. As a similar pattern begins again in Rev 10, the audience has an inkling of what to expect.

In addition to the seven-fold structuring, Rev 8:2–11:19 has an additional structuring device, three "woes" (Rev 8:13; 9:12; 11:14). Following the fourth trumpet plague, an eagle cries in midheaven "Woe, woe, woe to the inhabitants of the earth, at the blasts of the other trumpets that the three angels are about to blow!" (8:13). The fifth trumpet is identified as the first woe (9:12) and the passing of the second woe is announced following the story of the two witnesses (11:14). This additional structure helps the audience hold the long passage of Rev 10:1–11:13 together with the sixth trumpet.[93] The second woe reminds members of the audience of the sixth trumpet, with the result that they process Rev 10:1–11:13 in relation the sixth trumpet/second woe.

Rev 10:1–11:13 is usually divided into two units: 10:1–11 and 11:1–13.[94] Some scholars further separate Rev 11:1–2 and 11:3–13, but there are no formal delimiting markers separating these units.[95] While noting the ambiguity at Rev 11:1 and 11:3, I will take Rev 10:1–11 and 11:1–13 as the major unit divisions.

As with the analysis of Rev 7, I will use seven criteria for detecting signals of continuity and discontinuity: delimiting markers, communication axis, personal references, *dramatis personae*, spatial and temporal signals, and thematic vocabulary. As with Rev 7, the majority of signals indicate discontinuity with the trumpet series, especially in the first half (Rev 10:1–11). A few signals in the second half (Rev 11:1–13) suggest limited continuity with the trumpet series while the majority anticipate later scenes in Revelation. Of special significance to this investigation, Rev 10:1–11:13 develops characters and themes from Rev 7: John, the people of God, and the themes of delay, protection, separation, persecution, and vindication.

a) Delimiting Markers: Discontinuity and Ambiguity

The markers that delimit Rev 10:1–11:13 indicate discontinuity and an ambiguous relationship with the sixth trumpet. A new vision is introduced

---

[93] Bousset, 314; Bauckham, 11–2; Schüssler Fiorenza, *Justice and Judgment*, 54; F. D. Mazzaferri, *The Genre of the Book of Revelation from a Source-Critical Perspective* (BZNW 54; Berlin: de Gruyter, 1989), 337; E. Müller, 383; Pattemore, *Souls*, 137.

[94] Charles, *Revelation*, 1:256; Bauckham, *Climax*, 13; Boring, 142; Aune 2:555, 585; Beale, 520–521; Pattemore, *Souls*, 141. Lohmeyer, 89, and Mounce, 34, include 11:14 as the conclusion of the sixth trumpet but acknowledge 11:3–13 as separate from the woe. Schüssler Fiorenza, *Revelation*, 74, divides 10:1–11:13 into 10:1–11:2 and 11:3–13; similarly Caird, 133.

[95] Charles, 1:274; Bauckham, *Climax*, 12; Aune, *Revelation*, 2:585; Pattemore, *Souls*, 136.

by the marker καὶ εἶδον ἄλλον ἄγγελον ἰσχυρὸν ("and I saw another mighty angel," Rev 10:1). In Pattemore's hierarchy of connectives, καὶ εἶδον is the lowest level, used to connect elements within a series (e.g. Rev 8:13; 9:1).[96] It delimits Rev 10 from the sixth trumpet in the same way that the eagle flying in mid-heaven (Rev 8:13) separates the fourth from the fifth trumpet.[97] In addition, the reference to the seventh trumpet (10:7) further suggests that the trumpet series is the relevant context to understand it. The phrase καὶ εἶδον initiates a new vision, but suggests a relatively close relationship with the sixth trumpet and the trumpet series.

The end of this unit is not delimited by any of John's usual formulae. Pattemore lists καὶ ἐδόθη μοι ("and it was given to me," Rev 11:1) as the signal for a new unit, but nowhere else has John used this phrase in this way.[98] He uses this phrase to describe authority or objects given to characters that represent their role.[99] In Rev 11:1, the καί is the only connective signal, joining the previous sentence to this one. The lack of a formal marker suggests that Rev 11:1–13 would be understood as a continuation of the vision begun at Rev 10:1.[100] As I will discuss below, a division of the unit may be made at Rev 11:1 or 11:3 depending on which criteria are favored.

The identification of the second woe and announcement of the third in Rev 11:14 delimits the end of the unit. As noted above, the structure of the woes complements the numbered trumpet series, helping keep Rev 10:1–11:13 in the context of the sixth trumpet/second woe. The anticipation of the third woe opens the way for the seventh trumpet (Rev 11:15).

In summary, delimiting markers in Rev 10:1–11:13 establish a relationship with the sixth trumpet/second woe, but this relationship is ambiguous. John signals that it is a separate vision using the low-level marker καὶ εἶδον . What is the relevance of this new unit to the sixth trumpet? Given the audience's prior experience with Rev 7, it would not be surprised to experience an additional unit and delay before the seventh trumpet.

---

[96] Pattemore, *Souls*, 135 (cf. 117).

[97] It is striking how little the formula καὶ εἶδον is used in the trumpet series. It is used to introduce the seven angels (8:2), the eagle (8:13) and the star fallen to earth (9:1) but not to introduce each trumpet event, which are striking visual images (e.g. 8:7, hail and fire mixed with blood). In contrast the seal series uses this phrase with four of six elements (6:1, 2, 5, 8, 12).

[98] Pattemore, *Souls*, 141. Cf. Aune, *Revelation*, 2:555.

[99] A crown to the first rider (6:2), a great sword (6:4), authority (6:8), white robe (6:11), incense (8:3), key (9:1), authority like scorpions (9:3; cf. 9:5), mouth (13:5), and authority to act (13:5), to make war (13:7), breath (13:15), to scorch (16:8), and to be clothed (19:8).

[100] Beale, 599; Aune, "Apocalypse Renewed," 55; Schüssler Fiorenza, *Justice and Judgment*, 74; Kraft, 150; Hall, 288.

b) Communication Axis: Discontinuity

Discontinuity is strongly signaled by the shift of communication axis in Rev 10–11, which also reminds the audience of Rev 7. It is striking that heavenly agents again communicate directly with John. "A voice from heaven" instructs John not to write and to take the small scroll (Rev 10:4, 8). "Another mighty angel" (ἄλλον ἄγγελον ἰσχυρὸν) commands John to take and eat the scroll (Rev 10:9). An unidentified speaker commands him to prophesy (Rev 10:11) and to come and measure the altar but not the courtyard of the temple (Rev 11:1–2).

Rev 7 is the most immediately relevant, portraying a conversation between an elder and John. The episode in Rev 10–11 is different in at least two respects. John speaks, albeit briefly, in Rev 7:14 but not in Rev 10–11. The heavenly voices command John in Rev 10–11, but the elder explains the vision in Rev 7:13–17.

Revelation 5:1–5 is also relevant, portraying communication between an elder and John in the presence of a mighty angel (ἄγγελον ἰσχυρὸν). John does not speak, but weeps when no one is worthy to open the scroll. The elder points out the lion/lamb.

The command not to write (Rev 10:4) could also remind the audience of the initial command to write (Rev 1:11, 19) and the command to write the letters to the seven churches (Rev 2:1, etc.). In contrast, John is ordered in Rev 10:4 not to write what the seven thunders spoke.

Heavenly agents communicating with God's human agents continue in Rev 11:3–13. A "loud voice from heaven" commands the two witnesses to "come up" (Rev 11:12) that recalls the communication axis and vocabulary used to call John to witness the proceedings in the divine throne room (Rev 4:1).[101]

By embedding communication between heavenly agents and John/two witnesses, John separates Rev 10:1–11:13 from the sixth trumpet. The communication axis during the trumpet series is almost uniformly from John to the churches.[102] The contrast with Rev 10:1–11:13 is pronounced and emphasizes divine characters communicating with John and the two unnamed witnesses. Thus, John is juxtaposed with these two witnesses. By replicating the communication axis, the two witnesses are presented in a similar role as John, which I will discus further under *dramatis personae* below.

---

[101] Smith ("The Structure of Revelation in Light of Apocalyptic Literary Conventions") argues that the command to "come up" is a key structuring device that recalls a standard apocalyptic convention. Cf. Ladd, 33; Bauckham, *Climax*, 3–4; Beale, *Revelation*, 598.

[102] With the exception of the voice from the four horns of the altar to the sixth angel in Rev 9:14.

In summary, these communication situations remind the audience of when the elder spoke to John in Rev 7:13–17, the throne room vision (Rev 4:1, 5:1–5) and the initial command to write in Rev 1–3. Based on these connections, Rev 10:1–11:13 stands out from the trumpet series, reminding the audience of previous units that focused on communication with the people of God.

c) Personal References: Discontinuity

Personal references (those who do not act) in Rev 10:1–11 include God, seventh angel, slaves of God, peoples, nations, languages, and kings. Among these references, there are few connections to the trumpet series, a lack that signals discontinuity to the audience. God is a personal reference in Rev 10–11, but God is not named during the trumpet series (Rev 8:6–9:21) except in mention of the seal on the foreheads of the slaves of God (Rev 9:4).[103] In the trumpet series, God agency is obscured by the use of the divine passive (e.g. Rev 9:1).[104] By not using the word θεός except in the context of the saints (Rev 9:4; cf. 6:9), John implies God is distant from the trumpet series but present with the saints in Rev 10:1–11:13.

The seventh angel is mentioned in 10:7 but does not act. As discussed above, this has the effect of anchoring Rev 10:1–11 in the trumpet series.

The slaves of God are again brought to mind, but here refer specifically to the prophets. "[T]he mystery of God will be fulfilled, as he announced to his slaves the prophets" (Rev 10:7). John is clearly included in the group of prophets (Rev 10:11) as are the two witnesses (Rev 11:10). The audience is forced to reconcile this reference to the "slaves of God" with previous references that included the 144,000 sealed (Rev 7:3), believers at Laodicea (Rev 2:20), and the audience (Rev 1:1). A later reference will clarify that the slaves of God includes prophets and saints (Rev 11:18). The point, however, is that the reference to the slaves of God in Rev 10:7 particularly brings prophets to mind even as it more generally suggests the larger group of the saints described in Rev 7.[105]

John uses the four-fold description of humanity as "peoples, nations, languages, and kings" (Rev 10:11). The description recalls the positive description of those around the throne in Rev 7:9 and the origin of those redeemed by the lamb (Rev 5:10).[106] Although recalling humanity positively, the use in Rev 10:11 is ambiguous depending on how one translates ἐπί. If

---

[103] Likewise, θεός is only used once during the first six seals (6:9), again in context of the saints. In contrast, θεός is used seven times in Rev 7 and four times in 10:1–11:13. Cf. Bauckham, *Theology*, 43–47.

[104] Beale, *Revelation*, 529. Cf. Aune, *Revelation*, 1:ccii–cciii.

[105] Pattemore, *People of God*, 133–4.

[106] Bauckham, *Climax*, 27.

it means "over" then perhaps it is a positive call that more may be redeemed from the peoples, nations, languages, and kings.[107]

However, the last element, "kings," is new and suggests that "against" is the appropriate translation of ἐπί, although the ambiguity may be intentional.[108] Bousset argues that the reference to kings foreshadows their importance for the rest of the book as opponents of the Lamb and collaborators with the false prophet, beast, and dragon.[109] When "peoples and tribes and languages and nations" are mentioned again in 11:9, they are source of people who see the bodies of the two witnesses and refuse their burial.[110] These people are in parallel with the phrase "inhabitants of the earth" that consistently refers to people hostile to people of God (11:10; cf. 3:10; 6:10; 8:13; 13: 8, 14; 17:8).[111] In short, the negative connotations of the four-fold list in Rev 11:9 signals discontinuity with previous positive references.

"Those who worship" at the altar of the temple of God receive brief but important mention in 11:1. The motif of measuring is usually taken to refer to protection, a theme that some interpreters connect to the sealing of the 144,000 in Rev 7.[112] Aune concludes, "the worshipers in the temple of God, in my view, are analogous to the 144,000 whom God has sealed (7:3–8), for they too are divinely protected against the divine punitive plagues as well as the murderous intent of the enemies of God."[113] The scene of worshippers around an altar, even an earthly altar, may remind hearers of the heavenly scene around the throne in Rev 7 and the themes of protection and separation.

As observed in other categories (for example, communication axis), personal references in Rev 10:1–11:13 connect most clearly with Rev 7 and 5. The prominent reference to kings anticipates their role in Rev 16:12 and Rev 17 and 18. In contrast, there are few connections between Rev 10:1–11:13 and the sixth trumpet or the trumpet series.

---

[107] Charles, 1:cxxxiii; Kraft, 281.

[108] See discussion in Aune, *Revelation*, 2:573–4.

[109] Bousset, 313. Cf. Charles, 1:269; Aune, *Revelation*, 2:574; Beale, *Revelation*, 555.

[110] By using ἐκ + partitive genitive, Rev 11:9 suggests that only some of the peoples, tribes, languages, and nations refuse burial. The preposition plus partitive genitive is used as the subject without article or substantive (cf. 2:10; John 16.17). Charles, 1:58.

[111] Aune, *Revelation*, 2:622; cf. 1:240.

[112] Charles (*Revelation*, 1:274–275) notes three explanations for measuring: (1) rebuilding and restoring, (2) destruction, or (3) protection. Cf. Aune, *Revelation*, 2:604–5. Charles and Beale (*Revelation*, 558–9) emphasize that it is spiritual, not physical protection, but this is not so clear in context. Aune (*Revelation*, 2:598) argues it is both spiritual and physical protection.

[113] Aune, *Revelation*, 2:598.

d) Dramatis personae: *Discontinuity and Transformation*

The *dramatis personae* (those who act) dramatically separate Rev 10:1–11:13 from the surrounding units and strongly signal discontinuity to the audience. The event following the sixth seal concluded with a focus on humankind suffering the effects of the fiery cavalry and their failure to repent. Very differently, Rev 10 opens with another mighty angel coming down from heaven with accoutrements previously associated with God (rainbow) and Jesus (wrapped in cloud, face like sun, legs like pillars of fire, roar like lion), including a little scroll in his hand.[114] If the audience had forgotten the mighty angel and scroll from Rev 5:2, John draws attention to the repetition by pointing out this is "another" angel. Beale writes that "this angel is the first of several links between this chapter and ch. 5" and he concludes, "ch. 10 is parallel to ch. 5 and is to be interpreted in its light."[115]

The seven thunders are introduced as *dramatis personae* who speak (ἐλάλησαν) as other heavenly voices do (Rev 10:8; cf. 1:12; 4:1). They are introduced with the definite article, which suggests that John (and perhaps his audiences) is familiar with them.[116] Since the first living creature speaks with a voice like thunder (Rev 6:1), Beale's assertion is likely true. "[t]he thunders are to be viewed as metaphors for declarations of a heavenly being or beings."[117] Whether or not they reflect additional judgments (e.g. Caird, Mounce, Bauckham), these new characters indicate discontinuity with the previous unit and prompt the audience to search for their relevance.[118] The focus shifts to eating and prophesying instead of writing. As Ruiz notes, "eating is more important than writing."[119]

John is a major character in 10:1–11:2 in a way that signals discontinuity to the audience. When discussing communication axis, I noted that the

---

[114] Ezek 2–3 and Dan 12:7 are relevant here as well, but earlier references in Rev are primary. The depiction of this angel with symbols previously associated with God and Christ has led some interpreters to conclude it is an angelomorphic Christ, e.g., P. R. Carrell, *Jesus and the Angels: Angelology and the Christology of the Apocalypse of John* (SNTSMS 95; Cambridge: Cambridge University, 1997) and M. R. Hoffmann, *The Destroyer and the Lamb: the Relationship between Angelomorphic and Lamb Christology in the Book of Revelation* (Tübingen: Mohr Siebeck, 2005). Cf. Charles 1:259; Beale, *Revelation*, 522–6. Ladd, 141, stresses that in Revelation "angels are always angels; Christ is never called an angel….this angel plays the role solely of messenger; he is not given the rank of deity, nor is he worshipped." See similar comments by Bauckham, *Climax*, 253.

[115] Beale, *Revelation*, 522, 544. Cf. Caird, 125; A. Y. Collins, *Combat Myth*, 21; Bauckham, *Climax*, 257.

[116] Beale, *Revelation*, 535.

[117] Beale, *Revelation*, 533; cf. Aune, *Revelation*, 2:559.

[118] Bauckham, *Climax*, 259–260.

[119] Ruiz, "Hearing and Seeing," 104.

communication situation resembled Rev 7, 4–5 and 1.[120] Likewise, the focus on John himself makes his previous actions in Rev 7 and 5 more relevant to the audience to understand this unit.[121] Like the Lamb who approaches the One Sitting on the Throne to receive the scroll, John approaches the mighty angel to receive the scroll. Beale concludes, "John's similar action shows that he participates in and identifies with Jesus' authority in executing judgment and redemption."[122]

A critical point is that John's character is transformed by these actions.[123] The last time John acted (not counting hearing and seeing), he admitted ignorance and deflected the elder's question in Rev 7:14. In Rev 10:1–11, however, John gains knowledge of the seven trumpets. The command to "seal up" (σφράγισον) reminds the audience of the Lamb unsealing the scroll, and puts John in the opposite position of one who seals up a revelation. In this way, the sealing of the seven thunders contributes to John's ethos as knowledgeable. By taking the little scroll from the hand of the angel, John's actions recall the Lamb taking the scroll from the One sitting on the throne. By eating the scroll, John and the scroll become indistinguishable – its authority is his authority.[124] For the majority of the book, John is a passive observer, but in Rev 10 he is an active participant.[125] In short, Rev 10:1–11:2 builds on Rev 7 to develop John's character, moving him from ignorance to knowledge, passivity to action, and powerlessness to authority. I will argue in chapter 5 that this is one of the key functions of digressions in Revelation.

The focus on John further ties the two halves of Rev 10:1–11:13 together, seamlessly moving from the command to prophesy (Rev 10:11) to the command to measure (Rev 11:1–2) and the story of the two witnesses (Rev 11:3–13).[126] The lack of clear transitions juxtaposes John and the two witnesses closely together and makes it difficult to delimit the two halves.

New *dramatis personae* signaling that Rev 11:3–13 may be a new unit, which explains why some interpreters divide the unit at Rev 11:3 rather

[120] Noted in reverse order to highlight the most immediately relevant to Rev 10–11.

[121] Beale, *Revelation*, 548.

[122] Beale, *Revelation*, 548.

[123] See G. Carey, *Elusive Apocalypse: Reading Authority in the Revelation to John* (SABH 15; Macon, Georgia: Mercer, 1999), e.g. 123. Carey details the ways John constructs his ethos. Aune, *Revelation*, 2:563, concludes that the refusal to reveal lends credibility to the whole composition and that John is in a superior position to the audience.

[124] Ruiz, "Hearing and Seeing," 104, followed by Carey, 123–4.

[125] B. K. Blount emphasizes that John and the people of God become active witnesses in Revelation. See *Can I Get a Witness? Reading Revelation through African American Culture* (Louisville: Westminster John Knox, 2005), 46–67.

[126] E. Müller, 379.

than 11:1.[127] The appearance and action of the two witnesses separate Rev 11:3–13 from 10:1–11:2 and the trumpet series, recalling previous witnesses and anticipating the broadening of this group to include the audience. There has been much speculation about the identity of the two witnesses.[128] For our purposes the central issue is the relationship between them and the characters in surrounding units. No matter how many relevant figures may be found (e.g. Moses, Elijah, Enoch, etc.), they are identified as witnesses, olive trees, lampstands and prophets.[129] Witnesses, lampstands and prophets have relevance elsewhere in Revelation, while the olive trees are only intelligible if related to Zechariah 4:1–14.[130]

"Witness" (μαρτύς) is the first identification of Jesus (1:5; cf. 3:14) and is a role for believers (2:13). John is the one who witnessed (ἐμαρτύρησεν) to the testimony of Jesus Christ (1:2) and who was on Patmos because of the testimony of Jesus (1:9). Being a witness may result in death, as it did for Antipas and those seen under the altar (2:13; 6:9; cf. 17:6). Before Rev 11, the audience will have heard "witness" associated with Jesus, John, Antipas, and those slaughtered under the altar. By adding the two witnesses John continues to broaden the group of witnesses.[131]

After Rev 11, it becomes increasingly clear that all believers are to be witnesses to Jesus' testimony. A heavenly voice announces that believers have conquered the Dragon "by the word of their witness" (διὰ τὸν λόγον τῆς μαρτυρίας αὐτῶν, Rev 12:11). The children of the Woman clothed by the Sun are those who keep the commandments of God and hold the witness of Jesus (ἐχόντων τὴν μαρτυρίαν᾽Ιησοῦ, Rev 12:17; cf. 19:10). Witnessing may lead to death (e.g. beheading in Rev 20:4). In the end, the audience is expected to witness the book of Revelation itself for the sake of the churches. Jesus speaks through John to the audience, "I, Jesus, sent my angel to witness these things to you (pl.) for the congregations." (᾽Εγω ᾽Ιησοῦς ἔπεμψα τὸν ἄγγελόν μου μαρτυρῆσαι ὑμῖν ταῦτα ἐπὶ

[127] E.g. Richard, 78. Mounce, 211–5, Beale, *Revelation*, 557, and Osborne, 409, analyze Rev 11:1–2 separately but under the heading of 11:1–13.

[128] Aune, "Apocalypse Renewed," 57, suggests that John encourages such speculation. On various proposals for these figures see: Charles, *Revelation*, 1:281–2; Aune, *Revelation*, 2:599–603.

[129] For example, they are often identified with Moses & Elijah (Charles, Bauckham); Enoch & Elijah (Bousset). See the exhaustive summary in Aune, *Revelation*, 2:598–603.

[130] Jauhiainen, 150. Also Charles, *Revelation*, 1:282; Bauckham, *Climax*, 273–4; Pattemore, *People of God*, 162.

[131] Many interpreters quickly assumes that the two witnesses represent the whole Christian community (e.g. Mounce, 222–224; Bauckham, *Climax*, 274; Aune, *Revelation*, 2:586; Beale, *Revelation*, 573). Although an audience may draw this conclusion immediately, it is more likely that they would experience the expanding (and now anonymous) group and later come to identify themselves as witnesses. To jump to this conclusion misses the persuasive character of the subtle and gradual portrayal of witnesses.

ταῖς ἐκκλησίαις, 22:16). The members of the audience, the plural "you," receive Jesus' witness in order to become witnesses to the congregations.

Lampstands signal discontinuity with the trumpet series and also have prior reference in Revelation. They remind the audience of the inaugural vision of Jesus walking among the lampstands in Rev 1. Each lampstand is associated with a congregation that experiences Jesus' presence (1:20). Jauhiainen argues that John doubles the number of lampstands found in Zechariah 4 to distinguish his vision from Zechariah's and encourage the connection with Rev 1.[132] In addition, as witnesses they give testimony in a judicial sense (e.g. Num 35:30; Deut 17:6; 19:15).[133] In other words, 'lampstands' signals that these two witnesses are like two congregations, two assemblies that testify to the world with the veracity of two witnesses in a court.[134] This supports the conclusion that John uses the two anonymous witnesses to broaden the group that the audience associates with 'witnesses.'[135]

The last significant label for these two witnesses is that they are prophets (Rev 11:10), which also suggests discontinuity with the trumpet series. Prophets and prophecy are not mentioned in the trumpet series, but this is the third time that prophecy has been mentioned in Rev 10:1–11:13. The good news of the fulfillment of God's mystery was announced to the prophets (Rev 10:7). John was commanded to prophesy to peoples, nations, languages, and kings (Rev 10:11). And here, the two witnesses are called prophets. Similar to the word 'witness,' the title 'prophet' includes a larger circle of people, including John, that may be killed and humiliated for their testimony.

To be sure, some aspects of the two witnesses signal continuity with the trumpet series. They are given authority to inflict plagues that parallel the second and sixth trumpet plagues.[136] They have power to change the waters into blood (Rev 11:6), which recalls the second trumpet plague (Rev 8:9). Fire comes from the mouth of these two witnesses like the demonic horses of the sixth trumpet.[137] The two witnesses are able to inflict every kind of plague (ἐν πάσῃ πληγῇ), which recalls the same terminology for the sixth trumpet plague (Rev 9:18, 20). The inhabitants of the earth rejoiced and

---

[132] Jauhiainen, 89–93, cf. 149–150.

[133] Bauckham, *Climax*, 274.

[134] Pattemore, *People of God*, 162; Beale, *Revelation*, 574–5; Aune, *Revelation*, 2:615; Bauckham, *Climax*, 274.

[135] Bauckham, *Climax*, 274: "The story is more like a parable, which dramatizes the nature and result of the church's prophetic witness to the nations.... a call to the churches to play the role which God intends for them."

[136] Schüssler Fiorenza, *Justice and Judgment*, 54.

[137] Beale, *Revelation*, 585–6; cf. E. Müller, 381, also notes that a plague of fire comes from the mouths of horses (9:17–18) and from the mouths of the witnesses (11:5).

celebrated over the two witnesses because "these two prophets had tormented" them (Rev 11:10). The word "torment" (βασανίζω) connects this description to the fifth trumpet plague that describes locusts tormenting those who do not have the seal (Rev 9:5).

The beast from the abyss (Rev 11:7) is another important *dramatis persona* in Rev 11:3–13 that signals a degree of continuity with the trumpet series but predominantly anticipates the role of the beast in Rev 12–13.[138] Many have commented on the fact that the beast is presented with a definite article that suggests that the audience may be familiar with it, but this familiarity is not assumed up to this point.[139] Here it creates added ambiguity that sets the audience on a search for relevance that will be satisfied when the two beasts are introduced in Rev 13.[140] The mention of the "abyss" as the source for the beast reminds the audience that the abyss was the origin of the locust plague (Rev 9:1). The audience may relate this beast to the king of the abyss, named Apollyon and Abaddon (Rev 9:11).[141] Other aspects of the beast's character signal discontinuity. "Making war" weakly recalls the plague of locusts (Rev 9:9, 7) but more strongly anticipates the dragon's war against the Woman's children, who keep the commandments of God and hold the testimony of God (Rev 12:17). "Conquering" ironically recalls the title given to believers who repent and endure in Rev 2–3. "Killing" recalls Antipas and those under the altar (Rev 2:13; 6:11) as well as those who are killed by the plagues following the sixth trumpet (Rev 9:14, 18, 20). In general, mention of the beast anticipates Rev 13 and only weakly signals continuity with the trumpet series.

The population of the Great City is a *dramatis persona* that significantly connects the trumpet plagues to Rev 11:3–13. In Rev 11:13, seven thousand people were killed (ἀπεκτάνθησαν) in the Great City by an earthquake and the "rest" (οἱ λοιποὶ) of the city "give glory to the God of heaven" (ἔδωκαν δόξαν τῷ θεῷ τοῦ οὐρανοῦ). The audience may recall the sixth trumpet blast: "the rest (οἱ λοιποὶ) of humanity, those who were not killed (οἳ οὐκ ἀπεκτάνθησαν) by this plague, did not repent" (9:20). By repeating οἱ λοιποὶ and ἀπεκτάνθησαν, John contrasts those who did not repent (οὐδὲ μετενόησαν) after the sixth plague and those who give glory (ἔδωκαν δόξαν) to God after the witness, death and vindication of the two witnesses.

---

[138] Schüssler Fiorenza, *Justice and Judgment,* 73.

[139] Aune, *Revelation*, 2:616–7.

[140] Charles, *Revelation*, 1:286.

[141] This may yield the effect of associating the beast with Rome, who often identified Apollo as a patron deity. See Lohse, 57; Mounce, 191; Caird, 120; Schüssler Fiorenza, *Revelation*, 71–2; Aune, *Revelation,* 2:535; Beale, *Revelation*, 504. Charles, *Revelation*, 1:246–7, makes the connection with the cult of Apollo but not the Romans.

The impact of this connection is ambiguous, but the juxtaposition of the plagues and the witnesses suggests that witness is necessary for repentance. Schüssler Fiorenza and others argue that the earthquake anticipates but does not signal the final judgment, and so the rest (οἱ λοιποὶ) repented as a result of the testimony of the two witnesses.[142] When the plague following the sixth trumpet is juxtaposed with the story of the two witnesses, the implication is that plagues and disasters do not lead to repentance, but that the testimony of witnesses is necessary.[143] This conclusion is supported by the responses of people to the fourth, fifth, and seventh bowls: they did not repent and give God glory (ἔδωκαν δόξαν τῷ θεῷ, Rev 16:9), repent of their deeds (Rev 16:11), and people in the Great City cursed God (Rev 16:21). This group, who heard the two witnesses and experienced the earthquake that killed a tenth of the city, gave glory just as those gathered around the throne (Rev 4:9, 11; 5:12, 13; 7:12).

In summary, the *dramatis personae* are significant to the audience's experience of continuity and discontinuity. 'Witnesses' is the primary category of characters for this unit. John and the two witnesses are the *dramatis personae* in contrast to characters in the surrounding units. Revelation 7:1–17; 6:9–11; 4:1–5:14; 1:1–3:22 are the most relevant for understanding these characters. From the criteria of *dramatis personae* Rev 10:1–11:13 could be omitted without any loss to the logic of characters.

Although it could be omitted without loss to the logic of the characters, Rev 10:1–11:13 transforms the people of God in four ways. First, Rev 10:1–11:13 broadens the group of witnesses to include two unnamed people. The group of witnesses began with Jesus, then includes John and Antipas and those under the altar, but is broadened to include these two more. The trajectory is that more and more people are identified as witnesses. The designation as lampstands suggests that congregations are also witnesses.

Second, Rev 10:1–11:13 also gives clarity that being a witness may result in persecution and death. If these two witnesses are examples of what may happen, then the members of the audience should prepare themselves for death if they witness. In this way, Rev 10:1–11:13 plays a critical role in persuading the audience to become witnesses in the face of persecution and possible death.

Third, the story of the witnesses anticipates the narrative development of God's opponents. Little information is available about why Antipas

---

[142] Schüssler Fiorenza, *Revelation*, 79. Also Bauckham, *Climax*, 273–283, followed by Aune, *Revelation*, 2:628; Pattemore, *People of God*, 163.

[143] Bauckham, *Climax*, 279; Aune, *Revelation*, 2:587. In contrast, Beale (*Revelation*, 607) argues the remnant in the Great City only acknowledge God's power while remaining antagonistic.

(2:13) or the souls under the altar (6:9–11) were killed and by whom. Revelation 7:9–17 does not detail the nature of the "Great Persecution."[144] In Rev 11:3–13, however, the antagonist is revealed to be the beast from the abyss supported by some of the peoples, tribes, nations, and languages. As Pattemore observes, "[i]t is only at 11:7 that the enemies of the people of God are first clearly identified."[145] This enigmatic introduction anticipates the beast's development in Rev 13 and beyond.

Fourth, the impact of public witness becomes apparent by the repentance of the rest of the Great City (Rev 11:13). In contrast to rest of humanity not killed by the plague of the sixth trumpet (Rev 9:21), the rest who survive the earthquake give glory to God, which is the appropriate response of creatures to the Creator (Rev 5:12, 13; cf. 7:12). Plagues and disasters will not lead to repentance without witness.[146]

Despite the majority of discontinuous signals, some features about the *dramatis personae* that signal continuity between Rev 11:3–11:13 and the sixth seal. The fire from the mouths of the witnesses may remind the audience of the fire from the mouths of the horses (Rev 9:14–21;11:13). A disaster happens (plague from horses; earthquake) followed by enumeration of those killed and the reaction of the rest. These connections are made in the second half (11:3–13), but not the first (10:1–11:2). The *dramatis personae* in the first half (10:1–11:2) present new characters and situations for the audience to unravel, signaling discontinuity with the sixth trumpet. Therefore, when Rev 10:1–11:2 and 11:3–13 are juxtaposed, discontinuity is followed by continuity. The combined vision is independent of the sixth trumpet by virtue of the shift in *dramatis personae* but integrated with the sixth trumpet by the plagues and their results.

e) Spatial Signals: Discontinuity

Spatial signals throughout Rev 10:1–11:13 indicate discontinuity with the trumpet series. Space during the sixth trumpet (Rev 9:13–21) is marked by the Euphrates as the origin of the four angels and cavalry. No other location is given, except the remark that a third of humanity is killed (Rev 9:18) that implies a perspective of the whole world. In contrast, the action in Rev 10:1–11 is focalized from earth viewing the mighty angel coming

---

[144] So noted by A. Y. Collins, *Combat Myth*, 34.

[145] Pattemore, *People of God*, 91.

[146] This point forcefully argued by Bauckham, *Climax*, 258: "Where judgments alone have failed to bring the nations to repentance, the church's suffering witness, along with judgments, will be effective to this end. Thus God's kingdom will come, not simply by the deliverance of the church and the judgment of the nations, but primarily by the repentance of the nations as a result of the church's witness."

down from heaven.[147] Previously, the audience heard that the New Jerusalem will come down from heaven (Rev 3:12; cf. 21:2, 10) and this spatial signal anticipates other angels coming down (Rev 18:1; 20:1). The space in Rev 10:1 has heaven, sea and earth in view. It is further extended when John moves towards the angel and taking the scroll.

The space does not explicitly shift in Rev 11:1–2, but in direct discourse John is told to go and measure the temple, altar, and worshippers. There is no explicit fulfillment of this command, and so the audience is left wondering if there is a change in location. This temple is presented as a new location even if not explicitly described.[148] This ambiguity emphasizes the conflict with the nations and not its location. Whatever the specific location, the nations are trampling on and around the people of God.[149]

Like the angel coming down from heaven, the location of the two witnesses also moves from heaven to earth. The two witnesses are described as "standing" before the Lord of the earth (Rev 11:4), which is consistent with their role as "lampstands" in the presence of Jesus (Rev 1:12, 20). Yet, they are active on earth, not in heaven (Rev 11:5–6). This position of standing before God recalls the transformation of the question "Who will stand in the day of wrath?" (6:17) into "Who will stand before God?" (7:9–10).

The beast comes up from the abyss. As noted above, this location is a connection between the fifth trumpet and Rev 11:3–13. The locust came up from the pit to torment but not kill people without the seal of God, but the beast comes up from the abyss to conquer and kill the two witnesses. This signal is the only spatial signal of continuity.

The location of Rev 11:3–6 shifts to another tantalizingly specific yet ambiguous location: the Great City. There are no prior references to a Great City, and so audiences must search for relevance.[150] Many scholars

---

[147] Schüssler Fiorenza, *Justice and Judgment*, 75, cf. 53; Beale, *Revelation*, 522; C. H. Giblin, "Revelation 11:1–13: Its form, function and Contextual Integration," *NTS* 30 (1984): 435.

[148] Some interpreters see this as the temple in heaven (e.g. Feuillet, Giblin), others as the community as a spiritualized temple (e.g. Beale, Bauckham, Boring), and some as the literal temple in Jerusalem (e.g. Charles, Lohmeyer, Lohse). Charles notes that elsewhere in Revelation, ὁ ναὸς τοῦ θεοῦ is reserved for the temple in heaven (*Revelation*, 1:276–277, cf. 273). Charles also notes that τὸ θυσιαστήριον elsewhere in Revelation refers to the altar in heaven. "Holy City" elsewhere refers to the New Jerusalem (21:2, 10; 22:19).

[149] Beale, *Revelation*, 560–561; Aune, *Revelation*, 2:598. S. Friesen, *Imperial Cults and the Apocalypse of John* (New York: Oxford, 2001), 143, exhorts that "Revelation 11 should not be pressed too hard for historical purposes…."

[150] Charles (*Revelation*, 1:279, 287) and Beale (*Revelation*, 568) take the Holy City (11:2) to refer figuratively to the Christian community, but the Great City to be Jerusalem in 11:8 and Rome everywhere else in Revelation. Lupieri takes the Great City to always refer to Jerusalem. Aune (*Revelation*, 2:621) argues that the Great City is initially

concur with Pattemore who writes, "it is not one particular city, but 'every city' which opposes the people of God."[151] By avoiding naming Jerusalem specifically the Great City is none of them in particular.[152] The reference is ambiguous and anticipates the introduction of Babylon (Rev 14:8) and the unambiguous announcement that the Great City is Babylon (Rev 17:18).

The command to "come up" (ἀνάβατε ὧδε, Rev 11:12) signals the movement from heaven to earth and reminds the audience of John's similar ascent (Rev 4:1). The two witnesses go up to heaven in a cloud while John was transported in the Spirit.

In short, the action in Rev 10:1–11:13 takes place on earth, beginning with movement from heaven to a location on earth with land and sea and concluding with movement from earth (the Great City) to heaven. These shifts further separate Rev 10:1–11:13 from the plague of horses from the Euphrates after the sixth trumpet and the attendants around the throne following the seventh trumpet.

f) Temporal Signals: Discontinuity and Delay

Revelation 10:1–11 has three temporal signals that both separate and connect this unit to the trumpet series. Delay is an important theme developed from Rev 7 and, I will argue in chapter 5, is a critical part of the rhetorical strategy behind Rev 7:1–17 and 10:1–11:13.

The first temporal signal is the oath by the mighty angel that "there is no longer time" (χρόνος οὐκέτι ἔστιν, 10:6). Most simply, χρόνος refers to an interval of time.[153] The word χρόνος occurs only twice before this, the first time referring to the time given to Jezebel to repent (2:21), and the second to the time that the slaughtered under the altar would have wait before vindication (6:11).[154] In this context, it is not necessary to take this statement as sweepingly as Friesen, who suggests that it means "the end of

---

identified with Jerusalem, but with the reference to "peoples, tribes, languages and nations" it becomes a symbol for the world. However, the Great City is also identified as "spiritually Sodom and Egypt and where their Lord was crucified," not literal places, but the combined worst characteristics of these places. Cf. Pattemore, *People of God*, 163; Beale, *Revelation*, 591–2.

[151] Pattemore, *People of God*, 163; cf. Beale, *Revelation*, 592; Aune, *Revelation*, 2:586.

[152] Charles (*Revelation*, 1:288) throws up his hands saying, "It is impossible to reinterpret from the standpoint of the author the various details of this section, which originally set forth the expectations of an earlier time." He later acknowledges that the reference to "inhabitants of the earth" (11:10) makes the location even more ambiguous (1:289).

[153] Charles 1:263; Friesen, *Imperial Cults*, 155.

[154] Aune, *Revelation*, 2:568, and Beale, *Revelation*, 541, emphasize the conceptual link between 6:11 and 10:6b–7.

temporal space."[155] Recalling previous uses of the word χρόνος and observing the importance of repentance in 9:21, the angel seems to be saying, first, that there will not be any more time to repent and, second, that the time of waiting for vindication is over.[156] In this sense, it is accurate to translate the phrase as "There will be no more delay" (NRSV).[157]

Bauckham intimates that the angel in Rev 10:6 is announcing the time for repentance is over, consistent with the use of χρονός in Rev 2:21 that indicates Jezebel is running out of time to repent. He argues that it means there will be no more warning judgments. The seven thunders were seven potential warning judgments that would have delayed justice and been as ineffective in bringing repentance as the six trumpets.[158] "The point of the incident of the thunders is to make clear that there are to be no more warning judgments, but *instead* there is to be what the scroll will reveal."[159] The dramatic repentance after the ascension of the two witnesses (Rev 11:13) reinforces the conclusion that repentance is a purpose of the delay.

Some interpreters (e. g. Caird, Mounce, Bauckham) also take "no more delay" (Rev 10:6) to mean that there will be no more interruptions in the series of events leading up to the final judgment.[160] Rev 7:1–17 and 10:1–11:13 delay the forward progression of seals and trumpets towards the goal. Therefore, the announcement in Rev 10:6 explains why there are not lengthy units between the sixth and seventh bowl following the pattern of the seals and bowls. I consider this further in chapter 6.

The second temporal signal relates this unit to the seventh trumpet (Rev 10:7), suggesting continuity with the trumpet series. The angel announces the fulfillment of the mystery of God "in the days of the sound of the seventh angel..." (ἐν ταῖς ἡμέραις τῆς φωνῆς τοῦ ἑβδόμου ἀγγέλου). This is one of the few ties between Rev 10:1–11:13 and the trumpet series and reminds the audience that these units are embedded within the sixth trumpet/second woe.[161] It emphasizes that the seventh trumpet is a future event.[162] John uses τελέω ("fulfill," "complete") to indicate the end of a

[155] Friesen, *Imperial Cults*, 155; also Lupieri, 170.

[156] See discussion in Beale, *Revelation*, 539–41.

[157] Aune, *Revelation*, 2:568, argues that "delay" is an inappropriate translation if it "assumes that eschatological events have been postponed." I argue that eschatological events are not postponed but ordained in a way that may appear as delay to believers.

[158] Bauckham, *Climax*, 260.

[159] Bauckham, *Climax*, 260.

[160] Caird, 127–129; Mounce, 205–6; Bauckham, *Climax*, 263.

[161] Beale, *Revelation*, 540; Pattemore, *Souls*, 135.

[162] What is the "mystery of God" that is fulfilled when the seventh trumpet is blown? Interpreters offer various options: (1) the content of the scroll, (2) the series of visions beginning with 12:1, or (3) more generally God's plan. Bousset takes the mystery as Satan being cast down from heaven (12:8–9). Charles reports that Vischer, Völter, and

period of time with the connotation that God has ordained its duration (Rev 11:7; 15:1, 8; 17:17; 20:3, 5, 7; cf. 2:26).[163] The interval also reminds the audience of other delays: the delay in releasing the winds in order to seal the 144,000 (Rev 7:1–8) and the period of waiting for the souls under the altar (6:9–11).[164]

The third temporal signal in Rev 10:1–11 is John's command to prophesy again (πάλιν). It is not clear what previous testimony is being alluded to, and so the reference increases ambiguity and the processing effort to resolve it. It may refer to John's prophetic activity before the visions of this book, but known to the audience.[165] This is supported by the reference to "kings" that has not been included in other four-fold lists. Others (e.g. Charles, Beale, Hall) argue that πάλιν refers to prophetic activity earlier in the book.[166] If this is the case, Rev 5:9 and 7:9 are the most relevant, highlighting "people, nations, and languages" as the source for the people of God. In this context, Charles suggests that the force of πάλιν as "again" in Rev 10:11 may anticipate the negative role that the four-fold group will play in Rev 11:9 and the role of the kings in Rev 12–22.[167]

Revelation 11:1–11:13 also focuses on discrete intervals of time in a way that signals discontinuity from the trumpet series and anticipates the identical intervals in Rev 12–13.[168] Up to this point, John has not men-

---

Holtzmann takes it as a reference to the birth of the Messiah. Charles (1:265) argues that it refers to the "whole purpose of God in regard to the world" which has already been revealed to the prophets. Charles (1:260), Lohmeyer, 87, and Lohse, 56, argue that the little scroll is limited to 11:1–13. Others (e.g. Beale, *Revelation*, 527) argue it refers at least to the contents of Rev 11–16 if not Rev 11–22. Schüssler Fiorenza (*Justice and Judgment*, 53, 174–177) argues it is identical to 10:1–15:4. Bauckham (*Climax*, 257–266) and Aune (*Revelation*, 2:557) take it to refer to the bulk of Revelation. In any case, the scroll links Rev 10 to Rev 5 (with Beale, *Revelation*, 527, 530–532; Aune, *Revelation*, 2:557) and may be identical with it (with Bauckham, Boring), but the diminutive form makes the connection more ambiguous (a point made by Beale, *Revelation*, 531). See Aune, *Revelation*, 2:571–2 on the relationship between the little scroll and the scroll of Rev 5–6 and the contents of Revelation. As Beale (*Revelation*, 528) argues the pattern of conquering by perseverance through suffering applies first to the Lamb in Rev 5 and then is imitated by John in Rev 10. I am arguing that the purpose of the digressions is to persuade the audience gradually that conquering means persevering in testimony in the face of suffering and death.

[163] E. Müller, 379, notes that τελέω connects 10:1–11 to 11:1–13 but not to the trumpet series.

[164] Beale, *Revelation*, 587.

[165] With a different twist, Mazzaferri, 295, argues that John is supposed to prophesy "in turn" like OT prophets.

[166] Charles, *Revelation*, 1:269; Beale, *Revelation*, 555; Hall, 290.

[167] Charles, *Revelation*, 1:269.

[168] Schüssler Fiorenza, *Justice and Judgment,* 54–5, emphasizes that 10:1–15:4 are divided thematically but not temporally.

tioned a specific interval of time, and so the mention of 42 months, 1260 days, and 3 ½ days attracts special attention. The nations will trample the city, but not the temple or those sheltered there, for 42 months, which is equivalent to the time that the two witnesses will prophesy (1260 days). The informed audience will know Elijah's ministry lasted 42 months, the Israelite's wanderings included 42 encampments, and Daniel's period of eschatological tribulation lasted three and a half years.[169] They also may know that these are equivalent, and the most mathematically aware will know that 1260 is a square number.[170] But even an uninformed audience will be impressed by the number 1260 when compared to 42.[171] The length of time dedicated to the prophets seems greater and more significant than the time of persecution simply because of the size of the number. Further reflection (which may only be a moment) brings audiences to realize that the two periods are the same length.

These two temporal signals (42 months and 1260 days) do not relate to the trumpet series but anticipate other situations where an opponent of God is attacking agents of God.[172] The prophets will prophesy for the same time that the holy city is besieged (Rev 11:2–3).[173] The use of this length of time anticipates the woman's shelter in the wilderness (Rev 12:6, 14) from the dragon and the beast's slanderous speech and war on the saints (Rev 13:5–7). In this last situation, the agents are not protected but conquered (Rev 13:7), which recalls the same language used in Rev 11:7. When the testimony of the two witnesses is complete, the time of protection is over and the beast "makes war on them and conquers them" and additionally kills them (cf. 12:17). In this way, Rev 11:1–13 prepares the audience for the pattern of a fixed time of protection during persecution in which witnesses will testify and be nourished. When this time is over, however, the witnesses will be conquered and killed.

The last temporal signal is three and a half days (Rev 11:11), the length of time between their death and their resurrection and ascension. It also signals discontinuity with the trumpet series. The audience may find both internal and external data relevant to understand this interval. First, they may recognize the relationship between the time of protection and this in-

---

169 Bauckham, *Climax*, 266–273; Beale, *Revelation*, 565.

170 Bauckham, *Climax*, 400–1.

171 Charles, *Revelation*, 1:273, suggests that the two measures of time may indicate two sources.

172 Schüssler Fiorenza, *Justice and Judgment*, 73.

173 Charles, *Revelation*, 1:273, suggests that the period of the siege of Jerusalem and the interval of the two witnesses were two different situations in the original source, but that John has reinterpreted them so that "fidelity to Christ, while it ensures spiritual security against the demonic world, entails martyrdom, but that this martyrdom in its turn leads to ultimate victory in all things."

terval. 1260 days is three and one half years, or as said in Danielic language in 12:14, a time, times, and half a time.[174] Aune makes the point that three and a half days may seem a short time compared to the three and a half years of protection and testimony.[175] Second, they may connect these three and a half days to the tradition of Jesus lying in the tomb for three days before resurrection.[176] John has already presented martyrs under the throne who have been slaughtered (6:9–11), using the same verb (σφάζω) that described the Lamb (5:6, 9, 12).[177] The three and a half days may be another link with the souls under the altar and the Lamb.

The central point is that the temporal signals have their greatest relevance in recalling the delay introduced with the souls under the altar and the sealing of the 144,000 and anticipating the seventh trumpet and the beast. There are no temporal signals that directly connect Rev 10:1–11:13 to the sixth trumpet. In this situation, the audience must struggle to discover the temporal relationship with the units. The announcement of woe in Rev 11:14 helps the audience to understand that Rev 10:1–11:13 is embedded in the sixth trumpet, but does resolve the relevance problem.

g) Thematic Vocabulary: Standing and Prophecy

Many of the thematic vocabulary have been discussed above (e.g. "another mighty angel," scroll, sealing, witness, prophet, etc). E. Müller highlights a number of words that connect Rev 10:1–11 and 11:1–13. These include ἵστημι, δίδωμι, κατεσθίω/ἐσθίω, περιβάλλω, τελέω, τίθημι, στόμα, φωνή, νεφέλη, πούς and words with the stem *προφητ–. Müller notes that most of these words are not used in any other section of the trumpets.[178] Unique vocabulary signals discontinuity with the trumpet seals.

Only a few of these words are significant thematically.[179] περιβάλλω ("I clothe") is used with white robes (e.g. Rev 7:9, 13), the angel clothed in

---

[174] Also Dan 7:25. With Charles, *Revelation*, 1:279. Cf. Bauckham, *Climax*, 402–3, who connects the three and a half years to the Ascension of Isaiah 4:2–14 and the number of the beast.

[175] Aune, *Revelation*, 2:624.

[176] Beale, *Revelation*, 594; Aune, *Revelation*, 2:624. Aune notes that the relationship between "after three days" in the gospels and "three and a half days" is problematic.

[177] The slaughtered Lamb is of primary relevance for understanding the souls under the altar. Pattemore, *People of God,* 78.

[178] E. Müller, 379. See also Pattemore, *Souls*, 136 n. 63, 137 n. 64–66.

[179] Not significant thematically: δίδωμι is used in the passive voice to indicate a symbolic grant of authority from God (a connection with the trumpet series, 9:1, 3, 5, 11:1–3), but is not stylistically significant in the active voice (10:9). Although κατεσθίω and ἐσθίω occur in 10:1–11 and 11:1–13, it is not clear that such connection produces any significant contextual effects. It is hard to imagine the significance that John consumes the scroll (10:9–10) just as the fire consumes the enemies of the two witnesses

a cloud (Rev 10:1), and witnesses clothed in sackcloth (Rev 11:3). The relationship between these clothes is not clear. νεφέλη ("a cloud") is transportation between heaven and earth (Rev 1:7; 10:1 and 11:12; cf 14:14–16).[180] φωνή is used for human, animal (e.g. Rev 8:13) and heavenly voices (e.g. Rev 1:10) and noises (e.g. Rev 4:5; 9:9). The phrase φωνὴ μεγάλη is used thematically to describe loud heavenly voices (e.g. Rev 1:10; 5:2; 5:12; 7:9). This phrase links Rev 10:1–11:13 to previous loud voices from heaven in Rev 1, 4–5 and 7.[181]

More importantly, ἵστημι ("I stand") is a further link between Rev 7:1–17 and 10:1–11:13. Müller notes that this word does not occur during the trumpet events, and so Rev 7 is the most relevant.[182] The mighty angel is standing (ἑστῶτα) on the sea and land (Rev 10:5, 8) and the two witnesses are standing (ἑστῶτες) before the Lord of the earth (Rev 11:4) and stood (ἔστησαν) on their feet after the breath of God enters them (Rev 11:11). This pattern is similar to Rev 7 which portrayed angelic figures standing (Rev 7:1–3) in the first half, and human figures standing before the throne in the second half (Rev 7:9–17). In Rev 7, the question "who is able to stand" facing God's wrath was transformed into "who are these clothed in white" coming out of the great tribulation. In Rev 11:3–13 the two witnesses stand before God but are killed and lay in the street before being raised again. As in Rev 7, human characters will stand before God in their testimony, and ultimately only after coming through persecution or death.

Prophecy and prophets become significant in Rev 10:1–11:13 with *προφήτ– stems, which signals discontinuity with the trumpet series.[183] Before this unit, the audience was told that the entire book was a work of prophecy (1:3) and that one of John's opponents ("Jezebel") was a prophet

(11:5). The fire from the two witnesses may anticipate the consuming fire in 20:9 but as Aune (*Revelation*, 2:613) argues, fire is more likely a metaphor for speaking the judging word of God. τίθημι ("I put, place")is used in two different ways (10:2; 11:9; cf. 1:17) and is not significant. Feet (πόδες) like pillars of fire recalls the description of Jesus' feet (1:15; 2:18), but does not seem to be used thematically (compare falling to feet in 1:17; 3:9 with standing on feet in 11:11).

[180] Aune, *Revelation*, 2:557; Beale, *Revelation*, 523; Ladd, 141. Beale argues (*Revelation*, 599) that the cloud that transports the two witnesses (11:12) is to be identified with the mighty angel's cloud-clothing of 10:1. His strongest argument is that νεφέλη is anarthrous in 10:1 but has an article in 11:12, but otherwise the connection between clothing implied by περιβάλλω and transportation is not clear.

[181] Ruiz, "Hearing and Seeing," 97–98.

[182] E. Müller, 380. ἵστημι is used to describe the seven angels who receive the seven trumpets (8:2) and the angel in front of the altar (8:3).

[183] Giblin ("Revelation 11:1–13") and E. Müller emphasize prophecy as a key term and theme linking 10:1–11 and 11:1–13. Aune (*Revelation*, 2:555) agrees that this is a significant link here, and especially with latter sections of Revelation.

(Rev 2:20). Revelation 10:7 is the first time prophets are mentioned in the visions proper, as was briefly mentioned in the discussion of *dramatis personae*. "Prophet" becomes John's role explicitly in Rev 10:11. The testimony and violent death of the two witnesses anticipates the importance of prophets for the remainder of Revelation.[184]

h) Summary of Analysis of Rev 10:1–11:13

This analysis has explained why interpreters have identified Rev 10:1–11:13 as a deviation. The audience expected seven trumpets to be blown (Rev 8:2, 6) and experienced the first six trumpets in regular succession, with complex events after the fifth and sixth trumpets. Based on this pattern, the audience might be led to expect the seventh trumpet to be blown after Rev 9:21.

The members of the audience, however, have already had an experience of additional visions before the seventh element when they experienced the seven seals. There is less surprise when John changes the scene after the sixth trumpet, even using a low-level delimiter like καὶ εἶδον. John shifts the communication axis to feature communication between heavenly beings and himself and the two witnesses. He shifts temporal signals and spatial signals indicate new units. Besides a reference to the seventh angel (Rev 10:7), there are no signals to connect Rev 10:1–11 to the first six trumpets. So, the audience relies even more on other references, principally Rev 7:9–17, 6:9–11, and 5:1–5 and Rev 1–3, in that order, to make sense of this vision.

The second unit (Rev 11:1–11:13) is less clearly delimited from the first, but it has more clear signals relating it to the first six trumpets. The two witnesses are linked to the trumpet plagues by common vocabulary and ideas, such as plagues, fire from the mouth, blood to water, and torments. The beast comes out of the abyss like the locust plague released after the fifth trumpet. Common vocabulary also juxtaposes the results of the sixth trumpet plague and the testimony of the two witnesses. Humankind does not repent after the trumpet plagues, but strikingly does give God glory after the testimony, resurrection, and ascension of the two witnesses. These features recall the sixth trumpet and highlight the interruption caused by Rev 10:1–11, but there are many retrospective as well as prospective elements that refer beyond the trumpet series. The beast, Great City, 42 months, 1260 days, and prophetic roles are ambiguous signals to

[184] Prophets will be rewarded with the saints (Rev 11:18), with whom their blood is shed (Rev 16:6). With the saints and apostles, the prophets will rejoice over Babylon's demise (Rev 18:20) because Babylon shed their blood (Rev 18:24). Prophets are motivated by the spirit of God, so the audience may conclude that words of Revelation are trustworthy and true (Rev 22:6, 9; cf. 19:10; 22:7, 10, 18, 19).

be clarified later (what I am calling "discontinuity anticipating future units"). Because of these, we can see why Bousset, Charles, Collins, and Schüssler Fiorenza take Rev 10:1–11:13 with Rev 12–14.[185] Given the complexity of the relationships between Rev 10:1–11:13 and the surrounding units, it is no wonder that interpreters label it with various and divergent terms. It is untrue to say that Rev 10:1–11:13 is unrelated to the trumpet series, but at the same time it must be emphasized that it is strongly delimited and separated. The following table summarizes signals that contribute to the impression of continuity and discontinuity. The table expresses visually that the greatest number of signals recall units before the trumpet series and that the trumpet series is more relevant to 11:1–13 than 10:1–11.

[185] Bousset, 313; Charles, 1:xxvii; A. Y. Collins, *Combat Myth*, 19; Schüssler Fiorenza, *Justice and Judgment*, 34.

Table 3. Continuity and Discontinuity in Rev 10:1–11:13

	Continuity with Trumpet series	*Discontinuity Recalling Previous Units*	*Discontinuity Anticipating Future Units*	*Ambiguous*
10:1–11	καὶ εἶδον (9:1; 8:13) Seventh angel (10:7; 11:15)	ἄλλον ἄγγελον (5:2) Voice from heaven =>John Mighty angel => John (7:14; 5:1–5; 1:11, 19) God (ch. 7, 4–5) Slaves of God (7:3; 2:10; 1:1) Nation, tribe, people… (7:9; 5:10) Little scroll (5:1–2) John as actor (7:12–17; 5:4–5) Down from heaven (3:12; cf. 21:2, 10)	Slaves of God (11:18, etc) Prophets (11:18, etc.) Kings (chs 13–22) Down from heaven (18:1; 20:1)	καὶ εἶδον (8:13; 9:1) Seven Thunders
11:1–13	Plagues (9:20, 18) Fire from mouth (9:17–19) Water to blood (8:9) ἀδικέω (9:19, 10, 4) ἀποκτείνω (9:20, 18, 15, 5) βασανίζω (9:5) ἄβυσσος (9:11, 1) Inhabitants of the earth (8:13) Woe (11:14; 9:12; 8:13)	Unidentified speaker=>John (7:14; 5:1–5) Loud voice =>witness (4:1) Those who worship (7:3–8) Witnesses (John 1:2; Jesus 1:5; Antipas 2:13; souls 6:9) Lampstands (1:20; Zech 4:1–14) Peoples, nations trubes, languages (7:9; 5:9) Earthquake (8:5; 6:12) Giving glory (7:12; 5:12–13; 4:9, 11; 1:6) χρόνος (6:11; 2:21) φωνὴ μεγάλη (7:9; 5:2, 12; 1:10) προφήτ– (2:20; 1:3)	Temple (11:19; 15:5) τελέω (15:18, etc.) 42 months (13:5; Elijah) 1260 days and 3 ½ years (12:6; Daniel) προφήτ– (11:18; 16:6; etc.)	καὶ ἐδόθη μοι πάλιν

Rev 10:1–11:13 can be omitted without any loss to narrative logic. If the reader skipped from Rev 9:21 to 11:14 and announced the completion of the second woe following the failure to repent, the audience would not realize it missed anything.[186] None of the action, characters, or temporal or spatial signals are necessary to understand the following narrative.

Without Rev 10:1–11:13, audiences would not hear the signals repeated from Rev 7, 4–5, and 1–3. They would not hear the emphasis on witnessing and prophecy, the anticipation of conflict with kings, the beast, and the Great City (Rev 12–20), and the repentance of the city made possible by the testimony of the two witnesses.

The primary effect of Rev 10:1–11:13 within the trumpet series is contrast. The earth and sea are suffering plagues (Rev 8:7–9) and yet Rev 10:1–11 presents a divine angel who physically dominates earth and sea. Humankind does not repent or turn from their ways after the plagues (Rev 9:20–21), but John, the worshippers around the altar, and the two witnesses are obedient to God's commands. The plagues following the second and sixth trumpets are comparable to the potential effects of the two witnesses, but it is their testimony, death, ascension, and resulting earthquake that bring people to give God glory. In short, by embedding Rev 10:1–11:13 within the trumpet series, an alternative way is demonstrated: the way of witness, obedience to God that may lead to humiliation and death, but ultimately to resurrection and conversion. Without Rev 10:1–11:13, there would only be judgment and destruction in the seven seals.[187]

Revelation 7 is of primary relevance for understanding Rev 10:1–11:13. The people of God play a central role in these units, specifically John, those worshipping around the altar, and the two witnesses. As discussed above under *dramatis personae*, this focus on John further develops his character from Rev 7, the previous episode in which John was an agent. From Rev 7 to Rev 10–11, John moves from ignorant to knowledgeable, passive to active, powerless to authoritative. Likewise, the people of God (as a general category) are transformed in similar ways. Both Rev 7 and 10–11 describe the people of God as protected: in Rev 7, protected from the effects of the winds; in Rev 11:1–2, protected from the nations. Among the people of God, John reveals other prophets, and specifically two anonymous witnesses who testify and are killed. In Rev 7, those clothed in white robes came out of the great persecution and stood before the throne. In Rev 11, the two witnesses stand before the Lord of the earth and are conquered and killed by the beast, and humiliated by the inhabitants of the

---

[186] Minear, 95: "If one deletes the section he can move without apparent loss from 9:21 to 11:14."

[187] For this reason, some commentators find that 10:1-11:13 relieves the harsh destruction of the trumpet series, cf. Bousset, 314–5.

earth. The common theme is the suffering of witnesses following the example of Jesus, the Lamb. Rev 11 adds the further detail of the opponent, the Beast from the abyss, and the activity and authority of the witnesses and their final vindication and effect on the city. In other words, Rev 7 is of primary relevance for understanding the role of John and the people of God in Rev 10:1–11:13.

Rev 10:1–11:13 further focuses audiences on John's identity and the people of God. Pattemore concludes that these two scenes "focus attention on the prophets and the prophetic ministry."[188] The specific goal of this prophetic witness is the repentance and conversion of the nations. Bauckham likewise suggests that Revelation presents John and the two witnesses as models for the audience to imitate.[189] If audiences identify themselves with those worshipping around the altar, they will feel confident in protection from the trampling of the nations. If they identify themselves as witnesses, they will have a model of authority to testify and torment the inhabitants of the earth with knowledge of final vindication and success. In both of these cases, Rev 10:1–11:13 depicts characters with whom audiences are invited to identify. These characters – and by extension, John's audiences – are threatened but protected by God during their activity.

4. Conclusions and Questions

The primary result of this chapter is that Rev 7:1–17 and 10:1–11:13 are each embedded in a series of seven but significantly discontinuous from them. In chapter 1, I observed that interpreters either closely relate them to the seal series or sharply distinguish them based upon their emphasis on continuity or discontinuity. This analysis has explained why both positions are possible. Besides their embedded positions, these units gives a few signals of continuity, such as "stand" and "seal" for Rev 7:1–8 and the low-level delimiter καὶ εἶδον in Rev 10:1. The majority of signals, however, indicate discontinuity both recalling previous scenes and anticipating future ones. Given this interplay, it is not surprising that interpreters use a variety of terms that emphasize either continuity or discontinuity.

If the seals and trumpets are not the most relevant to understand Rev 7:1–17 and 10:1–11:13, what is more relevant? Rev 6:9–11 (the souls under the altar), 5:1–14 (The Lamb takes the Scroll) and 1:1–3:22 (Vision of Jesus and seven letters) are more relevant for understanding Rev 7:1–17 and 10:1–11:13. Lexical, semantic, and thematic repetitions remind the audience of these prior units, especially focusing on the character of John

188 Pattemore, *Souls*, 142.

189 Bauckham, *Climax*, 283.

and the people of God. The Exodus plague and Passover narrative also are relevant to the meaning of sealing in Rev 7. Zechariah 4:1–14 is necessary to understand the references to olive trees and lampstands in Rev 11. In chapter 4, I will return to Exodus and Zechariah as texts that illuminate the use of digressions in Revelation.

More specifically, this chapter has shown that Rev 7:1–17 and 10:1–11:13 are linked to one another independent of the seal and trumpet series. First, they share a common position between sixth and seventh elements. Second, these two passages are linked by the following signals:

communication axis	heavenly figures / voices => John/witnesses
personal references	God; slaves of God; four-fold "peoples, tribes, languages, nations"
dramatis personae	John; worshippers; witnesses
spatial signals	standing before Lord
temporal signals	delay/no delay
thematic vocabulary	standing; giving glory

Third, they are linked by the themes of protection and separation of God's people (Rev 7:1–8; 11:1–2; 11:3–6) and their suffering and vindication (Rev 7:9–17 and 11:7–13). These links confirm the argument that Rev 7:1–17 and 10:1–11:13 should be analyzed together. Might the audience have had other experiences of texts containing deviations that are linked together? Chapter 4 addresses this question.

This chapter has demonstrated how Rev 7:1–17 and 10:1–11:13 work together to develop the character of John and of the people of God, and the themes of delay, protection, persecution, death, and vindication. The way that Rev 7:1–17 and 10:1–11:13 develop these characters and themes anticipates my argument in chapter 5.

First, Rev 7:1–17 and 10:1–11:13 focus attention on the character of John and the people of God. The focus on John in these two passages is unique when compared to the seal and trumpet series and develops his character, or ethos, a rhetorical term I will discuss in the next chapter. John was transformed from ignorant (not knowing those clothed in white) to knowledgeable (knowing the message of the seven thunders). He was passive (observing events) and became active (prophesying, measuring). He was powerless and became authorized to witness.

These passages transform the people of God, the group that was first introduced as "slaves of God" (Rev 1:1). In Rev 7 and 10–11, the people of God are characterized in several different ways, as slaves of God, 144,000 sealed, innumerable crowd clothed in white who are coming out of persecution, prophets, witnesses, and worshippers. Like John, the people of God are transformed from passive (slaves, sealed) to active (worshipping, prophesying, and witnessing). They are transformed from powerlessness (needing sealing and shelter) to having authority to witness, even with the power of the plagues.

The group of witnesses is also expanded and their role developed from Rev 7 to Rev 10–11. Before Rev 7, Jesus is the faithful witness, followed by John and Antipas, and the souls under the altar. In Rev 7, the role of witness is extended to the innumerable crowd via the symbol of the white robe. Two anonymous witnesses in Rev 11 are added and in Rev 12–22 all saints are invited to consider themselves witnesses.[190]

Second, the content of Rev 7:1–17 and 10:1–11:13 develops the theme of delay. The souls under the altar introduced this topic when they asked how long until their vindication (Rev 6:10). In Rev 7:3, the destroying winds are delayed by the sealing of the slaves of God, meaning their protection and separation. Delay for protection is also a theme in Rev 11:1–13: the people around the altar and the two witnesses are protected for 42 months/1260 days. Revelation 10:1–11 develops the theme of delay by the angel who announces that, "there will be no more delay" (Rev 10:6). Both Rev 7:1–17 and 10:1–11:13 incorporate delay into their content.

Delay is also expressed structurally by the length of these two passages between the sixth and seventh seals and trumpets. Scholars agree that this translates into delay in the audience's experience but disagree whether it delays the progress of the action or enlarges the perspective. The temporal relationship with the seals and trumpets is ambiguous and can be interpreted in a variety of ways depending on which signals are privileged. However, since delay is incorporated in both content and structure and temporal signals primarily indicate discontinuity, one should emphasize the audience's experience of delay rather than the chronology of visions.

Third, Rev 7:1–17 and 10:1–11:13 gradually develop the theme of the persecution and death of witnesses that was hinted by Antipas' death (Rev 2:13) and introduced with the souls under the altar (Rev 6:9–11). Revelation 7:9–17 portrayed a crowd coming out of great persecution, but only in Rev 11:1–13 does John reveal who was killing witnesses and why. Rev 10:1–11:13 describes in further detail that the nations, the beast, the Great City, and the inhabitants of the earth opposed the witnesses because they were tormented by these prophets. As a result, the witnesses are killed and humiliated, but ultimately are raised from the dead and successful in bringing repentance. Progressively, Rev 7:1–17 and 10:1–11:13 present more and more detail about witnesses that face persecution and even death, confident that God will vindicate them.

---

[190] For example, Rev 12:17 is a strong signal in this direction. The children of the Woman Clothed by the Sun are "those who keep the commandments of God and hold the witness of Jesus."

Chapter 3

Digressions in theory

In order to understand how John's audiences experienced Rev 7:1–17 and 10:1–11:13 between the sixth and seventh trumpets and seals, we need to better understand communication patterns in late 1st century Asia Minor, especially how and why people deviated when they communicated.

From the 2nd century BCE to the 1st century CE, three rhetoricians (people who taught and discussed the theory of oratory) systematically discussed deviations under the Greek term παρέκβασις, 'digression.'[1] Hermagoras (2nd c. BCE), Cicero (1st c. BCE) and Quintilian (1st c. CE) used only παρέκβασις, and no other Greek term, to describe a section of a speech that did not contribute directly to its argument.[2] Prior to the 1st cen-

---

[1] Cicero and Quintilian associate three words with παρέκβασις: *digressio, egressus,* and *egressio*. Cicero *De inventione* I.51.97; Quintilian, *Inst.* IV.3.12. After the 1st century CE, other terms begin to be used. Anonymous Seguerianus (3rd c. CE) distinguishes παρέκβασις from παραδιηγήσις (II.61–2, 67). See section 3.f) below. This distinction was not continued by other rhetoricians. Fortunatus (4–5th c. CE) uses διέξοδος interchangeably with παρέκβασις (II.20). Παρέκβασις is the only Greek term used in the rhetorical handbooks by Greek rhetoricians Aelius Theon (4st c. CE?), Apthonius (4th c. CE), and John of Sardis (commenting in the 9th c. CE on Apthonius) and Latin rhetoricians Fortunatus (4–5th c. CE), Martianus Capella (5th c. CE), and Troilos (5th c. CE). For Theon, see L. Spengel, ed., *Rhetores Graeci* (3 vols; Leipzig: Teubner, 1854–56), 2:80–81. For Apthonius, and John of Sardis, see H. Rabe, ed., *Apthonii Progymnasmata* (Leipzig: Teubner, 1926), 17–20 and 21–22. English translations of Theon, Apthonius, and John of Sardis in G. A. Kennedy, trans., *Progymnasmata: Greek Textbooks of Prose Composition and Rhetoric* (Atlanta: SBL, 2003). For references in Fortunatus, Julius Victor, and Martianus Capella see C. Halm, ed., *Rhetores Latini Minores* (Leipzig: Teubner, 1863), 113.15, 429.2, 487.6. For Troilos see C. Walz, ed., *Rhetores Graeci* (9 vols; Osnabrück: Otto Zeller, 1968 [1832–1836]), VI.49. Cf. D. A. G. Hinks, "Tisias and Corax and the Invention of Rhetoric," *Classical Quarterly* 34 (1940): 67–69. For discussion of these rhetoricians and terms, see J. Martin, *Antike Rhetorik: Technik und Rhetorik* (München: Beck, 1974), 89–91; G. A. Kennedy, *A New History of Classical Rhetoric* (Princeton, New Jersey: Princeton University, 1994), 275–279; Heinrich Lausberg, *Handbuch der Literarischen Rhetorik* (München: Max Hueber Verlag, 1960) §§340–345. On the dating of progymnasmata, especially arguing Theon should be dated to the 4th century CE, see M. Heath, "Theon and the History of the Progymnasmata," *Greek, Roman and Byzantine Studies* 43.2 (2002/3):129–160.

[2] Cicero, *De inventione* I.51.97; *De oratore* II.19.80–3; II.77.310–312; Quintilian, *Inst.* IV.3.

tury, other rhetoricians such as Aristotle, the author of the *Rhetorica ad Alexandrum*, and the author of *Rhetorica ad Herennium* discouraged the practice of speaking "off subject" (ἔξω τοῦ πράγματος), but did not use a term to describe this experience.[3] In practice, orators used a variety of terms like παρέκβασις to connote a deviation from a path, as we saw in Oecumenius and will discuss further in chapter 4.

In this chapter, I investigate what rhetoricians, especially Hermagoras, Cicero, and Quintilian, mean by a digression (παρέκβασις). While they disagree about some aspects of a digression, they agree on a number of points. To summarize: Digressions interrupt and are unnecessary to the logical flow of the speech, so that an A-B-A' pattern may be discerned. Digressions may or may not make use of transitions. The primary reason to use a digression is to move the emotions of the audience and/or to construct the ethos of the parties involved. The point before the conclusion is often the most emotional, so this location is a common recommendation. Digressions often involve the orator directly addressing the audience, which further heightens the significance of the digression. Orators often use digressions to make oblique arguments, especially when the audience may not be sympathetic to the thesis. Because of these features, digressions can become more memorable than other parts of the speech.

This does not mean that every rhetorician approved of the use the term παρέκβασις or its technique. I will also investigate an alternate tradition that is most evident in Anonymous Seguerianus (3rd c. CE) that ridicules the paradox of a part of a speech that is unessential to the logic and yet essential to the effect of the speech. Anonymous tries to promote παραδιήγησις ('incidental narration') as an alternative term that has the same functions as attributed to παρέκβασις. The alternate term did not catch on and παρέκβασις continued to be used and debated until the 9th century CE.[4]

1. παρέκβασις in Biblical, Classical, and Literary Studies

Some Biblical scholars are aware of the use of παρέκβασις in Greco-Roman oratory and literature. In 1898, E. W. Bullinger wrote that "examples [of παρέκβασις] are not wanting in scripture," but he only gives examples in Genesis and one in Romans.[5] J. D. Hester suggests the temporal and spatial shifts in Galatians 2:11–14 signal it should be understood as a

---

[3] Aristotle, *Rhet.* I.1.1–3; *Rhet. Alex.* XXX.1438b.22–28; *Rhet. Her.* I.9.14.

[4] See n. 1.

[5] E. W. Bullinger, *Figures of Speech used in the Bible* (Grand Rapids, Michigan: Baker, 1968 [1898]), 906–7. He lists Gen 2.8–15; 36; 38; and Romans 1:2–6.

digression.[6] Craig Koester has done the most work with digressions by explaining the structure of Hebrews using Quintilian's *Institutio Oratoria.*[7] David Aune describes 'digression' under a heading in *The Westminster Diction of New Testament and Early Christian Literature and Rhetoric* but includes only one brief paragraph on New Testament examples, most of which deals with Koester's analysis of Hebrews. More work needs to be done in this area because digressions were widely used[8] and modern readers have trouble naming and understanding the structural anomalies they create. As a result, deviations that may have been identified in antiquity as digressions are thought in modernity to be evidence of redactional activity.

Classical scholars have examined digressions to greater depth. Josef Martin (1974) gives a brief overview of rhetorician's discussion of digressions from Hermagoras to Fortunatianus that informs our discussion below.[9] William Race (1980) wrote a brief article surveying the use of digressions in classical authors. His opening sentence may surprise Biblical scholars: "Everyone appreciates the fact that digressions (*parekbaseis*) are an important aspect of Greek literature, and are frequently the most striking and memorable part of a work."[10] The paucity of Biblical scholarship in this area shows not everyone appreciates the fact! Race concludes that modern scholars may be confused by digressions and warns not to "underestimate the subtlety of ancient authors."[11]

In general, classicists have focused on digressions in individual texts or as used by individual authors.[12] Their work provides foundational insights

---

[6] J. D. Hester, "The Rhetorical Structure of Galatians 1:11–2:14," *JBL* 103.2 (1984): 223–233.

[7] C. Koester, "Hebrews, Rhetoric, and the Future of Humanity," *Catholic Biblical Quarterly* 64 (2002): 103–123. See also his commentary in the Anchor Bible series, *Hebrews* (New York: Doubleday, 2001), 83–86, 89.

[8] See Appendix.

[9] J. Martin, *Antike Rhetorik*, 89–91. O. Navarre briefly discusses παρέκβασις in his discussion of the origin of rhetoric (*Rhétorique Grecque avant Aristote* [Paris: Librairie Hachette, 1900], 11–16).

[10] W. Race, "Some Digressions and Returns in Greek Authors," *The Classical Journal* 76.1 (Oct–Nov 1980): 1–8. See a similar comment by G. A. Kennedy (*Classical Rhetoric and its Christian & Secular Tradition: From Ancient to Modern Times* [Chapel Hill: University of North Carolina, 1980], 44) in a discussion of Plato's *Apology* 28a–34b: "Such 'relevant' digressions are highly characteristic of classical oratory."

[11] Race, "Some Digressions," 8.

[12] Studies on individual texts include: A. Barker, "The Digression in the 'Theaetetus'," *Journal of the History of Philosophy* 14.4 (Oct 1976): 457–462; J. M. May, "The *Ethica Digressio* and Cicero's Pro Milone: A Progression of Intensity from Logos to Ethos to Pathos," *The Classical Journal* 74.3 (Feb–Mar 1979): 240–246; cf. idem, *Trials of Character: The Eloquence of Ciceronian Ethics* (Chapel Hill : University of North Carolina Press, 1988), 28–30.

for this investigation: first, criteria for studying digressions and, second, recognition that digressions arise in oral patterns and that modern interpreters may misconstrue a digression as a sign of redactional activity. H. V. Canter (1931) listed and analyzed Cicero's digressions with criteria that I will use below.[13] Julia Haig Gaisser (1969) and Norman Austin (1966) analyzed how digressions are used in Homer's *Iliad* and *Odyssey* and provide evidence that digressions find their earliest expression in oral patterns of speech and not simply arising from rhetorical training.[14] Race (1978) analyzes Isocrates' *Panathenaicus*, arguing against classicists who attribute the digression on Agamemnon to redactional activity. He demonstrates how the digression about Agamemnon gives the impression of emotional spontaneity, contrasts between Spartan "crimes" and Agamemnon's virtue, and portrays himself as a defender of all Hellas like Agamemnon.[15]

These scholars make important contributions to this investigation, but they do not provide a comprehensive analysis of both rhetoricians and actual speeches. For example, Martin gives an excellent summary of rhetoricians, but does not analyze speeches or consider the implications of digressions on meaning.[16] Race surveys authors, but his treatment of Cicero and Quintilian is brief.[17] These two complement each other, but lack a clear definition of digressions, a way of detecting them, and a means of comparing digressions.[18] Canter addresses some of these needs by providing categories for comparing digressions, which are used in the analysis below.

---

[13] H. V. Canter, "*Digressio* in the Orations of Cicero," *The American Journal of Philology* 52.4 (1931): 351–361.

[14] N. Austin, "The Function of Digressions in the *Iliad*," *Greek, Roman, and Byzantine Studies* 7:4 (Winter 1966): 295–311; J. H. Gaisser, "A Structural Analysis of the Digressions in the Iliad and the Odyssey," *Harvard Studies in Classical Philology* 73 (1969): 1–43.

[15] W. Race, "Some Digressions," 2–3 and the complete treatment in "*Panathenaicus* 74–90: The Rhetoric of Isocrates' Digression on Agamemnon," *Transactions of the American Philological Association* 108 (1978): 175–185. See also the independent analysis of M. Laugaa, "La Théâtre de la Digression dans le discours classique," in *Semiotica IV* (The Hague: Mouton, 1971), 100–101, and R. Sabry, *Stratégies Discursives: digression, transition, suspens* (Paris: Les Éditions de L'École des Hautes Études en Sciences Sociales, 1992), 35–41.

[16] Martin discusses the digression in Antiphon's *On the Murder of Herodes* on p. 56, but otherwise examples of digressions are drawn from Quintilian's use of Cicero.

[17] Cicero and Quintilian are absent from Race's general survey of digressions ("Some Digressions"), and appear briefly in his analysis of *Panathenaicus*.

[18] Rather than these issues, classicists like Race seem most concerned with arguing that the explanations for digressions that orators provide should not be taken at face value. For example, Race argues that Isocrates' explanation in *Panathenaicus* 74–90 (that he's getting old) reflects a shrewd rhetorical strategy. See "*Panathenaicus* 74–90", and on a similar argument for Cicero's *Pro Milone*, see May, "*Ethica Digressio*" and D. A. Russell on Dio *Or.* 12 (*Dio Chrysostom: Orations VII, XII and XXXVI*, [Cambridge:

Literary critics have done the more comprehensive work on digressions in ancient rhetoric.[19] Randa Sabry's *Stratégies Discursives: digression, transition, suspens* (1992) is perhaps the most comprehensive analysis of rhetoricians and speeches from Lycurgus to Quintilian. The discussion of digressions in the present investigation largely follows Sabry, who tracks the use and discourse about digressions diachronically with attention to both the consistency and controversy surrounding their use. Sabry's analysis is based in part on Maurice Laugaa's work, exemplified in his article "La théâter de la digression dans le discours classique" (1971).[20] Laugaa deals sensitively with Cicero and Quintilian, and provides a basis (with Sabry) for our discussion of the function, location within a speech, and topics of digressions. Michael von Poser (1969) brings Pseudo-Longinus' *De sublimitate* into consideration, and discusses the relationship of digression and amplification.[21] In *Digressionen: Studien zum Verhältnis von Ordnung und Abweichung in Rhetorik und Poetik* (2000), Andreas Härter contributes a nuanced theoretical discussion of the relationship between order and deviation and provides the foundation for my theoretical reflections on the effect of digressions in Revelation.[22] Unlike Sabry, his analysis is largely synchronic, engaging Cicero and Quintilian while glossing over Aristotle and classical speeches.

When analyzing ancient authors, these literary critics focus especially on the paradox of a digression.[23] Sabry observes that it is a *coup de force* that digression is an integrated part of rhetorical speech because,

> [n]othing apparently justifies within this rigorously governed economy of τάξις or *dispositio* – according to which each part of the speech must contribute to the cohesion of the whole with a precise function – the presence of this floating part, foreign, autonomous, with the strange and confused status, and whose eccentricity burst through the se-

---

Cambridge University, 1992], 188). Martin, on the other hand, seems concerned with comparing various arrangements of speeches and describing the diachronic relationships between rhetoricians.

[19] The critics discussed below study digressions in ancient rhetoric as preparation to analyze the dynamics of 18th century Romance novels. Laurence Sterne's *Tristram Shandy* is the most common work analyzed.

[20] Laugaa, "Le théâter de la digression," 97–126.

[21] Michael von Poser, *Der abschweifende Erzähler: Rhetorische Tradition und deutscher Roman im achtzehnten Jahrhundert* (Berlin: Verlag Gehlen, 1969), 15–22; Laugaa, 105–126.

[22] A. Härter, *Digressionen: Studien zum Verhältnis von Ordnung und Abweichung in Rhetorik und Poetik* (Verlag: Wilhelm Fink, 2000). He briefly treats Aristotle on p. 19.

[23] E.g. Sabry, 17–18; Härter, 12; Laugaa, 97–98; Martin, 90; Barker, "The Digression in the '*Theaetetus*'," 457.

ries of terms selected to indicate it: παρέκβασις, διέξοδος, then later *digressio, digressus, egressio, egressus, excursio, excursus* and *excessus.*[24]

Simply put, a digression paradoxically arises from the subject matter and is at the same time outside the subject matter. Quintilian defines παρέκβασις as "the handling of some theme, which must however have some bearing on the case, in a passage that involves digression from the logical order of our speech" (IV.3.14),[25] the kind of definition that the rhetorician Alexander (2nd c. CE) mocks as laughable (*Anon. Seg.* 2.62). Put another way, if an author digresses, and assuming it does not reflect sloppy writing, then the author must have planned the digression.[26] How can a digression be outside the subject matter and at the same time planned? This paradox reveals a tension between order and chaos, a contest between the order of a speech and elements that disrupt that order. Härter makes this contest explicit, arguing that digressions represent the author's attempt to manage and control disorder.[27] The author may have divergent material to include, divergent goals to be met, or divergent aspects of the audience to be addressed. Digressions are a means for authors to manage this disorder, incorporating it into the speech and fencing it off with special terms, transitions, and apologies. Yet, by its very presence the digression still subverts the dominant order of the text and audience's expectations. Härter concludes that digressions form "not only an annoyance for the order, but also a danger, since their very existence undermines the validity claims of the order."[28]

Digressions create a further paradox for the critic who seeks coherence and logic in the flow of an argument. If a unit is outside the boundaries of the subject matter, it seems beyond theoretical reflection or must be

---

[24] All translations are my own unless noted otherwise. Sabry, 17–18: "Rien ne justifie apparemment au sein de cette économie rigoureuse régie par la τάξις ou *dispositio* – selon laquelle chaque partie du discours, pourvue d'une fonction précise, doit concourir à la cohésion de l'ensemble – la présence de cette composante flottante, étrangère, autonome, au statut insolite et confus, et dont l'ex-centricité éclate à travers la série des signifiants choisis pour la désigner: παρέκβασις..." διέξοδος is not a term used by Hermagoras, Cicero or Quintilian but is used by Fortunatus (4–5th c. CE).

[25] Παρέκβασις est, ut mea quidem fert opinio, alicuius rei, sed ad utilitatem causae pertinentis extra ordinem excurrens tractatio.

[26] Race ("Some Digressions," 1–2) uses Isocrates *Panathenaicus* to illumine the paradox. Isocrates says he is carried away in the moment, but spent three years writing this speech. The digression is simultaneously well-planned and presented as spontaneous.

[27] Härter, 9; cf. Sabry, 19; Laugaa, 99; M. E. A. Cruz, "Un Acercamiento a la Forma del Ensayo a la Luz del Concepto Retórico Quintilianesco de *Digressio*," in *Quintiliano: Historia y Actualidad de la Retórica* (2 vols; ed. T. Albadejo, et. al; Calahorra, Spain: Ayuntamiento de Calahorra, 1998), 2:463–472.

[28] Härter, 9: "sie bilden für die Ordnung nicht nur ein Ärgernis, sondern auch eine Gefahr, da ihre bloße Existenz den Geltungsanspruch der Ordung unterläuft."

rationalized into the interpreter's reconstruction of the argument. How does one analyze something that does not contribute to the argument? Sabry argues that some ancient rhetoricians reject digressions as inappropriate because they do not fit the "image of rigorism that essentially ended up being the dominant image of rhetoric."[29] Yet other rhetoricians describe digressions as an integrated part of speeches. Sabry posits that these rhetoricians recognize the there is a need to control "a certain inherent digressive force in the exercise of speech" and "to enclose it, channel it, codify it in order to better break its capacity of disorder."[30] By rationalizing or dissecting digressions, the rhetorician and interpreter attempts to control the chaos that a digression brings, replicating the author's attempts to tame disorder in the material or audience by using digressions, and replicating the author's attempt to control the digression itself with transitions, apologies and explanations.

2. An Overview of Ancient Rhetorical Theory

Before analyzing what ancient rhetoricians wrote about digressions, a brief overview of rhetorical theory provides basic definitions of technical terms, including terms for the basic genres of rhetoric, the tasks of the orator, the sources for things that persuade, and the basic arrangement of a speech.[31]

Speeches in ancient rhetorical theory were divided into three basic genres: forensic (γένος δικανικόν, *genus iudiciale*), deliberative (γένος συμβουλευτικόν, *genus deliberativum*), or epideictic (γένος ἐπιδεικτικόν, *genus demonstrativum*). Each correlates with a general communication situation: the forensic speech in a courtroom to accuse or defend someone before a judge or jury; the deliberative speech to persuade or dis-

[29] Sabry, 19. "l'image du rigorisme a fini par s'imposer comme l'image dominante de la rhétorique." Despite that image, "history knew an 'exuberant' rhetoric whose economy tolerated a certain luxury extremely well." (l'histoire a connu des rhétoriques 'exubérantes' dont l'économie s'accommodait fort bien d'un certain luxe.)

[30] Sabry, 19; "il se serait agi avant tout de maîtriser une certaine force digressive inhérente à l'exercice de la parole, de conjurer la menace qu'elle fait peser sur l'axe du discours, d'où cette place que lui concède le système, pour l'enclore, la canaliser, la codifier de façon à mieux briser son pouvoir de désordre." Cf. Laugaa, 99–100. Pseudo-Longinus (*De sublimitate*, 12.5) suggests that emotion inevitably introduces disorder, and implies that the orator must reckon with this in arranging the speech. See section 5 below.

[31] For a compact and clear summary, see H.-J. Klauck, *Ancient Letters and the New Testament: A Guide to Context and Exegesis* (trans. and ed. D. P. Bailey; Waco, Texas: Baylor, 2006), 211–227. See also various articles in D. Aune, *The Westminster Dictionary of the New Testament and Early Christian Literature and Rhetoric* (Lousiville: Westminster John Knox, 2003), especially "Rhetorical Genres," 418–420, "Rhetoric, divisions of," 415, "Ethos," 169–73, and "Pathos," 339–42.

suade a course of action before an assembly; the epideictic speech to praise or blame someone or something before a gathering at a festival or other occasion. Classifying actual speeches according to these three genres is often very difficult. Klauck gives the example of Isocrates' speech *On the Peace* that at the same time accuses, praises, and advises a popular assembly.[32] Genre is not significant to the present investigation because digressions are used across genres, as discussed below.

Following Aristotle (4th c. BCE), Cicero (1st c. BCE) describes five tasks (*officia oratoris*) for an orator preparing a speech: invention (εὕρεσις, *inventio*), arrangement (τάξις, *dispositio*), style (λέξις, *elocutio*), memory (μνήμη, *memoria*), and delivery (ὑπόκρισις, *actio* or *pronuntiatio*).[33] In invention, the orator discovers appropriate arguments, or means of persuasion, to persuade a particular audience in a particular situation. The means of persuasion (based on logos, ethos, and pathos) will be discussed in detail below because ethos and pathos are primary motivations for orators to digress. Arrangement is when the orator selects the means of persuasion that he thinks are most effective and orders them according to the rhetorical situation and goals. Arrangement is largely concerned with the macro-structure of the work.[34] Style, on the other hand, is concerned with microstructure, word choice, figures of speech, tone, and register.[35] Finally, after choosing the appropriate style, the orator memorizes the speech and delivers it. Of these five tasks of an orator, invention and arrangement are crucial for the discussion of digressions.

Invention is the stage of assessing the means of persuasion (πίστεις) that are available:[36] rational arguments (logos), arguments based on the moral character of the orator, audience, and others involved in the situation (ethos), and arguments to modify the audience's state of mind and their receptivity to the goals of the orator (pathos). Jacob Wisse gives a detailed description of how pathos and ethos were understood (or misunderstood) from Aristotle to Cicero, and the following definitions are based on his analysis.[37]

---

[32] Klauck, *Ancient Letters*, 214.

[33] Cf. *De oratore* I.31.142. Klauck, *Ancient Letters*, 215–6; Aune, "Rhetoric, divisions of," *Westminster Dictionary*, 415.

[34] Klauck, *Ancient Letters*, 217; Aune, "Arrangement," *Westminster Dictionary*, 63–65.

[35] Klauck, *Ancient Letters*, 217–8; Aune, "Style, or stylistics," *Westminster Dictionary*, 451–2.

[36] These means of persuasion could be either crafted (τέχνοι) or uncrafted (ἀτέχνοι). Aristotle (*Rhet.* I.15.1) lists five uncrafted proofs: laws, witnesses, contracts, torture, and oaths. I consider only proofs that are crafted by the orator.

[37] J. Wisse, *Ethos and Pathos: From Aristotle to Cicero* (Amsterdam: A. M. Hakkert, 1989).

'Logos' (λόγος) refers to rational arguments that are used to persuade.[38] Aristotle describes two kinds of logical proof: the enthymeme and the example (*Rhet.* I.2.8–22). An enthymeme is either a complete or shortened syllogism, e.g. "Those who see visions are prophets; John saw visions; therefore John is a prophet."[39] An example, or paradigm, is a special case of an enthymeme that uses a specific situation to draw a general conclusion. For example, one may prove that someone who sees visions is a prophet by giving specific examples of people who are acknowledged to be prophets and who saw visions (e.g. Ezekiel, Daniel).

'Ethos' (ἦθος) refers to means of persuasion based on the moral character of the orator, audience, or other person related to the case being argued.[40] Arguments based on ethos focus on trust. They attempt to persuade the audience that the orator, client, or witness is trustworthy (ἀξιόπιστος), or conversely that an opponent is untrustworthy. For Aristotle, these include three qualities: good sense (φρόνησις), virtue (ἀρετή) and goodwill (εὔνοια).[41] These three qualities may be expressed when the orator speaks of virtue and vice, the noble and the shameful,

> for when speaking of these, we shall make clear the means by which we will be taken to be of such and such a character (ἦθος), which, as we have said, is a second means of persuasion (δευτέρα πίστις); for it is by the same means that we will be able to make ourselves or others trustworthy (ἀξιόπιστον) with respect to virtue (*Rhet.* I.9.1; cf. II.1.4).

In Aristotle's theory, ethos does not refer to assumptions that the audience may have about the orator.[42] Cicero, on the other hand, includes the audience's assumptions about a person's reputation or social authority.[43] Taking Revelation as an example, John may assume that the audience views him as a prophet who is knowledgeable of the mysteries of God, and therefore is trustworthy. According to Cicero, John does not need to explicitly present himself as a prophet, but can build on assumptions about his ethos.

'Pathos' (πάθος) refers to means of persuasion designed to stimulate or suppress emotions.[44] Or, in Aristotle's words, it is necessary that orators know "how to put the judge into a certain frame of mind" (τὸν κριτὴν

---

[38] Wisse, 15.

[39] On John's use of enthymemes in Rev 2–3, see D. deSilva, "Out of our Minds? Appeals to Reason (Logos) in the Seven Oracles of Revelation 2–3," *JSNT* 31.2 (2008): 123–155.

[40] Wisse, 29–36. Wisse uses 'ethos' to specifically refer to the means of persuasion, while he uses ἦθος to more generically refer to the "delineation of character." See also Wisse, 60–61.

[41] *Rhet.* II.1.5–7. See Wisse, 29.

[42] See *Rhet.* I.2.4: "This kind of persuasion, like the others, should be achieved by the speech itself, not by any preconceived idea of the speaker's character."

[43] See Wisse, 234–40; Aune, "Ethos," *Westminster Dictionary*, 171–2.

[44] Wisse, 65–76.

κατασκευάζειν, *Rhet.* II.1.2). He describes 15 emotions: anger (ὀργή), calmness (πραότης), friendly feeling (φιλία), enmity (ἔχθρα), fear (φόβος), confidence (θάρσος), shame (αἰσχύνη), shamelessness (ἀναισχυντία), kindliness (χάρις), unkindliness (ἀχαριστία), pity (ἔλεος), being indignant (τὸ νεμεσᾶν), envy (φθόνος), emulation (ζῆλος), and contempt (καταφρόνησις) (*Rhet.* II.2–11).[45] For each emotion, Aristotle describes what state of mind inclines people towards each emotion, with whom they feel those emotions, and the situations that give rise to each. Emotions (τὰ πάθη) are a critical element in persuasion because they are "those things that transform people to change with respect to their judgments" (ἔστι δὲ τὰ πάθη δὶ ὅσα μεταβάλλοντες διαφέρουσι πρὸς τὰς κρίσεις). The assumption is that emotion colors judgment. An orator must take into account the audience's emotional state and modify it to become more sympathetic to the orator's message. For example, if fear of persecution hinders John's audience from being witnesses to Jesus, John must choose his arguments to suppress fear and stimulate confidence. Evoking emotion is a primary motivation for the use of digressions and is discussed further in section 5 below.

Two points should be stressed about the means of persuasion. First, one speech or work contains many "things that persuade" (πίστεις), all of which are based on one of the three πίστεις described above.[46] As a result, it is possible to outline and analyze a speech (or other kinds of ostensive communication) in three ways: the argument based on logos, the argument based on ethos, and the argument based on pathos. (I will outline the argument from ethos and emotion in Rev 7:1–17 and 10:1–11:13 in chapter 5.) Second, one passage may contain more than one means of persuasion.[47] A single line may include a rational argument (e.g. a syllogism), an argument from ethos (e.g. presenting the orator as trustworthy), and an argument from pathos (e.g. evoking confidence to mitigate the audience's fear). For example, "God told me in a vision that those who endure have no need to fear God's wrath. You are enduring faithfully, therefore you have no need fear God's wrath."

Arrangement is another key concept for the following discussion of digressions. Aristotle describes the basic four parts of a speech as (1) introduction (προοίμιον), (2) statement of the thesis (πρόθεσις), (3) argument

---

[45] The translation of these terms follows *Aristotle* On Rhetoric: *A Theory of Civic Discourse* (trans. G. A. Kennedy; New York: Oxford University, 1991). Cicero (*De oratore* II.51.206–11) lists love (*amor*), hate (*odium*), wrath (*iracundia*), jealousy (*invidia*), compassion (*misericordia*), hope (*spes*), joy (*laetitia*), fear (*timor*), and vexation (*molestia*). Among these, he briefly discusses love, hate, fear, jealousy and compassion.

[46] Wisse, 16.

[47] Wisse, 16.

or proofs (πίστις), and (4) conclusion (ἐπίλογος), but only the statement of thesis and proofs are necessary for every speech (*Rhet.* III.13). As discussed further in the next section, Aristotle seems to be reacting against others who are teaching that other parts are required in every speech.

> Therefore, if one would choose all such things, it will be how Theodorus and his school did it by distinguishing narrative, additional narrative, preliminary narrative, refutation, and additional refutation. But one must only adopt a name to express a distinct form or a real difference; otherwise it becomes empty and silly, like the terms introduced by Licymnius in his Art, where he names parts of speech as 'turning successfully,' 'wandering,' and 'offshoot' (Rhet. III.13.5).

Licymnius was teaching deviations as required sections. Aristotle reminds his students that, in theory, a speech only requires the statement and proofs. The structure of a speech should be appropriate to the particular orator, audience, and situation. The implication is that in the process of invention an orator may discover that a particular structure – including deviations that 'turn successfully,' 'wander,' or 'offshoot' from the basic four-part speech – may be persuasive in a particular situation.

3. Descriptions and Prescriptions by Rhetoricians

When Aristotle and Licymnius comment on deviations, they reflect the reality that orators are digressing, likely because audiences responded favorably. Rhetoricians had to respond, at least to prescribe how to use digressions according to their own theory of oratory.

As demonstrated below, digressions were part of the cognitive environment from which hearers could draw to understand communication. Poser argues that digression "was first copied from everyday life and seized as guidance in order to be reproducible with all its advantages."[48] In this environment, teachers naturally encouraged what they thought was effective, and criticized what was not.[49] Digressions were hardly irrelevant in courtrooms, council halls, marketplaces, and theaters. They were regular parts of an orator's repertoire and perhaps even expected by audiences.

In addition to reflecting actual practice, rhetoricians debated one another about digressions. Aristotle does not use the term παρέκβασις, but begins his treatise on rhetoric by criticizing rhetoricians who are teaching

---

[48] Poser, 17: "Die Sache war zunächst der Alltagspraxis abgeguckt und, um mit allen Vorzügen reproduzierbar zu werden, als Anleitung gefaßt worden."

[49] Sabry, 28, summarizes three concerns for Cicero and Quintilian: a concern for theorization, pragmatic concerns, and an aesthetic concern. The pragmatic and practical concern includes "appropriating the experience of orators, privileging the public space, and offering a range of tested techniques."

orators to emotionally digress "outside the subject matter" (ἔξω τοῦ πράγματος).[50] *Rhetorica ad Herennium* and *Rhetorica ad Alexandrum* seem to follow Aristotle's reasoning, encouraging orators to stick to the basics.[51] They do not discuss digressions under any term.[52] Others find digressions to be essential, such as Hermagoras (2nd c. BCE) who describes and critiques the use of digressions. Cicero (1st c. BCE) responds and critiques Hermagoras and unnamed others, Quintilian (1st c. CE) responds to even a broader array of rhetoricians.

Because of the interplay of replication and critique, the three teachers who discuss παρέκβασις (digression) must be assessed diachronically and must be accompanied by actual speeches and literature as M. Mitchell has advised.[53] Otherwise, we risk making 'digression' a static, monolithic, and disembodied concept by making a composite of what rhetoricians wrote or by isolating them from contemporary speeches.

In his study of Cicero's digressions, Canter suggests six primary areas of interest that offer a means for comparing rhetoricians and understanding the use of digressions. These criteria include extent, placement, genre, content, purpose of digression and the technique of its insertion. In addition, I suggest that we first ask how each rhetorician defines παρέκβασις.[54] Therefore, I examine how each rhetorician discusses (1) the definition of digression, (2) its functions, (3) length, (4) location in the arrangement, (5) relevance to surrounding material, (6) transitions into and out of the digressing unit, and (7) topics for digression. The following table summarizes the findings of this section.

---

[50] Aristotle *Rhet.* I.1.1–3. Aristotle is countering teachers like Licymnius who argues for a part of the speech that wanders (III.13.16–18). Sabry, 25–26, suggests that "Aristotle, by not considering [digressions], reduces them to a suspected manipulation of the passions of the audience." By not discussing digressions, he also is managing the disorder they introduce into speeches and rhetorical theory. "He proposes to reduce to silence these rhetors and their theories, to exclude them from the rhetorical field…."

[51] Martin, 89. See discussion below in section 3.f).

[52] *Rhet. Her.* I.9.14 teaches that a Statement of Facts (narration) should be brief, which means that orators use "no digressions and… do not wander from the account we have undertaken to set forth" (transitionibus nullis utemur,…non deerrabimus ab eo quod coeperimus exponere). Sabry, 43, suggests that after Quintilian, digressions were no longer a contested subject because speech making had become more mechanically constructed and rigidly conceived. Cf. Kennedy, *New History*, 201–229.

[53] A critical point made by Sabry, 19.

[54] I have renamed Canter's categories. He examines (1) Extent of digression (I have renamed "Length"), (2) Place of digression (Location), (3) Digression in different types of oratory (Omitted here. Canter's point is that Cicero does not use digressions in speeches that have minimal appeal to emotions.) (4) Content of digression (Topics), (5) Purpose of digression (Function) and (6) Insertion of digression technique (Transitions and Relevance). Canter, "*Digressio* in the Orations of Cicero," 353–361.

Table 4. Comparison of Rhetoricians on Digressions

	Hermagoras (2nd c. BCE)[55]	*Cicero (1st c. BCE)*[56]	*Quintilian (1st c. CE)*[57]
Definition	A part of speech between refutation and conclusion, unconnected to the case.	"Portion of speech proving no point by means of argument." (*De Orat.* II.77.311)	"The handling of some theme, which must have some bearing on the case, in a passage that involves digression from the logical order…" (*Inst.* IV.3.14)
Function	(1) Praise or blame (2) Amplify of proof	(1) Stimulate or curb emotion (2) Amplify (3) Entertain (4) Cover up weak argument	(1) Amplify a topic (2) Appeal to emotions (towards judge; to praise self or client, or denounce opponent) (3) Introduce topics for charm and elegance (4) Soften hard thesis
Length	A major part of speech	Implies only as long as necessary	Should be brief; With a preface, a longer digression
Location	Before conclusion	Introduction, conclusion, or all parts; interweaving	In any portion of speech
Relevance	Orator or opponent; amplification of element of proof	Exciting emotion related to facts given	person (orator, client, or audience), place, or amplification of topic
Transitions	Abrupt: "introduced unconnected with the case" (*De Invent.* I.51.97)	"neatly and tactfully effected" (*De Orat.* III.53.202; cf. III.54.207)	Follows naturally, not thrust in like a wedge; digression may be transitional
Topics	Praise of self; Abuse of opponent; confirmation or refutation not by argument but amplification	Related case that confirms or refutes. Commonplaces	(1) Ornamental (persons, places, regions, historical or even legendary events.) (2) Emotional (indignation, pity, hatred, rebuke, excuse, conciliation, or rebut invective) (3) Commonplaces (luxury, avarice, religion, or duty)

[55] Cicero, *De inventione* I.51.97. Cf. "Prolegomena to Hermogenes" in Walz, *Rhet. Graec.*, IV.12.

[56] Cicero, *De inventione* I.51.97; *De oratore* II.19.80–82; II.77.310–312; III.53.203–54.207; *Orator* xl.136–139; cf. ii.7–11; *Part. Orat.* iv.14–v.15.

[57] Quintilian, *Inst.* IV.3; IX.2.55.

a) Hermagoras of Temnos (2nd century BCE)

Hermagoras was perhaps the most well known rhetorician of the Hellenistic period.[58] He was born in Asia Minor in the city of Temnos (modern day Menemen), just north of Smyrna. It seems he studied at Rhodes before teaching rhetoric in Rome. Our primary sources for his life and work are Cicero's *On Invention*, the *Rhetorica ad Herennium*, Quintilian's *Institutio Oratoria* and other later rhetorical works. He is best known for his theory of determining the issue at stake in a case, called stasis theory.

Hermagoras included παρέκβασις as one of six fixed parts of speech, between the refutation and the conclusion.[59] Cicero writes in his early work *De inventione* that,

> Hermagoras puts the digression (*digressionem*) next, and then finally the peroration. In this digression he thinks a passage should be introduced unconnected with the case and the actual point to be decided; it might contain praise of oneself or abuse of the opponent or lead to some other case which may supply confirmation or refutation not by argument but by adding emphasis by means of some amplification. If anyone thinks this is a proper division of a speech, he may follow Hermagoras' rule.[60]

Hermagoras defines a digression as a section of a speech "unconnected to the case," which coheres with the etymology of the term digression but does not explain why it is an expected part of a speech.[61] The implication

---

[58] Kennedy, *New History*, 97.

[59] Cicero *De inventione* I.51.97. Cf. Sabry, 20. The *Prolegomena to Hermogenes* (Walz, *Rhet. Graec.*, IV.12.17) and *Prolegomena to Troilos* (Walz, *Rhet. Graec.*, VI.49) attribute the inclusion of παρέκβασις as a part of speech to Korax (5th c. BCE) and the earliest stage of rhetoric. Cf. Martin, 89; O. Navarre, *Rhétorique Grecque Avant Aristote* (Paris: Libraire Hachette, 1900), 15–16; Hinks, 67–69.

[60] Cicero, *De inventione* I.51.91 (Hubbell, LCL). Jean Cousin (*Études sur Quintilien* [Paris: Boivin, 1935], 1:245–6; cf. 2:114) suggests the school of Hermagoras is the source of the tradition of παρέκβασις displayed in the anonymous *Prolegomena to Hermogenes*. It describes the same five parts of a speech and similar definitions: "...these things are also called προοιμία. After calming and silencing the people, one begins to advise the people concerning the things that are necessary and [begins] to speak as in narration. And after recapitulating these things and reminding briefly about things that came first, then one [begins] to bring under their eyes the things spoken to the people, which are called προοίμιον, διήγησις, ἀγώνες, παρέκβασις, ἐπίλογος" (ἅτινα καὶ προοίμια ἐκάλεσε. μετὰ δὲ τὸ καταπραῦναι καὶ κατασιγῆσαι τὸν δῆμον ἤρξατο περὶ ὧν ἔδει συμβουλεύειν τῷ δήμῳ και λέγειν ὡς ἐν διηγήσει καὶ μετὰ ταῦτα ἀνακεφαλαιοῦσθαι καὶ ἀναμιμνήσκειν ἐν συντόμῳ περὶ τῶν φθασάντων και ὑπ' ὄψιν ἄγειν τὰ λεχθέντα τῷ δήμῳ, ἅπερ ἐκάλεσε, προοίμιον, διήγησιν, ἀγῶνας, παρέκβασιν, ἐπίλογον.) The *Prolegomena to Hermogenes* attributes this tradition to Korax, but as Sabry (21–22) says, this is "a quasi-minervan myth which is erased and lost in smoke." (Contra Navarre, 15.)

[61] The *Prolegomena to Hermogenes* also describes digressions in a similar way: "Now, a digression is when one attempts to show with assistance of things off the topic

is that orators and audiences expected digressions to be a part of speeches, and thus teachers like Hermagoras felt obliged to include it as a fixed part of a student's speech.[62] Kennedy suggests that it is "not so much a true digression as a discussion of some related matter that may affect the outcome or description of the moral character, whether favorable or unfavorable, of those involved in the case."[63] This fits the two functions that Hermagoras discusses, praise of self or blame of the opponent, or amplification of some topic. The relevance of the digression is not to the immediate argument but rather to the ethos of the parties involved: the orator, litigants, the audience and their relationships. The location of a digression is expected in the penultimate place, just before the conclusion. Transitions may be abrupt, emphasizing that the digression is seemingly unconnected to the surrounding material.

b) Teachers in Cicero's time (as he represents them) (1st c. BCE)

Cicero mentions other teachers of rhetoric who encourage digressions, but only names Hermagoras.[64] Although it is tenuous to reconstruct other rhetoricians in Cicero's day, Sabry, Laugaa, and Martin acknowledge their existence to illustrate the breadth of use and debate about digressions.[65]

---

that he is speaking the truth, and he is narrating the case." παρέκβασις δέ ἐστιν ἡνίκα τις πρὸς ἐπικουρίαν τῶν λεγομένων παρ' αὐτοῦ πειρώμενος δεῖξαι ὅτι ἀληθεύει, καὶ τὸ τοῦ πράγματος διηγεῖται (Walz, *Rhet. Graec.*, IV.12).

[62] G. Thiele (*Hermagoras: Ein Beitrag zur Geschichte der Rhetorik* [Strassburg: Verlag von Karl J. Trübner, 1893], 139–140) acknowledges, "Since Hermagoras prescribed these παρέκβασις so expressly, he seems to have regarded this place as the only one permissible for it in the speech. In this, his pedantic nature is to be felt and, in addition, in that he puts it, as it seems, as a necessary requisite of each speech, although it was nevertheless not at all always necessary." But Thiele is swayed by Quintilian and Cicero's presentation of παρέκβασις and concludes that the Hermagoras could not really think that a digression is a part of speech. "That is however hardly to be accepted that Hermagoras would have regarded these παρέκβασις as special part of the speech like the prooemium, the narration and the proof, since it was too insignificant an addition…" (Da Hermagoras diese παρέκβασις so ausdrücklich vorschrieb, scheint er diesen Platz als den einzigen für sie zulässigen in der Rede angesehen zu haben. Auch hierin ist seine Pedanterie zu spüren und ausserdem darin, dass er sie, wie es scheint, als ein notwendiges Requisit einer jeden Rede hinstellt, obwohl sie doch durchaus nicht immer nötig war. …Das ist jedoch kaum anzunehmen, dass Hermagoras diese παρέκβασις als besonderen Teil der Rede wie das Prooemium, die Erzählung und den Beweis angesehen hätte, da sie dazu zu unbedeutend war….)

[63] Kennedy, *New History*, 5.

[64] Aristotle is the most mentioned rhetorician other than Cicero's teacher Crassus, who is a featured speaker in the dialogues *De oratore*. For discussion of "maladroit theorizations" of minor rhetoricians and the bad taste of some orators in Cicero's time, see Sabry, 29.

[65] Sabry, 29; Laugaa, 101–2; Martin, 90.

Cicero portrays these other rhetoricians as having similarities and differences with Hermagoras. For example, like Hermagoras, they argue that a function of digression is to amplify some topic. Different than Hermagoras, they also emphasize securing the audience's attention or good will. Consistent with Hermagoras' advice, digressions should be placed before the conclusion (*peroratio*), but also argue that the introduction (*exordium*) should secure the audience's goodwill by any means, even if off-topic. More than Hermagoras, they emphasize that the primary relevance of digression is the audience's feelings about the orator.

c) Cicero (1st c. BCE)

Marcus Tullius Cicero (106–43 BCE) was a son of a wealthy and well-connected equestrian, educated in rhetoric and philosophy in Rome and Greece. He did not study, however, with Latin rhetoricians but only with Greeks.[66] By 55 BCE, when he wrote *De oratore*, he had direct knowledge of Aristotle's *Rhetorica*, which was perhaps retrieved from Asia Minor (probably Pergamum).[67] He earned a reputation for oratory in both the court and Senate, and published his speeches in 60 BCE, especially announcing in both Latin and Greek his role in stopping the Catiline conspiracy. In his later works such as *Brutus*, he argued with Roman teachers that he calls "Atticists" because they pursue "allegedly Attic Greek standards of purity and grace."[68]

Cicero was incredibly digressive in his speeches. This is remembered as one of his strengths.[69] Pseudo-Longinus (*De sublimitate*) compares the rhetorical abilities of Demosthenes and Cicero, noting that Cicero overwhelms his audiences with a flood of rhetoric

> well-fit with commonplaces, and perorations according to the best, and digressions (παρεκβάσεσι), all kinds of descriptions and epideictic, and historical and physiological examples, and not a few other kinds of material.[70]

[66] Kennedy, *New History*, 119, 143–4.

[67] Kennedy, *New History*, 143. On Asia Minor as the source, see 62.

[68] Kennedy, *New History*, 152.

[69] May, *Trials of Character*, 29: "Given the importance of character in Roman society and the Roman penchant for deploying ethos as a source of persuasion, it is not surprising to find that Cicero accepted the Greek tradition of an ethically based digression and adapted it to his own oratory."

[70] *De sublimitate* 12.5: τοπηγορίαις τε γὰρ καὶ ἐπιλόγοις κατὰ τὸ πλέον καὶ παρεκβάσεσι καὶ τοῖς φραστικοῖς ἅπασι καὶ ἐπιδεικτικοῖς, ἱστορίαις τε καὶ φυσιολογίαις, καὶ οὐκ ὀλίγοις ἄλλοις μέρεσιν ἁρμόδιος. W. Rhys Roberts' edition (originally published in 1899) reads παραβάσεσι (*Longinus On the Sublime* [New York: Garland, 1987], 78).

Canter counts 55 digressions in 43 speeches of various genres.[71] When offering examples of successful digressions, Quintilian describes Cicero's speeches *In Verrem*, *Pro Cornelio,* and *Pro Milone* as the models to follow (*Inst.* IV.3). Cicero's teaching and published works were influential into the 1st c. CE and beyond (e.g. Quintilian and his student Pliny the Younger), which suggests that many people experienced his theory and practice of digression.[72]

Cicero defines a digression (*digressio*) as a "portion of a speech proving no point by means of argument."

> [I]n spite of proving no point by means of argument…it is often useful to digress (*digredi*) from the subject one has put forward and is dealing with, for the purpose of arousing emotion ; and accordingly very often either a place is given to a digression (*digrediendi*) devoted to exciting emotion after we have related the facts and stated our case, or this can rightly be done after we have established our own arguments or refuted those of our opponents, or in both places, or in all the parts of the speech, if the case is one of this importance and extent; and the cases that are the weightiest and fullest for amplification (*augendum*) and embellishment (*ornandum*) are those that give the greatest number of openings for a digression (*digressionem*) of this kind, so allowing the employment of the topics which either stimulate or curb the emotions of the audience.[73]

Cicero indicates four functions in this passage.[74] The primary function is emotional, to stimulate or curb some emotion in the audience. In the case of judicial rhetoric, the prosecutor rouses the judge to anger at the defendant and the advocate softens the judge to favor the client.[75] Second, a digression may also amplify some proof or, third, embellish a speech in a way that demonstrates brilliance and entertains the audience.[76] He also suggests a fourth function, to obscure and cover up a weak case.[77]

Cicero discusses digression as both a part of speech and a figure of thought. The first refers to a passage long enough to stand as a major division among the usual parts of speech, which minimally include introduction, statement of thesis, proofs, and conclusions. The second, digression as a figure of thought, is shorter but shares with its longer sibling the impact on ethos and emotion. When evaluating elements of style in the *Ora-*

---

[71] 27 judicial, 7 deliberative, 4 demonstrative. Canter, 356.

[72] Cf. Pliny the Younger (a student of Quintilian and briefly governor of Bithynia) portrays Cicero as "the Master" to be copied.

[73] *De oratore* II.77.311.

[74] This discussion incorporates insights from Cicero's other works, as described in the footnotes below. These four functions are briefly discussed by Canter, "*Digressio* in the Orations of Cicero," 351 n.1.

[75] Cf. *De oratore* II.19.81–82.

[76] E.g. *Orator* ii.7–11, where Cicero digresses to demonstrate that he learned rhetoric "from the spacious grounds of the Academy" (iii.12). Cf. *De oratore* II.19.80–1.

[77] *Part. Orat.* iv.14–v.15. Cf. Sabry, 31.

tor, Cicero argues that "[f]igures of thought are more important" than other elements of style, since figures of thought contribute greatly to eloquence and embellishment is the essence of oratory.

> The orator, then, whom we are trying to discover will make frequent use of the following figures: he will treat the same subject in many ways, sticking to the same idea and lingering over the same thought; he will often speak slightingly of something or ridicule it; *he will turn from the subject and divert the thought...*[78]

The perfect orator will use digressions among other figures to display brilliance of style.

He takes issue with teachers (like Hermagoras) who argue that digressions are an essential part of a speech. Interestingly he does not argue that an 'essential' digression is oxymoronic, but is most concerned about departing from the main subject (*De inventione* I.51.97) and wearying the audience with length (*De partitione oratoria* IV.14). Since their primary use is to move the audience's emotions, digressions can be appropriate at any time during a speech, especially long and weighty speeches that have many openings for emotional appeals and embellishment. These speeches may have many digressions, which may be independent or related to one another.[79] Sabry marks this as a turning point in the history of rhetoric, giving new potential for amplification that can be grafted onto any part of speech.[80] Although Cicero argues that the location of digressions should suit the speech and not a fixed pattern, he ironically discusses digressions between the proofs and conclusion in *De oratore*, which suggests the practice and perhaps expectation of a digression in that arrangement. Cicero himself tends to digress in this location.[81] His character in *De partitione oratoria* argues that the prosecutor may deviate elsewhere in the speech but especially before or during the conclusion.

> [T]he prosecutor follows the order of the facts and after arranging his series of arguments ready in his hand like a spear, states them vehemently, draws his conclusions freely...employing the principles of perorating that are effective in arousing feeling, both in the rest of his speech when he diverges (*digrediens*) a little from his line of discourse, and with greater vehemence in the concluding peroration. For his object is to make the judge angry.[82]

---

[78] *Orator* xl.136 (Hubbell, LCL), my emphasis.

[79] Canter, 357, argues that digressions in *Pro Milone* and *Pro Sestio* work together to relieve the monotony of the speech and to familiarize the audience with philosophical ideas (for Cicero, one of the functions of oratory is to instruct).

[80] Sabry, 29.

[81] For example, Cicero digresses between *propositio* and *peroratio* in *Pro Milone* 72–91, which he explains as "outside the case" (*extra causam*) (§92). See May, "*Ethica Digressio*," 241–242; Härter, 19–20; Sabry, 29.

[82] *Part. Orat.* v.15 (Rackham, LCL).

This is exactly what Cicero does in his first criminal case, *Pro Roscio Amarino*, in which Cicero defends Roscio against the charge of parricide and attacks Chrysogonus as the real author of the charges. May comments that,

> The placement of an ethically based digression before the peroration is particularly effective, especially when one recalls the Roman belief in the affinity of ethos and pathos. As Cicero inveighs against Chrysogonus near the end of the digression (141), the tenor of his speech rises to fever pitch, transforming the mild emotions of ethos into more vehement feelings of pathos, which he further stokes in the peroration. In this way the *ethica digressio* provides an effective method for heightening the intensity of the speech – a progression that Cicero himself cautions should be gradual.[83]

In this example, Cicero digresses before the conclusion to attack the character of Chrysogonus and to sway the jury by emotion.

In his rhetorical treatises, Cicero argues that the audience's emotional state is the primary relevance of the digression, especially in relationship to the orator, his client or opponent. Although Cicero does not discuss specific situations, reference to his speeches gives a broader understanding of how digressions are designed to move the audience's emotions. If the audience is hostile to the orator, a digression may provide defense (e.g. *De domo* 3–31). If a list of horrible crimes threatens to numb the audience, a positive digression can gain their attention and provide ethical contrast (e.g. the praise of the Sicilians during the recital of Verres' crimes).[84] Sometimes the digression will be purely for "entertainment" (*delectatio*), but even here is designed to impress the audience with the orator's skill (*De oratore* III.53.203).

Unsurprisingly, appropriate topics for digressions include those that stimulate or curb emotions (*De oratore* II.77.312). These include praise or blame of people (e.g. Sthenius in *In Verr.* III.110–114), places (e.g. Pessinus in *De Harusp. Resp.* 28–29) and things (e.g. civil law in *Pro Caec.* 70–75).[85] Each topics is chosen to suit the particular case and audience in order to persuade the audience to acknowledge the orator and client's reputation and worth and, as a consequence, to accept the thesis being offered.

Cicero suggests 'interweaving' multiple digressions throughout a single speech to move the audience and affect the outcome of the case. The more

---

[83] May, *Trials of Character*, 30; cf. 167.

[84] See Canter, 357, for discussion of the digressions in *Pro Milone* and *Pro Sestio* to give relief to the audience and familiarize the audience with philosophical ideas.

[85] See Canter, 358–9, for a complete summary of the content of Cicero's digressions. Sabry, 30, suggests that the distribution of digressions throughout a speech is "accompanied by a liberation of the content of the digression" to include narrative, descriptive, ideological, and addressive contents, as well as commentary.

emotional the facts of the case, the more digressions can be expected.[86] When the character of the orator or client is central to the case, the more digressive the speech will be to develop their ethos. When the logical arguments are weak, digressions may serve to offset the weakness with emotional distractions.[87] In any of these situations, digressions in the structure become a way of infusing ethos and pathos "throughout the whole of the structure of the speeches like the blood in our bodies" (*De oratore* II.77.310). Thus, emotional and ethical digressions should be interwoven throughout the speech.

> But we do not think that [digression] should be listed among the regular parts of the speech, because we disapprove of digressing from the main subject except in case of 'commonplaces.' …Moreover, I am of the opinion that praise and vituperation should not be made a separate part but should be closely interwoven (*implicates*) with the argumentation itself.[88]

Even though Cicero defines digressions as proving no point, his digressions are interwoven with the argumentation and are a vital technique for persuading the audience.[89] In chapter 4, I draw on Cicero's description of interwoven digressions to identify what I call the 'systematic' use of multiple digressions in a single work.

Cicero's transitions are subtle and often inconspicuous. Canter shows that he uses a catch-word, phrase, or thought to introduce a digression and the same term to conclude it and signal the return to the main theme (34 of 55 cases), in an A-B-A' pattern.[90] The returning transition may also serve as a transition to a new phase of the main theme. In some cases, Cicero explicitly acknowledges the digression in the conclusion (what I call an 'articulated' digression in chapter 4). In other cases, he explicitly introduces the digression and marks its conclusion.

Cicero's digressions often are concentrated portraits of his rhetorical goals and a window into the rhetorical situation. In his most famously digressive speech, *Pro Milo*, he depicts the opponent Clodius as a danger to the Roman republic in contrast to his client Milo, whom he portrays as calm and deliberate. After Cicero formally concludes the plea of self-defense, which would naturally be followed by the conclusion, Cicero di-

---

[86] Canter, 357–8. Canter also suggests that if Cicero is too desperate or angry, he does not seem to digress and, conversely, the less emotional he is, the fewer digressions.

[87] Digression as distraction seems to be Cicero's strategy in *Pro Milo*. May notes that "Cicero never returns to his basic argument, that Milo killed Clodius in self-defense; this seems to reflect a deliberate strategy of first providing the jury with a legal out, and then inducing in them a patriotic desire to take it" ("The *Ethica Digressio*," 245).

[88] *De inventione* I.51.97 (Hubbell, LCL). Laudes autem et vituperations non separatim placet tractari, sed in ipsis argumentationibus esse implicates.

[89] Canter, 359.

[90] Canter, 360. Also, May, *Trials of Character*, 103.

gresses. May summarizes how the digression (§72–91) concentrates Cicero's goal of portraying Milo as incapable of committing the crime and Clodius as fully capable.

> Ethical narratives and numerous personifications in which Milo "speaks" for himself are effective means of revealing character in the speech. The beautifully constructed ethical digression presents perhaps the most concentrated and detailed picture of the antagonists. Much of the credibility of Cicero's plea of self-defense was based on the undergirding premise that the characters of Clodius and Milo made it probable that it was Clodius and not Milo who planned the ambush. Thus Cicero provides the jury with a legal escape of self-defense; in the digression, whose persuasive force relies almost entirely on ethos (and its close relative, pathos), Cicero offers the jury a patriotic reason for using that escape, by showing Clodius to be an un-Roman, criminal beast. The ethos, so vigorously expressed in the digression, is easily converted into the rousing pathos of the peroration.[91]

The digression offers a concentrated view into the rhetorical situation: the case is difficult to prove, and so an oblique argument must be made.[92] Cicero's final argument is not based on evidence of the crime, but on his portrayal of the characters. Towards this goal, he uses the digression to construct the ethos of the parties involved

d) Teachers in Quintilian's Time (as he depicts them) (1st c. CE)

In the time between Cicero and Quintilian, teachers in Rome continued to train orators to use digressions. Orators continued to use them as emotional appeals, especially to secure the favor of the audience, to enable the orators to flaunt their skill, and to mitigate a boring recital of facts or argumentative tone. Quintilian writes,

> Most of them are in the habit, as soon as they have completed the statement of facts, of digressing to some pleasant and attractive topic with a view to securing the utmost amount of favour from their audience. This practice originated in the display of the schools of declamation and thence extended to the courts as soon as causes came to be pleaded, not for the benefit of the parties concerned, but to enable the advocates to flaunt their talents. I imagine that they feared that if the slender stream of concise statement, such as is generally required, were followed by the pugnacious tone inevitable in the arguing of the case, the speech would fall flat owing to the postponement of the pleasures of a more expansive eloquence (*Inst.* IV.3.1–2 [LCL, Butler]).

Cicero had hinted that digressions were being used for entertainment and displaying brilliance; in Quintilian's time teachers were focusing on digressions as an opportunity for an otherwise restrained judicial speech to demonstrate eloquence. These teachers also seem to be emphasizing the

---

[91] May, *Trials of Character*, 139.

[92] See May, *Trials of Character*, 134–140.

contrast in tone and content between the digression and the surrounding material, a characteristic noted by Cicero.

After Cicero's time, digressions seem to have become more common earlier in the speech, between the statement of facts and proofs.[93] This perhaps reflects the increased use of digressions to liven up an otherwise boring or pugnacious recital of facts. The focus on the audience's pleasure, rather than other emotions, is emphasized by the choice of topics that are "pleasant and attractive," definitely not what Cicero often chose. (Scathing blame and denunciation were often his choices.)

e) Quintilian (1st c. CE)

Marcus Fabius Quintilian (c. 35–100 CE) was an advocate and teacher of rhetoric in Rome. He wrote the most comprehensive handbook on the training of an orator from childhood to adulthood, *Institutio Oratoria* (presented to Domitian c. 95 CE), synthesizing previous handbooks and teachers (especially Cicero) with his own descriptions and prescriptions about what made a virtuous and effective orator. Digressions were significant enough to merit a whole chapter in Book IV, between the discussion of the statement of facts (IV.2) and the *propositio* (IV.4).

As with Cicero, Quintilian discusses digression (*digressio*, *egressio*, παρέκβασις) under two headings: figures of thought and parts of speech. As a figure of thought, he includes digression in a broader category with interruptions and asides to the audience.

> Again it may be employed as a means of transition, as, for example, 'Cominus, however – nay, pardon me, gentlemen.' This last instance also involves digression (*digressio)*, if indeed digression is to be counted among figures, since some authorities regard it as forming one of the parts of a speech (*Inst.* IX.2.55 [Butler, LCL]).

In this brief example, the orator shifts *dramatis persona* to focus on himself ("me") and shifts the axis of communication to directly address the audience. The digression as figure of thought is short, and may include *aposiopesis* (stopping short so that the audience can complete the thought) and other figures.

When a digression is a part of a speech, he defines it to be both out of place and yet affecting the case, confirming the definition offered by Cicero and Hermagoras.

> Παρέκβασις may, I think, be defined as the handling of some theme, which must however have some bearing on the case, in a passage that involves digression from the logical order of our speech (*Inst.* IV.3.14 [Butler, LCL]).

---

[93] Quintilian, *Inst.* IV.3.1; Laugaa, 103; Martin, 90.

He seems to be aware of the paradox in this definition. Calling these units 'digressions' gives the impression of being off-subject, but in fact they are designed to have a bearing on the case.[94]

Quintilian describes five possible functions of digressions that illustrate their utility. Each function emphasizes the ethical and emotional appeal of digressions and varying relevance to the case. Agreeing with other teachers, Quintilian teaches that a first function of a digression is that it may be used to display eloquence. In practice orators are pleasing the judge with such topics, which Quintilian calls "ornamental" digressions, and he agrees they add charm and elegance and demonstrate the skill of the orator.

> I admit however that this form of digression can be advantageously appended, not merely to the statement of facts, but to each of the different questions or to the questions as a whole, so long as the case demand, or at any rate permit it. Indeed such a practice confers great distinction and adornment (*ornarique*) on a speech (IV.3.4 [Butler, LCL]).

The primary goal of these ornamental digressions is to please the judge or jury, and only slightly less to build up the character of the orator in the eyes of the audience. The ornamental digression is indirect in its method, not directly addressing the case, judge, self, orator, or opponent. These are not so much off-topic as subtly establishing the common values between orator, judge and the case being heard.[95]

A second function of a digression is to soften the elements of an argument that may be difficult for the judge or jury to accept (*Inst.* IV.3.9–11). These digressions target the judge's attitude and emotions about the case, but may be indirect in its appeal.

> But, though such digressions are not always necessary at the end of the statement, they may form a very useful preparation for the examination of the main question, more especially if at first sight it presents an aspect unfavourable to our case, if we have to support a harsh law or demand severe punishment. For this is the place for inserting what may be regarded as a second exordium with a view to exciting or mollifying the judge or disposing him to lend a favouring ear to our proofs. (IV.3.9 [Butler, LCL])

Such digressions can be like lotion on rough skin, softening a thesis that the jury may have difficulty accepting.

> We shall therefore employ such utterances as emollients to soften the harder elements of our statement, in order that the ears of the jury may be more ready to take in what we have to say in the sequel and to grant us the justice which we ask. For it is hard to persuade a man to do anything against the grain (IV.3.10 [Butler, LCL]).

---

[94] Härter, 42, notes this irony: a digression, although off-subject is still subordinated to the overall effect of the speech.

[95] For example, Quintilian quotes Cicero's spontaneous praise of Pompey (IV.3.13) that evokes a common sense of pride and gratitude, and reminds his audience of his relationship with the great general.

Quintilian prescribes that orators use digressions to address the audience's attitude towards the case, especially when trying to persuade the audience to do something that goes against their natural inclination.

A third function of digression makes a more direct appeal to the judge, praises self or client, or denounces the opponent. These 'ethical digressions' focus on the character of people involved in the case. Quintilian gives examples from two of Cicero's speeches.

As examples I may cite the praise of Sicily and the rape of Proserpine in the *Verrines*, or the famous recital of the virtues of Gnaeus Pompeius in the *pro Cornelio*, where the great orator as though the course of his eloquence had been broken by the mere mention of the general's name, interrupts the topic on which he had already embarked and digresses forthwith to sing his praises (IV.3.13 [Butler, LCL]).

Related to the ethical digression is the fourth function of a digression: to stimulate or curb emotion. These digressions express "indignation, pity, hatred, rebuke, excuse, conciliation or be designed to rebut invective" (IV.3.15 [Butler, LCL]). If the orator is a prosecutor, he hopes to arouse the anger of the audience against the opponent (as Quintilian cites Cicero's case against Verres), and if a defendant, he wants to soften the anger of the audience towards the client (as in *Pro Cornelio*). As with ethical digressions, the emotional digression may focus on the character of one of the parties, or respond to the emotions of the opposition.

A fifth function of digression is to amplify or abridge a topic of the case being heard. This kind of digression (which Cicero called "commonplace," *locus*, τόπος) takes a general topic under discussion (such as luxury, greed, religion, or duty) and explores it at greater length than would be normally required by the argument.

Other similar occasions for digression on points not involved by the question at issue arise when we amplify or abridge a topic, make any kind of emotional appeal or introduce any of those topics which add such charm and elegance to oratory, topics that is to say such as luxury, avarice, religion, duty (IV.3.15 [Butler, LCL]).

Quintilian warns that it is not always appropriate to call this a digression. "[T]hese would hardly seem to be digressions as they are so closely attached to arguments on similar subjects that they form part of the texture of the speech" (IV.3.15 [Butler, LCL]). This illustrates how a digression floats between relevance and irrelevance, sometimes so close to the case that it should not be so named, and other times so far away that it seems that it should not have been included.

The key for Quintilian is that a digression has little or no relationship with the surrounding material but does have an integral function in the speech's effect on the audience. On one hand, there is little continuity with the surrounding material.

There are however a number of topics which are inserted in the midst of matter which has no connexion with them, when for example we strive to excite, admonish, appease, entreat or praise the judge. Such passages are innumerable (IV.3.16 [Butler, LCL]).

After all, παρέκβασις "involves digression from the logical order of our speech" (IV.3.14). On the other hand, the digression may display the orator's ability, please the audience, directly address the character of those involved, appeal to the audience's emotions, or amplify or abridge a topic – all functions which relate to the whole speech and deeply affect the reception and outcome of the speech. In other words, there is little continuity between the digression and its immediate location, but the continuity with the speech as a whole has important rhetorical effects.

Length is a concern for Quintilian.[96] He does not want a digression – no matter how eloquent or pleasing – to distract the judge or jury so that they forget the facts.

But all these digressions should be brief. For as soon as he has heard the facts set forth in order, the judge is in a hurry to get to the proof and desires to satisfy himself of the correctness of his impressions at the earliest possible moment. Further, care must be taken not to nullify the effect of the statement by diverting the minds of the court to some other theme and wearying them by useless delay (IV.3.8 [Butler, LCL]).

Quintilian permits that long digressions may be appropriate if they follow the statement of thesis or proofs and are explicitly announced.

But the orator who makes some preface to the main question or proposes to follow up his proofs with a passage designed to commend them to the jury, may digress at some length. On the other hand, if he breaks away in the middle of his speech, he should not be long in returning to the point from which he departed (IV.3.17 [Butler, LCL]).

Under ordinary time constraints, long digressions may only weaken the case.

Quintilian appreciates digressions that follow naturally from what was said (IV.3.4). This implies that transitions were important for him, most likely catch-words that allowed the simulation of spontaneity. For example, Pompey's name is a catchword in Cicero's *pro Cornelio*, which Quintilian cites approvingly (IV.3.13). The mention of a place or topic may provide an opening for a digression that may allow for some pleasure and display of eloquence (IV.3.12). Although he stresses that spontaneous digressions are emotionally more powerful, he suggests that orators may

[96] The time limits on judicial oratory becomes the topic for Plato's digression in *Theaetetus* 172–177 which lifts up philosophers who are free and lawyer-orators who are slaves to the rules of their profession (Barker, 459). See also Dio *Or.* 12 who asserts that digression is a sign of a true philosopher, and Aelius Aristides *Or.* 2.73–4 (*Defense of Oratory*). Cf. Race, "Some Digressions," 3.

want to plan them in advance or at least be prepared in case the opportunity arises.

> Some will have been carefully prepared beforehand, while others will be produced to suit the occasion or the necessity of the moment, if anything extraordinary should occur in the course of our pleading, such as an interruption, the intervention of some individual or a disturbance. For example, this made it necessary for Cicero to digress even in the exordium when he was defending Milo... (IV.3.16 [Butler, LCL]).

An interruption may provide the orator an opportunity for emotion and eloquence.

f) An alternate tradition on digressions: παραδιήγησις

Hermagoras, Cicero, and Quintilian represent one rhetorical tradition that discusses digression (παρέκβασις and *digressio*, etc.), while other rhetoricians such as Aristotle and the author of *Rhetorica ad Herennium* do not. They represent an alternate way of dealing with deviations in a speech. I propose below that Anonymous Seguerianus is the heir of a tradition that rejected the paradoxical technique that rhetoricians described with the term παρέκβασις in favor of a less problematic technique and term, παραδιήγησις (incidental narration). The tradition represented by Hermagoras, Cicero, and Quintilian found παρέκβασις (digression) to be the best term for capturing the paradoxical nature of digressions, even as it evokes discomfort for ancient and modern interpreters.

Anonymous Seguerianus (3rd c. CE) uses παραδιήγησις to describe long deviations. As his appellative suggests, we know little of him. In their introduction to his work, Dilts and Kennedy conclude he is a rhetorician in the 3rd century CE older than Apsines, and after the rhetorician Alexander (late 2nd c. CE) whom he quotes extensively.[97] He briefly mentions παρέκβασις and contrasts it with another term, παραδιήγησις, translated "incidental narration."[98]

Anonymous believes παραδιήγησις, or "incidental narration," is appropriate but παρέκβασις is not. For the sake of brevity in a speech, παρέκβασις should be avoided along with ἐπεισόδιον (an addition)[99] or something that wholly wanders away from the subject (II.67).

---

[97] M. Dilts and G. Kennedy, *Two Rhetorical Treatises* (Leiden: Brill, 1997), x–xi, also notes that Johann Graeven identified him in 1891 as the third century rhetorician Cornutus. Laugaa, 101, assumes this in his discussion of this text. Cf. M. Patillon, in *Anonyme de Séguier: Art du Discours Politique* (ed. and trans. Michel Patillon; Paris: Les Belles Lettres, 2003).

[98] E.g. Harry Caplan's translation of παραδιήγησις in the Loeb edition of *Rhet. Her.* I.8.12 and H. E. Butler's in Quint. *Inst.* IX.2.107. Patillon translates "narrations digressives" (*Anonyme de Séguier,* 13).

[99] ἐπεισόδιον is also used in drama, see 4.6.a.

παραδιήγησις is unnecessary narration in contrast with narration that is an integral part of the subject being debated.

Of those addressed to judges, some are an integral part of the issue being debated, some are spoken to give particular accounts of the hypothesis, some, which they call *paradiēgēseis*, creep in to increase belief (πίστεως) or for amplification (αὐξήσεως) or prejudice (διαβολῆς) or something else of that sort (ἄλλου τινος τοιούτου).[100]

He lists four functions for παραδιήγησις that resemble what Hermagoras, Cicero, and Quintilian described as παρέκβασις (II.55). It is used for (1) credibility (πίστεως), (2) amplification (αὐξήσεως), (3) slandering opponent (διαβολῆς), or (4) "something else of the sort" (ἄλλου τινος τοιούτου). The topics of παραδιήγησις are chosen to provide material for enthymemes and for their persuasiveness (II.57).[101] This incidental narration is placed in one of three locations: the introduction, alongside the main narration or in the conclusion (II.57–60).[102]

He reports that some say παρέκβασις and παραδιήγησις are the same thing, but he disagrees (II.61).

One should know that some have supposed that the digression (παρέκβασις) is the same thing as the paradiegesis, but it differs; for the paradiegesis, as they say, seizes on things beyond the subject, but the digression is an excursus of words in terms of comparison or imitation of things that have happened. On the subject of the digression (παρέκβασις) Alexander has the following criticism: The term is ridiculous, he says: if what is being said is drawn from the subject itself, how is it a digression? But if from outside, how shall we speak about what is external to the hypothesis?[103]

---

[100] *Anon. Seg.* II.55. Translation by Dilts and Kennedy. τῶν δὲ ἐπι κριτῶν αἱ μὲν κατὰ τὸ ἀμφισβητούμενον αὐτὸ συνίστανται, αἱ δὲ πρὸς ἰδίας διηγήσεις τῆς ὑποθέσεως λέγονται, αἱ δὲ παρεμπίπτουσι πίστεως ἕνεκεν ἤ αὐξήσεως ἤ διαβολῆς ἤ ἄλλου τινὸς τοιούτου, ἅστινας καὶ παραδιηγήσεις τινὲς καλοῦσιν.

[101] ὅταν μὲν οὖν ἐμπέσῃ ἡ τῶν πραγμάτων διήγησις, τότε ἐμπεσεῖται παραδιήγησις ἐπιχειρημάτων μὲν ἔχουσα τόπον, πιθανὸν δέ τι συμπερομένη.

[102] "The species of paradiegeses are three: prodiegesis, paradiegesis, epidiegesis. It is prodiegesis whenever we narrate something else external to the fact before the fact itself, as in (Demosthenes' speech) *Against Timocrates*: 'For, men of Athens, since I have had an encounter with a wicked man...' It is paradiegesis whenever we narrate other facts with the main fact, as in *Against Meidias*: 'Contributions were made to Euboeia...' and so on. And epidiegesis whenever we give a narration after the proofs or in the epilogue." Trans. Dilts and Kennedy, 21. εἴδη δὲ τῶν παραδιηγήσεων τρία, προδιήγησις, παραδιήγησις, ἐπιδιήγησις. καὶ προδιήγησις μέν ἐστιν ὅταν πρὸ αυτοῦ τοῦ πράγματος ἔξωθεν ἕτερόν τι διηγησώμεθα, ὥσπερ ἐν τῷ κατὰ Τιμοκράτους· ἐγὼ γάρ ὦ ἄνδρες Ἀθηναῖοι, προσέκρουσα ἀνθρώπῳ πονηρῷ. παραδιήγησις δ' ὅταν περὶ τὸ αὐτὸ πρᾶγμα ἕτερα διηγησώμεθα, ὡς ἐν τῷ κατὰ Μειδίου· ἐγένοντο ἐπιδόσεις εἰς Εὔβοιαν, καὶ τὰ ἑξῆς. ἐπιδιήγησις δ' ὅταν μετὰ τὰς πίστεις ἢ τὸν ἐπίλογον διηγησώμετα.

[103] Trans. Dilts and Kennedy, 21. ἰστέον δὲ τοῦτο, ὡς τὴν παρέκβασίν τινες ταὐτὸν εἶναι ὑπέλαβον τῇ παραδιηγήσει, διαφέρει δέ· ἡ μὲν γὰρ παραδιήγησις,

Παραδιήγησις properly deals with things "beyond the subject" (παρὰ τὸ πρᾶγμα) but παρέκβασις is limited to "comparison and imitation of things that have happened" (καθ᾽ ὁμοίωσιν ἢ μίμησιν τῶν γεγονότων) (II.61). In effect, Anonymous limits the use of digressions by content to narrations that are integral to the issue under debate and by location to three places in the speech.

The paradox of the term παρέκβασις is a significant part of the problem. Anonymous quotes the 2nd c. CE rhetorician Alexander that the term παρέκβασις is laughable, since how could something be both drawn from the subject and external to the hypothesis of the speech? (II.62). In his commentary on Anonymous, Michel Patillon suggests that Alexander and Anonymous objects to the term in the specialized, technical sense used by other rhetoricians, such as Quintilian.

> Perhaps the criticism of Alexander aims at the one who takes παρέκβασις in a restricted sense, as is the case in the preceding lines (§61). The term παρέκβασις questioned in all this polemic is perhaps only one specialized meaning of the word designed for a certain narrative digression. For a specialization of the word, see Quintilian IV.3.14.[104]

In other words, the technique of unrestricted digression advocated under the term παρέκβασις is to be avoided, but παραδιήγησις is appropriate because it hews closely to the form of narrations and the issue being debated.

The author of *Rhet. Her.* describes an unnamed type of narration that seems to be related to Anonymous' discussion of παραδιήγησις. "There is a second type [of narration] which often enters into a speech as a means of winning belief or incriminating our adversary or effecting a transition or setting the stage for something" (I.8.12). These four functions are very close to what Anonymous wrote for παραδιήγησις (credibility, amplification, slander, or something else of the sort). It is striking that both *Rhet. Her.* and *Anon. Seg.* encourage the use of incidental narration with functions similar to what Hermagoras, Cicero, and Quintilian attribute to παρέκβασις.

ὥς φασιν, ἐφάπτεταί τινων παρὰ τὸ πρᾶγμα, ἡ δὲ παρέκβασις ἐκδρομή ἐστι λόγων καθ᾽ ὁμοίωσιν ἢ μίμησιν τῶν γεγονότων. περὶ δὲ τῆς παρεκβάσεως Ἀλέξανδρος ἀντιλέγει· γελοῖον γάρ ἐστι, φησί, τὸ λεγόμενον· εἰ μὲν γὰρ ἐξ αὐτοῦ τοῦ πράγματός ἐστι τὸ λεγόμενον, πῶς ἐστι παρέκβασις; εἰ δὲ ἔξωθεν πῶς ἐροῦμεν τὰ ἔξωθεν τῆς ὑποθέσεως;

[104] Patillon, 79: "La critique d'Alexandros vise peut-être une παρέκβασις prise dans un sens restreint, comme c'est le cas dans les lignes precedents (§61). Le terme παρέκβασις mis en question dans toute cette polémique n'est peut-être qu'une acception du mot specialize pour designer une certaine digression narrative. Pour une specialization du mot, voir Quintilien IV.3.14."

A common tradition is further suggested by the fact that both *Rhet. Her.* and *Anon. Seg.* use a series of "if..." statements to complete the conditional "the narration will be brief if...".[105] A variety of techniques contrary to brevity are mentioned, including digression.

Rhet. Her. I.9.14: "We will be able to make the Statement of Facts (*narrationem)* brief if we begin it at the place at which we need to begin...if we use no digressions and do not wander from the account we have undertaken to set forth..."[106]

Anon. Seg. II.64–68: "Now you will make the narration brief from the facts if you do not start from far back...and further if you were not to use a digression (παρεκβάσει) or describe episodes (ἐπεισοδίοις) or wander totally from the subject."[107]

The structure of the paragraph, the basic order and content of the "if" statements, and the treatment of digressions is similar in both *Rhet. Her.* and *Anon. Seg.*

I suggest that Anonymous and the author of *Rhet. Her.* are using a similar tradition that dismisses παρέκβασις as a term and technique.[108] Both dismiss digression as contrary to the virtue of brevity. Both prefer a kind of narration that does not wander too far from the issue, but function in

---

[105] Compare *Ad Herr.* I.9.14 with *Anon. Seg.* II.64–68. Both authors have a similar order for elements not contributing to brevity and share conclusions, although Anonymous inserts examples from Demosthenes.

[106] Trans. H. Caplan. "...et si transitionibus nullis utemur, et si non deerrabimus ab eo quod coeperimus exponere...."

[107] Trans Dilts and Kennedy, 23. ἐκ μὲν οὖν τῶν πραγμάτων σύντομον ποιήσεις τὴν διήγησιν, ἐὰν μήτε πόρρωθεν ἄρχῃ,... ἔτι τε ἐὰν μήτε παρεκβάσει χρῷο μήτε ἐπεισοδίοις μήτε ὅλως ἀπὸ τοῦ πράγματοκ πλανῷο· This paragraph is taken verbatim by John of Sardis' 9th c. CE commentary on Apthonius. See Kennedy, *Progymnasmata*, 186; Rabe, *Apthonii*, 21–22. This parallel is noted by Rabe, xxi. This is not to suggest direct dependence but intermediate sources and a common tradition, as suggested by Kennedy, *Progymnasmata*, 174.

[108] Two other likely witnesses to this traditions are the *Rhet. Alex.* (3rd c. BCE) and Aelius Theon (4th c. CE, on dating see Heath). The *Rhet. Alex.* does not discuss παρέκβασις or παραδιήγησις but does say about a narrative (διήγησις): "If the facts are moderate in number and not familiar, we ought to place the report or exposition or rediction of them bodily as an addition to the introduction (ἐπὶ τῷ προοιμίῳ); and we shall do this if we go right through from the beginning of the facts to the end, not introducing any side issue (συμπαραλαμβάνοντες) but merely stating the bare facts themselves" (XXX.1438b.22–28 [Rackham, LCL]). Aelius Theon uses the term παρέκβασις and does not completely dismiss it: "One should, moreover, avoid inserting long digressions (παρεκβάσεις) in the middle of a narration. It is not necessary simply to avoid all digressions (παρεκβάσεις), as Philistus does, for they give the hearer's mind a rest, but one should avoid such a lengthy digression that it distracts the hearers and results in the need for a reminder of what has been said earlier, as in Theopompus' *Philippica*. We find there two or three or more whole histories in the form of digressions where there is nothing about Philip and not even the name of any Macedonian." In Kennedy, *Progymnasmata*, 30. Greek from Spengel, *Rhetores Graeci,* 2: 80–81.

similar ways to what Hermagoras, Cicero, and Quintilian describe as παρέκβασις. This kind of narration, although outside the subject matter, improves credibility or disposes the audience favorably to the case. Avoiding the paradox of the term παρέκβασις and the freedom of location given by Cicero and Quintilian, the author of *Rhet. Her.* chooses not to give this kind of narration a name and Anon. Seg. chooses παραδιήγησις as a less problematic term that indicates its close relationship to the narration (διήγησις).[109] The author of *Rhet. Her.* assigns this kind of deviation to the narration only, while Anon. Seg. admits that they are being used in introductions and conclusions as well, and gives them names (προδιήγησις and ἐπιδιήγησις) that once again avoid the impropriety of παρέκβασις. One way to manage disorder is to name it, or refuse to name it. It is possible that the avoidance of discussion of digressions traces back to Aristotle.[110] Sabry suggests that Aristotle excludes rhetors who use digressions and rhetoricians who discuss them, relegating them "outside the circuit, outside combat."[111] She concludes that "[e]ven though he does not make an allusion to the parekbasis, one can nonetheless discern his attitude, judging by the hostility that he exhibits in regard to all fantastic divisions" of parts of a speech.[112] The author of *Rhet. Her.* and Anonymous share his disdain and his awareness that digressions wield emotional and ethical force.[113]

In summary, the paradox of digression is a lively subject in the 2nd and 3rd c. CE. Hermagoras, Cicero, and Quintilian attempted simultaneously to embrace παρέκβασις and to harness the contradictions of the term.[114] In contrast, the author of *Rhet. Her.* and Anonymous Seguerianus reject παρέκβασις but incorporate similar functions under the term παρα-

---

[109] Laugaa, 101.

[110] Further corroboration may be evident that the tradition of three kinds of narration (προδιήγησις, παραδιήγησις, ἐπιγιήγησις) used by Anon. Seg. and evident (but not named) in *Rhet. Her.* are traced to Aristotle, *Rhetoric*, III.13.1414b.5–1416b.10. Similar to Theon's moderate position, Aristotle suggests that during a narration, "even if the speaker wanders away (ἐκτοπίσῃ) from the point, this is more appropriate than that the speech should be monotonous." Cf. III.13.1415b.8 on arousing emotion with topics "outside the case" (ἔξω τοῦ λόγου). See Patillon, 78.

[111] Sabry, 27.

[112] Sabry, 28. "Même s'il ne fait jamais allusion à la παρέκβασις, on devine sans peine quelle aurait été son attitude, à en juger par l'hostilité qu'il affiche à l'égard de toute division fantaisiste."

[113] Compare Anon Seg. II.55 and Aristotle's *Rhetoric* I.1.1354a.3–5 which both refer to the emotional power of digressions.

[114] The persistence of this tradition can be seen in Apthonius, Julius Victor, Martianus Capella, and Troilos in the 4th and 5th century CE, especially by Troilos' efforts to show that the use of digression as a part of speech can be traced back to Korax. See Martin, 89; Hinks 67–69.

διήγησις while limiting its location and content. This alternate tradition may be linked back to Aristotle's rejection of rhetoricians who included digressions as parts of speech. Despite attempts to dismiss παρέκβασις as a term and technique, it was the premier term even in Latin rhetorical handbooks up until the 9th century CE.[115] The point is, however, that no matter what their tradition orators are digressing in practice to the point that teachers of rhetoric are compelled to respond by naming and attempting to control the practice.

4. Summary of Rhetoricians' Discussion of Digressions

From Hermagoras through Cicero to Quintilian and Anonymous, there are two traditions of handling digressions. One is less restricted and uses the term παρέκβασις (Hermagoras, Cicero, and Quintilian); the other limits the location and content of digressions and uses the term παραδιήγησις (*Rhet. Her.* and *Anon. Seg.*). The following points of consistency and controversy inform our understanding of communication patterns in 1st century Asia Minor:

(1) *Digressions were commonly used and taught* to the point that rhetoricians felt obliged to respond to their use and correct their excess. The majority of rhetoricians handled deviations in the order of a speech under the term παρέκβασις. From Hermagoras to Quintilian, many orators and teachers assumed that digressions were a necessary part of every speech. This highlights how effective and expected they were for audiences. Digressions aimed to please and move the emotions, and orators used them whether or not they had anything to do with the case. In the judicial setting, irrelevant digressions would result in the herald's rebuke, and so our rhetoricians caution against digressions that egregiously deviate beyond the case.

(2) Most simply, *a digression is a section of a speech that is unconnected to the surrounding argument but is used to affect the outcome of the speech.*[116] Hermagoras, Cicero, and Quintilian seem to assume three things about a digression:

---

[115] Using παρέκβασις are Greek rhetoricians Aelius Theon (4st c. CE?), Apthonius (4th c. CE) and John of Sardis (commenting in the 9th c. CE on Apthonius) and Latin rhetoricians Fortunatus (4–5th c. CE), Martianus Capella (5th c. CE) and Troilos (5th c. CE). See note 1 above. Cf. Martin, 89.

[116] Compare Bullinger, 906. Härter, 20, argues that rhetoricians develop the term digression as a way to include deviating material without contradicting the order of the speech, even serving the overall goals of the speech.

(a) *An A-B-A' pattern.* The content and even style varies between the unit and the surrounding text, which gives rise to the perception that a unit is a digression.[117] Unit A is interrupted by unit B before continuing with A'. One would expect these units to be delimited in ways that can be detected by the same criteria discussed in chapter 2 (delimiting markers, communication axis, etc).

(b) *A-A' logic.* The content of the preceding and following units match, so that the argument proceeds almost flawlessly if the digression is removed. This does not include transitions, which may link the digression to the surrounding material or when returning announce a new topic of the main theme.

(c) *Processing Effort.* Quintilian was especially concerned that digressions may try an audience's patience. Audiences hearing a digression will begin to ask how this may be relevant to the whole.[118] Digressions require more effort for the audience because they are left to make connections between the digression and the surrounding material even when there is an explanation.[119]

(3) *Digressions were used across all genres* although discussed most by rhetoricians assuming a judicial context.[120] Hermagoras, Cicero, and Quintilian were rhetoricians primarily concerned with speech in the law court, and so it is not surprising that their discussion of digressions primarily refer to a judicial context. Sabry argues that the earliest theoretical reflections on digressions began when the herald of the Areopagite court in 4th

[117] Race refers to this as the contrast between the digression and the surrounding material, for example the contrast in Pindar's *Pythian* 11 between the present celebration and the horrors that happened to great houses like Agamemnon's. Theon writes that in Theopompus' *Philippica* "We find there two or three or more whole histories in the form of digressions where there is nothing about Philip and not even the name of a Macedonian" (Spengel, 2:80). English in Kennedy, *Progymnasmata*, 30.

[118] For example, Cicero, *Orator* iii.11: "I know that this introduction of mine, which does not derive from the discussions on the subject of oratory, but from the heart of philosophy...will arouse criticism, or at least cause astonishment. For readers will either wonder how this can be relevant to our investigation...or will criticize us for leaving the well-trodden paths and hunting for new ones."

[119] See Race, "Some Digressions." Cf. Härter 8: "And if the speech is in order, the question arises: what does the phenomena of the deviation mean for the constitution of order. Is the deviation the last remains of some disorder, from which a certain order has been formed? Is the deviation a hint of some disorder from which the chaos of the cosmos proceeds?" (Und wenn von der Ordnung die Rede ist, stellt sich auch die Frage, was denn das Phänomen der Abweichung für die Konstitution der Ordnung bedeute. Ist die Abweichung der letzte Rest jener Unordnung, aus der eine jeweilige Ordnung gebildet worden ist? Ist die Abweichung die Spur jener Nichtordnung, die der Ordnung vorausgeht wie das Chaos dem Kosmos?)

[120] That digressions were used across genres is shown more fully in chapter 4. See the Appendix.

century BCE Athens censored speakers who deviated from the case at hand.[121] Quintilian, however, credits schools of declamation for the origin of digressions, which may represent his impression as well as an attempt to discredit the use of digressions (*Inst.* IV.3.2). Because he was so focused on the judicial context, he cites Cicero's digressions as examples and does not cite declamations, nor did he consider that one of his heroes, Isocrates (436–338 BCE), digressed in his famous epideictic speech, *Panathenaicus*, or that the poet Homer digressed in the *Iliad* and *Odyssey*.[122] Therefore, we should not take the courtroom as the sole context for digressions.[123] A survey of the use of digressions (see Appendix) confirms Quintilian's sense that digressions were used far beyond the courtroom.

(4) Of the various functions described by the rhetoricians, *the primary function is emotional*. Digressions evoke an audience's emotions and the characters of the people involved, although it does not contribute to the surrounding argument. In digression, the orator more clearly displays what is personally at stake for himself and his audience. In this way, digressions may be a unique window into the author's intentions and perception of the audience. It is too much to say that all digressions function with this kind of keen insight because some are so egregiously irrelevant and receive the rhetorician's (and sometimes the audience's) rebuke. A skillful digression, however, invites the audience behind the façade of the argument to see more clearly what is at stake

(5) Under the general motivation of moving an audience by emotion, the functions described by Hermagoras, Cicero, and Quintilian can be summarized under three headings that I will call Ornamental, Ethical/Emotional, and Amplifying digressions.

(a) *Ornamental* (not mentioned by Hermagoras): praise or blame of person not a party of the case, or place, historical or legendary occurrence. The overt function of these digressions is to please the audience, but they also allow the orator to display eloquence (as part of establishing ethos) and juxtapose values and ideas with the surrounding argument.[124] This

[121] Sabry, 22–26. See Aristotle *Rhet.* I.1.4–6.1354a. Lycurgus, *Contra Leocrates* 11–13. Quintilian, *Inst.* II.16.4; VI.1.7; X.1.107; XII.10.26. Lucian, *Anacharsis* 19, 21.

[122] Canter, etc. Race shows that the digression in *Panathenaicus* 74–90 has two purposes, one forensic and one epideictic. "*Panathenaicus* 74–90," 177.

[123] Cicero asserts that these rules apply to deliberative and epideictic speeches even though his focus is judicial. *De inventione* II.3.12–13; *De oratore* II.81.333.

[124] E.g. *Brutus* 82 describes Servius Galba as the first Roman who displayed distinguished traits of the orator such as using a digression for embellishment (ut egrederetur a proposito ornandi causa). Canter, "*Digressio* in the Orations of Cicero," 351 n.1. Laugaa, 103–104, distinguishes between five forms (ornament, common places, eulogy, description, and mythical story) and two functions (to move the audience or accuse the opponent).

kind of digression may include *ekphrasis* and *enargeia*, which are techniques usually associated with the epideictic species, but also occur in judicial or deliberative contexts.[125] Examples of ornamental digressions can be found especially in histories and in Homer's epics.[126]

(b) *Ethical/Emotional*:[127] praise or blame of person directly involved in the case, or spontaneous expression of emotion about some facet of the case. The primary function of these digressions is to stimulate or curb emotion in a way that will help the audience agree with the orator. The digression may emphasize either the argument from ethos, the argument from pathos, or both. The more ethical oriented digression characterizes a person involved in the case without evoking emotion, while the more emotional digression focuses on an audience's state of mind rather than a person's attributes. These digressions uses the standard topics of praise and invective usually associated with epideictic oratory, but also useful within other species of rhetoric. Ethical/emotional digressions are common in judicial oratory, being Cicero's favorite kind.[128]

---

[125] Cf. R. Cockroft, "Fine-Tuning Quintilian's Doctrine of Rhetorical Emotion: Seven Types of *Enargeia*," in *Quintiliano: Historia y Actualidad de la Retórica* (3 vols; ed. T. Albadejo, et. al; Calahorra, Spain: Ayuntamiento de Calahorra, 1998), 2:503–510.

[126] Historians such as Thucydides, Polybius, Diodorus, and Theopompus used ornamental digressions juxtaposed with narrative, providing pleasing variety but also insight into the values and behavior that the author prizes most. Sabry (p. 17) lists Thucydides 1.126.3–12 (on Kylon), 1.128–34 (on Pausanias), 1.138 (on Themistocles). Polybius *Histories* II.3.6.1, III.2.7, IV.9.1. See also Josephus on Ptolemais (*BJ* 2.10.2). On Theopompus, see G. S. Shrimpton, *Theopompus the Historian* (Montreal: McGill's-Queen University Press, 1991), 72–101; W. R. Connor, *Theopompus and Fifth-Century Athens* (Washington: Center for Hellenic Studies, 1968), 77–98.

Homer likewise used ornamental digressions this way, most famously the shield of Achilles and Odysseus' scar (see discussion in chapter 4). These digressions establish the ethos of his characters and provide pathos in contrast with the surrounding narrative. See Gaisser and Austin. Quintilian observes that Homer is a master of digressions, cf. *Inst.* X.1.49.

Aelius Aristides *Or.* 21 (Smyrnan II) §14–15 is an interesting example of an ornamental digression in an ostensibly epideictic speech. Aristides is giving an encomium of Smyrna in honor of Commodius, and adds a digression on the river Meles, saying that he was inspired by the river Nymphs. The effect of the digression is to subtly compare the emperors to the river, suggesting that the river is more constant and beneficial than the emperors. Aristides hopes the emperors can live up to the river's example.

[127] I am combining ethical and emotional here because the relationship of emotional appeal to character seems so intertwined in digressions. This may be in part because of what May calls the "the relationship of Ciceronian *ethos* (*delectare* or *conciliare*) and *pathos* (*movere*)." *Ethos* for Cicero is a milder form of *pathos* (May, "*Ethica Digressio*," 245). It may be possible to distinguish between ethical and emotional digressions, but Cicero's influence in this discussion makes it difficult. Cf. Wisse; section 2 above.

[128] Cf. May, *Trials of Character*. For another early example of ethical/emotional digressions: Lysias uses two ethical digressions in *Against Eratosthenes* as part of a strat-

(c) *Amplifying*: These digressions are most connected to the surrounding material and, as Quintilian suggests, arguably are not always really digressions.[129] They take some aspect of the case (not a person) and amplify it emotionally or as an opportunity to display eloquence. Cicero suggests that "commonplaces" (*loci*, τόποι) are appropriate topics for digressions, for example the value that Greeks put on works of art (*in Verres* 5.132–135). In *pro Caec.* 70–75, Cicero praises civil law. Quintilian names luxury, greed, religion, and duty as four possible topics for an amplifying digression.

(6) The *location* of digressions is a contentious issue. From Hermagoras' to Quintilian's time, digressions were used in fixed places, first just before the conclusion and later between the statement and proofs. This perhaps highlights how formulaic orators could be, or how strong audience expectations could shape the structure of a speech. Cicero and Quintilian argued against a fixed location for a digression because some orators spoke too far off topic or lacked the spontaneity that lent itself to an emotional appeal. Despite this argument, Cicero himself used digressions before the peroration.[130]

(7) *Transitions* were important to the rhetoricians. Hermagoras preferred an abrupt transition that emphasized the digressive nature of the unit, while Cicero and Quintilian preferred neat transitions, often based on catch-words that gave the impression of a spontaneous emotional outburst. Quintilian noted that some orators use digressions as a transition between two sections.

(8) Quintilian is most concerned about the *length* of the digression, that it not delay the progression of the case unnecessarily. A digression may be a short figure of thought or a major part of the speech.[131] Cicero hints

---

egy to systematically blame all of Athens' problems on Eratosthenes. Lysias, *Against Eratosthenes* §37–47, 70ff. Kennedy, *New History*, 67.

[129] For example, Plato identifies *Theaetetus* 172–177 as a πάρεργα, but Barker argues it is a digression "only in the sense that it develops ideas for their own sake beyond the needs of the general argument in which it is imbedded, and not in the sense that it has no direct relevance to the general argument at all" (Barker, "'*Theaetetus*'," 457). See Poser, 18–22, for a general discussion of how "amplification" became a category that included digression.

[130] E.g. *Pro Milone* 72–91. May suggests that this placement moves the audience in a sequence from logical argument (proofs) to *ethos* and finally *pathos* in the peroration. (May, "*Ethica Digressio,*" 246). Canter's analysis of Cicero's actual speeches suggests that he digressed at any point that served the case ("*Digressio*," 356).

[131] Cf. Lausberg §341.

at this concern by disapproving of digressions that go too far from the main subject, but he seems more concerned with content than length.[132] All of our rhetoricians assume that a digression is an identifiable unit more than one sentence. Cicero suggests that multiple digressions can be interwoven throughout a long and weighty speech at opportune points. I suggest in chapter 4 that this 'interweaving' of multiple digressions can create a series of what I will call 'systematic' digressions that relate to one another rather than the surrounding material.

5. Emotions (τὰ πάθη)

For the rhetoricians surveyed above, the primary motivation for digression was curbing or stimulating emotion. Interestingly, neither Hermagoras, Quintilian, the author of *Rhetorica ad Herennium*, nor Anonymous Seguerianus discuss emotion systematically or in detail.[133] The earliest and most detailed theoretical discussion of emotion is found in Aristotle's *Rhetorica*.[134] Cicero's most mature discussion of ethos and pathos in *De oratore* II.44.185–53.216 seems dependent on Aristotle, but is more prac-

---

[132] Canter, "*Digressio*," 354, notes the average length of Cicero's digressions is 76 lines. Cicero's digressions are generally longer if used in the exordium and shorter if used before the peroration.

[133] For a detailed discussion of how ethos and pathos were confused or omitted in rhetorical handbooks after Aristotle, see Wisse, *Ethos and Pathos*; cf. Aune, *Westminster Dictionary*, 340; Kennedy, *Classical Rhetoric*, 80. Cicero mechanically lists topics to evoke hatred and pity in *De inventione* I.52.100–54.105 and I.55.106–56.109. For Cicero, 'ethos' is an "ethos of sympathy," that incorporates Aristotle's concern for trustworthiness with the "milder emotions" that promote an audience's good-will. In Cicero's theory, 'pathos' refers only to the "violent emotions" (e.g. hate, jealousy, etc). As a result, it seems that Cicero is mixing ethos and pathos as defined by Aristotle. See Wisse for a complete discussion. For other brief treatments see Anon. Seg. 1.6, 4.224–228, *Rhetorica ad Herennium* I.5.8, II.31.50; *Rhet. Alex.* XXIV (1439b.15–1440b.3), XXVI (1442a.7–b.27); Quintilian *Inst.* VI.1–2. *De sublimitate* 44.12 promises a detailed discussion of τὰ πάθη, but breaks off (see also 17.1–2 on using figures with emotional intensity). See also Aristotle, *Poetics* VI.1449b.22–28, IX.1451b.32–1452a.10, XIII.1452b.27–1453b.1, XIV.1453b.13–1454a.14 on fear and pity in tragedy.

[134] For analysis of Aristotle's description of emotion see Wisse, 65–73; J. M. Cooper, "An Aristotelian Theory of the Emotions," in *Essays on Aristotle's* Rhetoric (ed. Amélie Oksenberg Rorty; Berkeley, California: University of California, 1996), 238–257; D. Frede, "Mixed Feelings in Aristotle's Rhetoric," in *Essays on Aristotle's* Rhetoric, 258–285; S. R. Leighton, "Aristotle and the Emotions," in *Essays on Aristotle's* Rhetoric, 206–237.

tical and less theoretical.[135] Later rhetoricians dealt with emotion only in passing, perhaps because of Stoic rejection of emotional appeal.[136]

Aristotle also seems ambivalent about analyzing this part of rhetoric because it is so powerful and overused. As discussed above, Aristotle connects digressions to emotional excess and derides speakers who only arouse emotion without attending to the rational argument (I.1.3).[137] Yet in book 2, he describes a number of emotions in detail because an audience's opinions vary based on their emotional state (II.1.4). People make decisions based on their disposition towards the orator and the topic. "The emotions are as many things that cause people to change with respect to judgments" (II.1.8). Given characteristics of both argument and audience, Aristotle describes various emotions, audiences, the state of mind of the audience, and the kinds of occasions, topics, and techniques for helping change the state of mind of the audience.[138] For example, if the audience is afraid of a certain misfortune and the orator wants them to act out of confidence (θάρσος) rather than fear (φόβος), then the orator should show that the fear is far off or applies to someone else (II.5.13). The key point is that Aristotle knows that an audience will not be persuaded by reasoned arguments alone. Emotion motivates and is an essential part persuading an audience.

This is why digressions are such a potent technique. Moving the emotions of the audience was the primary reason digressions were used in Greek and Latin oratory. In many contexts (especially judicial), it was not appropriate to openly make emotional arguments because they could be censored by the judge. In deliberative contexts it was more appropriate, and in epideictic most of all, but orators could demonstrate their skill by thinly veiling an emotional argument in a digression. The digression thus

---

[135] Wisse, 248, concludes: "In short, both authors are consistent, both in their own typical way. Aristotle gives us a model that is theoretically neat and that enables him to devote much attention to numerous psychological questions. Cicero gives us a model in which the importance of ethical and emotional appeal is fully recognized, but which, at the same time, is more practical. In the end, one might say, Aristotle seems chiefly interested in the psychological aspect of rhetoric, whereas Cicero's chief interest was the rhetorical aspect of psychology."

[136] Wisse, 80–83; Kennedy, *Classical Rhetoric*, 80–1.

[137] Other orators "chiefly devote their attention to matters outside the subject; for the arousing of prejudice, compassion, anger, and similar emotions has no connexion with the matter at hand" (I.1.3).

[138] Aristotle describes 15 emotions: anger (ὀργή), calmness (πραότης), friendly feeling (φιλία), enmity (ἔχθρα), fear (φόβος), confidence (θάρσος), shame (αἰσχύνη), shamelessness (ἀναισχυντία), kindliness (χάρις), unkindliness (ἀχαριστία), pity (ἔλεος), being indignant (τὸ νεμεσᾶν), envy (φθόνος), emulation (ζῆλος), and contempt (καταφρόνησις)

became a tool for incorporating both content outside the case as well as emotional appeal.

Further, digressions were useful because emotion was inevitable and introduced disorder. As Sabry and Härter argue, orators use digressions to channel and manage the audience's disorder.[139] Pseudo-Longinus (c. 1st CE) agrees, saying that emotion is "by disorder is the rush and commotion of the soul" (ἐν ἀταξίᾳ δὲ τὸ πάθος φορὰ ψυχῆς καὶ συγκίνησίς ἐστιν, *De subl.* 20.2).[140] The orator's "very order is disordered and equally his disorder involves a certain element of order" (ἡ τάξις ἄτακτον καὶ ἔμπαλιν ἡ ἀταξία ποιὰν περιλαμβάνει τάξιν, 20.3).

Three of the emotions that Aristotle describes are pertinent to the present investigation: fear (φόβος), confidence (θάρσος), and emulation (ζῆλος). The following definitions provide a basis for analyzing digressions in chapter 4 and Rev 7:1–17 and 10:1–11:13 in chapter 5.

a) Fear (φόβος)

Aristotle defines fear as

> a pain or trouble from sense perception of evil destruction or pain about to happen; for people do not fear all evils, such as becoming unjust or slow-witted, but those able to cause great pain or destruction, and only if they appear to be not far off but near at hand and about to happen, for people do not fear things that are far off; all know that they have to die, but as death is not near, they do not consider it (*Rhet.* II.5.1).

Three points are important. First, fear arises from a sense perception (φαντασία), which does not always correlate with reality; in fact the sense perception is warped by emotion itself.[141] If an audience perceives someone to be hostile and angry and to have the power to injure them, they will be afraid, whether or not the person actually intends harm. Second, fear is related to the proximity of the threat. The orator can heighten the audience's sense of fear by making a threat seem more imminent, or inversely, can reduce fear by making a threat seem more distant.[142] Third, the magnitude of the threat is proportional to the fear. Aristotle uses the adjective "great" to emphasize this point (great pain, great power of destroying, II.5.1). An orator who wishes to increase fear increases the size of the threat, and vice versa.

---

[139] Sabry, 19; Härter, 9; cf. Laugaa, 99.

[140] See discussion in Poser, 17–18.

[141] See *Eth. Nic.* 1149a24–31. Leighton, 212–216. Cf. Cooper; Frede.

[142] Where I discuss how an orator applies Aristotle's theory of emotion in practice, I am drawing an inference. Aristotle himself gives only hints at how his theory may be applied, instead focusing on the orator's ability to observe and analyze human emotions. Cf. Wisse; Leighton; Frede.

The state of mind (διακείμενος) conducive to fear is the expectation of misfortune. "It is clear that no one fears things they do not think they will experience" (*Rhet.* II.5.13). If the audience feels that a particular misfortune only happens to other people, they will not fear it. Therefore, the orator has to make the audience feel that they personally may suffer misfortune.

Aristotle further describes that another way of making an audience think they will suffer is to remind them that others greater than they have suffered.[143] When someone they respect suffers, the audience may feel that a similar threat applies to them.

However, the orator cannot allow them to despair but be offer some possibility to avoid the object of their fear. It is "a necessary incentive to fear that there should remain some hope of being saved from the cause of their distress. A sign of this is that fear makes people deliberate, whereas no one deliberates about things that are hopeless" (*Rhet.* II.5.15). Fear motivates deliberation about future action.

b) Confidence (θάρσος)

Although someone may be motivated to action by fear in the short term, confidence (θάρσος) provides better long term motivation. Aristotle writes that confidence is "the hope (ἡ ἐλπὶς) of things that lead to deliverance with sense perceptions that they are near at hand, while the things to feared are either non-existent or far off" (*Rhet.* II.5.16). Whereas the orator who evokes fear makes the threat imminent or large, confidence is evoked by making a threat seem distant or small. Audiences feel confidence before people who are a means of help (βοήθειαι), powerful friends who have done us good, when we have not committed wrong or have done good, or before those who share interests with us (II.5.17).

c) Emulation (ζηλός)

Emulation (ζηλός) is the desire to imitate someone who has highly valued goods or virtues. Aristotle's defines emulation as "pain at the apparent presence of honored good things, which also are possible for us to obtain, in the possession of those who are similar to us in nature. It is a pain not due to the fact that another possesses them, but because we do not" (*Rhet.* II.11.1). Emulation is aroused when people are presented who resemble the

---

[143] *Rhet.* II.5.15. Compare Cicero's brief description: "Fear (*timor*) again is struck from either the perils of individuals or those shared by all; that of private origin goes deeper but universal fear also is to be traced to a similar source" (*De oratore* II.51.209).

audience, and who have goods that the audience desires. Characters in narratives can be presented as models for imitation.[144] For example, Dio of Prusa used Nestor from Homer's *Iliad* as a model of an orator speaking in digression to powerful people (discussed further in chapter 4).

6. Conclusions

I have argued in this chapter that παρέκβασις is the most appropriate Greek term for deviations in the order of a speech, whether major sections of a speech or shorter figures of thought. Hermagoras, Cicero, and Quintilian are the primary witness of a rhetorical tradition that handled such units under the heading of the Greek term παρέκβασις or *digressio* in Latin. Another tradition represented by Anon. Seg. rejected this term as too paradoxical and unrestricted and embraced παραδιήγησις (incidental narration) that limited the location and content but nonetheless retained the same functions that the others attributed to παρέκβασις. In other words, rhetoricians reacted to the use of digressions by trying to name and control them. Despite this attempt to restrict and rename the phenomena, παρέκβασις was the term that persisted and the term that captured the paradox of an unessential unit that was essential.

Since digressions were used so widely that rhetoricians felt compelled to describe and evaluate the practice, many audiences must have been experiencing digressions. They did not need to be aware of the terms or rhetorical discussions in order to experience them. In terms of relevance theory, digressions were a part of audience's cognitive environment that they could relate to new communication situations.

Modern interpreters appropriately use the term 'digression' when trying to understand how an ancient audience would experience a deviation in structure. This term causes modern interpreters some discomfort because it suggests that a passage is not essential to understand the text,[145] but this discomfort replicates the audience's experience of a digression: the need to expend effort to understand its relationship to the whole. Many scholars have suspected that these passages are interpolations or incorporations

---

[144] Compare Quintilian *Inst.* IX.2.58: "The imitation of other persons' characteristics, which is styled ἠθοποιΐα or, as some prefer μίμησις, may be counted among the devices which serve to excite the gentler emotions."

[145] E.g., see J. M. G. Barclay's rationalizations for why Josephus calls *Apion* 1.47–56 a παρέκβασις (*Flavius Josephus: Against Apion*, [Leiden: Brill, 200], 40 n. 288; discussed further in chapter 4), or Race, "*Panatheniacus*," critiquing scholars who judge Isocrates as an old man losing control of his material.

from other traditions.[146] This suspicion is reminiscent of scholarly opinions about deviations in Revelation.

Most simply, a digression is a unit of text that does not contribute to or goes beyond the needs of the argument of the surrounding material. The text can be delimited in an A-B-A' structure. The logical progression of the surrounding text (A, A') is intact if the unit (B) is removed. This is not to say, however, that the meaning or impact of the whole text is the same. Digressions contribute to the overall meaning and reception of the text.[147] This does not mean that it lacks transitions that link to the surrounding material, but that the unit apart from transitions is unnecessary to the flow of the argument. In some cases, the return to the main subject is also a transition to the next topic.

The primary motivation for using a digression is to move the emotions of the audience to be favorably disposed to the orator and the thesis of the speech. Aristotle systematically details how an audience's opinion is related to its emotional state. Rather than furthering the logic of the argument, digressions attempt to evoke emotions like fear (φόβος), confidence (θάρσος), and emulation (ζηλός) in order that the audience may be receptive to the orator's goals.

Rhetoricians recommend that the location of a digression be chosen for maximum emotional effect. Cicero, and Quintilian stressed that the emotional power of digressions could be most effectively harnessed wherever the topics were emotional. This insistence on the orator's freedom to place a digression anywhere also helps explain why a digression before the last element in a series or speech may be advisable. A digression was routinely placed before the end of a speech to whip up the emotions of the audience to receive the conclusion most favorably. In this way, the emotional qualities of the whole speech are sustained and harnessed by the digression.

Since the content of a digression is 'off topic,' rhetoricians recommended that its content be used to obliquely introduce topics, to develop the author's ethos, and to directly address the audience and the contemporary situation. As Cicero and Quintilian suggested, digressions can be used to soften a difficult case and to persuade the audience to accept a difficult conclusion. In Quintilian's words, "it is hard to persuade a man to do anything against the grain" (IV.3.10 [Butler, LCL]). The orator is freed by a

[146] E.g. Gaisser's survey on Homer's digressions ("Digressions in the *Iliad* and *Odyssey*," 3). These units still may be redactional insertions, but when read aloud to an audience they would have been experienced as digressions.

[147] This is not to say that they all contribute equally, or that all digressions were relevant or well done. Certainly some authors must have digressed poorly and pointlessly to receive the rebuke of the herald and rhetoricians, but these sloppy examples may have been excised by time.

digression to choose material that will most favorably dispose the audience to the orator and the orator's goals.

As a result, digressions provide unique insight into the rhetorical situation because they illuminate the orator's concealed goals, evoke emotion, and often involve the orator directly addressing the audience. By heightening the emotions related to certain facts or a certain argument, a digression points to those facts or argument as the most significant for the audience. By directly addressing the audience in a digression, the orator develops a relationship, "with a view to exciting or mollifying the judge or disposing him to lend a favouring ear to our proofs" (*Inst.* IV.3.9). In this way, the digression offers interpreters a window into the orator's assumptions about the audience and his relationship with the audience.

Digressions are further significant to the audience because of they break with the order of the speech. On one hand, digressions are controlled by the order of the surrounding material while, on the other hand, they simultaneously are contesting that order. Sabry and Härter emphasize that the surrounding material harnesses the digression, controlling it, but in unresolved tension. The other aspect is that the digression wrests control from the order of the narrative. By interrupting the order of the narrative, the digression asserts supremacy over the rigid order of the speech. The audience's attention may be drawn to this contest between order and deviation. As a result, digressions may have more significant impact than the rest of the speech and become more memorable to the audience.

Chapter 4

Digressions in Practice

Margaret Mitchell exhorts those who study historic rhetoric to immerse themselves in actual speeches and literature in order to move beyond the narrowly descriptive and proscriptive rhetorical handbooks. In this chapter, I follow this advice to further refine our understanding of digressions. Examination of digressions in practice demonstrates that they were used across genres, languages, and locations. Digressions were utilized by Greek-speaking Jews and were generally accessible to first century audiences in Asia Minor. Josephus is a critical example of a Jewish author who uses digressions both with and without the technical term παρέκβασις. *Aristeas ad Philocrates* and 2 Maccabees provide further examples of their use by Greek speaking Jews. Audiences in Asia Minor were likely to be familiar with digressions through orators such as Dio 'Chrysostom' of Prusa and the enduring and influential Homeric epics. The Epistle to the Hebrews demonstrates that digressions were a part of the cognitive environment of this Christian author and his audience.

The last half of this chapter seeks to explore Jewish Apocalyptic and Hebrew literature that may be specifically relevant to John and his audiences. Digressions occur in *Jubilees* 23, *Sibylline Oracles* I/II, Exodus 12, and Zechariah 2, which are especially relevant to the book of Revelation. The passages in *Jub.* 23, *Sib. Or.* I/II, Exod 12 and Zech 2 focus on the ethos of the speaker and audience, address the contemporary situation, and evoke emotion. For these reasons, these digressions would likely have a greater impact on the audiences than the surrounding material.

Before analyzing these specific texts, I suggest some terms to describe how digressions are used in practice. Some works contain multiple digressions that repeat signals and themes while others use digressions in an isolated fashion. In the following section, I suggest that we distinguish between 'simple' digressions that do not relate to other digressions and 'systematic' digressions that are interwoven throughout a work. In addition, some digressions are clearly identified while others are not. Following Longenecker's terminology for chain-link transitions, I distinguish between 'articulated' and 'unarticulated' digressions.

1. Distinguishing Simple and Systematic Digressions

Authors sometimes used more than one digression in a work. Cicero uses three digressions in *Brutus* in order to obliquely comment on the contemporary Atticist controversy that sought to repristinate 'pure' oratory. George Kennedy writes, "[t]he chronological sequence of *Brutus* is varied by carefully placed digressions that relate to the Atticism controversy." [1] The first (§§70–76) interrupts the account of Roman oratory after the discussion of Cato the Elder to compare the history of oratory to sculpture, painting, and poetry. The second digression (§§183–200) is in the middle of the speech and deals with how to judge oratory. Rather than judge oratory by aesthetic standards (which diminishes Cato), Cicero argues that orators should be judged by their effectiveness. This topic relates directly to the subtle juxtaposition of Cato with developments in art and poetry. The theme of the digressions becomes clear when Atticus mocks the idea that Cato is a Roman Lysias in the last digression (§§292–300). Kennedy says it is "closely connected and balanced" with the first digression and concludes,

> The objective of the [first] digression is to suggest that Cato should be viewed as a Roman counterpart to Lysias, though Atticists ignore him. Balancing this is a third digression (292–300) in which Atticus is allowed to ridicule Cicero's glorification of early Roman orators, including the assertion that Cato was a Roman Lysias. Cicero sticks to his guns, but the digression adds liveliness to the dialogue and shows that he did not mean his claim to be taken too literally. *Brutus* is one of Cicero's more carefully written works; he seems to have sought a prose style that would be approved by his opponents.[2]

Three points are salient: first, Cicero used multiple digressions, i.e. multiple passages of the speech with an A-B-A' structure in which the B section could be omitted without loss of the logical flow of the narrative. Second, these digressions did not stand alone but were balanced and related to one another. Third, these digressions were designed to present a thesis to opponents in a way they might approve it. In short, Cicero's digressions in *Brutus* are carefully placed to work together to make a difficult thesis more palatable. Cicero suggested in theory that digressions can be interwoven in a text and *Brutus* puts that advice into practice.[3]

A term such as 'systematic,' rather than 'interwoven,' better expresses how multiple digressions in a single text work together as a system to develop vocabulary, topics, and ideas from one digression to another. For example, the digressions in *Brutus* develop the contrast between aesthetic

---

[1] G. A. Kennedy, *A New History of Classical Rhetoric* (Princeton: Princeton University, 1994), 155.

[2] Kennedy, *New History*, 155.

[3] *De Inventione* I.51.97. See discussion in chapter 3.c.

quality and rhetorical effectiveness in order to subtly promote Cicero's high view of Cato in the face of opposition. 'Systematic' captures the sense that Cicero's multiple and connected digressions are a part of a methodical and coherent strategy. The digressions are not simply isolated incidents, but work together as a system towards the author's rhetorical goals. For this reason, I will use 'systematic' to describe this kind of digressions in contrast to 'simple' digressions that have no relationship with other digressions.[4]

Systematic digressions share common delimiting signals and themes. For example, the three digressions in Cicero's *Brutus* reflect common topics, *dramatis personae*, spatial signals, temporal signals, and thematic vocabulary. Each digression in *Brutus* compares oratory to other arts: the first digression to sculpture, painting, poets and playwrights (§§70–73), the second to music (§§187,192), and the third compares Cato directly to painters (§298). Each deals with the topic of judging art. In the first and third digression, Cato is a *dramatis persona*. In each, temporal signals shift from the historical recital of Greek and Roman oratory to a synchronic discussion of artists, theoretical discussion of judging oratory, and explicit comparison of Cato and Lysias.[5] In contrast to surrounding material, spatial signals are quickly blurred and ambiguous by rapid listing of artists without locations or theoretical discussions.

By interweaving digressions throughout the speech, Cicero is able to address his Atticizing opponents obliquely and progressively while ostensibly giving a history lesson on Roman oratory. Systematic digressions are a powerful technique for achieving goals that are not the explicit purpose of the speech. They allow the orator, under the guise of talking "off topic," to gradually introduce and develop themes and ideas, even a second line of argument, that the audience may resist if openly announced.[6]

2. Articulated and Unarticulated Digressions

Some authors and orators explicitly acknowledge that they digress. Others do not, transitioning in and out of digressions like a fish jumping in and out of the water. Longenecker's use of the terms 'articulated' and 'unarticulated' to describe the chain-link technique is helpful to distinguish be-

[4] Cf. Kennedy, *New History*, 67. Other examples of speeches with systematic digressions include Lysias, *Against Eratosthenes* and *Against Agoratus*. See Appendix.

[5] Kennedy, *New History*, 155.

[6] This feature has led some to think digressions are a kind of σχιζόμενος or 'covert allusion.' For criticisms of this interpretation, see W. Race, "Some Digressions and Returns in Greek Authors," *The Classical Journal* 76.1 (Oct–Nov 1980): 1–8.

tween these two kinds of digressions.[7] An 'articulated' digression is one that identifies a unit explicitly as a digression (usually at the end). The identification confirms what the audience has felt about the unit – that the author has strayed beyond what was expected. Josephus articulates a digression using the technical term παρέκβασις twice (discussed below in detail).[8] In other places, he indicates the digression without a term, noting that he is departing from his main topic.[9] When preparing to digress on the three "philosophies" of the Jews in the *Antiquitates Judaicae*, Josephus uses the phrase "concerning these things I plan to discourse a little" (περὶ ἧς ὀλίγα βούλομαι διελθεῖν, *AJ* 18.10).[10]

Other authors use a variety of terms to acknowledge a digression. These other terms are often compounds of the prepositions *παρα- and *ἐκ- with some noun or verbal form denoting movement or a path (such as –βάσις, –βαίνω, –ὁδός, –τροπή, –τρέπω, –δρομή, etc).[11] These terms, although not the technical term παρέκβασις, give the impression that the speech is a path and the orator the audience's guide. When the orator noticeably goes off the path, articulation confirms the audience's suspicion and helps the orator and audience to continue together through the speech. At the same time, the articulation confirms the author's control of the material. In some cases, the orator apologizes or explains the purpose of the digression and its relationship to the rest of the speech.[12] These explanations and apologies draw more attention to the deviation and further heighten their memorability and importance for understanding the whole speech.[13]

An unarticulated digression, on the other hand, makes no explicit note that the orator has deviated from the expected path. Instead, the orator returns to the previous topic and the audience is left to discern the relationship between the digression and surrounding material. This is a more risky procedure, requiring the audience to expend more effort to make the connections and increasing the possibility of multiple experiences of the di-

---

[7] B. W. Longenecker, *Rhetoric at the Boundaries: The Art and Theology of the New Testament Chain-Link Transitions* (Waco, Texas: Baylor University, 2005), 45–46.

[8] παρέκβασις: *CA* 1.57; *V* 367; cf. *CA* 2.254 (not in Latin mss, so not counted).

[9] For examples of unarticulated digressions see *AJ* 13.171–73; *BJ* 1.9; 3.70–100; 7:259; *V* 36–42. See Appendix.

[10] Josephus uses a similar phrase to introduce the digression in *Vita* §336: μικρὰ διέλθειν. Cf. S. Mason, ed. and trans., *Flavius Josephus: Translation and Commentary, Volume 9: Life of Josephus* (Leiden: Brill, 2001), 135–136 n. 1368.

[11] For example, διέξοδος, παρεξόδος, ἐκβάσις, ἐκδρομή, ἐκτροπή.

[12] E.g. Josephus in *CA* 1.57 discussed below, or Dio of Prusa *Or.* 7.

[13] See how Aristides' explanation of the digression in *Defense of Oratory* (*Or.* 2.66–74) draws more attention to his enthusiasm for divine healing, his emotion, and his character in relationship with the divine. Cf. Race, "Some Digressions," 4.

gression and multiple ways to construe its relationship to the surrounding material.[14] The benefit of this ambiguity, however, may be a pleasant distraction, a minimal awareness of the author's role, or a more subtle revelation of the author's rhetorical goals. Josephus' first digression in *Vita* (discussed below) is unarticulated but the second is articulated. In *Contra Apionem*, the reverse is true: the first is articulated and the second is not.

3. A Greek-speaking Jew in 1st c. Rome: Josephus' *Vita* and *Contra Apionem*

Scholars such as Shaye D. J. Cohen, Tessa Rajak, Steven Mason, and John M. G. Barclay have noted that Josephus, the Jewish historian (c. 37–100 CE), used digressions.[15] Although they are "off-topic" and unessential to the logic of the argument, scholars agree that these digressions are essential to his rhetorical goals. Cohen argues that in Josephus' autobiography the *Vita* "[t]he most important passage is *V* 336–367, the long digression (παρέκβασις, 367) against Justus."[16] On this passage, Steve Mason notes, "[t]his digression forms something of a symmetrical counterpart to §§34–42, where Iustus and his rival account are introduced in the *Life*."[17] Rajak studies the digressions in *Vita*, *Contra Apionem* and Josephus' other works, including *Bellum Judaicum* 3.70–109. On the passage in *BJ*, she concludes that "Josephus' long digression on the efficiency of the Roman army" emphasizes the futility of the Jewish revolt.[18] In *Contra Apionem* 1.57, Josephus explicitly calls the preceding section a digression (παρέκβασις). Barclay concludes, "The 'digression' is both admitted and justified, indicating Josephus' control of his discourse."[19] In each of these

[14] See Härter and Sabry on the dangers of digressions.

[15] S. J. D. Cohen, *Josephus in Galilee and Rome: His Vita and Development as a Historian* (Leiden: Brill, 1979), 114; T. Rajak, *Josephus* (2nd ed.; London: Duckworth, 2002), 79, 81, 152–154. Cf. D. E. Aune, s.v. "Digression," *The Westminster Dictionary of New Testament and Early Christian Literature and Rhetoric* (Louisville, Kentucky: Westminster/John Knox, 2003), 189.

[16] Cohen, 114; also Rajak, 152–154.

[17] Mason, 135 n. 1367.

[18] Rajak, 180; cf. 160.

[19] J. M. G. Barclay, ed. and trans., *Flavius Josephus: Translation and Commentary, Volume 10: Against Apion* (Leiden: Brill, 2007), 41 n. 228. Cf. C. Gerber, *Ein Bild des Judentums für Nichtjuden von Flavius Josephus: Untersuchungen zu seiner Schrift* Contra Apionem (Leiden: Brill, 1997), 68; D. Labow, *Flavius Josephus: Contra Apionem Buch I: Einleitung, Text, Textkritischer Apparat, Übersetzung und Kommentar von Dagmar Labow* (Stuttgart: W. Kohlhammer, 2005), 41 n. 116.

cases, scholars emphasize that Josephus is in control of his material. Although the term 'digression' suggests disorder, Josephus harnesses them to further his rhetorical goals.

It is not clear how or where Josephus might have learned παρέκβασις as a term or technique. Rajak argues that he learned Greek in Palestine but received assistance in Rome when he translated the *Bellum Judaicum* from Aramaic into Greek.[20] Although no Aramaic version is extant, Rajak suggests that he did not use digressions in the Aramaic *Bellum Judaicum* because it is not a common structure in Hebrew or Aramaic.[21] Josephus most likely learned digression as a rhetorical technique in Rome,[22] but given the widespread use and discussion of digressions we cannot rule out that he first experienced them in Palestine. No matter where he learned to digress, it is notable that he uses the Greek technical vocabulary for digression (παρέκβασις). Josephus digresses in all four of his extant works, articulated and unarticulated, both simple and systematic.[23] I will focus only on the two digressions in the *Vita* and the two in *Contra Apionem*.

a) Vita *36–42: Josephus Introduces his Opponent Iustus*

Josephus appends the *Vita* at the end of the *Antiquitates Judaicae*. We cannot be certain it was read by the Jews of Asia Minor, although it seems that was his intent for the *Antiquitates* and so also for this appendix.[24] In the *Vita,* he defends his role in the Jewish War and portrays himself as an honorable participant, eyewitness of events, and living example of a Jewish way of life. Rajak argues that in the context of the 90's CE, "Josephus'

---

[20] Rajak, 177–8.

[21] Rajak, 180.

[22] Some examples of digressions in Hebrew are in Exod 12 and Zech 2, discussed below in sections 8.c and 8.d. Arguing that Josephus received some Roman rhetorical education: R. G. Hall, "Josephus, *Contra Apionem* and Historical Inquiry in the Roman Rhetorical Schools," in *Josephus'* Contra Apionem (eds. Louis H. Feldman and John R. Levison; Leiden: Brill, 1996), 229–249; D. M. Hay, "What is Proof? – Rhetorical Verification in Philo, Josephus and Quintilian," in *Society of Biblical Literature 1979 Seminar Papers* (ed. P. J. Achtemeier; vol II; Missoula, Montana: SBL, 1979), 87–100.

[23] E.g. *BJ* 1.9; 2.10.2; 7.259; *AJ* 13.171–73; 18.1.2–6; *CA* 1.46–56; 2.145–286; *V* 36–42; 336–67.

[24] *BJ* 1.6. Rajak 176. S. Mason ("The *Contra Apionem* in Social and Literary Context: An Invitation to Judean Philosophy," in Feldman and Levison, eds., *Josephus'* Contra Apionem, 187–228) argues that *Contra Apionem* is protreptic, but this does not explain the structure and content of the whole speech. For a detailed discussions of the genre of *Contra Apion*, see Gerber, 34–42, and Barclay, *Against Apion*, XXX–XXXVI, who conclude it is an apology, but not a direct apology to a specific accuser. Cf. D. Balch, "Two Apologetic Encomia: Dionysius on Rome and Josephus on the Jews," *JSJ* 13 (1982): 102–122. For a discussion on a non-Jewish and Jewish audience, see Barclay, *Against Apion*, XLV–LI.

failure to master the Galilee, and his rejections as an official commander by Jerusalem were the major issues."[25] Cohen emphasizes that the *Vita* is a continuation of the themes of the *Antiquitates* (the reluctance of the Jewish people to fight Rome, the circumstances and incidents which compelled them, and Josephus' role). What is new in the *Vita* is an emphasis on Josephus' character. "He was a religious Jew who followed Pharisaic rules and maintained piety throughout his life."[26] Mason emphasizes this last point arguing that Josephus' primary goal is to "offer his life as the final exhibit in his presentation of the Judean constitutions."[27] Since character is at issue, ethical digressions against his emblematic rival Iustus[28] seem natural.

Steve Mason finds two digressions in the *Vita*, first near the beginning (§§36–42) in Josephus' survey of the situation in pre-war Galilee and then near the end (§§336–67) before reciting his successes. The first digression is unarticulated, what Mason calls "informal and unannounced." The second is articulated using the technical term παρέκβασις. Mason writes,

> Josephus devotes two digressions to his literary adversary Iustus of Tiberias: near the beginning (§§ 36–42) and near the end (§§ 336–67) of the book. The first digression is informal and unannounced, but may count as a digression because it is noticeably disproportionate in his crisp summary of factions at Tiberias. The latter is a formal, announced digression.

The first digression is unarticulated, but evident by the disproportionate length of Josephus's description of Iustus. Ostensibly, Josephus is summarizing the leadership of three factions he found when he arrived in Galilee (§§32–42). The first two factions he summarizes in 97 words in the Greek text, but he spends 279 words describing Iustus' words and deeds.[29] The sheer length and detail of Josephus' description of Iustus is beyond the sparse summary of the factions.

In order to provide a full example of an unarticulated digression, I quote *Vita* 34–42 in its entirety below, including sections before and after the digression (§§36–42).

> (§34) at that time all of those mentioned counseled [the people] to stand firm in loyalty to the Romans and to the king.
>
> But Pistus did not concur with this opinion, being influenced by his son Iustus; besides, he was by nature somewhat crazed. (35) So the second faction, comprising the most insignificant, was determined to make war.

---

[25] Rajak, 154, cf.150.

[26] Cohen, 170.

[27] Mason, *Life*, XLVIII.

[28] I follow Mason's transliteration of Ἰοῦστος except in citation of other scholars.

[29] Greek text of *Vita* from Josephus, *Aus meinem Leben (Vita)* (eds. and trans. F. Siegert, H. Schreckenberg, M. Vogel; Tübingen: Mohr Siebeck, 2001), 36–39.

(36) Iustus, son of Pistus, the chief of the third faction, on one hand pretended to waver on the war, but on the other hand he desired newer government from the transition, thinking to manufacture power for himself. (37) So he came along into the [city] center and tried to teach the mob that the city had always been the capital of Galilee since the times of Herod the Tetrarch, who was its builder, and who had wanted the city of the Sepphorites to submit to that of the Tiberians. They had not relinquished this primacy under King Agrippa the father, but it remained until Felix was put in charge of Judea. (38) Now, he was saying:

"You yourselves just happen to have been given to the younger Agrippa as a gift from Nero! And because it submitted to Rome, Sepphoris immediately became the capital of Galilee, and both the royal bank and archives, having been dismantled, are with them."

(39) These and many other things against King Agrippa he said to them, for the sake of provoking the populace to defection. He added:

"Now is the time to take up weapons after welcoming the Galileans as allies – for they are willing to begin, because of the hatred they have towards the Sepphorites for maintaining loyalty to the Romans – and with a large force to execute vengeance because of them."

(40) By saying these things, he won over the mob. For he was rather good at manipulating the populace and at overcoming the better arguments of disputants by craftiness and a kind of guile through words. In fact, he was well trained in the Greek sort of education, on the basis of which he audaciously took it upon himself to record also the history of these events – as if he could overcome the truth itself by means of this speech-craft. (41) But concerning this man – how sordid his life became and how he was, with is brother, the cause of almost complete ruin – we shall explain as the story unfolds. (42) At that time, when he had persuaded the citizens to take up weapons and compelled many who did not so desire, Iustus came out with all of these men and set fire to the villages of the Gadarenes and also of the Hippenes, which happened to lie on the frontier between Tiberias and the territory of the Scythopolitans.

(43) So Tiberias was in such a state. At Gischala, matters took this turn. Ioannes son of Levis ...[30]

Josephus does not acknowledge that he is going beyond the needs of his summary of the Galilean situation. He begins the discussion of Iustus simply enough as the leader of the third faction:

Iustus, son of Pistus, the chief of the third faction, on one hand pretended to waver on the war, but on the other hand he desired newer government from the transition, thinking to manufacture power for himself (§36).[31]

He concludes with an abrupt summary that does not acknowledge the lengthy treatment of Iustus: "So Tiberius was in such a state" (§43).[32] By using an unarticulated digression, Josephus does not draw additional atten-

---

[30] Translation modified from Mason, *Life*, 41–47. Other translations are my own unless noted.

[31] Ἰοῦστος δ᾽ ὁ Πιστοῦ παῖς ὁ τῆς τρίτης μερίδος πρῶτος ὑπεκρίνετο μὲν ἐνδοιάζειν πρὸς τὸν πόλεμον νεωτέρων δ᾽ ἐπεθύμει πραγμάτων ἐκ τῆς μεταβολῆς οἰόμενος δύναμιν ἑαυτῷ περιποιήσειν.

[32] Καὶ Τιβεριὰς μὲν ἐν τοιούτοις ἦν.

tion to the length, but leaves it to the audience to determine the relevance of the digression to the whole.[33]

Although unarticulated, Josephus signals this digression in various ways. The communication axis shifts to include direct speech by Iustus (§§38, 39). He includes personal references to Herod Antipas and King Agrippa (§§37, 39) who have not appeared before in the *Vita*. Other leaders of factions were personal references (§§32–34), but Iustus is the principal *dramatis persona* in §§36–42. Sepphoris and the city center of Tiberias are specific spatial signals that distinguish this unit (§§37–39). Josephus also gives specific temporal signals to the time period of the rule of Agrippa I to Felix (§37). Finally, Josephus uses thematic vocabulary that is reprised at the end of the book, for example "desiring newer government" (νεωτέρων δ' ἐπεθύμει πραγμάτων).[34] These shifts signal to the audience that Josephus has digressed.

The function of this digression is ethical and emotional. It is ethical as Josephus attacks Iustus' character as a rival historiographer.[35] Josephus tries to depict him as "manufacturing power for himself" to take control of Galilee (§36).[36] Iustus is a demagogue (§40) and scoundrel (§41), inciting the Tiberians to revolt against Agrippa and attack neighboring cities (§42). It is emotional because he describes in terms designed to evoke anger (ὀργὴ):[37] Iustus writes histories "as if he could overcome the truth by means of this speech-craft. But concerning this man – how foul his life became and how he was with his brother the cause of almost complete ruin – we shall explain" (§§40–41).[38] Iustus opposes truth (περιεσόμενος τῆς ἀληθείας), and his life is foul (φαῦλος). Josephus excites the audience's anger against Iustus as the cause of almost complete ruin (μικροῦ δεῖν καταστροφῆς αἴτιος).

[33] Thus some commentators (E. Schürer, B. Niese, R. Laqueur, H. Thackeray) have argued that the *Vita* is written primarily against Iustus, while others (Cohen, Mason, and Rajak) argue that Iustus is only an incidental target. See the review of scholarship in Mason, *Life*, XXVII–XXIV.

[34] Mason, *Life,* 42 n. 217–219, notes the many parallels between this passage and the end of the book, especially the second digression. He translates νεωτέρων πραγμάτων as "revolutionary activities."

[35] Mason, *Life*, XXVII and XLIX, argues that Iustus receives too much attention by commentators because of these digressions. Iustus, similar to Ioannes of Gischala, "fits the general pattern: a power-hungry, self-serving demagogue (*Vita* 40, 391–3)."

[36] Cohen, 128; Mason, *Life*, 42 n. 218.

[37] Aristotle, *Rhetoric*, II.2.1378a.1–1380a.27.

[38] τὴν ἱστορίαν τῶν πραγμάτων τούτων ἀναγράφειν ὡς τῷ λόγῳ τούτῳ περιεσόμενος τῆς ἀληθείας ἀλλὰ περὶ μὲν τούτου τοῦ ἀνδρός ὡς φαῦλος τὸν βίον ἐγένετο καὶ ὡς σύν τῷ ἀδελφῷ μικροῦ δεῖν καταστροφῆς αἴτιος ὑπῆρχεν προϊόντος τοῦ λόγου δηλώσομεν.

In summary, Josephus uses this digression to introduce and attack a rival historiographer. Similar to Josephus, Iustus had written a history of the Jewish War. When Josephus describes the factions that he found in Galilee, it is a natural occasion to deviate in order to portray his rival Iustus negatively and to rouse his audience to anger. It is an unarticulated digression; perhaps Josephus does not want to draw more attention than necessary to the fact that he has interrupted his stated purpose to describe the situation in Galilee. He keeps the authorial hand hidden until his audience is ready to accept his full-fledged attack on Iustus, which he saves for a second digression near the end of the *Vita*.

b) Vita *336–67: Iustus of Tiberius, Lying Historian*

The central episode in the *Vita* describes how Josephus handles the delegation sent from Jerusalem to replace him (§§189–335). Next, Josephus narrates his opponents' humiliation and his successes (§§336–413). He begins this unit, however, with a lengthy 1175 word digression. Rajak, following Cohen, calls this "the Great Digression."[39]

He begins by announcing that he will not discuss the events following the delegation but instead liars who write history, Iustus being chief among them.

> Having come to this part of my narration, I want to go through a few things against Iustus, who has himself written a history concerning these matters; and against others who profess to write histories, but have little regard to truth, and are not ashamed to tell lies either out of hostility or favor (§336).[40]

He ends the digression by articulating it using the technical term παρέκβασις.

> But let the matters with reference to Iustus that make the digression (παρέκβασιν) necessary (ἀναγκαίαν) be said by us with these words (§367).[41]

Consistent with the definitions used by Hermagoras, Cicero, and Quintilian, this digression does not further the argument. It does not describe nor

---

[39] Rajak, 152–3; Cohen, 114–120.

[40] Γεγονὼς δ' ἐνταῦθα τῆς διηγήσεως βούλομαι πρός Ἰοῦστον καὶ αὐτὸν τὴν περὶ τούτων πραγματείαν γεγραφότα πρός τε τοὺς ἄλλους τοὺς ἱστορίαν μὲν γράφειν ὑπισχνουμένους περὶ δὲ τὴν ἀλήθειαν ὀλιγώρους καὶ δι' ἔχθραν ἢ χάριν τὸ ψεῦδος οὐκ ἐντρεπομένους [μικρὰ διελθεῖν].

[41] ἀλλὰ τὰ μὲν πρὸς Ἰοῦστον ἀναγκαίαν λαβόντα τὴν παρέκβασιν μέχρι τούτων ἡμῖν λελέχθω. Mason, *Life*, 150, seems to take ἀναγκαίαν as an adverbial accusative, and τὴν παρέκβασιν in apposition to τὰ λαβόντα: "But let the matters that had necessarily to be raised against Iustus – this digression – be said by us with these words." I am taking τὴν παρέκβασιν as the object of the participle and ἀναγκαίαν as a predicate adjective to τὴν παρέκβασιν.

defend his actions during the Jewish War. Instead, it attacks his rival Iustus as a historiographer, a rival witness and chronicler of those times. A digression by definition is unnecessary, yet paradoxically Josephus says that it was necessary (ἀναγκαίαν). This paradox – unessential to the argument but essential to the effect – is also consistent with how rhetoricians described digressions.

As with the first digression in the *Vita* (§§36–42), this is an ethical digression. Josephus attacks Iustus character and portrays himself as virtuous. It is striking that in this passage, Josephus uses the rhetorical device of speaking directly to Iustus. He changes communication axis to address Iustus directly as "you," making accusations as if in court. For example, he mocks Iustus and announces the use of this technique:

> How then, (I speak in this way in order that I may speak to him as if present) Iustus, most awesome among composers – for this is what you boast about yourself … (§340)[42]

Next, he accuses Iustus as if in front of a jury of those who will peruse the historical accounts (τοῖς ἐντυγχάνειν μέλλουσιν ταῖς ἱστορίαις, §345; cf. §367). He directly addresses the audience in the second person plural in the digression, e.g., "Do you (plural) not remember how so often, I, being self-controlled, destroyed no one…?" (§353).

In this digression, Josephus develops his ethos, his trustworthiness in the eyes of his audience. On one hand, Josephus attacks Iustus; on the other, scholars have noted that Josephus is more interested in his relationship with the audience than in Iustus. Cohen argues that Josephus had to defend his pedigree and piety against not only Iustus but attacks from fellow Jews.[43] Likewise, Rajak suggests that Josephus' issue is less Iustus and more his audience's questions about Josephus' management of the situation in Tiberias that reflected negatively on his character.[44] Mason proposes that Iustus must be dealt with as a detractor to Josephus' self-depiction as "the final exhibit in his presentation of the Judean constitution" begun in the *Antiquitates*.[45] To this end, Josephus uses the digression to establish himself as the truthful historiographer and virtuous Jew in contrast to Iustus. The digression gives a unique view into this rhetorical situation.

Mason argues that *V* 336–367 is a counterpart to §§36–42, which suggests that they are what I am calling systematic digressions. The location of each digression is significant. Josephus introduces Iustus in the first di-

---

[42] πῶς οὖν ἵνα φῶ πρὸς αὐτὸν ὡς παρόντα Ἰοῦστε δεινότατε συγγραφέων τοῦτο γὰρ αὐχεῖς περὶ σεαυτοῦ…

[43] Cohen, 144; cf. 136–137.

[44] Rajak, 154.

[45] Mason, *Life*, XLVIII.

gression as a rival leader of the Jews in Galilee and as a rival historiographer. By presenting Iustus at length in the beginning as a warmonger, demagogue, and deceitful historiographer, Josephus builds himself up in contrast. The second digression follows Josephus' triumphant description of expelling the Jerusalem delegation that was sent to remove him. He demonstrates that he was in control of the situation. From that confidence, he launches into a sustained digression to attack Iustus. Iustus becomes a foil for him to promote himself as the superior historiographer and example of Jewish virtue. In this second, articulated digression, Josephus recalls the seeds of the comparison that he planted in the first digression, now allowing them to grow fully into a *synkrisis* that leaves Josephus the superior.

In summary, Josephus uses two digressions in his *Vita*. The first is unarticulated and the second articulated. He explicitly states the paradox of digression: it is unessential to the logic of the argument being made, but necessary for the effect. Josephus uses these digressions as a system to develop his ethos in the eyes of the audience in comparison to a rival historiographer and general, Iustus. By directly addressing Josephus' contemporary situation and opponent, the digressions provide unique insight into the rhetorical situation motivating the *Vita*.

c) Contra Apionem *1.47–56: Josephus, Eyewitness*

In his last work, which we know as *Contra Apionem*, Josephus writes explicitly to defend Judaism against slander by those of the likes of Apion.[46] This work was often known as "On the Antiquity of the Judeans" (περὶ τῆς τῶν Ἰουδαίων ἀρχαιότητος), a title that captures Josephus' defense against the charge that Judaism is a new religion.[47] Although he was writing in Rome, he was oriented to the east, demonstrating the antiquity of Judaism in relationship to eastern cultures, such as those of the Babylonian, Phoenician and Egyptians, which were venerated by the Greco-Roman world.[48] Given his emotion about the slander it is not surprising that *Contra Apionem* is digressive.

---

[46] *CA* 1.2: "Now, since I see many giving heed to the slanders having been spoken by some with ill-will and not believing the things written by me concerning the ancient history..." (ἐπεὶ δὲ συχνοὺς ὁρῶ ταῖς ὑπὸ δυσμενείας ὑπό τινων εἰρημέναις προσέχοντας βλασφημίαις καὶ τοῖς περὶ τὴν ἀρχαιολογίαν ὑπ᾿ ἐμοῦ γε–γραμμένοις ἀπιστοῦντας).

[47] This title was used by Origen, Eusebius, and Jerome. See Barclay, XXVIII–XXX; Labow, LXXIII.

[48] Rajak, 177–8.

Josephus's digressions in *Contra Apionem* are similar in many respects to those in his *Vita*, a fact noted by Cohen, Mason, Barclay, and Labow.[49] In both his *Vita* and *Contra Apionem*, he uses digressions systematically to promote himself as the superior historiographer and virtuous Jew. The digressions in *Contra Apionem* explicitly promote Judaism as the superior way of life, with Josephus being a chief exhibit, of course.

Josephus' first digression in *Contra Apionem* is articulated within a defense of the antiquity of the Jewish scriptures. He elaborates on the age and transmission of the twenty-two books of the canon, and emphasizes that Jews are willing even to die for them (*CA* 1.42–3). This emotional topic leads him to compare Jewish histories with Greek histories. He sarcastically suggests that no one would die for Greek histories, which are not based on eyewitness accounts, and especially no one would die for the recent histories of the Jewish war that were based on hearsay (*CA* 1.44–46). So subtly, Josephus slides from the original topic (the antiquity of the Jewish faith) to an independent topic (the veracity of Josephus' account of the war). If this was all he did, his audience would have thought this a pointed aside at his personal detractors, but he turns the new subject into a full-fledged digression. It is related to the case by the theme of writing histories, but no longer deals with ancient but contemporary history.

To provide a full example of an articulated digression, the following quote is given in its entirety, with a few passages before and after the digression (1.47–56).

(46) In fact, even in relation to the war that happened recently to us, some have published works under the title of histories without either visiting the sites or going anywhere near the action; rather, concocting a few things on the basis of misinformation, they have given it the name of 'history' with the complete shamelessness of a drunk.

(47) Now, I also have made a true record of the whole war and of the things that happened during it in each part, since I myself happened to be present in all matters. (48) For I was in command of those we call 'Galileans' for as long as it was possible to resist, and after being captured lived among the Romans as a prisoner. When they had me under guard, Vespasian and Titus compelled me to be continually in attendance on them, initially bound; then, when I was released, I was sent from Alexandria with Titus to the siege of Jerusalem. (49) During that time none of the action escaped my knowledge; for I watched and carefully recorded what happened in the Roman camp, and I alone understood what was reported by deserters. (50) Then, when I had leisure in Rome, and when all the work was prepared, having made use of some collaborators for the Greek language, I thus constructed my account of the events. So confident was I of its truthfulness that I decided to use as my witnesses, before everyone else, the commanders-in-chief during the war, Vespasian and Titus. (51) For I presented the books to them first of all; after them I sold copies to many Romans who had fought with them in the war, and to many of our own people, men also steeped in Greek wisdom, among whom were Julius

[49] For a helpful table comparing *Vita* 336–367 and *CA* 1.47–56 see Labow, 9. Cf. Cohen, 116–117; Mason, *Life*, 136 n. 1370; Barclay, *Against Apion*, 34 n. 191.

Archelaus, the most distinguished Herod, and the most renowned king Agrippa himself. (52) These all bore witness that I had carefully safeguarded the truth, and they would not have held back or kept silent if, out of ignorance or bias, I had altered or omitted any of the facts.

(53) But certain despicable characters have attempted to libel my history, thinking they have been set an exercise, as are boys at school, of an extraordinary form of accusation and libel. They ought to know that it is incumbent on the person who promises to give others an account of true occurrences that he first himself acquires an accurate knowledge of these, either by having followed events or by gaining information from those who know about them. (54) This I consider I have accomplished very well in both my works: the *Ancient History*, as I said, I translated from the sacred writings, being a priest by ancestry and steeped in the philosophy contained in these writings; (55) and I wrote the history of the war having been personally involved in many events, an eyewitness of most of them, and not in the slightest deficient in my knowledge of anything that was said or done. (56) So how could one consider other than reckless those who have attempted to challenge my truthfulness – who, even if they claim to have read the field-notes of the commanders-in-chief, were certainly not present in the affairs on our side as well, in the opposite camp.

(57) I have been compelled to make the digression (τὴν παρέκβασιν) about these things because I desire to indicate the recklessness of those who announce that they write histories. (58) Now that I have made it sufficiently clear, I think, that the recording of ancient history is a tradition more among 'barbarians' than among Greeks…[50]

The digression begins to become apparent when Josephus turns to the first person, away from the third person defense of Judaism (*CA* 1.47):[51]

Now I also have made a true record of the whole war and of the things that happened during it in each part, since I myself happened to be present in all matters.[52]

---

[50] Translation modified from Barclay, *Against Apion*, 33–41.

[51] Scholars have not agreed about the extent of the digression, and understandably so. It is somewhat difficult since the digression is not articulated until the transition back to the main topic. S. Mason ("*Contra Apionem* in Social and Literary Context," 209) has suggested that 1.6–59 should be considered a programmatic digression that argues that "[o]riental historians are the best, and the Judeans are the best of them." Barclay (p. XVIII, 41 n. 228) identifies 1.53–57 as the digression because it contains explicit polemics, but acknowledges that the topic departs in 1.47. "This justification of Josephus' history of the War, in 1.47–52, at first looks out of place in a text whose advertised concern is Judean antiquity…Why does he now depart into what he recognizes as a 'digression' (1.57)…?" (p. 34 n. 191; cf. XXII). C. Gerber (68) suggests 1.47–57, including the articulation of the digression (1.57). D. Labow and S. D. H. Cohen suggest 1.46–56 for the extent of the digression, excluding the articulation but including 1.46 because it turns towards contemporary historiographers (Cohen, 116; Labow, 36). Applying Pattemore's delimiting criteria confirm the general consensus by Cohen, Labow, and Gerber that 1.47–56 is the extent of the digression, while 1.45–46 and 1.57–59 are transitions.

[52] Ἐγὼ δὲ καὶ περὶ τοῦ πολέμου παντὸς καὶ περὶ τῶν αὐτῷ κατὰ μέρος γενομένων ἀληθῆ τὴν ἀναγραφὴν ἐποιησάμην τοῖς πράγμασιν αὐτὸς ἅπασι παρατυχών. Greek text from Labow, 36. Translation is my own unless noted. I have not yet been able to get access to the most recent critical edition, which is F. Siegert, H.

He then details his own participation in the Jewish War for the next 10 sections in a way that validates his claim as an eyewitness.[53] He marks the transition back to the main subject by using the term παρέκβασις to acknowledge he has digressed and explains its relevance (*CA* 1.57). Therefore this is what I am calling an articulated digression.

I have been compelled to make the digression (τὴν παρέκβασιν) about these things because I desire to indicate the recklessness of those who announce that they write histories...[54]

Following this explanation, he resumes and concludes the preceding topic of the antiquity of the transmission of Jewish histories and announces the next topic (the antiquity of the "constitution," *CA* 1.58). The digression about himself (*CA* 1.47–56) adds nothing to the argument about the antiquity of the transmission τοῦ νομοῦ, and could have been omitted.[55] He picks up in *CA* 1.58 exactly where he left off, offering a second exordium describing the plan that follows.[56] This fits the form that rhetoricians prescribed for a digression, a unit that proves no point of the immediate argument.[57]

In terms of function, this is an ethical/emotional digression because Josephus' character is the focus of the digression. The attacks on the antiquity of the Jews are no longer abstract and impersonal. Josephus brings the real contemporary attacks against Judaism and himself into view. He intertwines his reputation with the integrity of Jewish scriptures, presenting himself as a representative of all those who have faithfully transmitted Jewish history in the past. He emphasizes his unique role in interviewing Jewish prisoners (*CA* 1.49), receiving assistance in writing in Greek (*CA*

Schreckenberg, and M. Vogel, *Flavius Josephus, Über das Alter des Judentums (Contra Apionem)* (Tübingen: Mohr Siebeck, 2006). Barclay uses this critical edition for his translation.

[53] Labow, LXXVII: Josephus "emphasizes his own abilities as a historiographer in an excursion, which is directed against the slanders and the representation of the Jewish war by Justus of Tiberias (46 [8] – 56 [10])." [e]r in einem Exkurs, der sich gegen die Verleumdungen und die Darstellung des Jüdischen Krieges durch Justus von Tiberias richtet, seine eigenen Fähigkeiten als Geschichtsschreiber hervorhebt (46 [8] – 56 [10]). Cf. Labow, 36–40, "Josephus als Geschichtsschreiber."

[54] Περὶ μὲν οὖν τούτων ἀναγκαίαν ἐποιησάμην τὴν παρέκβασιν ἐπισημήνασθαι βουλόμενος τῶν ἐπαγγελλομένων τὰς ἱστορίας συγγράφειν τὴν εὐχέρειαν.

[55] With Gerber, 68, and Cohen, 116.

[56] Labow, 41. Barclay notes that 1.58–59 functions as a second *exordium*, and suggests it is uncommon to digress at the beginning of a treatise (*Against Apion*, XVII–XVIII). However, Quintilian advises using a digression as a second exordium after the statement of the case, especially to excite or mollify the judge in a difficult case (*Inst.* IV.3.9).

[57] Labow, 4 *inter alia.*

1.50), and appealing to the emperors Vespasian and Titus as witnesses.[58] As further witnesses of his character and the quality of his history, he lists names of prominent people who received copies and their willingness to vouch for the veracity and impartiality of Josephus' accounts (*CA* 1.51–52).[59] He rebuts invective against his history and reputation (*CA* 1.53) and underlines his role as priest and his knowledge of Jewish "philosophy" (*CA* 1.54) before returning to the original topic of his role as eyewitness (*CA* 1.55) and final invective against his opponents (*CA* 1.56). Josephus deploys this digression consistent with rhetoricians' recommendations that ethical digressions praise self and blame opponents.[60]

The length of the digression is significant: 343 words long in Greek. By way of comparison, his description of the transmission of Jewish scriptures (*CA* 1.30–41) is 389 words. Although the ostensible topic is the antiquity and reliability of transmission of the Jewish Scriptures, Josephus spends almost as much time defending his role as reliable historian of the Jewish War. Because of its length, an audience may be impressed by the significance of the digression, which reveals that Josephus thought his character is almost as important as the transmission of Jewish scripture!

The location of the digression is immediately before the conclusion of the topic of transmission. This is consistent with the advice given by Hermagoras and teachers during Cicero's time that a digression is useful to heighten emotion before the conclusion, although they were referring to the end of a speech. In this case, Josephus heightens the emotion of the work by contrasting Jews who die for their history with Greeks who do not. This allows him to make the ethical digression that sustains a high level of emotion, currying the sympathy of his audience, until released by the conclusion of the section.

With respect to relevance, the digression does not lie completely outside the logic of the case. The surrounding argument is that Jewish histories have been accurately transmitted through the line of priests who maintained them faithfully. By means of the digression, Josephus presents himself as typical of those priests (*CA* 1.54) who record what they saw and transmit the "sacred writings" faithfully.[61] Just as Moses and the prophets wrote what they saw in their times (*CA* 1.40), Josephus recorded what he

[58] Rajak, 187; Barclay, 37 n. 205. See Rajak, 233–236, on question of Josephus' assistants.

[59] Barclay, 38 n. 212–3.

[60] On praise and blame in this passage, see Barclay, 34 n. 191, 38 n. 214.

[61] Barclay, XXII, 34 n. 191; Labow, 40.

saw. Although off the main subject of the antiquity of Jewish histories, this digression is a key to Josephus' defense of Judaism – and himself.[62]

The transition begins in *CA* 1.42 quite subtly, gradually introducing tangential topics (dying for history, contrast with Greeks) before turning the subject on himself. To hearers and readers, the gradual transition makes the beginning of the digression seem to be a natural consequence – an expansion even – of the previous topics. To scholars, it is difficult to identify where the digression precisely begins.

In contrast, the transition back to the main subject is abrupt, clearly delimited by the articulation of the digression and its explanation. Barclay argues that Josephus has to admit to the digression because he could not find a way to transition from the polemic of 1.53–56 back to the subject matter.[63] This is unlikely since Josephus has returned to the topic of eyewitnesses (1.55–56), which forms an *inclusio* with the transition into the digression (1.45–46). If the transition was the problem, he could have simply summarized the point (Jewish historians are reliable eyewitnesses) and move on. For example, when Josephus uses an unarticulated digression to summarize the three "sects" of Jews in *AJ* 13.171–173, he merely summarizes the point and moves on without further comment. The problem in *Contra Apionem* is that he has inserted himself and the contemporary contest over the representation of the Jewish War into a defense of the antiquity and reliability of Jewish scriptures. The audience expected Josephus to play the role of defense attorney, but instead finds him playing witness in the digression. Reverting to his prior role required acknowledging the difference.

d) Contra Apionem *2.145–286: Praise for the Jewish Constitution*

Some interpreters suggest that the conclusion of another digression is marked by Josephus' phrase in *CA* 2.151: "To resume my discourse from a little way back…" (Μικρὸν οὖν ἀναλαβὼν τὸν λόγον). Barclay argues that *CA* 2.147–150 is the digression, that Josephus is resuming "[p]resumably from the end of *CA* 2.146; taking *CA* 2.147–50 as a digression."[64] Müller takes *CA* 2.145–50 as the digression.[65] In contrast, C. Ger-

---

[62] Cohen, 118, concludes that this digression (along with the similar one in *Vita* §336–367) responds to direct attacks on Josephus "the man, his character and actions." He does not go as far as saying that Iustus is the target in both texts. Also Mason, 135–6 n. 1367; Labow, 41 n. 116; Barclay, 38–9 n. 214.

[63] Barclay, 41 n. 228.

[64] Barclay, *Against Apion*, 253 n. 566.

[65] J. G. Müller, *Des Flavius Josephus Schrift gegen den Apion. Text und Erklärung aus dem Nachlass von J. G. Müller* (eds. C. J. Riggenback and C. von Orelli; Basel: Bahnmeier, 1877), 289.

ber takes *CA* 2.147–150 as the exordium of the third major part of the discourse.[66]

Rather than a digression, *Contra Apionem* 2.145–150 is best understood as an example of the chain-link transition technique described by Longenecker. Against Müller and those who take *CA* 2.145–150 as a digression, Gerber persuasively argues that this passage transitions from the argument against Apion (*CA* 2.1–144) and functions as an introduction to the third major section (*CA* 2.145–286).[67] She details how Josephus' argument in *CA* 2.145–150 moves back and forth between the antithesis and thesis. He begins by recalling two opponents, Apollonius Molon and Lysimachus (*CA* 2.145a; cf. 2.16, 79), then introducing the encomium on the Law (*CA* 2.145b–147). He then returns to refuting Apollonius and Apion (*CA* 2.148–149) before returning to the encomium on the law, the primary topic of *CA* 2.145–286.

This is the classic structure of a chain-link A-b'-a'-B transition described by Longenecker:[68]

A (2.145a Apion)
    b' (2.145b–147 encomium on Law)
a' (2.148–150 refutation of Apollonius/Apion)
    B (2.151ff encomium on Law).

Given this back and forth structure, Josephus' comment, "To resume my discourse from a little way back," refers simply to the introductory encomium on the law given in *CA* 2.145b–147 that becomes the plan for the entire unit of *CA* 2.145–286: "I wish to speak briefly, as best I can, about the whole structure of our constitution and about its individual parts."[69] Josephus articulates the chain-link transition in *CA* 2.151 to remind the reader that the brief refutation of Apollonius and Apion is not the main topic. The structure and parts of the constitution is the announced topic. By using an articulated chain-link, Josephus simultaneously avoids and pro-

---

[66] Gerber, 134–135; cf. 137: she interprets μικρὸν οὖν ἀναλαβὼν τὸν λόγον (2.151) to mean "Briefly I want to say now, if I take up the speech, this as the first that..." (Kurz will ich nun, wenn ich die Rede aufnehme, dies als erstes sagen, daß...) rather than an interrupted speech has been resumed. This supports the conclusion that 2.145–150 is better understood as a chain-link transition than a digression.

[67] Gerber, 133–136. Barclay, *Against Apion,* 247 n. 524 also calls 2.145–150 an introduction.

[68] Without using Longenecker's term, Barclay, *Against Apion*, 297 n. 892, suggests that Josephus often uses this technique. "We have already seen many cases in which he places in the last sentence of one paragraph a phrase that anticipates the next (e.g. 2.156, 163, 174, 189)." (Commenting on 2.219.)

[69] Cf. Gerber, 70, 76–77; cf. 133–4.

motes the impression that the encomium is a response to Apollonius.[70] He links the encomium inexorably to the apology by using a chain-link, but the length and depth of the encomium magnifies the virtues of the Jewish constitution far beyond what is necessary for the apology.

The whole passage *CA* 2.145–286 is best understood as a digression. The evidence is, first, that scholars agree that *CA* 2.145–286 signals primarily discontinuity with the preceding argument and, second, that it fits the description of a digression as described by Hermagoras, Cicero and Quintilian. Identifying *CA* 2.145–286 as a digression helps to explain the difficulty interpreters have had relating this unit to the whole structure. It is also an example of (a) the location of a digression before the conclusion (as suggested by Hermagoras and practiced by Cicero and Quintilian) and (b) a systematic digression that works with another digression (*CA* 1.47–56) to obliquely address the rhetorical situation.

The first point is that scholars are in agreement that the long passage *CA* 2.145–286 goes far beyond what is necessary for the defense against Apion and Apollonius Molon. Gerber writes that it "goes far beyond the goal" of dealing with Apollonius Molon.[71] As a result she argues that it is a third major section of the treatise with its own introduction and argument.[72] Mason agrees that *CA* 2.145–286 should not be taken with the preceding defense against Apion but as part of an extended conclusion that positively summarizes Jewish culture and welcomes converts.[73] Based on the same signals, Barclay agrees that *CA* 2.145–286 is different in many ways from what preceded.

> It is frequently noted that the style, tone, and content of this segment of the treatise are different from the preceding segments, a shift summarized in the perception that here, after being defensive, Josephus offers a "positive" portrayal of the Judean tradition, its constitutions and laws.[74]

Barclay, however, rejects that this section is a third main part of the treatise because Josephus presents it as an ἀπολογία (*CA* 2.147). He labels this section an *apologetic encomium*, i.e. an encomium embedded in the structure of an apology.[75] Although he does not call it a digression, Bar-

---

[70] Gerber, 76, makes a similar conclusion: "With reproaches, here now he deals with Apollonius Molon, but he pursues beyond the goal to prove the quality of the Jewish politeuma in itself and in comparison with other." (Auf Vorwürfe, hier nun des Apollonius Molon, geht er ein, verfolgt aber darüber hinaus das Ziel, so die Güte des jüdischen Politeuma an sich und im Vergleich mit anderen zu erweisen.)

[71] Gerber, 76.

[72] Gerber, 70, 94–99.

[73] Mason, "*Contra Apionem* in Social and Literary Context," 212–216.

[74] Barclay, *Against Apion*, XIX; cf. 247 n. 524.

[75] Following Balch.

clay's description is reminiscent of the struggle scholars have with continuity and discontinuity in Rev 7:1–17 and 10:1–11:13.

> Thus, even if Josephus' content is sometimes only loosely connected to its present apologetic use, this is not always the case, and *even if it were*, our understanding of the work in its final, Josephan form must pay primary attention to *his* depiction of his aims and argumentative structure.[76]

CA 2.145–286 is loosely connected to the defense against Apion but is nonetheless embedded in it. In short, Barclay suggests that *CA* 2.145–286 signals discontinuity through the shifts in style, tone and content, but functions continuously when taken with the whole work and its overall effect.

The elements of discontinuity become clear when summarizing the argument of *CA* 2.145–286. The end of the previous unit is sharply delimited. After attacking Apion and describing his death (*CA* 2.142–144), he concludes, "here let us bring our argument to an end."[77] Josephus begins a long section of different style, tone and content. Rather than defending against specific attacks, Josephus provides an independent, positive description of Judean traditions.[78] The main topics are the Judean 'constitution' and its lawmaker Moses. These are announced in *CA* 2.145b–147 and summarized in *CA* 2.287. Josephus insists that it is not an encomium (*CA* 2.147, 2.287), but the topics, style and tone of *CA* 2.145–286 fit an encomium:[79] Moses' deeds (*CA* 2.157–60), character (*CA* 2.161–163), the structure and virtues of the law (*CA* 2.164–189), a summary of the laws (*CA* 2.190–218), Judean faithfulness to the law even to death (*CA* 2.219–35), concluding with Judean attitudes towards different beliefs (*CA* 2.236–86).[80] The majority of signals indicate discontinuity to the audience.[81]

This is an ethical-emotional digression. Josephus uses this long passage to obliquely further his goal of extolling the Jewish way of life.[82] Josephus refers to an amorphous crowd of "others" headed by Apollonius Molon and Lysimachus who libel Moses and Jewish law.[83] This reference pro-

---

[76] Barclay, *Against Apion*, XX. His emphasis.

[77] τοῦτο ἡμῶν ἐνταῦθα τὸ πέρας ἔστω τοῦ λόγου.

[78] Barclay, *Against Apion* XIX.

[79] Barclay, 243, cf. xix; cf. Balch; Gerber, 37–38.

[80] For this structural outline, see Barclay, *Against Apion*, 242–330.

[81] The few points of continuity are noted by Barclay, *Against Apion*, 247 n. 524.

[82] Mason, "*Contra Apionem* in Social and Literary Context," 212, argues that "Josephus' assumptions about the audience and his own aims become clearest in the second half of volume 2 (2.145–286)."

[83] Barclay (*Against Apion*, 243) notes this discontinuity between 2.145–286 and the preceding passage, writing that "its structure and rhetorical tone are quite different from the preceding apologetic arguments. Instead of citing and refuting accusations one by one, Josephus bundles them together at the start (2.145, 148) and then follows his own structure, which meets all these charges, but indirectly and on his own terms. In fact, the

vides a pretext for the following encomium that might normally have aroused suspicions of self-praise.[84] He knows it is a risk and so he minimizes the risk by implying that the discussion of Moses and the law is in response to Apollonius Molon's charges. The specific charges, however, are not revealed until *CA* 2.255–261 when it becomes clear that the whole unit *CA* 2.145–286 goes far beyond what is necessary to refute them.[85] In order to claim in his conclusion that he has not offered an encomium or attacked other people's beliefs (*CA* 2.287), he packages his encomium and invective as a digression with refuting Apollonius and Lysimachus as the ostensible motivation.

As noted above, scholars have a difficult time describing the relationship of *CA* 2.145–286 to the whole.[86] Gerber labels it a third section (Dritte Hauptteil) and Mason a Peroration, but Barclay argues that these terms do not fit such a long and internally coherent segment.[87] The debate over terminology is reminiscent of discussions about the place of Rev 7:1–17 and 10:1–11:13 within the structure of Revelation, and further suggests how an unarticulated digression creates tension for the reader/hearer and focuses more attention on that segment of the text.

Contra Apionem 2.145–286 fits the expectations of a digression described by Hermagoras, Cicero and Quintilian. The topics and argument of this passage are beyond what is necessary for the case to refute slander against Judaism. Its function is to praise Moses, the Jewish Constitution and the Jewish way of life, i.e. the ethos of Judaism and Josephus. It is a long unit, called by some a third part of the speech. The passage occurs after refuting the charges of Apion and before the conclusion, consistent with Hermagoras' advice. The transitions are not abrupt but smoothly use a chain-link technique to conclude the previous major unit and begin the digression.

This digression has many unique relationships with the first (*CA* 1.47–56) that suggests that Josephus is using multiple digressions in a single text

apology is at the same time an encomium (2.147, 287), using summary, paraphrase and comparison to extol Moses, the Judean constitution and the Judean laws."

[84] Barclay, XXXII. See Pliny the Younger's resistance to publish self-praise, *Epist.* I.8; also Plutarch's "On Praising Oneself Inoffensively" (*De Laude Ipsius*) in *Moralia* VII.540c–f.

[85] *CA* 2.236–254 may be a digression of invective within the digression of encomium. Josephus admits "he would have preferred not to examine the laws of other nations" (2.236) and later denies that he censures other people's customs (2.287; cf. 2.144). As stated above, Josephus is trying to minimize the herald's censure that he has gone beyond refutation. In Greek manuscripts this is an articulated digression (using παρέκβασις in 2.254), but not in Latin mss. See Barclay p. 297 n. 892.

[86] Barclay, XIX.

[87] Barclay, XIX n. 5.

to develop vocabulary, topics, and ideas in what I am calling 'systematic digressions.' As with the first digression, *CA* 2.145–286 is an ethical digression on the character of the Judean legislator, Moses, and the faithfulness of the Judeans who keep the law. It is also an ethical digression on the character of the law, asserting its rigor and piety. The character of the law is presented as further evidence of the piety of Moses and practicing Judeans. The bravery, piety and faithfulness of Judeans were also foci of the first digression, and these themes emerge dominant here. The willingness of Judeans to die for the law was the spark that led to the first digression (1.42–43), and here in the second digression is a key theme (e.g. 2.219–235, 283; cf. 2.150). Barclay speculates that this would have been appealing to a sympathetic Roman audience who valued toughness, commitment to ancestral customs, and contempt of death.[88]

The tone of the two digressions is also similar, moving away from directly refuting charges to positive portrayal of deeds and virtues. In the first digression, Josephus portrays himself as a faithful priest in the line of other eyewitnesses, while surrounding material deals with refuting charges that Judaism is a new religion. In this second digression, Moses and the law are described in the most favorable light, while the material immediately before the digression refuted Apion point by point (*CA* 2.137–144).

In summary, Josephus uses two digressions (1.47–56 and 2.145–286) in *Contra Apionem* as a way to praise himself, Moses, and the Torah while refuting attacks against Judaism. Overt self-praise would be inappropriate, but digressions are an acceptable way to include this material. They work together as a system, reinforcing the themes of the superiority of Judaism and the willingness of Judeans to die for the Law. These go beyond the needs of refuting slander, instead towards a larger goal: appealing to Epaphroditus and other sympathetic non-Judeans who want to know more about Judeans.[89] This appeal is concentrated in these two digressions, and reveals that Josephus believes his audience is sympathetic to hearing about the superiority of Judaism. Overtly, the goal is to refute charges against Judaism, but the digressions are a key part of Josephus' strategy to appeal to non-Judeans. This observation supports the contention that digressions can offer a unique view into the rhetorical goals and strategy of an author.

---

[88] Barclay, 244. When presenting Clearchus and Hecataeus' reports supporting of Judaism's antiquity (*CA* 1.161–218), Josephus hints at the shift from defending the antiquity of Judaism to encouraging admiration (esp. 1.161–2). See Barclay, 92, for discussion.

[89] See Barclay, XLVIII–XLIX; Mason, "*Contra Apionem* in Social and Literary Context." All of the passages cited by Barclay to support an appeal to a non-Judean audience are from these two digressions.

4. Greek-speaking Jews in Alexandria: *Aristeas* and 2 Maccabees

Other Greek-speaking Jews used digressions, notably the authors of *Aristeas ad Philocrates* and 2 Maccabees. Ostensibly, *Aristeas* is about the translation of the Law into Greek, but surprisingly five-sixths of *Aristeas* is taken up by digressions (§51–82, 83–120, 128–171, 187–300).[90] Sylvie Honigman notes that these digressions have often been taken as interpolations rather than compositional techniques.

> Needless to say, the assumption sometimes articulated by scholars at the beginning of the twentieth century completely misses the compositional quality of *B. Ar.*, which may well have been the aspect its author was most proud of. However, literary enjoyment is not incompatible with utility, quite the contrary. While the main narrative in *B. Ar.* focues on a narrow, albeit central, topic – the translation of the Jewish Law into Greek – the digressions allowed the author to broaden the scope of his work to include a comprehensive presentation of this Law, as well as, of the people abiding by it.[91]

This description is consistent with rhetorician's discussion of digressions and the above examples from Josephus. Although he does not articulate his digressions using any term, he apologizes to Philocrates, "If I have dwelt at length on these matters, Philocrates, I beg your pardon" (§295).[92] Although 'off topic' and unessential to the main narrative, the digressions express the oblique goals of the author, in the case of *Aristeas*, to present the Law and the ethos of those who live by the law.

2 Maccabees also uses digressions. In his analysis of its "temple propaganda," Robert Doran relates the use of digressions in 2 Maccabees to Greek historiography, which he calls 'reflections' by the author in 4:16–17; 5:17–20; and 6:12–17.

> Digressions were part of Herodotus' plan (4.30), Thucydides used them, and they became a traditional feature of Greek historiography. Polybius remarks that many earlier writers

---

[90] S. Honigman, *The Septuagint and Homeric Scholarship in Alexandria: A study in the narrative of the* Letter of Aristeas (London: Routledge, 2003), 13; R. J. H. Shutt, "Letter of Aristeas," in *OTP* 2:10. Cf. A. Wasserstein and D. J. Wasserstein, *The Legend of the Septuagint: From Classical Antiquity to Today* (Cambridge: Cambridge University, 2006), 24: "A reader coming to the *Letter of Aristeas* for the first time after having known of it only by report would be surprised to find how very small a part of it is concerned with the translation or the translators."

For another example, see Philo of Alexandria, *De opificio mundi* §§45–52 (an amplifying digression on the number four) and §§89–128 (an amplifying digression on the number seven). See discussion by D. T. Runia in Philo of Alexandria, *On the Creation of the Cosmos according to Moses* (Leiden: Brill, 2001), 187–196, 260–308.

[91] Honigman, 19. Cf. A. Pelletier, *Lettre d'Aristée a Philocrate* (Paris: Les Éditions du Cerf, 1962), 53–54.

[92] Εγὼ δὲ [εἰ πεπλεόνακα,] τούτοις, ὦ φιλόκρατες, συγγνώμην ἔχειν.

used such digressions to entertain their readers with myths and stories (Plb 38.5–6)...The author of 2 Maccabees also uses reflections at 4:16–17; 5:17–20; 6:12–17. These reflections are used to instruct the reader.[93]

As with Greek historians, the author of 2 Maccabees uses digressions to instruct the reader.[94]

2 Maccabees 7:20–29 fits the description of a digression and may be significant to understanding the book of Revelation because it interrupts the story between the sixth and seventh element of a numbered series.[95] 2 Maccabees 7 describes how each of Eleazar's seven sons are killed. Before the last one, however, their mother has two extended speeches which form the B section in an A-B-A' pattern. The account of her speeches is 262 words long in Greek, compared to the 35 words to describe the brief speech and death of the sixth son.[96] If one omitted 2 Macc 7:20–29, there would be no loss in the narrative logic.

Discontinuity is signaled to the audience especially by shifts in communication axis, personal references, *dramatis personae*, and temporal signals. The communication axis shifts as the narrator intrudes to evaluate the mother for the audience.

The mother was exceedingly admirable and worthy of good memory. Although she saw her seven sons perish within a single day, she bore it with good courage because of her hope in the Lord. (2 Macc 7:20).

In 2 Macc 7:1–19, the communication axis is dominated by speech between each son and Antiochus. 2 Macc 7:20–29 begins with the author addressing the audience, followed by direct speech by the mother to her sons.

By focusing on the mother as subject in 2 Macc 7:20–29, personal references and *dramatis personae* signal discontinuity with the prior pattern of the sons' deaths. The mother is a personal reference in 2 Macc 7:1, 4,

---

[93] R. Doran, *Temple Propaganda: The Purpose and Character of 2 Maccabees* (Washington D.C.: Catholic Biblical Association, 1981), 95–96. See his discussion of the "two major digressions or reflections of the epitomizer" on pp. 52–55.

[94] Doran does not mention the authorial prologue (2:19–32) and epilogue (15:38–9) as other examples of digressions.

[95] Doran did not analyze this text, probably because he confined himself to digressions that directly address the reader.

[96] Compare with her brief and very different role in 4 Maccabees 12:6 (still an interruption between the sixth and seventh son, but far less emotionally potent). The mother has no direct speech between sixth and seven sons' death, but receives an emotional encomium in 4 Macc 14:13–17:8. Her speech of exhortation is suspended until 17:16–22. The author of *Josippon* seems to follow the structure of 2 Maccabees, but changes her speech into a prayer. See S. Zeitlin, ed., *The Second Book of Maccabees* (trans. S. Tedesche; New York: Harper, 1954), 49.

and 5, depicted as merely present with her sons.[97] She is not mentioned at all during the death of the second through sixth sons, but becomes the subject and *dramatis personae* in 2 Macc 7:20–29. As she becomes a *dramatis persona*, her sons become personal references, characters that do not act but receive their mother's exhortations. Her son's speech in 2 Macc 7:30 also signals the return to the familiar pattern: a son's speech followed by his death.

Temporal signals in 2 Macc 7:20 also indicate discontinuity. Rather than the time between the sixth and seventh son's death, the whole day is signaled: "her seven sons in a single day." The temporal perspective is that of the audience looking back in time at that day. Likewise, 2 Macc 7:21–23 is also retrospective, summarizing a speech to each son that is not revealed until this point in the story. "She encouraged each of them in the language of their ancestors" (2 Macc 7:21). Because of its A-B-A' structure and discontinuity of communication axis, personal references, *dramatis personae*, and temporal signals, 2 Macc 7:20-29 is a digression.

Emotion seems to be a primary reason for the location of the mother's speeches between the sixth and seventh deaths. The mother exhorts her son to accept death with courage, trusting in God's justice and the promise of resurrection.[98] (In chapter 2, I observed these themes in Rev 7 and 10–11). When the mother's exhortation interrupts the series it sustains the emotion of the six sons who have died and builds suspense for the anticipated seventh death. The heroic and pious nature of their death is highlighted by the mother's expectations, as well as the sheer pathos of a mother watching her sons die horrible deaths. Similar to other digressions, this is a memorable passage.[99]

---

[97] English translations disguise how the mother is de-emphasized in prepositional phrases. In 2 Macc 7:1, the Greek text literally says "seven brothers along with their mother" (ἑπτὰ ἀδελφοὺς μετὰ τῆς μητρὸς); 2 Macc 7:5, "they kept exhorting one another, together with their mother" (ἀλλήλους παρεκάλουν σὺν τῇ μητρὶ). The mother does not become a subject until 7:20.

[98] J. Goldstein discusses at length how the mother shows her knowledge of philosophy, but does not comment how odd it is that the speech is placed on the mother's lips and in between the death of sixth and seventh son (*II Maccabees* [AB 41A; Garden City, New York: Doubleday, 1983], 307–315).

[99] Cf. J. R. Bartlett, *The First and Second Books of the Maccabees* (Cambridge: Cambridge University: 1973), 273: "The mother was the most remarkable of all, and deserves to be remembered with special honour."

5. Speeches in 1st c. Asia Minor: Dio of Prusa

Dio of Prusa demonstrates the use of digressions in Asia Minor around the time of John's ministry. Dio is an example of orators who spoke throughout Asia Minor in the 1st century. He was accessible to a variety of social groups and classes and widely imitated (e.g. Or. 42).[100] I will briefly describe three orations in which he uses digressions. He does not use the technical term παρέκβασις, but articulates digressions using terms such as ἐκτροπή and ἐκβαίνω, while others are unarticulated. As with other digressions explored above, he uses them to obliquely promote himself in front of his audiences.

In Or. 7 (*Euboean*), spoken around 96 CE, Dio begins with a long narration about his encounter with a hunter.[101] The hunter is the ideal in contrast to the depravity of the city dwellers who jeer and mock the man. After this long introduction, Dio apologizes for the long story (7.81) and later entreats the hearer that,

> It is not necessary to be annoyed at the digressions (ἐκτροπὰς) of speeches, even if they do seem excessively long, if only they are not about trivial or unworthy or irrelevant things, since the speaker has not abandoned the theme of the whole…(7.128)[102]

Reminding the audience of his long introduction, he explains that orators may be compared with hunters have to go off the path to catch the big prey (7.129). On one hand, the digression is ornamental, giving pleasure in the richness of its description, and on the other it is also ethical – presenting the hunter as an ideal to be emulated and, in fact, the basis for Dio's commonplace critiques of the city.

In Or. 12 (*Olympian)* given around 104 CE, Dio cleverly uses the famous statue of Zeus as a basis for discussing the nature of the gods, the appropriateness of images of the divine, and the quality of Greek life.[103] In

---

[100] On the relevance of Dio's speeches for understanding the book of Revelation, see P. Perry, "Critiquing the Excess of Empire," *JSNT* 29.4 (2007): 473–496.

[101] On Or. 7, see C. P. Jones, *The Roman World of Dio Chrysostom* (Cambridge: Cambridge Unversity Press, 1978), 56–61; D. A. Russell, *Dio Chrysostom*; John Ma, "Public Speech and Community in the *Euboicus*," in *Dio Chrysostom: Politics, Letters, and Philosophy* (ed. S. Swain; Oxford: Oxford University, 2000, 108–124.

[102] χρὴ οὖν τὰς ἐκτροπὰς τῶν λόγων, ἂν καὶ σφόδρα μακραὶ δοκῶσι, μὴ μέντοι περί γε φαύλων μηδὲ ἀναξίων [λόγων] μηδὲ οὐ προσηκόντων, μὴ δυσκόλως φέρειν, ὡς οὐκ αὐτὴν λιπόντος τὴν τῶν ὅλων ὑπόθεσιν τοῦ λέγοντος ἕως ἂν περὶ τῶν ἀναγκαίων καὶ προσηκόντων φιλοσοφίαι διεξίηι. Greek text from Russell, *Dio Chrysostom*, 55.

[103] H.-J. Klauck and B. Bäbler, *Dion von Prusa: Olympische Rede* (2nd ed; Darmstadt: Wissenschaftliche Buchgesellschaft, 2002); B. F. Harris, "The Olympian Oration of Dio Chrysostom," *Historical Studies* 10.38 (1962): 85–97; Jones, 53; Russell, *Dio Chrysostom*; Perry, "Excess of Empire."

the midst of describing the nature of the gods (12.27–35), he begins to attack the antitheistic beliefs of the Epicureans (12.36–38).[104] He confesses that he has digressed (ἔκβας) and needs to turn the "ship" of his speech back on course (12.38).

> Now to explain this digression (ἐκβάς): my argument is responsible, having turned aside of itself; for perhaps it is not easy to check the course of a philosopher's thoughts and speech, no matter what direction they may take; for whatever suggests itself to his mind always seems profitable, nay indispensable, for his audience, and my speech has not been prepared to "suit the water-clock and the constraint of court procedure," to use somebody's expression, but allows itself a great deal of license. Now then, it is not difficult to run back again, just as on a voyage it is not difficult for competent steersmen who have got a little off their course to get back upon it.[105]

In explaining his digression, he focuses on his *ethos* as a philosopher, with the implication that he is a true philosopher and Epicureans are not.[106] The digression is one of the ways that Dio amplifies the theme of the superiority of philosophers (himself specifically) over sophists, painters, sculptors and poets.

In Or. 36 (*Borysthenes),* given around 98 CE, Dio recounts to his native city Prusa a visit to a small struggling community on the Black Sea.[107] He uses a series of systematic but unarticulated digressions (36.33–35; 36.39c–h; 36.43a–e; 36.48; 36.50) to develop the theme of his superiority over even Plato and Homer for knowledge about the gods, presenting him self as the representative of the Magi.[108] Some of these digressions are short, simply "figures of thought" as Cicero and Quintilian call them. The Magi, he relates, understand the true nature of the cosmos (which conveniently coincides with popular Stoic doctrine). Dio, of course, cannot simply come out and say that he is superior to cultural icons such as Homer and

---

[104] Race, "Some Digressions," 4.

[105] Trans. J. W. Cohoon, LCL, modified. Ταῦτα μὲν οὖν ἐπεξῆλθεν ὁ λόγος καθ' αὑτον ἐκβάς· τυχὸν γὰρ οὐ ῥάδιον τὸν τοῦ φιλοσόφου νοῦν καὶ λόγον ἐπισχεῖν, ἔνθα ἂν ὁρμήσηι, τοῦ ξυναντῶντος ἀει φαινομένου ξυμφέροντος καὶ ἀναγκαίου τοῖς ἀκροωμένοις, οὐ μελετηθέντα πρὸς ὕδωρ και δικανικὴν ἀνάγκην, ὥσπερ οὖν ἔφη τις, ἀλλὰ μετὰ πολλῆς ἐξουσίας καὶ ἀδειας. οὐκοῦν τό γε ἀναδραμεῖν οὐ χαλεπόν, ὥσπερ ἐν πλῶι τοῖς ἱκανοῖς κυβερνήταις οὐ πολὺ παραλλάξασι. Greek text from Russell, *Dio Chrysostom*, 73.

[106] Cf. Russell, *Dio Chrysosom*, 188.

[107] Jones, 61–64; Russell, *Dio Chrysostom*; G. Salmeri, "Dio, Rome, and the Civic Life of Asia Minor," in Swain, ed., *Dio Chrysostom*, 53–92; Graham Anderson, "Some Uses of Storytelling," in ibid, 143–160 [esp. 157–160]; Michael Trapp, "Plato in Dio," in ibid, 213–239 [esp. 214–219].

[108] For example, Russell, *Dio Chrysostom*, 228, summarizes 36.33–5 as "The poets – at least the earliest poets – have a certain understanding of this, which they communicate to their hearers, though they are not the true initiates." The true initiates are the Magi, whose myth Dio bears (36.39–61).

Plato, but uses the digressions as a way to promote his ethos and move their emotions. Josephus used digressions in a similar way in *Contra Apionem* as an oblique rhetorical strategy to promote his identity as the superior eyewitness and to promote his lifestyle to sympathetic audiences.

Speaking in Rome, Greece, and Asia Minor, Dio demonstrates the use of digressions consistent with what we have seen in Josephus and the rhetoricians. He articulates some digressions and not others. He uses them both simply and systematically. His digressions are most often ethical: constructing himself as the ideal philosopher and exhorting his audiences to virtue. He is concerned about their length, but argues that their location is the most relevant to his argument and his audience. He chooses topics consistent with his ethical self-construction. Josephus in Rome and *Aristeas* in Alexandria are examples of Jews who used digressions as a part of their rhetoric. Dio provides examples of digressions used in speeches in Asia Minor.

6. Digressions in Drama and Poetry?

It is difficult to gauge the extent that poetry, tragedies, and comedies influenced the use of digressions. The issue is pertinent for two reasons. First, there was clear interaction of the orator, poet, and dramatist. Second, many scholars (e.g. Eichhorn, Brewer, Bowman, Blevins, Schüssler Fiorenza, Smalley) have suggested that Rev 7:1–17 and 10:1–11:13 are comparable to choral interludes in Greek tragedy.[109]

Oratory influenced drama and poetry, and vice-a-versa. Some of the earliest reflections on Greek oratory are found in the tragedies of Aeschylus, Sophocles and Euripides.[110] Division of a speech into logical parts and distinction of speaking styles can be discerned in Homer's epics, and Homer

[109] J. G. Eichhorn, *Einleitung in das Neue Testament* (2 vols; Leipzig: Weidmannische Buchhandlung, 1810), 2:334–65; R. Brewer, "The Influence of Greek Drama on the Apocalypse of John," *Anglican Theological Review* 18 (1936): 74–92; J. W. Bowman, *The Drama of the Book of Revelation* (Philadelphia: Westminster, 1955); J. L. Blevins, *Revelation as Drama* (Nashville: Broadman Press, 1984) and "The Revelation to John: Its Dramatic Structure and Message," *Interpretation* 9.4 (1955): 436–53; E. Schüssler Fiorenza, *The Book of Revelation: Justice and Judgment* (Minneapolis: Fortress, 1998), 172; S. S. Smalley, *The Revelation to John* (Downers Grove, Illinois: InterVarsity Press, 2005), 21–22. See the critical response by M. A. Harris, *The Literary Function of Hymns in the Apocalypse of John* (Unpublished PhD dissertation; Southern Baptist Theological Seminary, 1988), 7–11; cf. A. W. Wainwright, *Mysterious Apocalypse: Interpreting the Book of Revelation* (Nashville: Abingdon Press, 1993), 143–144.

[110] Kennedy, *New History*, 17, 24–26. The earliest discussion of different styles is not found in rhetorical handbooks, but Aristophanes' comedy *The Frogs*.

is a constant source of material for orators (e.g. Dio of Prusa and Quintilian, discussed below). Both drama and poetry are sources for observing deviations in practice, although dramatists use different terms.

a) ἐμβολίμον *and* ἐπεισόδιον *in Drama*

In drama, the most obvious kind of deviation is when the chorus interrupts the narrative by coming out to sing. The chorus provides new dramatis personae, and time and place may shift. Vocabulary, topics and style shift. The communication axis changes from characters in the story to communication between the chorus and audience. In many cases, these interruptions could be removed without changing the logic of the surrounding narrative, but their presence affects the audience's reception of the whole. Some songs provide commentary on the action and characters, and perhaps in some cases could be considered a kind of amplificatory digression.[111] Others are radically disconnected from the surrounding narrative.[112] Theoreticians, however, do not call these παρέκβασεις, but instead use ἐμβολίμον for choral interruptions and ἐπεισόδιον for dialogue between choral songs.[113] The dramatists, as with the orators, used these deviations to heighten emotion, develop character, and focus on direct communication between the actors and the audience.

Aristotle, Dionysius of Halicarnassus, and Anon. Seg. provide some evidence that an audience could connect deviations in poetry and speeches

---

[111] E.g. Sophocles, *Antigone* 1115–54, a ὑπόρχημα (dance-song) to Dionysus that Creon has taken the advice to go free Antigone from her prison. This upbeat song makes the coming tragedy seem all the more terrible. R. Jebb, *Sophocles: The Plays and Fragments – Part III: The Antigone* (Amsterdam: A. M. Hakkert, 1971), xvi: "The substitution of this lively dance-song ('hyporcheme') for a choral ode of a graver cast here serves the same purpose of contrast as in the *Oedipus Tyrannus*, the *Ajax*, and the *Trachiniae*. The catastrophe is approaching." Cf. 198.

[112] E.g. Euripides, *Elektra* 432–486, which describes the details of Achilles' shield in a kind of imitation of Homer's digression. The description, although not necessary, builds up the ethos of characters and emotionally affects the audience. C. H. Keene, *The Electra of Euripides* (London: George Bell & Sons, 1893), xxvii: "The Chorus have learned by hearsay of the wonders depicted on the famous shield, and describe them in detail, the better to exalt our idea of the character of the men Agamemnon had under his command..." Keene, 45, comments further on the paradox that the description of the shield is not necessary but has important effect on the audience: "Paley says that the present [432–486] is one of the Choral odes of Euripides which seem merely ἐμβόλιμα, i.e. inserted to mark the intervals in the action without any reference to the plot. Its drift, however, is to enhance the enormity of Clytaemnestra's crime and so prepare the way for her approaching punishment."

[113] Aristotle, *Poetica* XIX.1456a.28–31; cf. XII.1452b.13–27, IX.1451b.33–37. Cf. Lausberg, §1195 who describes ἐπεισόδιον as a choral song in the middle of a play, contrasted with πρόλογος and ἔξοδος, the entrance and exit songs for the chorus.

to interludes in drama.[114] Aristotle uses ἐπεισόδιον for both the Catalogue of Ships in the *Iliad* (*Poetica* XXIII.1459a.34–37) and for dialogue between two songs in tragedy (XII.1452b.20). Dionysius of Halicarnassus (*Comp.* 19, *Isocr.* 4, *Thuc.* 7) uses ἐπεισόδιον for both epic poets and orators to describe units with variations of rhythm, figures, and pitch of voice.[115] *Anon. Seg.* II.67 juxtaposes ἐπεισόδιον with παρέκβασις, which may be another link between deviations in oratory and drama.

b) Digressions in Poetry

Ancient audiences identified digressions in poetry, especially in Homer.[116] Quintilian praises Homer as a master of digressions, among other rhetorical techniques.

> Then consider [Homer's] similes, his amplifications, his illustrations, digressions (*digressus*), indications of fact, inferences, and all the other methods of proof and refutation which he employs. They are so numerous that the majority of writers on the principles of rhetoric have gone to his works for examples of all these things (*Inst.* X.1.49 [Butler, LCL]).

As further evidence of the impact of Homer's digressions (and evidence of a digression in the letter genre), Pliny the Younger justifies his digression about his house in Tuscany in a letter to a friend by comparing it to Homer description of Achilles' shield.[117] Pliny argues for both Homer and himself that the digression is not irrelevant but essential and a sign of artistry.

Norman Austin and Julia Haig Gaisser have shown how Homer uses digressions interwoven throughout the narrative for emotion and characterization.[118] Gaisser considers twenty-four digressions in the *Iliad* and

---

[114] Cf. W. D. Furley and J. Maarten Bremer, *Greek Hymns: Volume I: The Texts in Translation* (Tübingen: Mohr-Siebeck, 2001), 59–60; W. Race, "Aspects of Rhetoric and Form in Greek Hymns," *Greek, Roman, and Byzantine Studies* 23 (1982): 5–14, esp. 6.

[115] Dionysius does not discuss changes in the criteria we are using for detecting digressions. Although Stephen Usher translates ἐπεισόδιον as 'digression' in the Loeb volume, the context suggests 'episode' as a more appropriate translation to communicate the overlap between epic poet, tragedian, and orator.

[116] Modern readers have also detected digressions in Pindar's poetry, which I will not discuss here for sake of brevity. See Appendix; cf. Race, "Some Digressions and Returns."

[117] Pliny, *Epist.* 5.6.43.

[118] N. Austin, "The Function of Digressions in the *Iliad*," *Greek, Roman, and Byzantine Studies* 7:4 (Winter 1966) 295–311; J. H. Gaisser, "A Structural Analysis of the Digressions in the Iliad and the Odyssey," *Harvard Studies in Classical Philology* 73 (1969): 1–43. Although overlapping, Austin and Gaisser identify some different units in the *Iliad* as digressions, most notably in Book 1. See Appendix. The differences may be explained by the fact that Gaisser provides a clearer method for detecting digressions.

twenty-seven in the *Odyssey*.[119] Concerning himself only with the *Iliad*, Austin argues that

> the digressions of the *Iliad* are not haphazard accretions, but neither are they merely ornamental decorations subject to the whims of poet or his audience. There is a consistency in their themes, their occurrence and their degree of elaboration which indicates an ordering principle in their use. Both thematically and dramatically they are relevant to the structure of the whole poem.[120]

For example, Austin shows that four of the five digressions in *Iliad* book 1 are paradigmatic stories told by one character to another to persuade or dissuade another character.[121] Homer also uses digressions systemati-

---

What rhetorical criticism identifies as digressions, others may analyze in terms of redaction history or narratology. These methodologies are not mutually exclusive. A passage identified as a digression may have been inserted from another source or reflect a different performance (Parry and Lord's understanding of way the epics were composed). The Catalogue of Ships in *Iliad* 2 is likely a redactional insertion but has undeniable rhetorical function in the current structure. Gaisser and Austin identify it as a digression (cf. G. S. Kirk, *The Iliad: A Commentary: Volume I: books 1–4* [Cambridge: Cambridge University, 1985], 168–9). Some consider Nestor's speech during the victory feast for Aias (*Il.* 7.327–337) to be a later addition, but Bruce Louden argues it looks ahead to the funerals for Patroclus and Hector (B. Louden, *The Iliad: Structure, Myth, and Meaning* [Baltimore: Johns Hopkins, 2006], 47–8). I. J. F. de Jong uses Narratology to analyze many of the passages listed by Austin and Gaisser as analepsis and prolepsis (*Narrators and Focalizers: The Presentation of the Story in the Iliad* [Amsterdam: B. R. Grüner, 1987], 81–90, 149–179). Similar to my argument about digressions, she concludes,

> Analepses and prolepses found in the simple narrator-text can be considered *surplus*-passages ... This surplus status might account for the fact that so many of these passages have been athetized or, in the case of digressions, have been considered purely ornamental element characteristic for the "epische Breite." However, in this section I hope to have demonstrated that analepses and prolepses find their *raison d'être* ...: they create dramatic irony and suspense, incite pathos, elicit pity, signal the importance or symbolic value of objects, recall important information and provide background information necessary for the appreciation of following speeches (90).

The *Doloneia* (*Iliad* 10) is another passage that may be considered from both a redaction history and rhetorical perspective. It is absent from some versions, and deviates in style, tone, and vocabulary. It can be skipped without loss of narrative logic, but nonetheless Hainsworth argues that it is necessary to create urgency. "Whether the poet invented, retained, or imported Dolon from another episode ... seems to be an open question, but without an oracle or an *aristeia* Dolon is essential." (B. Hainsworth, *The Iliad: A Commentary: Volume III: books 9–12* [Cambridge: Cambridge University, 1993], 152.) Hainsworth (152) calls the *Doloneia* an 'interpolated episode,' Richardson calls it an 'interlude' (N. Richardson, *The Iliad: A Commentary: Volume VI: books 21–24* [Cambridge: Cambridge University, 1993], 12).

[119] Gaisser, 6.

[120] Austin, 297.

[121] Austin, 300.

cally.[122] Nestor's speeches (*Il.* 1.260–73; 7.124–60, 11.670–790, 23.629–43) are examples of what I am calling systematic digressions, digressions that repeat and amplify the exhortation for the Greek men to live up to his heroic ideal.[123] Under the guise of a garrulous old man, Nestor presents himself as an example to follow and a warning to Achilles and Agamemnon.[124] These digressions are not simply edifying examples, however, but Nestor's "most persuasive form of rhetoric" offering "positive proof of a present possibility."[125] In the present crisis, Nestor shows there can be a positive outcome if the Greeks follow his example.

In 1st century CE Asia Minor, Dio of Prusa understood this point and presents himself as a kind of Nestor, an orator who is not bragging but wisely advising powerful people (*Or.* 57).[126] Dio may be responding to those who consider Nestor's speeches digressive when he says, "Does it seem to you that Homer put these words into Nestor's mouth by chance (ἀπὸ τύχης)...?" (57.8, cf. 9). However, he is more likely taking up a sophistic topic ("Did Homer make Nestor a braggart?" 57.2). In any case, Dio took Nestor's digressions as a strategy to persuade powerful people to change their opinions.[127] For this 1st century orator, a character in Homer using digressions became an example to imitate.

Homer's use of digressions corresponds with the advice of rhetoricians to sustain emotion. Digressions in the *Iliad* and *Odyssey* are delimited using catch phrase and ring-composition transitions and an A-B-A' structure identifiable by shifts in *dramatis personae*, temporal, and spatial shifts.[128] They are often long, and their very length is a form of amplification.[129]

---

[122] See Gaisser's discussion of the repeated theme composition in the *Odyssey* (e.g. Gaisser, 31, 39).

[123] Austin, 301; cf. Richardson, 237; Hainsworth, 305. Nestor becomes not only an ideal within the Homeric story world but also to audiences who hear the *Iliad*. For example, see Dio of Prusa's *Or.* 57, which presents Nestor as the model for leadership in the 1st/2nd century CE. See discussion below.

[124] Austin, 302–303; Richardson, 237; Hainsworth, 295, 296–309.

[125] Austin, 303. Louden, 119–20, argues that Nestor's attempts to guide the Achaeans is ineffective.

[126] Jones, *The Roman World of Dio Chrysostom*, 122.

[127] See the thinly veiled self-reference in *Or.* 57.10 describing an orator telling "ordinary men" about speeches to "others who are far superior." He is not bragging, Dio says, but imitating Nestor (μιμούμενος τὴν τοῦ Νέστορος).

[128] Gaisser shows how Homer prefers ring-composition for the *Iliad* and for the *Odyssey* catch-phrase/theme transitions. She notes that Nestor's digressions are especially clear because of temporal signals. See Gaisser, 10.

[129] Austin, 306. For example, "Nestor's anecdote is long precisely because the situation is desperate."

They are often placed where the action is most intense, sustaining the emotion of previous narrative. According to Austin, they function as a paradigm for action (i.e. an ethical/emotional digression) within the story.[130] Dio is an example of someone who was persuaded to emulate Nestor's example outside the story. In Austin's judgment, these digressions, far from being irrelevant or demonstrating the poet's loss of control, are Homer's most forceful passages. The digression in the *Iliad* "brings time to a complete standstill" and locks the audience's attention on that particular moment.[131]

In summary, there is some evidence that dramatic interludes affected the use and reception of digressions but more evidence for poetic deviations. Pliny the Younger and Dio of Prusa demonstrate that Homeric digressions influenced letters and speeches. Homeric digressions became an example of developing ethos for Pliny's letter and for Dio's self-presentation. Impacting both epistolary and epideictic genres, Homeric digressions were often memorable, received more focus than the surrounding material, and provided examples to emulate.

7. Digression in the New Testament: Epistle to the Hebrews

Do authors in the New Testament use digressions? They do not use παρέκβασις or any comparable term; from this we can only conclude the New Testament lacks articulated digressions. Are there examples of unarticulated digressions?

The author of the epistle to the Hebrews is an example of one who uses an unarticulated digression in Heb 5:11–6:12.[132] The preacher begins the central argument about Jesus as High Priest in Heb 4:14 and develops it in 5:1-10. Unexpectedly, and quite emotionally, the preacher stops, "About this we have much to say that is hard to explain, since you have become unambitious (νωθροὶ) in hearing" (5:11).[133] George H. Guthrie highlights the significance of this interruption.

---

[130] Austin, 306, cf. 311: "The digressions are not, then, a release from tension but a concentration of tension."

[131] Austin, 312.

[132] One might also consider the so-called intercalations of Mark as digressions. Cf. F. G. Downing, "Markan Intercalation in Cultural Context," in *Narrativity in Biblical and Related Texts* (eds. G. J. Burke and J.-D. Kaestli; Leuven: University Press, 2000), 105–117.

[133] On translating νωθρός as "unambitious," see P. S. Perry, "Making Fear Personal: Hebrews 5.11–6.12 and the Argument from Shame," *JSNT* 32.1 (2009): 1–27.

For the author to give an introduction to the appointment of the Son as high priest (5:1–10) and then suddenly to break off and confront the hearer's directly with their immediate problem (5:11–6:3) may do damage to our outlines, but it would have made a rhetorical impact.[134]

The digression is delimited by an *inclusio* of the key word νωθρός (5:11, 6:12). The communication axis shifts to direct address between the author and the audience. Members of the audience become the *dramatis personae*. They are characterized as infants who need milk and who are still unskilled and not in a mature state to distinguish between good (5:12–14). They are described generally with all believers who have experienced the benefactions of God: they have been enlightened, have tasted the heavenly gift, shared in the Holy Spirit, and tasted the message of God and power of the age to come (6:4–5). Spatial signals shift from the location of Jesus' suffering to the audience's location. Temporal signals shift from Jesus' time to the present time of the hearers and their recent experiences. Thematic vocabulary shifts to language about maturity, Christian instruction and experiences of God's benefactions, agricultural imagery, and the threat of burning for unproductive ground.

Craig Koester argues that Hebrews uses digressions to transition between various units, and identifies Heb 5:11–6:20 as one example.[135]

---

[134] G. H. Guthrie, *The Structure of Hebrews: A Text-Linguistic Analysis* (Grand Rapids: Baker, 1994), 146; cf. C. Koester, *Hebrews: A New Translation with Introduction and Commentary* (AB 36; New York: Doubleday, 2001), 307; H. W. Attridge, *The Epistle to the Hebrews* (Hermeneia; Philadelphia: Fortress, 1989), 157; G. Gelardini, *"Verhärtet eure Herzen nicht": Der Hebräer, eine Synagogenhomilie zu* Tischa be-Aw (Leiden: Brill, 2007), 257.

[135] C. Koester, "Hebrews, Rhetoric, and the Future of Humanity," *CBQ* 64 (2002): 103–123; idem., *Hebrews* (New York: Doubleday, 2001), 83–86, 89. As with other digressions, modern interpretations vary according to the emphasis on signals of continuity or discontinuity. Cynthia L. Westfall acknowledges that most scholars emphasize discontinuity: "[T]here seems to be a consensus among scholars concerning 5:11–6:20 that infers a lack of coherence (or at least disorganization) in the discourse" (C. L. Westfall, *A Discourse Analysis of the Letter to the Hebrews: The Relationship between Form and Meaning* [LNTS 297; London: T & T Clark, 2005], 141). She emphasizes continuity, however, and argues that Melchizedek is still the topic of 5:11–6:3. She arrives at this conclusion by reading περὶ οὗ (5:11) to mean "about Melchizedek" (Westfall, 144), which is a tenuous since Melchizedek was only ambiguously mentioned in 5:6, 10 and the priesthood of Christ is the primary topic of 5:1–10 (see Koester, *Hebrews*, 296–9; Attridge, 156–7). Emphasizing discontinuity, Paul D. Landgraf argues that the structure mirrors the movement of the High Priest going into the temple on the Day of Atonement (P. D. Landgraf, "The Structure of Hebrews: A Word of Exhortation in Light of the Day of Atonement," in R. Bauckham, et. al., eds., *A Cloud of Witnesses: The Theology of Hebrews in its Ancient Contexts* [LNTS 387; London: T & T Clark, 2008], 19–27). He notes the signals of discontinuity in 5:11–6:12, but is reluctant to call it a digression. Instead,

> These digressions do not move the larger argument forward in a direct way, but allow the author to turn and address the listeners with words of warning and encouragement. The digressions resemble each other in that they admonish the listeners to pay attention, and warn about the dangers of neglect, sluggishness, apostasy, and persistent sin, since divine judgment is inescapable (2:1–4; 5:11–6:20; 10:26–39; 12:25–27). Rather than trying to fit the digressions into the flow of the argument, as is common in outlines of Hebrews, we can better treat them as digressions that seek to retain the audience's attention during the transition between sections. At the same time, the importance of the digressions in the author's rhetorical strategy should be recognized.[136]

Koester argues that Heb 10:26–39 and 12:25–27 are also digressions, but these passages do not exhibit discontinuous signals from the surrounding units. He labels them as digressions based upon similar exhortation and warnings as 5:11–6:12. Although this is true, there are no shifts in communication axis, personal references, *dramatis personae*, spatial or temporal signals. Thematic vocabulary (e.g. "enlightened," 6:4; 10:32; fire as judgment, 6:8; 10:27; 12:29) does connect 5:11–6:12, 10:32–39, and 12:25–27, but this only demonstrates how 5:11–6:12 anticipate the repetition of exhortation and warning.

Hebrews 6:13–20 is a transition back to the main topic of the high priesthood of Jesus, and not part of the digression.[137] It signals a return to the topic of 5:1–10, the high priesthood according to the order of Melchizedek, and preparation for the full discussion of that subject in 7:1. Thematic vocabulary focuses on God's oath to Abraham that anticipates God's oath to make Jesus a High Priest (6:13, 16, 17; 7:20-1). The introduction of Abraham in 6:12 signals a shift in communication axis, personal references, *dramatis personae*, temporal and spatial signals that set the stage for discussing Abraham's encounter with Melchizedek in Heb 7.

Hebrews 5:11–6:12 is an ethical digression, focusing specifically on the character of the audience rather than Jesus the High Priest.[138] The initial transition is abrupt, while the concluding transition (6:13–20) gradually

---

mirrors the movement of the High Priest going into the temple on the Day of Atonement (P. D. Landgraf, "The Structure of Hebrews: A Word of Exhortation in Light of the Day of Atonement," in R. Bauckham, et. al., eds., *A Cloud of Witnesses: The Theology of Hebrews in its Ancient Contexts* [LNTS 387; London: T & T Clark, 2008], 19–27). He notes the signals of discontinuity in 5:11–6:12, but is reluctant to call it a digression. Instead, he suggests that it replicates a pause for exhortation as the High Priest goes from the Holy Place to the Most Holy Place (Landgraf, 25).

[136] Koester, "Hebrews, Rhetoric, and the Future of Humanity," 113.

[137] With D. deSilva, *Perseverance in Gratitude: A Socio-Rhetorical Commentary on the Epistle "to the Hebrews"* (Grand Rapids, Michigan: Eerdmans), 248; Gelardini, 250–252. Scholars arguing that 5:11-6:20 is a unity include Koester, *Hebrews*, 306–7; Attridge, 156; cf. Guthrie, 110, who at the same time acknowledges that 6:13–20 is different, "another intermediary transition."

[138] Koester, *Hebrews*, 306–7.

leads back to the topic of the high priesthood. The location of the digression is after the beginning of the central section and its thesis about the high priest. This is consistent with Quintilian's advice that a digression occurs wherever it has the greatest emotional impact. The preacher confronts the audience with the consequences of rejecting Christ in order that they may personally fear God's wrath.[139]

Hebrews provides one example of an unarticulated digression in the NT, and there are more candidates. Other passages that have been identified include 1 Cor 2:6–16; 6:1–11; 9:1–27; 10:1–13; 13:1–13; 2 Cor 5:14–6:2; 6:13–7:1; Gal 2:11–14; and Eph 3:2–13.[140] These passages have been subject to the same terminological and methodological problems as Rev 7. As one example, 2 Cor 6:13–7:1 has been called a digression by one scholar and interpolation by another, but has not been analyzed using handbooks and actual speeches.[141]

8. Apocalyptic and Hebrew Literature

Digressions were used by the author of Hebrews, Greek-speaking Jews in Rome (Josephus) and Alexandria (*Aristeas* and 2 Maccabees) and by orators such as Dio in 1st century Asia Minor. The focus on Greek-speaking authors begs the question: Are digressions only a Greek-speaking technique (and Latin by derivation)? Since the Hebrew Bible (and its Greek translations) is of primary relevance to the book of Revelation, are there examples there? Are there any examples in Jewish apocalyptic?

These are difficult questions because few have examined the Hebrew Bible or Jewish Apocalyptic with the awareness that digressions may be a common technique in oral cultures.[142] If there are digressions, they are un-

[139] Perry, "Making Fear Personal"; cf. Koester, *Hebrews*, 318.

[140] See Appendix for a complete list of NT passages that have been identified as digressions. On Gal 2:11–14 (the Antioch episode), see J. D. Hester, "The Rhetorical Structure of Galatians 1:11–2:14," *JBL* 103.2 [1984]: 223–233). On Eph 3:2–13 see T. Gombis, "Ephesians 3:2–13: Pointless Digression, or Epitome of the Triumph of God in Christ?" *Westminster Theological Journal* 66 (2004): 313–23. Also of interest, A. W. F. Blunt identifies a digression in Justin Martyr's *First Apology* §63. A. W. F. Blunt, *The Apologies of Justin Martyr* (Eugene, Oregon: Wipf & Stock, 2006 [1911]), lvii, 94.

[141] Aune, s. v. "Digression," *Westminster Dictionary*, 134.

[142] Along a similar line of thought, Bruce Longenecker's study of chain-link techniques in the Hebrew Bible is pioneering, but I have not found Hebrew Bible scholars that have responded to his analysis.

As noted with Homeric scholarship, the identification of digressions in the Hebrew Bible does not exclude analysis of redaction history or form criticism (cf. O. H. Steck, *Old Testament Exegesis: A Guide to the Methodology* [trans. J. D. Nogalski; SBLRBS 33; Atlanta: Scholars, 1995]; J. Barton, *Reading the Old Testament: Method in Biblical*

articulated and more difficult to detect. What follows suggests the need for additional research. This analysis relies on O. S. Wintermute who calls *Jubilees* 23:9–32 a "digression on Abraham's death"[143] and John J. Collins, who observes that the "schematization of history [in Sibylline Oracle I] is used by the Sibyllist as a framework for exhortation."[144]

Before examining these examples, one may ask if there are digressions in numbered series, as occurs in 2 Maccabees between the death of the sixth and seventh son (2 Macc 7:20–29). Some works of Jewish Apocalyptic are arranged in series of seven, similar to the seals, trumpets and bowls of Revelation, but digressions have not been observed. 4 Ezra is arranged in seven sections, but proceeds in a very orderly fashion from vision to *aporia* to interpretation.[145] 2 Baruch is also arranged in seven sections, but

---

Study [Rev. ed.; Louisville, KY: Westminster John Knox, 1996]; K. Koch, *The Growth of the Biblical Tradition* [trans. S. M. Cupitt; New York: Macmillan, 1988]). Historical rhetorical criticism (as I have conceived it with Relevance Theory) takes the extant text as evidence of communication events within a cognitive environment designed to strengthen or change audiences' behavior, attitude, or values (see Introduction: Methodology). The text may be the result of a complex process of growth, including insertions, reductions, transpositions, and composition. Historical rhetorical criticism may assist analysis of literary layers, for example, by explaining the rhetorical value of inserting material in a particular place. Both rhetorical and redaction critics are interested in "analyzing how the author/editor achieves his effects, why he arranges his material as he does, and above all what devices he uses to give unity and coherence to his work" (Barton, 52).

A detailed discussion of rhetorical criticism of the Hebrew Bible is beyond the scope of the current project, which would need to include a nuanced discussion of the relationship between Greco-Roman rhetorical theory and Hebrew communication patterns. For a foundational study, see G. Kennedy, *Comparative Rhetoric* (New York: Oxford University, 1998) and articles in *Rhetoric before and beyond the Greeks* (eds. C. S. Lipson and R. A. Binkley; Albany, NY: State University New York, 2004). For a discussion of rhetoric and redaction and application of Kennedy's rhetorical method see K. Möller, *A Prophet in Debate: The Rhetoric of Persuasion in the Book of Amos* (JSOTss 372; London: Sheffield, 2003), esp. 1–152. Other resources include D. M. Howard, "Rhetorical Criticism in Old Testament studies," *Bulletin for Biblical Research* 4 (1994): 87–104; Y. Gitay, "Rhetorical Criticism," in *To Each Its Own Meaning: An Introduction to Biblical Criticisms and Their Application* (ed. S. L. McKenzie and S. R. Haynes; Louisville: Westminster John Knox, 1993), 135–149; D. Patrick and A. Scult, *Rhetoric and Biblical Interpretation* (JSOTSup 82; Sheffield: Almond, 1990); D. F. Watson and A. J. Hauser, *Rhetorical Criticism of the Bible: A Comprehensive Bibliography with Notes on History and Method* (Leiden: Brill, 1994), esp. 110–112; C. C. Black, "Keeping up with Recent Studies, pt. 16: Rhetorical Criticism and Biblical Interpretation," *Expository Times* 100.7 (1989): 252–258.

[143] O. S. Wintermute, "Jubilees," in *OTP* 2:35.

[144] J. J. Collins, "The Sybilline Oracles, Books 1 and 2," in *OTP* 1:332–3.

[145] T. W. Willett, *Eschatology in the Theodicies of 2 Baruch and 4 Ezra* (JSPSup 4, Sheffield: JSOT, 1989), 54–65. Gustav Volkmer seems to be the first to argue for a

without interruption.[146] The War Scroll (1QM) found at Qumran depicts seven orders of battle, but without digression. Other apocalyptic works have complex structures, but again without evidence of digressions. 1 Enoch, although structurally complex, completes each series before beginning a new unit.[147] Daniel is complicated by the use of two languages, but it is also free of digressions.[148] Text critical issues make analyzing apocalypses difficult, but it seems most are uninterrupted by digressions,[149] with the exception of *Jub.* 23.9–32 and *Sib. Or.* I.125–282 discussed below.

a) Jubilees *23.9–32: The Future Evil Generation*

The book of *Jubilees* relates what happened to Moses during the forty days he spent on Mount Sinai. A Jew in Palestine most likely wrote it during the middle of the second century BCE, after the Maccabean crisis.[150] It is an example of the "re-written scripture" of the Second Temple Period.[151] *Jubilees* re-shapes the Genesis–Exodus story to appeal to the author's generation to observe the Torah, especially the observance of the sacred calendar (Sabbath and other festivals), purity laws, and circumcision.[152]

Jubilees 23.9–32 is an example of a digression in apocalyptic literature.[153] O. S. Wintermute describes, "the digression at 23:9–32 [is] marked

seven-fold structure in 4 Ezra (*Handbuch der Einleitung in die Apokryphen* [Tübingen: Fues, 1863]).

[146] F. J. Murphy, *Structure and Meaning of Second Baruch* (SBLDS 78, Atlanta: Scholars, 1985), 11–29. Willett, 80–95.

[147] For example, consider the series of ten weeks in the Apocalypse of Weeks, or the seventy weeks of the Animal Apocalypse. Neither series is interrupted. 1 Enoch has five major divisions and two appendices. G. Nickelsburg, *1 Enoch 1: A Commentary on the Book of 1 Enoch, Chapters 1–36; 81–108* (Hermeneia, Minneapolis: Fortress, 2001), 7.

[148] J. J. Collins, *Daniel: A Commentary* (Hermeneia, Minneapolis: Fortress, 1993), 24–25; W. H. Shea, "Further Literary Structures in Daniel 2–7: An Analysis of Daniel 5, and the Broader Relationships Within Chapters 2–7," *Andrews University Seminary Studies* 23.3 (Autumn 1985): 277–295; J. P. Tanner, "The Literary Structure of the Book of Daniel," *Bibliotheca Sacra* 160 (July–Sept 2003) 269–82.

[149] Others include: the five heavens of 3 Baruch, seven visions of Apocalypse of Abraham, and the seven days of creation in Jubilees 1–2.

[150] Wintermute, 44–45; M. Segal, *The Book of Jubilees: Rewritten Bible, Redaction, Ideology and Theology* (Leiden: Brill, 2007); S. W. Crawford, *Rewriting Scripture in Second Temple Times* (Grand Rapids, Mich: Eerdmans, 2008), 61–2; J. C. VanderKam, *The Book of Jubilees* (Sheffield: Sheffield Academic, 2001), 21.

[151] On Jubilees as "rewritten scripture" see Segal; Crawford, esp. 60–83; J. C. VanderKam, *Introduction to Early Judaism* (Grand Rapids, Mich: Eerdmans, 2000), 88–115, esp. 97–100 on Jubilees.

[152] Wintermute, 48; Crawford, 67.

[153] Wintermute, "Jubilees," in *OTP* 2:35; cf. VanderKam, *Jubilees*, 57–9. Crawford, 79, identifies it as an 'interpolation' along with 1.7–18 (future prediction of faithlessness and witnesses), 7.34–38 (future establishing of cities and agriculture) and 15.31–34 (fu-

off...the author looks beyond the time of Moses to describe what happens in the distant future."[154] The previous unit (*Jub.* 11.1–23.8) contains Abraham stories, and the following unit continues in chronological order to consider Jacob (*Jub.* 24.1–45.15). In contrast, *Jub.* 23.9–32 looks beyond the patriarchs and matriarchs to a future evil generation that will receive punishment and to the children who will search the Torah, repent, and receive God's blessings. The transition (*Jub.* 23.9–10) connects the digression to the previous unit by emphasizing the unique righteousness and longevity of Abraham in contrast to the generations to come. These future wicked generations and some especially cruel leaders (*Jub.* 23.23) are the new *dramatis personae* of the digression, not Abraham. Destruction will come on the people before white haired "children" will search the law and repent (*Jub.* 23.26).

Temporal signals mark a shift from the time of Abraham to "future generations" (*Jub.* 23.11) and the general spatial signal of "the land" (*Jub.* 23.18) shifts from the specific location of "the cave of Macnpelah" (*Jub.* 23.7). Thematic vocabulary includes "old age," "evil," "no peace," "plagues," and "wounds," and "pollute." Personal references shift from Sarah, Rebecca, Isaac, Ishmael to the amorphous "evil generation that sins in the land" (*Jub.* 23.14). The communication axis, however, remains unchanged through the digression, although the concluding transition (*Jub.* 23.32) recalls the narrative framework of God speaking to Moses on Mt. Sinai (*Jub.* 1.1).

The digression capitalizes on the emotions generated by the death of Abraham, and his pious example in the presence of evil (*Jub.* 23.10). It sustains and amplifies grief by contrasting Abraham with the wickedness of the future generation. It also amplifies fear by depicting first destruction caused by their wicked ways (*Jub.* 23.13–21) followed by punishment from God (*Jub.* 23.22–25).[155] However, a way out of fear is offered. If the audience imitates the children of the wicked generation by searching the

---

ture failure to observe circumcision). Segal adds 6.32–38 (Future failure to observe 365 day calendar). I also suggest these digression are used systematically in Jubilees. Segal (see esp. 319–322) makes a similar argument for these passages calling them "the redactional layer." These digressions take the original prediction of faithlessness, witnesses, repentance, and restoration in Moses' generation (1.7–25) and project them far beyond the patriarchs and matriarchs to apply to the author's time. Moses is established at the beginning of Jubilees as the type of leader to emulate, who will witness to a wicked generation and intercede on their behalf. The digressions take him as an example in the author's generation. Wintermute (46–48), Crawford (79–80), and Segal (*ad loc*; e.g. 37, 320–1) draw their conclusions about the author's time from these very texts, supporting my thesis that digressions offer a unique window into the rhetorical situation.

[154] Wintermute, 35.

[155] Consistent with Aristotle's advice (*Rhet.* II.5.15). See chapter 3.5 on Emotion.

law and returning to righteousness (*Jub.* 23.26) and then God will bless them (*Jub.* 23.27–31).

For Wintermute, Segal, and Crawford *Jub.* 23.9–32 is central to understanding the purpose of the whole book. "The writer anticipates an age of increased blessings in his own time which will result from renewed loyalty to the Law."[156] Segal affirms the importance of this passage for understanding the book. "As a number of scholars have already noted, the key for dating the book can be found in the apocalypse in *Jub.* 23:9–32."[157] For a book concerned with chronological matters, this interruption of a future time stands out prominently and becomes an interpretive key, suggesting that audiences in the author's time can experience God's blessings by being obedient to the Law as emphasized in *Jubilees* and emulating righteous ancestors such as Abraham. Facing the threat of destruction and punishment, the author of *Jubilees* exhorts the audience to obey the Law. The digression serves to get the audience's attention, address their situation, excite their emotions, and provide characters to emulate.

b) Sibylline Oracles *I.125–282: Noah the Moral Preacher*

The *Sibylline Oracles* are a complex collection of twelve books of oracles (usually numbered 1–8 and 11–14) attributed to pagan prophetesses. Hellenistic Jews produced the core of these documents in imitation of the pagan oracles; Christians heavily redacted them into their present state.[158] *Sib. Or.* III is usually thought to have the oldest and most Jewish core. Buitenwerf argues that it should be located in Asia Minor and dated in the second century BCE.[159] The Jewish core of *Sib. Or.* I/II is the next oldest (now numbered treated as one book even though numbered separately in the first manuscripts discovered). John J. Collins and Paul Trebilco date *Sib. Or.* I/II between 30 BCE and 70 CE and locate it in Asia Minor, specifically in Apamea in Phrygia.[160] Despite its Christian redactions, *Sibyl-*

[156] Wintermute, 38; Cf. Crawford, 80, who underlines how these passsages are discontinuous: "None of these passages of predictive history is tied closely to the Genesis–Exodus narrative."

[157] Segal, 320.

[158] J. L. Lightfoot, *The Sibylline Oracles: With Introduction, Translation and Commentary on the First and Second Books* (Oxford: Oxford University, 2007), vii–viii, cf. 18–23; J. J. Collins, "The Sybilline Oracles, Books 1 and 2," in *OTP* 1:330.

[159] R. Buitenwerf, *Book III of the Sibylline Oracles and its Social Setting: With an Introduction, Translation, and Commentary* (Leiden: Brill, 2003); contra Collins, who argues for Egyptian provenance of the Jewish core (III.97–349 and 489–829) in the early 2nd century BCE. See J. J. Collins, *The Sibylline Oracles of Egyptian Judaism* (Missoula, Mont: SBL, 1974), 21–71.

[160] Collins, "The Sybilline Oracles, Books 1 and 2," 332; P. Trebilco, *Jewish Communities in Asia Minor* (Cambridge: Cambridge University, 1991), 95–96.

line Oracles I/II is critical to understanding Judaism in Asia Minor. Collins concludes, "The Jewish substratum is the only extensive document we have from the Judaism of Asia Minor in this period."[161]

In his recent commentary, J. L. Lightfoot suggests that the length, content and location of *Sib. Or.* I.125–282 sets it apart. This passage is

> remarkable on several grounds. The first is its sheer length, and the prominence the flood receives by virtue of its central placement.... The second is that the flood story receives a local context. The Ark comes to land in Phrygia, at the source of the Marsyas: this locates it at Apamea Kibotos, hinted at by the name in 266...The location of Ararat is startling.[162]

To Lightfoot, the length, topics, and location all signal discontinuity from the surrounding framework of the seven generations in Book I.

An analysis of other delimiting signals further suggests that this passage is a digression. The fifth generation (lines 120–124) is announced predictably as a further degeneration from the first four. Abruptly, Noah is introduced (line 125). Noah is the first and only human named – a new *dramatis persona.* Personal references shift from Giants to "all the peoples" (ἅπαντες, line 129) and "people sated with faithlessness" (ἄνδρες ἀπιστοκόροι, line 150).[163] The communication axis shifts when, for the first time, God speaks to an individual human (compare line 57–58). New thematic vocabulary is introduced: repentance, wooden house, and flood. God commands Noah to preach repentance, and threatens that if humanity does not repent, they will be destroyed.[164] The Noah unit is 157 lines long – more than the first 4 generations combined. The transition from the Noah narrative includes the announcement of the sixth generation and identification of Noah's wife as the author (the Sibyl) and three kings (usually identified as Noah's three sons, although it is not clear).[165] In short, the author of *Sib. Or.* I has interrupted the orderly narration of generations with the Noah narrative. The progressive decline continues then in the seventh generation (line 307). By all these signals, *Sib. Or.* I.125–282 is a digression.

---

161 Collins, "The Sybilline Oracles, Books 1 and 2," 332.

162 Lightfoot, 364–5; also Trebilco.

163 Greek text from Lightfoot.

164 Lightfoot, 376–77, observes that "the Sibyl wastes few words on the insolence of Noah's generation" because the point is its message to her readers. "[T]he Sibyl's emphasis is all on Noah's message, with its elements of moral exhortation, urgent calls for repentance and prophecy. There is a clear change of register between the previous races with their Enochic, giant-like characteristics, and this race, with its urgent ethical message directed at real people."

165 Lightfoot, 380: "It is striking that Noah fades from view so soon after the flood. His importance is exhausted after his warnings of the coming calamity and experience of it."

One may object to identifying *Sib. Or.* I.125–282 as a digression for two reasons. First, there is no temporal shift. The Noah narrative is in chronological order in the fifth generation, preceding the sixth. Second, the plot of the Noah narrative (saving a righteous few and cleansing the wicked world by flood) is necessary to understand the emergence of the "golden" sixth generation.

However, amplifying digressions in theory may lack temporal shifts but exceed the length and detail necessary for the argument.[166] In practice this is borne out. Aristeas gives every question and answer during the 72 days of symposia, which does not introduce a temporal shift but goes far beyond what was necessary. Pliny's description of his house in Tuscany did not involve a temporal shift and was one of his main points in the letter to his friend, yet he apologizes and explains this digression.[167]

Therefore, *Sib. Or.* I.125–282 is both an amplifying and ethical digression. It amplifies the cleansing of the world that makes the golden sixth generation possible and exhorts the contemporary audience to moral behavior through Noah's preaching.[168] J. Collins concludes that the Noah narrative indicates the primary function of the Jewish core, and that the framework of the generations has been shaped to serve the rhetorical goals expressed in the Noah narrative.

> The schematization of history is used by the Sybillist as a framework for exhortation. The impending destruction of the world provides an occasion for presenting he crucial ethical values on which the judgment is based. So in *Sibylline Oracles* I.150–70 and again in 174–98 Noah preaches to his contemporaries about the sins which lead to destruction and the way to avoid it.[169]

As I am arguing is true of many digressions, the Noah narrative offers unique insight into the rhetorical strategy and goals of the whole book. Trebilco makes the point forcefully.

> The whole structure of I.1–282 was designed to give weight and urgency to the thrust of Noah's preaching. The five generations build up to the judgment, with the imminence of the flood providing the occasion for presenting these crucial ethical values. Judging by the structure of the first half of the Jewish substratum, the message of Noah's preaching was a vital reason for the book's composition....Noah is a 'preacher of repentance' be-

---

[166] See chapter 3.4, summarizing ancient rhetoricians' advice on digressions.

[167] Pliny, *Epist.* 5.6.43.

[168] Trebilco, 98: "We see, therefore, that the work is basically hortatory and attempts to discourage the sins which lead to condemnation and to encourage the behaviour of which the author approves."

[169] J. J. Collins, "The Sybilline Oracles, Books 1 and 2," in *OTP* 1:332–333; similarily Lightfoot, 376–7.

cause the book mirrors the situation in Apamea. It is hard to see any other explanation for such long, detailed and unique sermons.[170]

In summary, *Jub.* 23.9–32 and *Sib. Or.* I.125–282 are examples of digressions in Jewish apocalyptic literature. Each of these passages signals discontinuity with the unit preceding it and, to a lesser extent, continuity as well. Each locates the digression within the structure to maximize its impact on the audience. Each offers concentrated insight into the rhetorical situation that the book seeks to address. Each portrays characters to imitate in order to avoid destruction, and therefore function as ethical digressions. Although it is not clear that either *Jubilees* or *Sib. Or.* I/II is relevant in the technical sense to Rev 7:1–17 and 10:1–11:13, these characteristics suggest that they share a common understanding of how digressions may be used to move an audience.

c) Exodus 12:1–28

Two units in the Hebrew Bible (Exod 12:1–28 and Zech 2:6–13) are digressions as defined in chapter 3, both of which are relevant (in the technical sense) to hearers of the book of Revelation.[171] The first is the Passover narrative (Exod 12:1–28), which Martin Noth argues is "a primary and independent element," U. Cassuto calls "an interval," John I. Durham "an intrusion," and Cornelis Houtman a "digression."[172]

Moreover, the Passover narrative, which occurs before the last plague in Exodus, may be a model for Rev 7:1–17 and 10:1–11:13 occurring before the last seal and trumpet. As discussed in chapter 2, the plague narrative (Exodus 7–12) is a part of the mutual cognitive environment assumed by the book of Revelation. However, rather than the ten-fold series in Exodus, John seems to have used a seven-fold tradition of plagues similar to that preserved in Psalm 78 and 105 as a model for the series of seven seals,

---

[170] Trebilco, 98.

[171] As discussed in the Introduction, relevance in the technical sense means that an external text or context that can be accessed with minimal processing effort by the audience with significant contextual effects.

[172] M. Noth, *Exodus: A Commentary* (trans. John Bowden, London: SCM Press, 1962), 88; U. Cassuto, *A Commentary on the Book of Exodus* (trans. I. Abrahams; Jerusalem: Magnes, 1967), 136; J. I. Durham, *Exodus* (WBC 3; Waco, Texas: Word, 1987), 152; C. Houtman, *Exodus* (trans. J. Rebel and S. Woudstra; 4 vols; Kampen: Kok, 1993–2002), 2:141. Cf. T. Fretheim, *Exodus* (Interpretation; Louisville: John Knox, 1991), 132–136; G. W. Coats, *Exodus 1–18* (FOTL 2a; Grand Rapids, Mich.: Eerdmans, 1998), 79–89. On scholars' agreement that both Passover and Feast of Unleavened Bread were independent traditions from the plague narrative, also see B. S. Childs, *Exodus: A Commentary* (London: SCM Press, 1974), 186–187.

trumpets, and bowls.[173] Both Exodus and Revelation have passages that interrupt a series of destructive events before the last element, and I argue below that there are significant contextual effects for audiences who are aware of this connection.

The instructions for the Passover meal (Exod 12:1–13, 21–28) and Feast of Unleavened Bread (Exod 12:14–20) interrupt the sequence of the plagues and exodus from Egypt (Exod 11:1–12:42).[174] The last plague is announced to Moses in Exod 11:1 while he is still speaking to Pharaoh (note the last spatial signal is in Exod 10:23, "Then Pharaoh summoned Moses").[175] Moses warns Pharaoh of the last plague before he departs (Exod 11:4–8). Next, God informs Moses that Pharaoh will not listen. In other sequences, such as the plague of locusts (Exod 10:1–20), the plague immediately follows the announcement. Instead, the *concluding* formula is used: "the LORD hardened Pharaoh's heart, and he did not let the people of Israel go out of his land" (Exod 11:10; compare 10:20).[176] In an *inclusio* around the Passover narrative, the fulfillment of the last plague (A': Exod 12:29–32) is marked by almost verbatim phrasing of Moses' prediction (A:

---

[173] D. Aune, *Revelation* (3 vols; Waco, Texas: Word, 1997–8), 2:502–6. M. Greenberg argues that the redactor of the Exodus plagues overlapped two seven-fold versions of the plagues ("The Redaction of the Plague Narrative in Exodus," in *Near Eastern Studies in Honor of William Foxwell Albright* (ed. Hans Goedicke; Baltimore: Johns Hopkins, 1971), 243–252. Perhaps John is replicating two seven-fold plague series by having the bowl plagues overlap with the trumpet plagues. On the two seven-fold plague traditions in Exodus, see also W. Johnstone, "The Two Theological Versions of the Passover Pericope in Exodus," in *Text as Pretext: Essays in Honour of Robert Davidson* (ed. R. P. Carroll; JSOTss 138; Sheffield: Sheffield Academic, 1992), 160–178. On the seven-fold plague series in Ps 78 and 105, see J. M. Leonard, "Identifying Inner-Biblical Allusions: Psalm 78 as a Test Case," *JBL* 127.2 (2008): 241–265; A. F. Campbell, "Psalm 78: A Contribution to the Theology of Tenth Century Israel," *CBQ* 41.1 (1979): 51–79; cf. Houtman, 17–21.

[174] Further instructions about the Passover, Festival, and consecration of the firstborn interrupt the escape from Egypt (12:43–13:16). Some interpreters have seen these as "appendices" (e.g. Cassuto), but Childs argues that the structure disrupts the pattern to call future generations to "an ongoing experiential appropriation from the heart in response to what God has done" (204, cf. 202–204). Although a full analysis is necessary, this tentative conclusion supports the argument that the digressions in Exodus directly address the contemporary audience and seek to relate their experience with the characters in the surrounding historical narrative and imitate these characters. Fretheim suggests this point when he argues that the alternating structure of story and ritual is the hermeneutical key to the structure of Exod 12:29–15:21 (*Exodus*, 133–4).

[175] With Childs, 133 (cf. 161), *pace* Noth, who argues that 11:4–8 is a speech to Israel. On the difficulty of delimiting the plagues and especially 11:1–10, see B. Lemmelijn, "Setting and Function of Exod 11, 1–10 in the Exodus Narrative," in *Studies in the Book of Exodus: Redaction – Reception – Interpretation* (ed. M. Vervenne; Leuven: Leuven University Press, 1996), 443–460.

[176] Childs, 132.

Exod 11:4–6). The command to celebrate the Passover sacrifice and feast of unleavened bread intervenes (B: Exod 12:1–28) before the plague is fulfilled, so that Exod 11:4–12:32 has an A-B-A' pattern.[177] As William H. C. Propp writes, the "paschal legislation severely disrupts narrative chronology."[178]

Houtman and Cassuto describe other signals of discontinuity. The length and content of Exod 12:1–28 lead Houtman to call it a digression.

> The crushing blow to Pharoah is imminent (11:1). Mindful that YHWH himself will soon directly intervene, the reader eagerly anticipates the events to come. But again, for the umpteenth time, the writer keeps him in suspense....Meticulously it is laid out how the people are to celebrate the Passover and the feast of the unleavened bread (= Matzoth). At first the wordiness is unsettling to the reader. The digression comes across to him as postponement, delay of the deliverance, and anxiously he wonders whether stalling is not tantamount to shelving. But gradually it dawns on him that the celebration of Passover and Matzoth are a necessary component of the departure.[179]

Houtman emphasizes the length of Exod 12:1–28 and the effect of delay on the audience. Cassuto summarizes other signals of discontinuity.

> After the completion of the preceding section there is an interval, which is followed, as stated, by a transformation in the character of the narration; the story changes its aspect, assuming a new form. Pharaoh is forgotten, and so are his servants; Pharaoh's palace and the entire environment in which we found ourselves throughout the whole of the preceding section disappears, as it were, from our sight. The epic now has its center in the midst of the people of Israel, and the commands given to Moses and Aaron are directed towards the Israelites. What has to be done vis-à-vis Pharaoh, the Lord will do. Moses and Aaron must concern themselves only with their people.[180]

Discontinuity is signaled by shifts in communication axis, personal references, *dramatis personae*, temporal and spatial signals, and thematic vocabulary. As Cassuto observed, the communication axis shifts from God to Moses to Moses to the "elders of Israel" (Exod 12:21; a phrase which had not been used since Moses' call in Exod 3:16–18). Pronouns shift from the third person to second person imperatives, e.g. "Your lamb" (Exod 12:5). Previously, Pharaoh was the recipient of God's words mediated by Moses (e.g. Exod 10:25). In Exod 12:1–28, Pharaoh has no role and the "whole congregation of Israel" (a unique phrase found in Exodus only here, 12:3, and 12:47; cf. 12:6) is now addressed as the *dramatis personae* receiving the Lord's words. The temporal axis shifts between instructions for future Passover sacrifices and feasts in the promised land (Exod 12:2–11, 14–20,

---

[177] To Childs, 161, this gives the impression that "the slaying of the first-born is both the culmination of the plague narrative and the beginning of the Passover tradition."

[178] W. H. C. Propp, *Exodus 1–18* (Anchor Bible, New York: Doubleday, 1998), 382.

[179] Houtman, 141.

[180] Cassuto, 136.

24–27) and the specific night of the plague ("that night," 12:12–14, 21–23). The spatial signals follow a similar pattern, alternating between "in Egypt" (Exod 12:1, 12–14, 21–23) and in the "land that the Lord will give you" (ambiguous in Exod 12:1–11, specific in 12:19–20, 25). Thematic vocabulary shifts to concerns of the calendar, sacrifice of a lamb or goat, and unleavened bread. Any continuity with the surrounding plague narrative is suggested by references to Egypt, the plague and firstborn humans and animals (Exod 12:12–13, 17, 23, 27). Lastly, the narrative can be read coherently by skipping from Exod 11:10 to 12:29. By all criteria, Exodus 12:1–28 is properly called a digression.[181]

Martin Noth argues that the Passover narrative was originally independent, and was placed here before the final plague as the climax and focus of the entire plague narrative.[182] While it may have been originally independent, Noth's observation about the point of the plague narrative has bearing on how we understand Exodus 12:1–28 functioning as a digression. He argues that the plagues have no real point because they end with Moses leaving Pharaoh in the same situation that they began (Exod 11:9). To Noth, the only point of the plagues is to prepare for the Passover Narrative.[183]

In other words, the plagues build suspense and provide evidence of God's protection and power, but the Passover narrative is more important to the audience. At the beginning of the plague sequence, God implies that the plagues may lead to Israel's freedom (Exod 7:4), and each plague builds suspense as they fail to achieve that goal.[184] As the narrative progresses, Israel is protected from the effects of the plagues, but it is clear by the conclusion in Exod 11:9 that they will not be freed by these "signs and wonders" even if the plagues add to God's honor (and Moses' honor as God's agent, cf. Exod 11:3).[185] The author has skillfully brought the audi-

---

[181] Childs, 143, allows but minimizes the possibility that oral patterning explains the structure of the plagues. When discussing the Passover narrative, however, he says it "took shape in an oral stage" (p. 194).

[182] Noth follows Pedersen ("Passahfest und Passahlegende") in arguing that the Plagues are secondary to the Passover narrative. See discussion in Childs, 190–192. Childs, 194, agrees that "The P account reflects a period in which the Passover had assumed a new importance." Cf. Coats, 85–6; Fretheim, 133.

[183] Cf. Fretheim (*Exodus*, 136): "The break provides a hermeneutic for interpreting the entire narrative."

[184] Childs, 135; Cf. Fretheim, 135–6.

[185] Childs, 144–149, discusses Buber's theory that the structure of the plague narratives is shaped by a typological struggle between a prophet and a king. Although he ultimately rejects the details of Buber's proposal, he affirms that a prophetic legend is a secondary influence on the structure of the plagues. (The hardness of Pharaoh's heart is the primary motif for Childs.) He argues that Moses' role is as prophet to speak God's word to the king and to demonstrate divine power. This dual role is mirrored especially by John and the two witnesses in Rev 10–11. (See esp. Childs, 146.)

ence to an impasse: how will Israel be freed?[186] At the end of Exod 10, the plagues have not lead to freedom and the tension is at its highest point. B. Lemmelijn puts it this way:

> At this point the reader is disappointed. He gives up hope. All the plagues, which YHWH sent upon Egypt to free his people, were without result. Israel still has not been liberated and Pharaoh continues to be stubborn. Moses, YHWH's mediator is threatened with death. What hope is left, if even YHWH does not succeed?[187]

The first nine plagues do not change Pharaoh and do not lead to the liberation of the people of God. The Passover narrative interrupts the last plague, which suggests that even the last plague is insufficient to lead to freedom. I will return to this point later for its significance to understand the book of Revelation.

The structure of the Passover narrative itself shapes the ethos of the audience by blending past and future observances of the feast. The structure of Exodus 12:1–28 juxtaposes the past *dramatis personae* with the contemporary audience. This passage has an a-b-c-b'-a' pattern with the festival of unleavened bread in the central position.[188]

a:	12:1–11	Instructions for the Passover sacrifice (delimited by "The Lord said...," "This month...," and "This is the Passover of the Lord") –General Future, spatial signals ambiguous
b:	12:12–13	Announcement of last plague (cf. 11:4–6) – Specific future, spatial signals = Egypt
c:	12:14–20	Instructions for Feast of Unleavened Bread (delimited by "This day...," and next unit "Then Moses...") – General future, spatial signals "in land" and "settlements" (12:19–20)
b':	12:21–23	Moses speaking to elders – past, with specific future in direct discourse, Egyptians
a':	12:24–27a	Instructions for children regarding Passover sacrifice – general future, spatial signals = "land that LORD will give you" (12:25)
	12:27b–28	Obedient response of the people/Transition

The structure juxtaposes the instructions for the first Passover and feast of Unleavened Bread with the activities of the audience in the promised land.

[186] See Childs, 135–137, on the author's composition skill.

[187] Lemmelijn, 449; cf. Houtman, 141.

[188] Following Noth, 92–93. He is concerned about sources more than literary structure. Childs, 196–197, segments the text into 12:1–13, 14–20, 21–27a and 27b–28, but stresses that 12:1–20 is a coherent whole. His detailed analysis, however, confirms the structure above: the definite article in 12:21 corresponds to 12:11, so that 12:21–23 represents the event announced in 12:12–13. Following Moses words, Childs notes that "the narrative momentarily pauses" in 12:24 turning "briefly from the historical setting into a parenetic style" answering the question "How does Israel transmit its faith to the next generation?" (p. 200).

It creates the sense that the contemporary audience is joined with the first audience for Moses' instructions.[189]

Because this structure is embedded in the last plague, Israel and the contemporary audience's identity and activity are central in a way missing from the previous plagues. They must take action to be spared from destruction.[190] Houtman writes, "the Passover celebration is necessary to shield Israel from the impending plague (12:12f., 23) and that the eating of unleaven bread is the necessary bridge towards a new existence."[191] The required action is cultic; they must sacrifice a lamb or goat and put its blood on the lintel of their doorpost. Future generations will practice this explicitly to remember protection from this last plague (Exod 12:27). The Feast of Unleavened bread is subtly different. It is the remembrance of liberation from Egypt (Exod 12:17) without reference to the last plague.[192] In the Feast of Unleavened bread identity construction is made explicit when it instructs that people will be "cut off from the congregation" if they eat leavened bread (Exod 12:19). By joining these two observances, the digression joins Israel's identity to protection from God's wrath and to liberation from slavery.[193]

The memory of fear of God's wrath and slavery is evoked, but to what extent does this apply to the contemporary audience? Noth argued that the audience of Exodus lived in a peaceful, settled time.[194] If they are an established cultic community, a purpose of blending of historical recollections and cultic instructions may be to evoke fear of God's future wrath and to motivate annual observance so no plague will destroy them. In this way, the plagues have a contemporary function, reminding the audience of God's power to inflict devastation as well to save.[195] The plagues cumulatively evoke fear and awe, one on top of another. God is shown as mighty and capable of inflicting terrible suffering. It is great motivation to obey the ordinances of the Passover and Feast of Unleavened Bread, which contain the hint that the last plague may apply to them if they do not obey. "[W]hen I see the blood, I will pass over you, and no plague shall destroy you" (Exod 12:13). Likewise, the threat against those who eat leavened bread evokes fear of loss of communal identity. "[W]hoever eats what is

---

[189] With Childs, 198: "For this biblical narrator the historical distinction between earlier and later Passovers was lost." Cf. Coats, 82–3; Fretheim, 136.

[190] So Cassuto, 138; Noth, 88.

[191] Houtman, 141.

[192] Noth, 89.

[193] Durham, 155; Coats, 88–9; Fretheim, 135–6.

[194] Noth, 94.

[195] This is the use of the plague tradition in Ps 78:40–53 (see n. 173 above). Also, Deut 28:60: "[God] will bring back upon you all the diseases of Egypt of which you were in dread…"

leavened shall be cut off from the congregation of Israel" (Exod 12:19). Although the primary focus is cultic instructions, their importance is underlined by bringing old fears into the present. Evoking these fears, the digression also show how these threats can be avoided and gives examples of leaders and people who obey.

This digression is a unique window into the rhetorical strategy and goals of the author, in this case elevating the significance of the Passover traditions and connecting them to the Plague narrative and liberation from slavery. For Noth, the plague narrative is "directed exclusively towards the account of the Passover night and makes no sense without it."[196] The plagues demonstrate the "signs and wonders" of God (Exod 7:3, 11:9 in an *inclusio* around the plague narrative).[197] "This situation leads us to the conclusion that the account of the Passover night occupies a primary place in the tradition in comparison with the plague narrative."[198]

The digression is more important to the contemporary audience than the surrounding narrative.[199] The plagues are important as reminders of God's "signs and wonders," but it is the Passover sacrifice and Feast of Unleavened Bread that become determinative of Israel's identity for the audience.[200] Durham concludes,

> The point of the connection [between the festivals and the exodus deliverance], and the reason for the insertion, is the provision of authoritative and didactic means of bringing

---

[196] Noth, 68. Childs, 191 (following Fohrer) contests Noth's analysis of the tradition history arguing that Ex 12:21–24 lacks a reference to the first-born, and thus confirming the independence of the Passover narrative. While this is true for the tradition history, this does not affect Noth's point that in its final form, the Passover narrative has become the focus and the plagues secondary.

[197] So Childs, 132, cf. 161–2; Durham 149; Lemmelijn, 454; W. H. Schmidt, "Die Intention der beiden Plagenerzählungen (Exodus 7–10) in ihrem Kontext," in *Studies in the Book of Exodus: Redaction – Reception – Interpretation* (ed. Marc Vervenne; Leuven: University Press, 1996), 240–1.

[198] Noth, 69.

[199] On the primary significance of the Passover narrative for forming identity, see Walter Brueggemann, "Passion and perspective: Two dimensions of education in the Bible," *Theology Today* 42.2 (July 1985): 172–180; Dianne Bergant, "An Anthropological Approach to Biblical Interpretation: The Passover Supper in Exodus 12:1–20 as a Case Study," *Semeia* 67 (1994): 43–62; cf. Fretheim, 133, 136; Houtman, 144–5.

[200] Durham, 153, writes that it insists upon "Yahweh's Passover as a commemoration of Israel's beginning as a people freed by Yahweh." Noth, 94, says that the situation envisaged is "peaceful times in a cultivated land and takes scant consideration of the critical situation in Israel immediately before the Exodus." Durham, 153, writes that it insists upon "Yahweh's Passover as a commemoration of Israel's beginning as a people freed by Yahweh." For the first time in the Hebrew Bible, the word 'congregation' (עדה) is used to describe Israel as a cultic community (12:3).

the exodus deliverance into the experience of Israel of the generations beyond settlement and the unified monarchy.[201]

Durham comments on the didactic language of 12:24–27, "Quite simply, it amounts to an attempt to make the past present, to teach through a repetition that aims to create experience rather than simply transmit information."[202]

Exodus 12 is specifically relevant to Rev 7 and 10–11. In general, Exodus provides primary motifs of Revelation, including theophany language, God's people as "kingdom and priesthood," the slaughtered lamb, and the plagues.[203] Specifically, the Seer has adapted the series of plagues in Exod 7–11 into the events following the seven trumpets and the seven bowls of plagues.[204] Protection, persecution, and vindication are also common themes. In Exod 12 and Rev 7 and 10–11, God's people are protected from divine agents and vindicated after persecution and oppression.

The placement of the Passover narrative within the plague structure is the most striking result of this analysis. First, the audience expects the last element in the series but receives a digression instead. The last plague is announced before the Passover narrative (Exod 11:1–9) but not enacted until after it (Exod 12:29). Likewise, the audience expects the seventh seal and trumpet but receives Rev 7:1–17 and 10:1–11:13 instead. Second, Rev 7 and 10–11 occupy a position before the final element of the series, just as the Passover narrative occurs before the final plague that leads to Israel's release. Structurally, Rev 7:1–17 and 10:1–11:13 occupy the same position in the seals and trumpets as the Passover narrative does in the plague narrative.

Another result of this analysis is recognition that plagues do not lead to liberation or oppressor's hearts being changed. Noth, Lemmelijn, and others emphasize that the first nine plagues did not lead to liberation. Likewise, the first six trumpet plagues in Revelation did not lead to repentance (Rev 9:20–21), but the faithful testimony of the two witnesses and their vindication led to the rest of the Great City giving glory to God (Rev 11:7–13). With the Exodus plague narratives in mind, audiences of Revelation may know that plagues alone will not change hearts or lead to liberation.

There are, of course, significant differences between Rev 7 and Exod 12. God's people are asked to make no sacrifice for protection in Rev 7. They are protected by a seal on their foreheads (a la Ezek 9), not blood on the lintel. The Lamb's blood is shed apart from their actions, which has

---

201 Durham, 159–160.

202 Durham, 163.

203 See *ad loc* Charles, Schüssler Fiorenza, Beale, Pattemore, Aune, Richard, etc.

204 See note 173 above and Childs, 163, who suggests that they are mediated through Enochic traditions.

bought them out of slavery (Rev 5:9) without their effort. They have washed their robes in its blood assuring their place before the throne. They go through a "great tribulation" and not departure from Egypt. They do sing hymns of victory (a la Exod 15), but it is not after passing through the sea and escaping from Pharaoh's army. Most notably, neither Rev 7 nor 10–11 contain any instructions for sacrifice or celebrating a feast.[205]

Revelation 10–11 and Exod 12 also have few similarities and many differences in content. On one hand, the two witnesses are modeled to some extent on Moses' role as prophet, speaking God's word and demonstrating divine power (Rev 11:3–6). On the other, they do not explicitly speak to kings as Moses and Aaron spoke to Pharaoh, but John is told to accept this dramatic role (Rev 10:11). Rev 10–11 does not evoke fear of God's wrath, but it evokes fear of the nations that will trample the court around the temple (Rev 11:1–2), of the beast that will kill the two witnesses, and of the inhabitants of the earth that will celebrate their death. The content of Exod 12 is only loosely related to Rev 7 and 12.

In summary, Exodus 12:1–28 is a digression with characteristics that suggest it may have been a model for the structure, themes, and function of Rev 7:1–17 and 10:1–11:13. The Passover narrative occurs before the last element of the series of plagues.[206] It presents the themes of protection from divine destruction and vindication after coming out of persecution. In contrast to the preceding narrative, it addresses the contemporary audience's situation and constructs their ethos as the people of God by providing characters for the audience to imitate. It evokes confidence and fear to persuade the audience to follow the instructions.

d) Zechariah 2:6–13 (2:10–17 Heb)

Zechariah is a 6th century prophet in Judah (often paired with Haggai) who announced the restoration of the Temple under the high priest Joshua and governor Zerubbabel. As discussed in chapter 2, Zechariah is a part of the mutual cognitive environment assumed by the book of Revelation. Interpreters have detected allusions to Zechariah throughout Revelation, including Rev 7 and 10–11. Marko Jauhiainen's investigation of these allusions, *The Use of Zechariah in Revelation*, is a primary resource here.[207]

---

[205] Håkan Ulfgard (*Feast and Future: Revelation 7:9–17 and the Feast of Tabernacles* [Stockholm: Almqvist & Wiksell, 1989]) argues that Rev 7:9–17 is modeled after the Feast of Tabernacles. See discussion and critique in Pattemore, Beale, and Aune.

[206] The parallel of plagues fits the series of trumpets and bowls better than the seals, which seem less like Exodus plagues than announcements of disasters. Nonetheless, the deviation before the last element fits.

[207] Marko Jauhiainen, *The Use of Zechariah in Revelation* (WUNT 2.199; Tübingen: Mohr Siebeck, 2005).

Of special interest is Zechariah 1:7–6:8, a series of eight unnumbered visions.[208] The prophet experiences dream visions (1:8) that are introduced by vision formulas (e.g. "I saw," "I looked up and saw," "then he showed me") and interpreted by an angel.[209]

Zechariah 2:6–13 (2:10–17 Heb) is a digression in this series of eight visions.[210] Jauhiainen calls it an 'oracular supplement.'[211] Mike Butterworth supports this conclusion when he concludes his structural analysis by remarking that Zech 2:6–13 is "marked off from the preceding section not only by its opening *hôy* but, more surely, by the difference in form and content."[212] Similar to Revelation 7:1–17 and 10:1–11:13, Zech 2:6–13 been labeled with many terms. Butterworth calls it an 'exhortation and promise' and 'supplement.'[213] Meyers and Meyers use the term 'expansion.'[214] The New Revised Standard Version gives this unit the superscription 'an interlude.' Given these diverse titles, Zech 2:6–13 is a deviation as defined in chapter 1.

Analysis of delimiting signals demonstrates the discontinuity and continuity of Zech 2:6–13 with its surrounding units. The previous vision (the third) is of a man with a measuring line and two angels (Zech 2:1–5). The unit is introduced by the formula "I looked up and saw" and concluded by the change in vocabulary, personal references, communication axis, and spatial references in Zech 2:6. The fourth vision shows the high priest

---

[208] C. L. Meyers and E. M. Meyers, *Haggai, Zechariah 1–8* (AB 25B; Garden City, NJ: Doubleday, 1987), liv. M. Butterworth, *Structure and the Book of Zechariah* (JSOTss 130; Sheffield: Sheffield Academic, 1992), 62–70. Edgar W. Conrad suggests that we call them 'seeing-sayings' since they are never described using the word for 'visions.' The text helps the reader/hearer to see the world through the prophet's eyes. Nonetheless, to avoid introducing new jargon, even if slightly more accurate, I will continue to use 'visions' with Conrad's sense. E. W. Conrad, *Zechariah* (Sheffield: Sheffield Academic, 1999), 19; cf. 58.

[209] See Meyers and Meyers, lvii, for a helpful chart of the distribution of formulaic language in these visions. Conrad, 59–62, argues that מלאך should be translated 'messenger' not angel, because these are not heavenly beings but prophets such as Haggai that appear in a new guise (cf. Haggai 1:13). A messenger's presence is tantamount to divine presence, which evokes fear. "The point is that messengers appear in the world of human beings, are involved in human activities, and are often indistinguishable from human beings themselves" (61). Two way communication happens between the LORD and people through the messengers, which is distinguished from the one way communication of prophetic announcements (66).

[210] Verse numbers for the remainder of this section are given according to the English version of Zechariah.

[211] Jauhiainen, 44.

[212] Butterworth, 65.

[213] Butterworth, 65, 110.

[214] Meyers and Meyers, lix.

Joshua reclothed and commissioned (Zech 3:1–10).[215] The common thread throughout these units is Jerusalem: the direction to Jerusalem (Zech 2:2, 7) and the choice of Jerusalem (Zech 2:12; 3:2). Throughout, Zechariah sees visions of restoration of Jerusalem and the temple.

The discontinuity in signals from Zech 2:1–5 to Zech 2:6–13 demonstrate it is a digression, despite the continuity of orientation towards Jerusalem and its restoration.

(Zech 2:3–5 NRSV) Then the angel who talked with me came forward, and another angel came forward to meet him, and said to him, "Run, say to that young man: Jerusalem shall be inhabited like villages without walls, because of the multitude of people and animals in it. For I will be a wall of fire all around it, says the LORD, and I will be the glory within it."

(Zech 2:6 NRSV) Up, up! Flee from the land of the north, says the LORD; for I have spread you abroad like the four winds of heaven, says the LORD.

The most striking is the shift in *dramatis personae*. In v. 6, the prophetic interjection הוי (NRSV translates as "up") is followed by the plural imperative "Flee!"[216] In v. 6 it is unclear who is being commanded to flee. In v. 4, the first angel commands the second angel to "Run" and "say." The ambiguous second-person plural is then clarified in v. 7 as "you that dwell with daughter Babylon" is commanded to escape.[217]

(Zech 2:7–13 NRSV) Up! Escape to Zion, you that live with daughter Babylon. For thus said the LORD of hosts (after his glory sent me) regarding the nations that plundered you: Truly, one who touches you touches the apple of my eye. See now, I am going to raise my hand against them, and they shall become plunder for their own slaves. Then you will know that the LORD of hosts has sent me.

Sing and rejoice, O daughter Zion! For lo, I will come and dwell in your midst, says the LORD. Many nations shall join themselves to the LORD on that day, and shall be my people; and I will dwell in your midst. And you shall know that the LORD of hosts has sent me to you.

The LORD will inherit Judah as his portion in the holy land, and will again choose Jerusalem. Be silent, all people, before the LORD; for he has roused himself from his holy dwelling.

---

[215] Butterworth calls it 'exhortation and promise' (65) and then 'a supplement' (110). Meyers and Meyers, lix, use the term 'expansion.' They also identify other passages in Zechariah: Zech 3:8–10 is a 'supplementary oracle' and 4:6b–10a is a 'Zerubbabel insertion' and an oracular insertion into the final crowning scene (6:9–15). As I have been arguing for the term 'digression,' they argue that 'expansion,' 'supplement,' and 'insertion' are paradoxically integral to the narrative. They describe these textual units as simultaneously amplifying themes and incorporating features of the surrounding visions. These sound similar to what we have called systematic amplifying digressions. Further research on these other passages would be necessary to see if they fit the criteria for a digression described here.

[216] See Meyers and Meyers, 162, on the use of הוי in these verses as a call to attention.

[217] "Escape" and "you that dwell" are both singular in Heb, plural in LXX.

The speaker of the command to flee must be God. The "I" who spread them abroad in v. 6 is the LORD, the same "I" who will be a wall of fire and glory for Jerusalem (v. 5). The effect is a blurring in v. 5 between the angel speaking and God speaking. In v. 5, the angel's identity fades and it is the LORD who is speaking. By v. 6, the LORD is addressing the exilic community, not a messenger running to Jerusalem. Verse 5 thus functions as a transition between the vision and the digression.

As I have noted for other digressions, this one directly addresses the audience. The communication axis shifts so that God is directly speaking to the exilic community through the mouth of the prophet.[218] E. Conrad observes that Zechariah's words and the word of the Lord converge in Zech 2:6–11, suggesting that the presence of the messenger is "tantamount to divine presence."[219] This convergence is most evident in the switching of 1st person referents in v. 9 from God ("I am going to raise my hand") to Zechariah ("Then you will know the LORD of hosts has sent me").[220] By conflating Zechariah's voice with the LORD's and allowing Zechariah's distinct voice to interrupt God in v. 8 and 9, the digression legitimates Zechariah's visions and role as the messenger of God.[221]

This is an amplifying digression, although the role of Zechariah suggests a subtle construction of ethos. The motif of "running to Jerusalem" (v. 4) is amplified and transformed into a call for the exiles to leave "Babylon" (used symbolically since Zechariah is explicitly speaking during Persian rule).[222] The structure of the digression reveals that it is amplifying the themes of the preceding three visions.[223]

2:6–7	Flee Babylon to Zion	2:1–5	Run to Jerusalem
2:8–9	Nations will be plundered	1:18–21	God will strike horns of nations
2:10–13	Lord dwells, chooses Jerus.	1:7–17	Lord dwells, chooses Jerusalem

The key difference between the digression and the visions is the direct address of the audience. God speaks directly to the exiles (via Zechariah), and in this way fulfills the command to Zechariah to proclaim the message

[218] Conrad, 80; Butterworth, 65.

[219] Conrad, 43.

[220] See also the 'prophetic interjection' (Meyers and Meyers' term) in v. 8, "after his glory sent me." Conrad 82–83.

[221] Conrad, 80.

[222] Meyers and Meyers, 164.

[223] As argued by Meyers and Meyers, 162–163. Conrad, 81, associates "those spread abroad" with the four horns that scattered the people of Judah. This confirms Meyers and Meyers' argument that 2:6–13 amplifies themes of the first three visions, but undermines the neat inclusio described in this table. Conrad, 83, agrees that God's raised hand connects with striking the nations in the second vision (1:21).

(1:14, 17). The digression promotes Zechariah's character as an obedient messenger even while it amplifies key themes.[224]

Emotion plays a role in the digression, especially confidence, benevolence and shame, but differently than the digressions studied above. Other digressions have occurred at a point of high emotion, sustaining and focusing it on the author's rhetorical goals. It is not clear that this digression is preceded by any attempt to arouse emotion.

Zechariah 2:6–13 is designed to evoke confidence in the LORD and in Zechariah as God's messenger. It begins with the emphatic interjection הוי, which usually indicates lament, but here seems to call the audience to attention.[225] The audience is assured that whoever "touches" them, touches God's eye (v. 9) and that their plunderers will be plundered. Confidence in God's great power mitigates any fear of foreign oppressors. Benevolence is evoked by God's service to the exiles in their time of need.[226] God's sovereignty – and the audience's honor – will be recognized by the nations as they "join themselves to the Lord" (Zech 2:11).[227] If there is any shame or fear, these exhortations and promises lead to confidence and honor. The final exhortation to silence before the LORD (Zech 2:13) brings these emotions to a climax and prepares for the introduction of Joshua, the first named *dramatis personae* since Zech 1:7.[228]

These emotions add force to the sequence of imperatives that urge the audience from exile into a visionary temple. The sequence of "flee" and "escape" evoke fear of the nations while in exile (v. 6–7), "Sing" and "rejoice" (v. 10) express the confidence and benevolence in response to God's display of power. Finally, "be silent" retains these emotions, tingeing it with fear of God's power. (This pattern of replacing fear of oppression with confidence and fear of God is also evident in digressions in the Epistle to the Hebrews, as discussed above, and Revelation, discussed in the next chapter.)

Although many commentators have found allusions in Revelation to Zech 2:6–13, it is difficult to say whether the Seer of Revelation intends to evoke Zechariah or is simply adapting stock prophetic language (including Zechariah's) even as a musical composer borrows phrases and notes to demonstrate their pedigree.[229] With Jauhiainen, I have argued that the

---

[224] Conrad, 86: "Zechariah begins to emerge as a character in this scene."

[225] Meyers and Meyers, 162.

[226] Aristotle *Rhet.* II.7.1–3. See esp II.7.3: "That is why those who help a man who is poor or an exile...are regarded with favor owing to the urgency and occasion of the need."

[227] Meyers and Meyers, 169.

[228] Conrad, 85–86, 88.

[229] Jauhiainen, 29–35, follows Z. Ben-Porat in defining allusions as "a device for the simultaneous activation of two texts." The interpreter goes through up to four stages: (1)

"four winds of heaven" (Zech 2:6) are not relevant to Rev 7:1 because they are "of heaven," not earth, and because the context is gathering not destroying.[230] However, both Rev 7 and Zech 2:6–13 share a pattern: gathering God's people, gathering the nations, a cry of praise, God's presence followed by silence. This pattern is argued by Randolph R. Rogers,[231] but is contested by Jauhiainen who argues that neither text envisages a gathering of God's people, and that the gathering of the nations occurs before the cry of praise in Rev 7.[232] Jauhiainen's critique can be further refined: both Rev 7:2–8 and Zech 2:7–9 depict protection, but more specifically Rev 7:2–8 depicts protection from God's wrath and by means of a seal. Zech 2:7–9 is protection, but not from divine forces. It depicts justice (*lex talonis*) on the nations for plundering. If there is an allusion in Rev 7, the Seer has radically changed the pattern.[233]

If taken in isolation, there is no clear allusion of Zech 2:6–13 in Rev 7. If these elements are taken together with the structure of digression followed by silence, Zech 2:6–13 may be specifically evoked by Rev 7.[234]

---

recognizing a marker, which is an element or pattern belonging to another text. (2) Identifying the evoked text that has the marker. (3) Modifying the interpretation of the alluding text on the basis of the marker. (4) Optionally, activating the whole evoked text in order to draw broader connections between the alluding and evoked texts. When the interpreter reaches stage 4, this is called an 'allusion' and if only reaching stage 3, a 'simple allusion.' When an interpreter is not able to reach stage three, the marker is called an 'echo.' The cognitive process described by Ben-Porat and utilized by Jauhiainen corresponds well to the processing effort and generation of contextual effects, as described by Relevance Theory.

[230] Jauhiainen, 70–72. Compare G. Beale, *The Book of Revelation* (NIGTC; Grand Rapids, Mich: Eerdmans, 1999), 406–407. See chapter 2.2 under d) *Dramatis Personae.*

[231] Jauhiainen refers to Randolph R. Rogers, "An Exegetical Analysis of John's Use of Zechariah in the Book of Revelation: The Impact and Transformation of Zechariah's Text and Themes in the Apocalypse" (Ph.D. diss.; Southwestern Baptist Theological Seminary, 2002), 100–103.

[232] Jauhiainen, 72–73.

[233] The silence following the digression (2:13) is strikingly similar to the opening of the seventh seal in Rev 8:1. Conrad argues that Zechariah is about to enter the temple and the crowd is called to silence just as when the high priest enters the holy of holies (Conrad, 43). Jauhiainen notes that the silence is on earth in Zech 2:13 and not in heaven (Jauhianen, 78). Although this is true, he does not consider that both Rev and Zech portray silence before a throne room/temple scene. In Zechariah, the silence occurs as he is entering the temple on earth to witness an angel commissioning Joshua (Conrad 43). In Revelation, the silence occurs before an angel at the altar comes out.

[234] Jauhiainen, 134–135, notes four simple allusions between Rev 7 and Zech 2:6–13, but dismisses the suggestion that Zech 2:6–13 provides a model for Rev because it does not match the order of Zech but more generally matches the order of apocalyptic events (151–153, cf. 72–73). He accurately criticizes Rogers for overstating the parallels between Rev 7 and Zech 2:6–13, but does not consider the wind and digressive structure in his analysis. He acknowledges that Farrer is right in saying John is using more than one

Both are digressions. Both begin with four winds. Both include elements of protection, rejoicing, gathering of nations, and dwelling of God. Both are followed by reverential silence before God.

If it is an allusion (which is not clear) the differences show that John has reworked these elements and inserts radically different content. John adds angels in control of punishing winds, sealing as protection from God's wrath, a list of tribes, rejoicing before the throne, direct description of their songs, a dialogue about those clothed in white, and the dwelling theme. At best, it seems that Zech 2:6–13 provides an example of the structure of a digression followed by silence, and the constellation of elements that include four winds, protection of God's people, rejoicing, gathering the nations, and God dwelling. The Seer has reworked these so thoroughly that there is only a verbal echo of their original content and function in Zechariah.

Looking more broadly than the digression in Zech 2:6–13, Zech 2–4 is a significant source for images of measuring and the two olive trees that are used to characterize the people of God in Rev 10–11.[235] The image of two olive trees is the stronger allusion.[236] When John identifies the two witnesses as "two olive trees" and "two lampstands," these images would be confusing without Zechariah 3 and 4 which identify Joshua the high priest and Zerubbabel the governor in these roles.[237] John's use of this verse is consistent with Zechariah's sense. The lampstands and olive trees are necessary for the functioning of the temple, the rebuilt temple in Zech and heavenly one in Revelation. In both texts, the number "two" refers to two individuals, although in Revelation the two witnesses also symbolize the churches and every witness. In both texts, the temple is not built by human might or power but by God's spirit. Finally, the lampstands represent people (and congregations in Rev) who are able to fulfill their prophetic vocation only when their lamps are burning.

There are significant differences that confirm the sense that if Zechariah is a model, it is a model that John has radically reconfigured. Joshua is clothed with festal robes in Zechariah, the two witnesses with sackcloth in Revelation. The two witnesses breath fire that consumes their enemies.

---

prototype. The Seer creatively combines and modifies texts so that Jauhiainen expects too much when he looks for slavish adherence to order to demonstrate the use of a prototype. Instead the repeated activation of Zech 2:6–13 is enough of a signal that it is a prototype for the text (along with others, we should note, such as census lists). As also shown by Jauhiainen, we should note the repeated activation of Zech 2:6–13 again in the conclusion of the book (Rev 22:7, 12, 20). This digression in Zech is important to the Seer.

[235] A. Farrer, *A Rebirth of Images* (Westminster: Dacre, 1949), 128–30.

[236] Jauhianien, 67–8, 90.

[237] Jauhiainen, 92–93.

They shut the sky and can turn waters to blood. They are killed by the beast, lie in the street, and become a cause for celebration by those afflicted by their prophecy. They are raised after three and a half days and are called up to heaven in the same way John was (cf. 4:1). The two witnesses in Rev 11 have a very different purpose and fate than Joshua and Zerubbabel in Zech.

e) Relevance to Revelation 7 and 10–11

Jubilees 23.9–32, *Sib. Or.* I.125–282, Exod 12:1–28, and Zech 2:6–13 provide evidence that the technique of digression was a part of the cognitive environment of communities using the Hebrew Bible and Jewish Apocalyptic, even if they did not know or use the term 'digression.' John assumes Exodus and Zechariah are accessible to his audience for optimal relevance.[238] Audiences who recalled Exod 12 and Zech 2 while hearing Revelation could connect the digressions in these two passages to Rev 7 and 10–11.

If they recalled the pattern of the Exodus plagues interrupted by the Passover instructions before the last element, they would have received the amplification of an Exodus typology. The Passover narrative (Ex 12) is placed in position before the last plague in a way that heightens suspense, sustains, and modifies emotion. Simultaneously, the digression evokes confidence in God's saving hand while it transfers fear of the Egyptians to fear of God, who will take their firstborn if they do not sacrifice as prescribed. The placement of Rev 7 and 10–11 before the seventh element replicates the pattern of sustaining and modifying emotion between the penultimate and ultimate elements. This is most persuasive for Rev 10:1–11:13, which occurs after six events resembling the Exodus plagues.

A significant effect of this connection is to highlight the practices of the community that comes out of slavery. The plague narratives are past events, but the Passover and Feast of Unleavened Bread are perpetual ordinances. Likewise, the digression in Rev 7 puts the turmoil of the seals into the past and focuses on the practice of the community gathered around the throne. Unlike Exod 12, Rev 7 does not prescribe any new rituals for their identity. Their role is the same as for all creation, as established in Rev 5: worship of God and the Lamb. On the other hand, Rev 10–11 gives commands to the Seer and describes two witnesses who testify to God's

---

[238] With Beale (*Revelation,* 193–5; cf. 90) and Aune (*Revelation*, 47–48, 55–56), Exodus 19:6 is first activated in Rev 1:6 ("kingdom and priesthood"). Zechariah 12:10–13:1 is activated in Rev 1:7 (seeing and mourning the one whom they pierced), a key location following the epistolary opening and doxology. Jauhiainen, 142–144, 166, argues that this allusion activates Zechariah's eschatological framework, and places Jesus in the role traditionally reserved for YHWH.

will. Rev 10:1–11:13 moves the audience beyond their fear of plagues to be witnesses to the world of God's sovereignty and justice. The community can imitate the two witnesses and trust in the same divine vindication that raised them dramatically from dishonorable death.

In this way, awareness of Exod 12 amplifies the audience's experience of Rev 7 and 10–11 as digressions that interrupt tragic events, communicate protection from God's wrath, evoke the emotion of confidence in the fulfillment of God's promises, and identify the people of God who are brought out of slavery. The 144,000, those robed in white, John, and the two witnesses are examples for audiences to emulate, just as the first celebrants of the Passover were meant to be examples for the audience to imitate. In this Exodus typology, Rev 7 and 10–11 portrays the people of God not yet out of slavery, but living in the period just before freedom. For hearers who identify themselves with the people of God, Rev 7 and 10–11 stands out as more important to be remembered just as the Passover instructions were determinative for the hearers of Exodus.

If audiences activated the pattern of Zechariah 2:6–13 interrupting visions, they would receive Zechariah's expectations for the coming of the LORD, restoration of the people of God, and rebuilding Jerusalem.[239] The digressions in Zech 2:6–13 and Rev 7 begin with a reference to four winds and is concluded by silence before God and include the topics of justice for God's people, punishment and gathering of the nations, and dwelling with God. These echoes suggest that the audience consider fleeing and escaping from 'Babylon' (cf. Rev 18:4). Rev 10:1–11:13 adopts Zechariah's juxtaposition of the angel measuring Jerusalem with Jerubbabel rebuilding the city to portray Christian witnesses as these types of leaders. John measures the space and the time with his prophetic activity. Then, as with the priest Joshua and the governor Jerubbabel, Christians are exhorted to become a "priesthood and kingdom" for God through their witnessing and willingness to die. At this point, Exodus and Zechariah meet: portraying leaders and community coming out of exile to the place promised by God.

What is described above is the maximalist case of the effects on an audience that activates Exodus and Zechariah's digressions. If audiences were familiar with *Sibylline Oracles* I/II, *Jubilees*, Exodus 12, or Zechariah 2 but did not activate any allusions, they still had experience with unarticulated digressions. Because of their length, amplification, and emotional intensity, these digressions dominate the interpretation of the sur-

[239] Jauhiainen, 142, lists these as John's three uses of Zechariah. He argues that John transfers the motifs of building the eschatological temple to the New Jerusalem (149).

rounding material, whether it is Noah's preaching during the six degenerate generations in *Sib. Or.* I, the wicked future generation during the history of the patriarchs in *Jubilees*, the Passover narrative during the plague narrative in Exodus, or the call to come out of exile during the visions of restoration in Zechariah. In each case, the authors directly address the audiences' situation, evoke emotions, construct the ethos of the author and audience, and offer examples for imitation.

Through these experiences of digressions, John's audiences likely were familiar with digressions even if they would never use the term. Consciously or unconsciously they likely were aware of the form, content, and function of digressions that are consistent with the prescriptions of rhetoricians and examples from other literature. They would expect that the Seer's digressions may most directly address their situation, evoke emotions, construct the ethos of the author and audience, and offer examples for imitation. As a result, the audience would find the digressions more relevant than the surrounding material.

9. Conclusions

Digressions were common in the Greco-Roman world by the 1st century. From the survey in this chapter, digressions were used in practice in various genres, languages, and locations. They were used in poetry, letters, histories, speeches, prophecy, and apocalyptic. They were used in Greek, Latin, and Hebrew. They were used in Rome, in Asia Minor, and in Palestine. Dio of Prusa is our key witness of their use in Asia Minor during the 1st century. Josephus is an example of a Jew who wrote in Greek in Rome and used articulated and unarticulated digressions as a rhetorical strategy. The authors of *Aristeas* and 2 Maccabees demonstrate the use of digressions by Jewish authors in Alexandria. The Noah narrative in the first *Sibylline Oracle* and the future wicked generation in *Jubilees* are examples of digressions in Jewish Apocalyptic. Exodus and Zechariah, both relevant to Revelation, seem to use digressions. From these many examples and various sources, I propose that John's audiences likely were familiar with digressions even if they were not familiar with the theoretical discussions by rhetoricians.

Orators and authors used ethical/emotional digressions to obliquely introduce themes, to develop the author's ethos, and to directly address the audience and the contemporary situation. Cicero and Quintilian suggest that digressions can be used to soften a difficult case. Josephus instructs his sympathetic audience about the piety and virtues of the Jewish constitution and to evoke friendliness towards the Jews. Dio of Prusa uses digressions to present himself as superior to other philosophers and sophists (even Homer and Plato!) in knowledge of the gods. These goals are not the explicit occasion for the work, but are discernable through digressions.

These digressions are a unique window into the rhetorical situation. Josephus' digressions in *Contra Apionem* and *Vita* are the primary sources for describing Josephus' construction of himself and the problem. In *Contra Apionem*, the digressions make it clear he is addressing both attacks on his credibility and non-Jewish sympathizers. In the *Vita*, the digression makes it plain that Iustus is the exemplar of his contemporary opponents. In both Josephus and Dio, digressions uniquely construct and reveal the author's identity, his conception of the audience, and the rhetorical situation.

In effect, digressions can become more important for understanding the author's rhetorical strategy and goals than the material in which they are embedded. *Jubilees* 23.9–32 is a key to understanding the author's strategy to persuade his audience to study the law and repent of their parent's wickedness. The six generations are a framework to communicate Noah's preaching in *Sibylline Oracles* I.125–282. Exodus 7–12 uses the plagues to build up to the Passover narrative and persuade the people of God to imitate the example of the Israelites. Zechariah 2:6–13 amplifies the critical themes of leaving exile, justice for the nations, and the promise that God will dwell with the people of God. These digressions are unessential since they can be removed without changing the narrative logic. At the same time, they are essential to the rhetorical effect of the whole.

Chapter 5

Revelation 7:1–17 and 10:1–11:13 as Digressions

How does understanding the use of digressions illuminate how ancient audiences experience Rev 7:1–17 and 10:1–11:13? To answer this question, I apply the six delimiting criteria (function, length, location, transitions, relevance, topics), first, to demonstrate that Rev 7:1–17 and 10:1–11:13 cohere with the theory and practice of ethical/emotional digressions and, second, to investigate the implications of this finding.

Understanding Rev 7:1–17 and 10:1–11:13 in the light of other digressions reveals how these passages become more important than the seal and trumpet series in which they are embedded. They work together as a system of digressions to develop the ethos of John and the people of God and the themes of protection, persecution, death, and vindication. These two passages are part of an argument from emotion to overshadow fear of persecution by evoking fear of God's wrath, to diminish fear of God's wrath by encouraging confidence in God's protection and vindication, and to provide examples for the people of God to emulate.

In this way, Rev 7:1–17 and 10:1–11:13 play a critical role in John's rhetorical strategy. John urged his audiences to disassociate from the Roman Empire and from Christian leaders who encouraged assimilation.[1] Some in the seven assemblies in Asia Minor disagreed whether Christians should eat sacrificial meat, should participate in imperial commerce, and should fear violence by the Empire against Christians. The digressions in Rev 7:1–11 and 10:1–11:13 especially address the last point, gradually revealing forces hostile to Christian life. Digressions are a key to John's strategy to persuade audiences that witnesses to Jesus must be prepared to suffer and even be killed.

The chapter concludes by discussing theological implications for Revelation. The use of digressions suggests that God's judgment is not rigidly ordered but may be delayed for protecting God's people and for providing opportunities to worship and witness. In this way, confidence in God's grace is promoted over fear of God's wrath. Digressions also have an impact on ecclesiology. Revelation 7:1–17 and 10:1–11:13 separate God's people from the inhabitants of the earth, embed God's people in earthly

[1] See the Introduction, section 2, "The Cognitive Environment."

events, and give them the roles of worshippers and witnesses that may result in their death.

1. Terminology: παρέκβασις

Chapters 3 and 4 demonstrated that ancient authors were deviating in the expected order in speeches, histories, letters, and poetry, by Jews, Greeks, and Romans, in Rome, Alexandria, Palestine, and Asia Minor. When theoreticians of oratory described and prescribed this technique, the dominant term they used was παρέκβασις, or digression. Another tradition called it παραδιήγησις, literally 'near narration,' a name which itself indicates the attempt to control the phenomena by limiting its location and restricting its content to topics appropriate to narration. Παρέκβασις became the dominant term in part because of the influence of renowned rhetoricians such as Cicero and Quintilian and because παρέκβασις better captures the paradox of a digression: an unessential section that is essential to the rhetorical impact of the whole.

For this reason, παρέκβασις, or simply 'digression,' is an appropriate term as we seek to understand how a 1st century audience would understand Rev 7:1–17 and 10:1–11:13. It is not necessary to assume that John or his audience had any knowledge of technical discussions about παρέκβασις or even that they would have used the term. Because they had opportunity to experience the technique in speeches and literature in Greek and Hebrew, digressions were a part of their cognitive environment and could be accessed to understand Rev 7:1–17 and 10:1–11:13.

Consistent with how rhetoricians defined παρέκβασις, audiences who heard Revelation 7:1–17 and 10:1–11:13 experienced them as the B unit in an A-B-A' structure in which B deviates from the expected A-A' order.[2] The number of seals and trumpets are announced, which signals that an audience should expect that order of events. The first six events fulfill that expectation. However, Rev 7:1–17 and 10:1–11:13 deviate from these expectations and the audience must expend greater effort to relate the digression to the surrounding material.[3] This additional effort can increase the significance of the digression for the audience.

The term παρέκβασις or 'digression' is not unproblematic for ancient or modern critics. In chapter 3, I discussed how rhetoricians struggle with

---

[2] See chapter 3.4, "Summary of Rhetoricians' Discussion of Digressions."

[3] The audience is further challenged by the fact that the digression themselves are each divided into two loosely related parts. Their structure is A-B-B'-A', or more precisely representing the series of seven, A^1, A^2, A^3, A^4, A^5, A^6, B, B', A^7. See chapter 2 for discussion of the ambiguous relationships between B and B' in each digression.

how a unit of text is simultaneously off subject and yet contributes to the rhetorical effect. Some modern scholars (e.g. Boring) reject the term 'digression' for Rev 7:1–17 and 10:1–11:13 because it seems to imply that the units are not well integrated into their location or that they are unessential. But digressions can be both continuous and discontinuous with the preceding unit, and both unessential to the narrative logic and yet essential to the rhetorical effect.

In both theory and practice, digressions were both continuous and discontinuous in their immediate literary context. This tension explains why interpreters use a variety of terms to describe these units, in effect reproducing the audience's struggle to interpret the digression in its immediate literary context. Chapter 2 demonstrated that the majority of signals in Rev 7:1–17 and 10:1–11:13 (delimiting markers, communication axis, etc.) were discontinuous with the surrounding seal and trumpet series but that enough signals were continuous with the previous unit to relate each digression to the surrounding series. This minimal continuity coheres with rhetorician's advice about fitting a digression into its context,[4] as well as the examples by Josephus and others given in chapter 4.

In his study of digressions, Härter explains the ambiguous relationship between the digression and its surroundings as the relationship between chaos and order. A deviation cannot occur unless there is order. At the same time, the digression resists order and represents danger to the order, undermining its validity claims.[5] In the case of Revelation, order is expressed by the numbered opening of the seals and blowing of the trumpets, each revealing judgment and plagues. To use Härter's conception, the orderly sequence of judgment is threatened by scenes of protection, persecution, and vindication. These scenes delay judgment and undermine its claim for supremacy. I consider this insight further below when discussing the theological implications of digressions.

2. Unarticulated Digressions

When examining the use of digressions in practice, I observed articulated and unarticulated digressions. Some ancient authors explicitly identified

[4] For example, see Quintilian's comment: "Indeed such a practice confers great distinction and adornment on a speech, but only if the digression fits in well with the rest of the speech and follows naturally on what has preceded, not if it is thrust in like a wedge parting what should naturally come together." (*Inst.* IV.3.4; cf. 14). See discussion in chapter 3.

[5] A. Härter, *Digressionen: Studien zum Verhältnis von Ordnung und Abweichung in Rhetorik und Poetik* (Verlag: Wilhelm Fink, 2000), 8–9.

passages as digressions, which I called 'articulated,' following Longenecker's terminology for the chain-link transition. Other authors digressed without comment. Rev 7:1–17 and 10:1–11:13 are unarticulated, which is consistent with digressions used by Josephus and Dio and found in the Hebrew Bible and Jewish apocalyptic texts.

By not drawing attention to the digression, these authors minimize and manipulate the audience's awareness of authorial control. For John, this is a key point. He portrays the book of Revelation as the revelation of Jesus Christ, not sprung from the mind of John of Patmos.[6] John's role is carefully managed (especially in the digressions) to reflect his role as authoritative mediator who obediently recorded (or not, cf. Rev 10:4) what he saw and heard.[7] The digressions of Rev 7:1–17 and 10:1–11:13 are not the result of the author's awareness of effective rhetoric. These digressions between the sixth and seventh elements occur because that is how God wanted it.

John presents the material as divinely structured. He tacitly claims that both the content and structure are from God. However, even if audiences accepted that the structure was divinely inspired, Rev 7:1–17 and 10:1–11:13 are consistent with digressions in other genres. For John and his audiences, these digressions are unarticulated in a profound sense: John disguises any role he had in creating, selecting, and arranging the material. If asked what he was doing, he might say, "to God be the glory… and the structure!"

3. Experiencing Revelation 7:1–17 as a digression

If Revelation 7:1–17 and 10:1–11:13 match the experience of an unarticulated digression as an unannounced B section in an A-B-A' structure, how do they compare with other digressions using the criteria developed in chapter 3? How does understanding them as digressions illuminate Revelation's rhetorical strategy and the experience of hearing Revelation read aloud?

---

[6] E. Schüssler Fiorenza, *Revelation: Vision of a Just World* (Minneapolis: Fortress, 1991), 40; D. Aune, *Revelation*, (3 vols; Nashville: Thomas Nelson, 1997–8), 1:12; cf. 2:563.

[7] On the construction of John's ethos, see G. Carey, *Elusive Apocalypse: Reading Authority in the Revelation to John* (Macon, Georgia: Mercer University Press, 1999).

a) Function: Ethical/Emotional

Digressions could be used for an argument from ethos. Hermagoras, Cicero, and Quintilian prescribe an ethical/emotional digression to praise or blame someone directly involved in the case, especially the orator and the audience.[8] In practice, ethical/emotional digressions also developed characters with whom an audience could identify. Dio of Prusa used a hunter as a model of virtue for his audience (*Or.* 7). The Sibyl of *Sibylline Oracle* I/II used Noah as a moral preacher to reach her generation. The author of *Jubilees* held up a future generation that repented in contrast to the previous wicked generation. Exodus 12 is more direct in addressing the descendants of those in the story; but this also requires audiences to identify themselves as descendants before the directions are personally relevant. Zechariah 2 includes direct appeals through second person imperatives to "those who live with daughter Babylon" (Zech. 2:7), a description that an audience can apply to itself when living under foreign rule. In these examples, ethical/emotional digressions used characters to shape the audience's conception of themselves and the author.

Rev 7:1–17 coheres with the expectations of an ethical/emotional digression described above.

(1) Ethos.[9] One of the ways that Rev 7:1–17 stands apart from the six and seventh seal is its focus on the ethos of John and the people of God. Personal references (non-acting) signal discontinuity by referring to the "slaves of God," 144,000 sealed. *Dramatis personae* (acting characters) also signal discontinuity: the great crowd dressed in white, and John himself.[10] The communication axis includes speech between John and an elder (Rev 7:12–17), the only time John's direct speech is recorded (2.2.2). Each of these signals characterizes John or the people of God, or, in rhetorical terms, construct an argument from ethos. The people of God are portrayed as protected, separated, persecuted, and vindicated. John is portrayed as moving from ignorance to knowledge.

The vision of the sealing of the 144,000 (Rev 7:1–8) develops the ethos of the audience by characterizing the people of God as the "slaves of God" who are protected and separated. Four angels are about to unleash destroying winds against earth, sea, and trees, when another angel ascends to focus the angels' (and the audience's) attention on the slaves of God by saying, "Do not damage the earth or the sea or the trees, until we have sealed the slaves of our God with a seal on their foreheads" (7:3). "Slaves of God" is the primary way the audience and author are identified in the

[8] See chapter 3.4, "Summary of Rhetoricians' Discussion of Digressions."

[9] Although ethos and pathos overlapped for Cicero and Quintilian, I will distinguish them here for the sake of analysis.

[10] See chapter 2.2 for a full discussion of these and other signals.

opening of the book. "The revelation of Jesus Christ, which God gave him to show his slaves what must happen soon; he made it known by sending his angel to his slave, John" (1:1). If members of the audience understood themselves to be slaves of God, then Rev 7 applies to them in a way the first six seals did not.[11] Characters like them are sealed before damaging winds are released.

In this way, the audience is encouraged to identify with characters who are protected and separated. The themes of protection and separation are made more memorable by evoking the Passover narrative. The Passover narrative illuminates the seal in Rev 7 because of the similar context of destruction targeting land, sea, and trees, protection from divine agents, and separation from the surrounding population.[12] First, the people of God are protected from destructive winds that threaten earth, sea, and trees. The protective function of the seal is made explicit in Rev 9:4:

> [The locusts] were told not to damage the grass of the earth or any green growth or any tree, but only those people who do not have the seal of God on their foreheads (Rev 9:4).

The Israelites were protected from the first nine plagues that afflicted the Egyptians and protected from the tenth plague by the sign of the Lamb's blood on the doorpost.[13] In the same way, the slaves of God in Revelation are protected from the destroying winds and coming trumpet plagues.

The second theme is separation. Most simply, a seal on a slave implies ownership; in Revelation the impact of ownership is separation from the surrounding populations. The first indication of separation in Rev 7:3 is very general, that the slaves of God are separated from those who will be affected by winds destroying earth, sea, and trees. In Rev 7:4–8, the general focus on the slaves of God shifts to the more specific separation of the 144,000 from the tribes of Israel. Separation within the tribes may remind an audience that some Israelites may not observe the Passover, but more likely recalls the way the lamb's blood separates Israelites from Egyp-

---

[11] With S. Pattemore, *The People of God in the Apocalypse: Discourse, Structure and Exegesis* (MSSNTS 128. Cambridge: Cambridge University, 2004), 89; *inter alia,* Schüssler Fiorenza, *Revelation*, 68, 77, 78; G. Beale, *Revelation* (Grand Rapids, Michigan: Eerdmans, 1999), 413–4; 570–1, 573; G. Caird, *The Revelation of St. John the Divine* (New York: Harper, 1966), 100–103; M. E. Boring, *Revelation* (Louisville: John Knox, 1989), 66; P. Richard, *Apocalypse: A People's Commentary on the Book of Revelation* (trans. P. Berryman; Maryknoll, New York: Orbis, 1995), 74–75. Others take unspecified 'slaves' as referring only to prophets, e.g. R. H. Charles, *Revelation* (London: T & T Clark, 1985 [1921]), 1:6; R. H. Mounce, *The Book of Revelation* (rev. ed.; Grand Rapids, Michigan: Eerdmans, 1998), 65.

[12] See chapter 2.2.h, "Summary of Analysis of Rev 7:1–17."

[13] Israelite protection from the first nine plagues is implicit (Exod 7:24; 8:4; 9:11; 10:6) and explicit (8:22–23; 9:4; 9:26; 10:23). The narrative is ambiguous if gnats affected Israelites (8:17–18).

tians.[14] The relevance of the 144,000 is ambiguous in Rev 7, except to give the impression of a military muster list separating combatants from non-combatants.[15] In Rev 12–20, separation is emphasized more than protection, contrasting those who have the seal of God with those who have the mark of the beast.[16] In light of the contrast with the mark of the beast, the question of ownership is implicit in the last half of the book: whose slaves are you, God's or the beast's? This question is nascent in the theme of separation found in Rev 7:1–8.

The slaves of God described in Rev 7:1–8 are juxtaposed with vision of the great crowd around the throne in heaven in Rev 7:9–17. This passage also develops the ethos of the audience through characterization of the people of God and the ethos of John through his interaction with an elder.

In contrast to the finite 144,000 in Rev 7:1–8, the vision of the great crowd portrays the people of God in its most inclusive form:

> After this I looked, and behold! a great crowd that no one could count, from every nation and tribes and peoples and languages, standing before the throne and before the Lamb, robed in white, and palm branches in their hands (Rev 7:9).

Members of an audience who include themselves in the people of God can identify themselves in this group, a group not limited by size, clan, ethnicity, or language. The four-fold pattern of nation, tribe, people, and language further identifies this group with those who the Lamb "bought for God from every tribe and language and people and nation" (Rev 5:9). This image of slave manumission strengthens the way the seal on the slaves of God signals ownership and separation from the rest of humanity.

This great crowd is the first group of human beings explicitly to praise God and the Lamb. This characterization develops the people of God from passivity to activity. The four living creatures chant day and night (Rev 4:8) and the twenty-four elders extol the worthiness of God and the Lamb to receive praise (Rev 4:11; 5:9–10). A huge, but numbered (ten thousand times ten thousand and a thousand times a thousand) band of angels likewise extols the Lamb (Rev 5:12) and finally all creation joins in praise of God and the Lamb (Rev 5:13). Although their participation is implied in Rev 5:13, in Rev 7:10 the people of God explicitly praise God for the first time. The great crowd praises God and the Lamb for victory (σωτηρία). They are crying out in a loud voice (κράζουσιν φωνῇ μεγάλῃ), which recalls those under the altar who cried out in a loud voice (ἔκραξεν φωνῇ

[14] See chapter 2.2.g, "Thematic Vocabulary: Ambiguous Standing and Seals."

[15] With Bauckham, *Climax*, 217–20; Aune, *Revelation*, 2:443–4; Beale, *Revelation*, 422–3. The relevance is clarified by the depiction of the messianic army on Mt. Zion (Rev 14:1–5). See chapter 2.2.c, "Personal References: Discontinuity then continuity."

[16] See chapter 2.2.h, "Summary of Analysis of Rev 7:1–17."

μεγάλῃ) to ask for justice. The implication is that this great crowd has been vindicated.

The identity of those robed in white is the crucial question for this vision. The elder asks John, "Who are these, robed in white, and where have they come from?" (Rev 7:13). In context, the symbol of the white robe suggests persecution.[17] "White robes" (στολή λευκή) most immediately recalls the souls under the altar who had been slaughtered for the sake of their testimony (Rev 6:11). If this is the most relevant to understand the great crowd in Rev 7:9, does this mean that the whole crowd has been slaughtered for their testimony? The question is not explicitly answered, but the elder's answer to John confirms the threat of persecution against a large number of believers.

> I said to him, "Sir, you are the one that knows." Then he said to me, "These are they who have come out of the great persecution (θλίψεως); they have washed their robes (τὰς στολὰς) and made them white (ἐλεύκαναν) in the blood of the Lamb" (Rev 7:13).

The great crowd has come through persecution. The association with the blood of the Lamb suggests that the great crowd will be tested and purified by persecution that mirrors the slaughter of the Lamb (cf. Rev 5:6).[18] Therefore, an audience that identified with the great crowd in Rev 7:9 should prepare itself for persecution and even death.

Persecution and death are not the last words. The people of God are characterized again in Rev 7:15–17 as vindicated and actively serving God, returning to the themes that were emphasized in Rev 7:9–12. "Who are these clothed in white robes?" The elder concludes his answer by saying that they stand before the throne of God and serve God day and night in God's temple. Whatever persecution they faced is minimized by the vindication of standing before God and serving in God's temple. These people are given everything they need, most importantly dwelling with God: "the one sitting on the throne will shelter (σκηνώσει) them" (7:15). They will not hunger or thirst and the sun will not strike them nor any heat (7:16; cf. Isa 49:10). The Lamb will shepherd them and guide them to the springs of living water (7:17).

---

[17] The white robes also suggest reward, although more weakly than the theme of persecution. The glorified Jesus promised white garments (τὰ ἱμάτια λευκὰ) to those in Sardis who had not soiled their garments (Rev 3:4). Likewise, the assembly in Laodicea is urged to buy white robes (ἱμάτια λευκὰ) from Jesus (Rev 3:18; cf. 16:15). The twenty-four elders are also robed in white garments (περιβεβλημένους ἐν ἱματίοις λευκοῖς) (Rev 4:4; cf. the rider of the white horse, Rev 19:13, 16). These references are linked by the use of white (λευκός), but the relevance is weakened by different terms being used for the clothes (στολὴ vs. ἱματίον).

[18] Bauckham, *Climax*, 227–9; Aune, *Revelation*, 2: 474–5; Beale, *Revelation*, 436–9.

Rev 7:13–17 develops John's ethos from ignorant to knowing in a way that bonds him with his audiences. When the elder asks him, "who are these clothed in white robes," John responds, "my lord, you know" (Rev 7:13). This ignorance puts John and his audiences on the same level – neither understands the identity of the great crowd until it is explained.[19] Listening to the elder's response, John and his audiences together become knowledgeable.

In summary, the people of God are portrayed as protected, separated, praising, persecuted, and vindicated. The argument from ethos can be outlined as follows, focusing on how humans are characterized:

6:12–17	Kings, magnates, etc.	Threatened, hiding
7:1–3	Slaves of God	Protected
7:4–8	144,000	Separated
7:9–12	Great crowd	Praising God and Lamb
7:13–14	Great Crowd	Coming out of persecution
	John	Ignorant => knowledgeable
7:15–17	Great Crowd	Vindicated and serving

As with digressions discussed in chapter 4, there is contrast in personal references and *dramatis personae* between the digression and the surrounding material.[20] Like other ethical/emotional digressions, Rev 7:1–17 focuses on characters with whom John's audiences can identify.

(2) Emotion. The second aspect of an ethical/emotional digression is emotion. As discussed in chapter 3, Aristotle describes various emotions, the kind of people who have those emotions, their state of mind, and the kinds of occasions and topics for helping change the state of mind of the audience. Fear (φόβος), confidence (θάρσος), and emulation (ζηλός) are three emotions relevant to the book of Revelation.

By outlining the structure of the argument from emotion in Rev 7:1–17, the rhetorical strategy behind the structure becomes apparent. The sixth seal evokes fear of God's wrath on all people, climaxing with the dramatic question "Who will stand?"[21]

---

[19] Ironically, the prophet not knowing is a standard *topos* (e.g. Ezek 37:3, see section 3.f below). It bonds John and his audience in ignorance and simultaneously presents him as a prophet comparable to other prophets.

[20] For example, Josephus focuses on himself in *Contra Apionem* 1.47–52 in the midst of a discussion of the antiquity of the Jewish histories.

[21] Schüssler Fiorenza, *Revelation*, 65, Beale, *Revelation*, 371, and Pattemore, *People of God*, 74, argue that the audience would understand themselves to be a part of the humanity that suffers the effects of the four riders.

Then the kings of the earth and the magnates and the generals and the rich and the powerful, and everyone, slave and free, hid in the caves and among the rocks of the mountains, and they said to the mountains and the rocks: "Fall on us and hide us from the face of the one sitting on the throne and from the wrath of the lamb, for the great day of their wrath has come and who is able to stand?" (Rev 6:15–17)

Fear is "a painful or troubled feeling caused by the impression of an imminent evil that causes destruction or pain" (Arist., *Rhet.* II.5.1). One way to evoke fear is to show that others greater have suffered (*Rhet.* II.5.15). In Rev 6:12–17 even the most powerful in society are hiding and fearful of God's wrath.

In contrast, the digression that follows (Rev 7) evokes confidence, emulation, and a new fear. Confidence[22] is inspired by sealing the slaves of God (Rev 7:1–8), even if it does not specifically answer "who will stand."[23] The angel stops the coming destruction, ordering "Do not harm the earth nor the sea nor the trees until we have sealed the slaves of God on their foreheads" (Rev 7:3). Even if it does not directly address the threat of the sixth seal, this angel and seal represent help against the destructive winds.[24]

Emulation is evoked by presenting goods to be desired.[25] In Rev 7:1–17, these 'goods' include the seal of the living God, the white robes, and the people's role worshipping around the throne. These have been offered as rewards to the seven assemblies (Rev 2–3). Believers in Philadelphia were promised that they will be marked with the name of God and they will stay in the temple and never leave it (Rev 3:12). White garments were promised to those in Sardis (Rev 3:4) and offered to the Laodiceans (3:18). Each of these is presented as something that the assemblies should desire. By associating these goods with characters in Rev 7, John evokes audiences to emulate people who are sealed, clothed in white robes, and worshipping around the throne.

A new fear is intimated by the revelation that they are coming out of a great persecution and their robes have been washed in blood. "These are the ones who are coming out of the great persecution and they have

[22] Confidence is "the hope (ἡ ἐλπὶς) of things that lead to deliverance with sense perceptions that they are near at hand, while the things to feared are either non-existent or far off" (*Rhet.* II.5.16).

[23] See chapter 2.2.h, "Summary of Analysis of Rev 7:1–17."

[24] *Rhet.* II.5.17: Confidence is evoked "if there are means of help, either many or large or both." The question of who will stand is finally resolved in the vision of people from every nation, tribes, peoples and languages robed in white and around the throne.

[25] Emulation is "pain at the apparent presence of honored good things, which also are possible for us to obtain, in the possession of those who are similar to us in nature. It is a pain not due to the fact that another possesses them, but because we do not" (*Rhet.* II.11.1).

washed their robes and they have made them white in the blood of the lamb" (7:14). The precise nature of the threat is not clear in Rev 7, which I argue below is a deliberate omission to give an audience time to accept that they too can face this threat.

This new fear is diminished by evoking confidence in the help provided by God and the Lamb. Those clothed in white have endured through the "Great Persecution" and are vindicated. God will dwell with them. They will not hunger or thirst or fear the sun or any heat, because the Lamb will shepherd them (7:15–17). As Aristotle writes, "We are also reassured when a thing does not inspire fear in our equals, our inferiors, or those to whom we think ourselves superior" (*Rhet.* II.5.19). The great crowd – with whom the audience is invited to identify – endured through the Great Persecution. The implied message is that if they could do it, the audience can as well.

The argument from emotion can be summarized as follows:

6:12–17	Sixth Seal	Fear of God's wrath
7:1–8	Sealing of 144,000	Confidence in God's protection from winds
7:9–12	Multitude	Confidence standing before throne Emulation of worship, white robes
7:13–14	Great Persecution	Fear of persecution, death
7:15–17	Explanation	Confidence in help from God and the Lamb Emulation of robes, role, water of life

Like other ethical/emotional digressions, the emotion being evoked distinguishes the digression from the preceding material.[26] In particular, this digression diminishes fear of God's wrath with confidence in protection. Although the sealing of the 144,000 does not answer the question of who will stand in the day of God's wrath, it nonetheless provides confidence in the face of fear. Because of its ambiguity, the sealing sustains some element of that fear.[27] The great crowd robed in white, however, clearly stands and shouts "Victory!" after coming out of the Great Persecution. They are promised a future without homelessness, hunger, thirst, or sunstroke. John

[26] For example, in his *Vita* 36–42, Josephus shifts from a more neutral tone to evoking anger as he introduces Iustus (see chapter 4.3). 2 Macc 7:20–29 shifts from the pity for the death of the woman's sons to confidence in God (see chapter 4.4). Hebrews 5:11–6:12 interrupts confidence in Christ by shaming the audience for considering to reject Christ and by evoking fear of the consequences (see chapter 4.7).

[27] On the ambiguous answer of Rev 7:1–8 to the question "Who will stand?" see 2.2.h, "Summary of Analysis of Rev 7:1–17."

evokes emulation by presenting these figures with valued 'goods' that the audience desires. A fear of persecution is hinted by mention of "Great Persecution" and washing robes in blood, but these references are surrounded by confidence in God's promises. Overall, confidence is the emotion most evoked by Rev 7:1–17 in contrast with the fear of the series of seals.

b) Length means delay

Rhetoricians caution against using digressions because they delay the argument. Their concern is principally the water clock that measures the length of judicial speeches, but others express a similar concern when they apologize for the delay caused by their digressions.[28] At the same time, these apologies and explanations are careful strategies to persuade the audience to accept material that may seem (in the immediate context) to be outside the case.

Revelation 7:1–17, in contrast, integrates delay as essential in structure and content and, as a consequence, in the audience's experience. In content, the four angels are told to delay the release of the four winds and their destruction of earth, sea, and trees in order to protect the slaves of God. Structurally, it delays the seventh trumpet as well as the four winds. When members of an audience hear the text read aloud, they have an experience of delay: 400 words from Rev 7:1 to 7:17.[29] These three kinds of delay (structure, content, experience) are a further connection between the audience and the slaves of God in the story. In this way, John encourages members of the audience to identify their experience of delay outside the story with the protection of the slaves within the story. If they wonder why the expected progression of God's judgment seems delayed in the world, the answer given by Rev 7 is that God's slaves are being sealed.

Delay is a critical element to understand how Rev 7:1–17 function as a digression.[30] With their eyes on the water clock, rhetoricians advised minimizing delay. However, the digression in Rev 7 makes delay an explicit topic, focusing on the cause and purpose of delay. Rather than reflecting any failure of God's promises, delayed judgment is caused by God

---

[28] Isocrates blames his old age for his digression in *Panathenaicus* (§74–90). Josephus explains that it is worth the time to explain the three 'philosophies' of the Jews in the middle of retelling their history (*Ant* 18.10). Dio of Prusa mollifies any sense of delay in *Or.* 7 by acknowledging that the story of the hunter was long.

[29] R. Bauckham, *Climax of Prophecy: Studies in the Book of Revelation* (London: T & T Clark, 1993), 12: "such delay would be particularly felt in oral performance. [These lengthy interruptions] serve to incorporate the issue of delay of judgment into the structure of the book."

[30] This corroborates interpreters surveyed in chapter 1 who emphasized the role of delay.

and announced by God's agents (the angel from the rising sun). The purpose of this delay in Rev 7:1–17 is protection of the slaves of God, specifically the 144,000.

c) Location for maximum emotional impact

Cicero and Quintilian advised against fixing the location of a digression, emphasizing that the digression should serve the purposes of the speech and not a preordained pattern.[31] Since moving the emotions was a primary goal, they recommended placing the digression where it would maximize the emotional impact. In practice Cicero often used a digression before the conclusion of the speech, following Hermagoras' advice.[32] He found that the conclusion was more effective if the emotions of the audience were stirred up favorably towards the orator and against the opponent.

Similarly, Rev 7:1–17 is placed at the emotional climax before the conclusion of the series of seals. Each seal resulted in suffering for someone, and the sixth seal led to the most dramatic event yet, bringing fear to a pinnacle when even the kings hid from fear and asked the mountains and rocks to hide them from the wrath of God and the Lamb. The location of Rev 7:1–17 coincides with the peak of emotion. By anticipating the conclusion of the seal series, this point between the sixth and seventh seal also harnesses the cumulative tension of the first six elements to maximize the fear of the seal events. As a result, this location achieves the highest possible contrast between the fear of God's wrath evoked by the seal series and the confidence expressed in Rev 7.

d) Minimal use of transitions

Minimal transitions are typical for unarticulated digressions.[33] Transitions used in both Rev 7:1–17 and 10:1–11:13 offer little to suggest their relationship with surrounding units. The transitions from Rev 6:17 to 7:1

[31] Cf. Aristotle's prescription that only the thesis and proof are absolutely necessary, and even the introduction and conclusion should be included only if they serve the purpose of the speech (*Rhet.* III.13). Härter, 38, notes that this flexibility in position still attempts to subordinate the digression, but now to the effect of the speech as a whole rather than one location within a speech.

[32] See chapter 3.4, "Summary of Rhetoricians' Discussion of Digressions."

[33] For example, Cicero's digressions begin typically with a catch-word (such as mentioning Pompey's name in *Pro Milone* 72–91; cf. chapter 3.3.c above) or emotional topic that launches the digression, and returns to the argument without comment. Likewise, when Josephus first digresses on Iustus in *Contra Apionem* 1.46–56, he interrupts the narrative about factions in Galilee with only a few words, and abruptly returns to his subject in 1.57. The digressions in the Hebrew Bible and Jewish Apocalyptic that were discussed in chapter 4 (*Sib. Or.* I, *Jub.* 23, Exod 12, and Zech 2) are all unarticulated and have minimal transitions.

tionship with surrounding units. The transitions from Rev 6:17 to 7:1 and from 7:17 to 8:1 delimit these units, but give few clues how to relate these units. The transition from 6:17 to 7:1 is delimited by the ambiguous μετὰ τοῦτο ("after this"), which may refer to the sixth seal or the whole seal series. Otherwise, the audience experiences the transition through the shifts in communication axis, personal references, *dramatis personae*, and spatial and temporal signals described in chapter 2. The seventh seal is opened in Rev 8:1 without any transition from the direct speech of the elder (Rev 7:14–17).

Like unarticulated digressions in general, minimal transitions reduce the awareness of the author's role in shaping the material and suggest to the audience that the digression is naturally continuous with what preceded. If the author indicates that the material is a digression, the audience will be relieved of some motivation to search for its relevance. By minimal transitions, the audience is stimulated to search for the relevance of the new material. The transitions in Rev 7:1–17 and encourages the audience to make links that will later be dissolved or clarified. For example, the sealing of the 144,000 ambiguously answers the question "who will stand before God's wrath?" but in Rev 7:9–17 this question is dissolved into "who are these who stand before the throne?"

e) Relevance to whole more than part

The tension between continuity and discontinuity between Rev 7:1–17 and the series of seals is consistent with the theory and practice of digressions. Hermagoras, Cicero, and Quintilian insist that digressions be related to the argument in some way, whether by an element of the proof (Hermagoras), emotion related to the facts of the case (Cicero), or a person, place, or topic (Quintilian). Most of all, it is this tension combined with a focus on the author and audience that makes the unit more memorable than the surrounding units. As Race suggested generally, digressions "are frequently the most striking and memorable part of a work."[34] Aune said something similar of Revelation, that these passages are "more important to the author-editor" than the surrounding material.[35]

---

[34] W. Race, "Some Digressions and Returns in Greek Authors," *The Classical Journal* 76:1 (Oct–Nov 1980): 8.

[35] D. Aune, s.v. "Revelation," in *The Westminster Dictionary of New Testament and Early Christian Literature and Rhetoric* (Louisville, Kentucky: Westminster/John Knox, 2003), 404. Cf. P. Richard, *Apocalypse* (trans. P. Berryman; Maryknoll, New York: Orbis, 1995), 87; P. Minear, *I Saw a New Earth* (Washington: Corpus, 1968), 75; E. Wendland, "7 x 7 (x7): A Structural and Thematic Outline of John's Apocalypse," *OPTAT* 4 (1990), 378.

Like other ethical/emotional digressions, Rev 7:1–17 is more relevant to the whole book than to their immediate literary context.[36] The first half of the digression (Rev 7:1–8) recalls the audience's identity as "slaves of God" from the prologue and letters (Rev 1–3) and anticipates 144,000 as a messianic army and the development of the seal as a sign of ownership by God rather than the mark of the beast.[37] The second half (Rev 7:9–17) returns the focus on the throne room and the attendants around the One who is sitting on the throne (Rev 4–5) and also looks forward to the opening of the temple (Rev 11:19; cf. 15:5) and the fulfillment of God's promise to dwell with the people of God (Rev 21–22). These signals make most sense within the context of the whole book of Revelation rather than the seal series.

f) Topics: ethos of author and audience

Topics deployed in Rev 7:1–17 are consistent with other ethical/emotional digressions. They address the moral character (ethos) of the author and the audience. Many of these topics may also be found in Jewish literature, including:

(1) The *topos* of the sealing of God's people against destructive divine forces is used in Revelation to develop the people of God as protected and separated in a way congruent with the Israelites' exodus from slavery (see Exodus 7–12; cf. Ezek 9).[38]

(2) The *topos* of the military census list is used to encourage the people of God to imagine themselves as chosen for military duty, further evoking continuity with the Exodus (see Num 1:3, 18, 20; cf. 1QM 6:11).[39]

(3) The *topos* of the crowd welcoming a victorious king with palm branches is used to evoke confidence in God's help (see Jn 12:13; cf. 1 Macc 13:51; 2 Macc 10:7).[40]

(4) The *topos* of the prophet's ignorance is used to bolster confidence that the prophecy comes from God (see Ezek 37:3; cf. Dan 7:16).[41]

Differently from some other authors who use ethical/emotional digressions, John does not use Rev 7:1–17 to attack his opponents. Cicero's digressions were often filled with invective against his opponents. Josephus used the digressions in the *Vita* to directly attack Iustus. Dio of Prusa subtly suggested in *Or.* 36 that Homer and Plato were less qualified than he to

[36] For a summary of signals of continuity and discontinuity, see table 2.

[37] Pattemore, *People of God*, chapter 5 "Companions of the Lamb – A Messianic Ecclesiology," esp. 117–118.

[38] See 2.2.h, "Summary of Analysis of Rev 7:1–17."

[39] Bauckham, *Climax*, 217–220; Aune, *Revelation*, 2:443–4; Beale, *Revelation*, 422–3.

[40] Aune, *Revelation*, 2:468–9; Beale, *Revelation*, 428; Charles, 1:211.

[41] Aune, *Revelation*, 2:472; cf. Beale, *Revelation*, 432–3.

understand the nature of the divine. In this light, the absence of John's rivals (e.g. 'Jezebel,' the 'Nicolaitans') suggests his primary interest is his audience and how his audience perceives him.

4. Experiencing Revelation 10:1–11:13 as a digression

Revelation 10:1–11:13 also coheres with other ethical/emotional digressions. This passage develops many of the same characters and emotions as Rev 7. Specifically, Rev 10:1–11:13 characterizes John as a knowledgeable, active, and authorized prophet, it depicts the people of God as worshipping during persecution, and it provides the example of two witnesses who are persecuted, killed, and ultimately vindicated.

a) Function: Ethical/Emotional

(1) Ethos. Similar to Rev 7, Rev 10:1–11:13 coheres with the expectations of an ethical/emotional digression, particularly developing the ethos of the author, John, and the audience. John's ethos is developed by direct characterization, while the audience is encouraged to identify with characters included in the people of God.

A shift in personal references (non-acting) and *dramatis personae* (acting characters) in Rev 10:1–11 signals discontinuity from the trumpet series. The sixth trumpet event ends with the announcement that one third of humanity was killed by the plague and the rest did not repent. Is the audience included in 'humanity'? The scope of the term 'humanity' (οἱ ἀνθρωποί) is ambiguous in Rev 9:18–21.[42] When John wants to designate humans who oppose God, he uses "inhabitants of the earth" (οἱ κατοικοῦντες ἐπὶ τῆς γῆς; cf. 11:10),[43] but this designation does not occur during the trumpet plagues (except the eagle's cry in 8:13). It is unclear if the audience is included in the humanity who is killed by the plagues or if 'humanity' is equivalent to only the inhabitants of the earth.

Rev 10:1 shifts the focus to John's encounter with another mighty angel. As in Rev 7, John becomes a major character. In Rev 10:1–11:2, he is

[42] 'Humanity' is a larger category in Rev 9 that includes the people of God, as shown in Rev 9:4: "and they were told not to inflict harm on the grass of the earth, nor any green thing, nor any tree, but only the humans (τοὺς ἀνθρώπους) who do not have the seal of God on their forehead." Pattemore notes that the mention of sealed believers in Rev 9:4 "presupposes the presence of the people of God throughout this plague, without giving any suggestion about how they fare." Pattemore, *People of God*, 160. Cf. Schüssler Fiorenza, *Revelation*, 71; Beale, *Revelation*, 496.

[43] Aune, *Revelation*, 1:240; Beale, *Revelation*, 595–6; Pattemore, *People of God*, 86.

characterized as going from ignorance to knowledge, passivity to activity, and powerlessness to authority.[44]

John receives unique knowledge when he hears the seven trumpets and is commanded not to write their words. "And when seven thunders spoke, I was about to write, but I heard a voice from heaven saying, 'Seal the things that the seven thunders spoke and do not write them'" (10:4). In Rev 7, John and the audience shared the journey from ignorance to knowledge; in Rev 10, John alone knows what the thunders said. John is characterized here as having more knowledge than the audience.

He is also portrayed as transformed from passivity to activity. In previous visions, John was merely an observer. In Rev 7, he was asked a question. In Rev 10, John becomes a full-fledged agent: He is about to write (10:4), he moves to receive the little scroll from the angel, and he receives and eats it (10:9). For the first time, we hear John explicitly told to prophesy (10:11).

John's transformation from passivity to activity is accompanied by a move from powerlessness to authority. He is given the little scroll to eat and commanded to prophesy (10:10–11). He becomes a representative of the divine, a role enacted by the command to measure the temple (11:1–2). John is no longer a powerless by-stander, but an authorized representative of the divine court.

The people of God are characterized in Rev 11:1–2 as "those worshipping (τοὺς προσκυνοῦντας) in [the temple]" (11:1). As people worshipping God, they are characters with whom an audience can identify. The description recalls the great crowd worshipping God and the Lamb (Rev 7:9–11; cf. 5:13; 4:10) and reinforces the primary role of the people of God as worshippers.

However, these people of God are being persecuted by the nations (τὰ ἔθνη): "it was given to the nations that they may trample the holy city for 42 months" (11:2).[45] Previously the nations were a source for the people of God (5:9; 7:9), but now they are the first explicit persecutors. John is gradually disclosing more information about forces hostile to the people of God.

The next passage (Rev 11:3–13) characterizes two anonymous witnesses. They are separated for service, protected from hostile forces, persecuted, killed, humiliated, and finally vindicated. They are separated in time and space. They are given 1260 days to witness and prophecy and clothed in sackcloth (11:3). Evoking the *topos* of God's agents as olive tree

[44] See discussion in 2.3.d, "*Dramatis Personae*."

[45] On the *topos* of trampling as a symbol of persecution, see Luke 21:24; Zech 12:3 LXX; Dan 8:13. Bauckham, *Climax*, 217; Aune, *Revelation*, 2:608; cf. Schüssler Fiorenza, *Revelation*, 77.

and lampstand from Zechariah 4 (see chapter 2.3.d, "*Dramatis personae*"), they stand before the Lord of the earth like Joshua and Zerubabbel, leaders of the restoration of Jerusalem. The combination of these symbols communicates that these two witnesses are distinguished by the time allotted for their work and by their location before God.

The two witnesses are also protected. During the 1260 days of their witness and prophecy, anyone who tries to harm them will be killed by fire proceeding from their mouths (11:5). John reveals at the end of the scene why they need protection. Their prophecy is not easy for the surrounding population to hear: "The inhabitants of the earth rejoiced over them and celebrated and sent gifts to one another because these two prophets tormented the inhabitants of the earth" (11:10). "Torment" (βασανίζω) is the same word used to describe the effect of the fifth trumpet plague of locusts (9:5). With this detail, John explains why the witnesses are persecuted, and why they need protection.

When this protection ends, the two witnesses will be persecuted, killed, and humiliated. "And when they complete their witness, the beast that rises from the abyss will make war on them and conquer them and kill them. And their bodies will be on the street of the great city…" (11:7–8). Their protection was limited, but allowed them to fulfill their vocation to witness.

These two witnesses are finally vindicated and their witness brings about repentance. "After three and one half days, a living spirit from God entered them and they stood on their feet, and a great fear fell on those watching them" (11:11). Even killing the witnesses will not stop them. They are raised publicly to life and in plain view ascend to heaven. A great earthquake punctuates their vindication and is the final element leading to the remainder of the city giving glory to God.

Although they seem to resemble two particular people, the two anonymous witnesses are introduced in ways that subtly allow an audience to identify with them.[46] First, the number of people labeled as witnesses increases throughout Revelation, beginning with John (1:2), typified in Jesus (1:5), and expanded to include Antipas (2:13) and then the two witnesses. Second, the two witnesses are juxtaposed structurally and temporally with those worshipping around the altar (11:1–2).[47] There are few delimiting signals that structurally separate 11:1–2 and 11:3–13, and the temporal signal of 42 months for the trampling nations is equivalent to 1260 days for the two witnesses to witness. Third, the two witnesses are "lampstands" (λυχνίαι) that stand before the Lord of the Earth just as each of the seven assemblies has a lampstand that stands before Jesus (Rev 11:4; 1:12–13;

[46] See discussion in 2.3.d, "*Dramatis Personae*: Discontinuity and Transformation."

[47] For a similar argument, see Pattemore, *People of God*, 111–2.

cf. 2:5). The risen Jesus even says that "the seven lampstands are the seven assemblies" (1:20), which encourages these two witnesses to be understood as personifications of the people of God.[48] As argued in chapter 2, the broader connection with the people of God is ambiguous until made explicit in Rev 12:11, when it is disclosed that believers have conquered the dragon by the word of their witness.

Ambiguity about the connection between the audience and the two witnesses is strategic. Through these anonymous characters, John reveals key information about who persecutes witnesses and why. An audience could feel overwhelming fear if they over-identify with characters who are killed by the beast and left on the streets in shameful exposure. By suggesting that these are two specific people, John allows his audiences to dissociate from them and not take their threat personally. At the same time, he subtly signals that the audience should identify with these characters. In this way, John allows the audience to gradually accept the thesis that witnesses should prepare for persecution and death.

The argument from ethos can be outlined as follows:

9:18–21	"Rest of humanity"	Not repentant
10:1–11	John	Knowledgeable, Active, Authorized
11:1–2	Those around altar	Persecuted
11:3–4	Two witnesses	Separated
11:5–6	Two witnesses	Protected
11:7–10	Two witnesses	Persecuted, killed, humiliated
11:11–13	Two witnesses	Vindicated
	Rest of the City	Giving Glory to God

(2) Emotion. The sixth trumpet climaxes with the death of one third of humanity (9:18–21), and so Rev 10 opens with that fear fresh in the audience's mind.

In contrast, the emotional thrust of the first half of the digression (Rev 10:1–11) is confidence in God's help and confidence in John's role as prophet. God's help comes in the form of the mighty angel who dominates land and sea and promises the fulfillment of the delayed mystery of God. John's message is trustworthy, first, because it comes from God's agent and, second, because he receives it like Ezekiel did (Ezek 2:8–3:3). Just as Ezekiel can be trusted as a prophet of God, so also the image of eating a scroll inspires confidence in John. In addition, the bitter effect on his

[48] Bauckham, *Climax*, 273–4. Cf. chapter 2.3.d, "*Dramatis Personae*: Discontinuity and Transformation."

stomach and the command to prophesy against kings foreshadows the fear that is elaborated in Rev 11 and the hostile response to the two witnesses.[49]

The second half of the digression (Rev 11:1–13) arouses the emotions of emulation, confidence, and fear of persecution followed by confidence in vindication. The description of worshippers around the altar evokes emulation, recalling previous scenes of believers worshipping in the temple (e.g. Rev 3:12, the promise to Philadelphians; Rev 7:9–17, those clothed in white). The witnesses are likewise identified as standing before God, juxtaposing the witnesses (Rev 11:4) and the worshippers around the altar (11:1–2; cf. 7:9–12; 5:1–13; 4:4–11). Confidence is further aroused by the protection extended to the witnesses. "And if anyone wants to harm them, fire pours from their mouth and consumes their foes; anyone who wants to harm them must be killed in this manner" (Rev 11:5).

However, those who identify themselves as witnesses will experience fear at the threat of the beast and humiliation by people who would leave bodies unburied and rejoice over the death of the two witnesses.

> When they have finished their witness, the beast that comes up from the bottomless pit will make war on them and conquer them and kill them and their dead bodies will lie in the street of the great city...and the inhabitants of the earth will gloat over them and celebrate and exchange presents, because these two prophets had been a torment to the inhabitants of the earth (Rev 11:7–10).

The details are general enough to apply to any city and time, but the suffering and humiliation is clear enough to evoke fear in anyone considered to be a witness.[50]

The episode ends in vindication, which arouses confidence that, even through humiliation and death, the witnesses and their message will be vindicated by resurrection and repentance.

> But after the three and a half days, the breath of life from God entered them, and they stood on their feet...Then they heard a loud voice from heaven saying to them, "Come up here!" And they went up to heaven in a cloud while their enemies watched them... and the rest were terrified and gave glory to the God of heaven (Rev 11:11–13).

---

[49] On translating ἐπί as "against" in Rev 10:11, see chapter 2.3.c, "Personal References: Discontinuity." That this verse foreshadows hostility towards the two witnesses, see Bauckham, *Climax*, 265; Schüssler Fiorenza, *Revelation*, 77; *inter alia*, Aune, *Revelation*, 2:574; Beale, *Revelation*, 555.

[50] See discussion in chapter 2.3.e, "Spatial Signals." Aristotle advises, "Whenever it is best that they should be afraid, it is necessary to make them think they are likely to suffer, ...and showing that their equals are suffering or have suffered, and that at the hands of those from whom they did not expect it, in such a manner and at times when they did not think it likely" (Arist., *Rhet.* II.5.15).

In contrast to the fear evoked by the beast, the population of the great city are terrified (ἔμφοβοι) by the ascension of the two witnesses and the great earthquake.

Taking Rev 10:1–11:13 as a whole, the pattern of the argument from emotion is:

9:13–21	Sixth Trumpet	Fear of plagues
10:1–11	Angel Commissions John	Confidence in God's help and John as prophet
11:1–2	Measuring Temple	Emulation of Worshippers Fear of nations
11:3–6	Protection of Witnesses	Confidence in God's protection
11:7–10	Death and Shame	Fear of beast and shaming
11:11–13	Resurrection & Repent.	Confidence in vindication

The argument from emotion is structured to overshadow fear evoked by the trumpet plagues with confidence in help from the mighty angel and John as prophet. This confidence allows John to introduce the new fear of the nations, the beast, and people who shame the witnesses. John develops these fears by giving detail of who is persecuting the people of God, how they do it, and why. He avoids overwhelming the audience by implying that the two witnesses are specific people but gives subtle signals evoking fear of persecution for audiences. Fear of persecution is diminished, however, by showing the witnesses raised from the dead and the success of their testimony: those who survive the great earthquake give glory to God. This is a similar pattern as Rev 7, which moved the audience from fear of the earthquake and cosmic disasters following the sixth seal to fear of "the great persecution" (Rev 7:14). The significance of this pattern will be discussed further below in section 6.

b) Length means delay

Rev 10:1–11:13 provides its audiences an experience of delay between the sixth and seventh trumpet. In this way, Rev 10:1–11:13 matches experience to content and structure. The mighty angel announces that there will be no more time, that is, no more delay in completing the mystery of God (Rev 10:6) and, by implication, no more time to repent.[51] In Rev 11:1–13, the delay is given a specific limit: 42 months or 1260 days for the protection of the worshippers and the work of the two witnesses.

---

[51] See chapter 2.3.f, "Temporal signals," for a discussion about the meaning of the delay in Rev 10:6.

These various descriptions of a limited delay helps audiences identify with John, the worshippers, and the two witnesses. Everyone has tasks to perform during the limited time remaining. Some are worshipping, symbolically around the altar in the temple (11:1–2).[52] John and the two witnesses prophesy. Prophecy and witness will be met with resistance and hostility, and when the time is up, persecution and death. But, the promise is that witnesses will be vindicated and their message will lead to repentance.[53] Members of an audience that identify themselves as worshippers and witnesses can see these as their primary tasks during delay of God's expected judgment.

c) Location for maximum emotional impact

Similar to Rev 7, the location of Rev 10:1–11:13 between the sixth and seventh trumpet maximizes the emotional impact before the conclusion of the series. Each trumpet plague led to suffering, and the sixth led to a third of humanity killed (Rev 9:20–21). Revelation 10:1 opens at the point of maximum fear in the trumpet series. This fear makes the confidence evoked by the mighty angel and John receiving the little scroll all the more attractive and desired.

d) Minimal use of transitions

Revelation 10:1–11:13 uses minimal transitions with ambiguous delimiting markers. The transition from Rev 9:21 to 10:1 uses the low-level delimiter καὶ εἶδον but a dramatic shift in personal references, *dramatis personae*, and spatial and temporal signals. In Rev 11:13, the repentance of the remnant of the city recalls similar vocabulary at the end of the sixth trumpet. Revelation 11:14 signals the closing frame of the sixth trumpet/second woe without explaining the relevance of the preceding unit.

e) Relevance to whole more than part

Revelation 10:1–11:13 has many signals that recall Rev 1–5 or are ambiguous until resolved in Rev 12–22.[54] Revelation 10:1–11 recalls the descriptions of Jesus from Rev 1–3 and God in Rev 4, the mighty angel and the scroll from Rev 5, and the slaves of God in these chapters and Rev 6:9–11. The mention of kings anticipates their role in Rev 13–22. Rev 11:1–13 recalls the worship around the throne in Rev 5 and 7 and the role of witnesses in Rev 1–3 and 6:9–11. The role of the beast in Rev 11:7 anticipates

[52] On the symbolism, see Bauckham, *Climax*, 277; Schüssler Fiorenza, *Revelation*, 77; Aune, *Revelation*, 2:597–8; Beale, *Revelation*, 564.

[53] Bauckham, *Climax*, 13, cf. 278–9. See 2.3.f, "Temporal Signals."

[54] See chapter 2.3.h, "Summary of Analysis of Rev 10:1–11:13."

the beasts of Rev 13–20. The resurrection and vindication of the two witnesses anticipates the resurrection and vindication of other witnesses in Rev 20:4–6 and 20:11–15.

In other words, Rev 10:1–11:13 relates more to the whole book than to its immediate context in the trumpet series. As shown in chapter 4, this would not surprise audiences who heard digressions in other literature. The effect is that the digression simultaneously seems unessential yet is essential for the impact of the whole.

f) Topics: ethos of author and audience

The topics used in Rev 10:1–11:13 are appropriate to a digression developing the ethos of the author and audience. The focus of the characterization is John and characters with whom the audience is invited to identify, as discussed in section a) above. Specifically, many of these topics are chosen from Jewish literature. Some examples include:

(1) The *topos* of the prophet commanded not to write is used to develop John's ethos as obedient messenger of God and the credibility of the whole book (see *T. Sol.* 6:6; *Apoc. Zeph.* 5:6).[55]

(2) The *topos* of the prophet eating the scroll is used to develop John's ethos as a trustworthy prophet like Ezekiel (see Ezek 2:8–3:3).[56]

(3) The *topos* of measuring for protection is used to develop the audience's ethos as protected people of God (see Ezek 40:1–6; 42:20; Zech 2:5).[57]

(4) The *topos* of fire proceeding from the mouth is used to develop the ethos of witnesses as protected by divine power (see Jer 5:14b; 2 Kings 1:10–14).[58]

The audience does not need to be aware of these *topoi* in other literature to be moved by their argument from ethos.

---

[55] Aune (*Revelation*, 2:562) writes, "This prohibition to write reflects a curious convention in ancient revelatory literature in which *all but one thing is revealed.*" He concludes, "First, in a document filled with revelations, a refusal to reveal some possibly important detail lends credibility to the whole composition. Second, since the ostensible author is forbidden by supernatural intervention to reveal something to his audience, he is therefore more knowledgeable…." (2:563). Schüssler Fiorenza (*Revelation*, 75) connects this with Jesus' teaching that no one knows the day or hour (Mk 13:32; Mt 24:36). Beale (*Revelation*, 536) argues it indicates the beginning of judgment.

[56] Schüssler Fiorenza, *Revelation,* 76; Aune, *Revelation*, 2:571; Beale, *Revelation*, 548.

[57] Schüssler Fiorenza, *Revelation,* 77; Bauckham, *Climax*, 272–3; Aune, *Revelation*, 2:604; Beale, *Revelation*, 559–60.

[58] Bauckham, *Climax*, 275; Aune, *Revelation*, 2:613–4; cf. Schüssler Fiorenza, *Revelation,* 78; Beale, *Revelation*, 581.

5. Systematic Digressions

Using the terminology I have suggested, digressions in practice can be classified as either simple or systematic. What I am calling 'systematic digressions' are multiple digressions in a single work that share personal references, communication axis, *dramatis personae*, spatial signals, temporal signals, or thematic vocabulary. Together the multiple digressions develop characters, themes, and ideas independent of the surrounding units. As discussed in chapter 2, Rev 7:1–17 and 10:1–11:13 share a focus on (1) John and the people of God as *dramatis personae* and personal references, (2) communication between divine agents and the people of God, (3) spatial signals of protection on earth and worship around the throne and altar, (4) temporal signals relating to delay and (5) themes of protection, persecution, death, and vindication.[59] In this way, Rev 7:1–17 and 10:1–11:13 are consistent with other systematic digressions (discussed in chapter 4). These two passages in Revelation work together obliquely to develop a thesis that audiences may find difficult to accept: as witnesses they should be prepared to suffer and die.

First, Rev 7:1–17 and 10:1–11:13 work together as a system to develop the ethos of John and the people of God. John passively observes the 144,000 and the multitude in heaven in Rev 7, but actively writes, takes, eats, and prophesies in Rev 10. The people of God are passively sealed in Rev 7:1–8 but then actively worship in Rev 7:9–17 and 11:1–2 and two of them actively witness, which torments the inhabitants of the earth and leads to their war with the beast. John is ignorant and defers to the elder in Rev 7:14, but is knowledgeable of the seven thunders and the little scroll in Rev 10. John is powerless to do anything except observe in Rev 7, but in Rev 10 is given the little scroll to eat, empowering him to prophesy against peoples, nations, languages, and kings. Likewise, the people of God seem powerless to do anything except worship in Rev 7 and 11:1–2, but the two witnesses breathe fire and cause plagues, and most importantly testify to the Great City and the inhabitants of the earth.

The themes of protection, persecution, death, and vindication are also developed from Rev 7:1–17 to 10:1–11:13. The 144,000 are protected from winds and demonic locusts (cf. 9:4) and juxtaposed with the multitude dressed in white who are identified with the slaughter of the lamb and coming out of the great persecution. Those around the altar in Rev 11:1–2 are protected for 1260 days from the trampling of the nations. This group is juxtaposed with the two witnesses who stand before the Lord of the earth and are protected for the same amount of time before they are killed

[59] See especially the chart in chapter 2.4, "Conclusions and Questions." I discuss the theme of separation when considering theological implications in section 8 below.

by the beast, left shamefully unburied, only to be vindicated by resurrection and ascension. Rev 11:1–13 further develops the pattern of protection, persecution, death, and vindication by giving increasing detail about the source of persecution (the nations and the beast), the humiliating nature of their death, and the manner of vindication.

The pattern of protection, persecution, death, and vindication reveals the underlying message that the digressions are obliquely developing: witnesses need to be prepared for persecution and death. Cicero suggested that digressions are an effective means to persuade an audience of a difficult thesis. John's message is difficult to swallow by people who are intimately involved with Greco-Roman society through social meals (in Pergamum and Thyatira) and commerce (in Laodicea) or are generally trying to avoid conflict (in Smyrna, Philadelphia). As S. Friesen argues, John disagrees with the congregations about the violent nature of the empire.[60] Thus he slowly unveils the violence of the beast. At the same time, however, John has to persuade his audience to be willing to suffer when they are faithful witnesses, even up to death, but with confidence that God will vindicate them. The digressions therefore work as the key strategy towards this goal. The orderly, by-the-numbers judgment of the wicked is expected. Cosmic destruction is expected. Public witness leading to death is not expected. The digressions develop this difficult thesis.

The digressions do not initiate the case that witnesses should be prepared for suffering and death. The themes of persecution and death are introduced through characterization of Jesus, Antipas and the souls under the altar. Jesus is the "faithful witness," "firstborn from the dead" (Rev 1:5), and the "lamb who was slaughtered" (Rev 5:9) just as the souls under the altar were witnesses who were slaughtered (Rev 6:9–11). Antipas is specifically named as a faithful witness who was killed (Rev 2:13). In these brief strokes, John hints that being a witness may end in death in a manner similar to Jesus. Most specifically, the two witnesses die in the streets of the Great City, which among other things has the characteristics of the city "where their Lord was crucified." Being a witness is modeled on Jesus, the prototypical witness who was slaughtered.

Rev 7:1–17 and 10:1–11:13 work together as a system to broaden these themes to characters with whom the audience can identify: the multitude who come out of the great persecution and wash their robes in the blood of the Lamb, those who gather around the altar, and the two witnesses that are two lampstands. Experiencing the digressions, the audience gradually can identify with witnesses who suffer and die.

---

[60] S. Friesen, "Satan's Throne, Imperial Cults and the Social Settings of Revelation," *JSNT* 27.3 (2005): 351–373.

The digressions also systematically develop the theme of delay of vindication. The themes of the death and vindication of witnesses are developed in tandem beginning with Jesus, but the digressions increasingly illustrate a delay between death and vindication. In Rev 1:5, Jesus' vindication is introduced at the same time as his identity as a witness who died: he is the faithful witness and the firstborn from the dead. In Rev 5:6, the Lamb was slaughtered but now stands. Vindication, however, is delayed for the souls under the altar who are given white robes and told to wait (6:9–11). It is promised and not yet realized. Rev 7:15–17 emphasizes the promise of shelter, food, water, and protection from the sun that is not fulfilled until Rev 21. Likewise the vindication of the two witnesses is delayed three and a half days but has dramatic power for those who see it. In short, imminent vindication is emphasized initially in Revelation but tempered by delay as details about persecution and death are revealed. The effect is to build confidence in vindication while gradually acknowledging its delay.

John portrays the people of God in ways to allow the audience both to identify and to disassociate with characters in order to gradually reveal that fate of witnesses. If John simply announced, "Witnesses will be persecuted and be killed," it is unlikely that many would want to be witnesses. Instead, he presented their exemplar, Jesus, as the prototypical witness who suffers death and is vindicated. John describes specific characters before general groups in order to slowly persuade the audience to identify themselves. At first, the characters who suffer persecution and death are specific. The audience is able to acknowledge that Jesus and Antipas (with parallel language) were witnesses who are killed without admitting that they are models to imitate. The souls under the altar are anonymous as are the multitude around the throne.[61] This multitude, however, begins to show to the audience that an unnumbered host will come out of a great persecution, having washed their robes in the blood of the lamb. Audiences can have thought of Antipas as one of those souls under the altar and could have disassociated themselves from that group.[62] However, they could identify with the great multitude around the throne, those gathered to worship God and the Lamb. It is only late in Rev 7 that John and the audience learn that this group has experienced persecution. A similar assembly faces persecution around the altar in Rev 11:1–2 for a limited time. The specificity of two witnesses allows the audience to disassociate themselves somewhat, but their anonymity, their role as lampstands (representing congrega-

---

[61] Aune, *Revelation*, 2:406; Pattemore, *People of God*, 89; cf. Charles, *Revelation*, 1:172–3; Schüssler Fiorenza, *Revelation*, 64–5. Beale, *Revelation*, 390–1, argues that "slain" is metaphorical and the image applies to all Christians.

[62] Pattemore, *People of God*, 79.

tions in Rev 1–3), and juxtaposition with the assembly around the altar suggests that the audience should be prepared for the witnesses' fate. By moving from specific individuals to general groups with whom the audience can identify, John gradually presents every witness as facing the threat of persecution and death. This becomes most explicit in Rev 12:11: "they have conquered [the dragon] by the blood of the Lamb and by the word of their testimony, for they did not cling to life even in the face of death."[63] As digressions, Rev 7:1–17 and 10:1–11:13 make this argument obliquely, preparing the audience to identify with this group who conquers the dragon by witness, even willing to die.[64]

6. Emotion: Minimizing Fear, Maximizing Confidence

The major reason orators and authors used digressions was to stimulate or curb emotions. The argument from emotion that is developed systematically in Rev 7:1–17 and 10:1–11:13 is a crucial element in John's strategy to minimize fear of persecution. In order to persuade people to be willing to die for being a witness, John must address the fear of persecution and death. Revelation 7:1–17 and 10:1–11:13 first mitigate fear of God with confidence in God's protection and promises and with emulation of those who are protected and vindicated. Working together as a system, these two digressions slowly introduce fear of public persecution so that it is overshadowed by fear and confidence in God.

In the midst of evoking confidence (the dominant emotion evoked in Rev 7:1–17 and 10:1–11:13), fear of public persecution and death is subtly but systematically developed in the digressions. This fear is subtly evoked by, first, broadening the set of characters who suffer persecution and, second, gradually providing more information about threats against the people of God. The souls under the altar (Rev 6:9–11) make it plain that the inhabitants of the earth had something to do with their death, but audiences are not given enough information to determine if the threat applied to them as well. Rev 7:9–17, however, begins to hint that audiences should also be afraid. They can identify with these people from every tribe, language, people, and nation praising God and the Lamb, desiring to emulate those

[63] The association of death and all who testify becomes explicit in 12:11 followed by 12:17; 13:7, 9–10; 16:5–7; 17:6; 18:24; 19:2; 20:4–6. Cf. Pattemore, *People of God*, 96–113; Beale, *Revelation*, 665–6.

[64] This conclusion may be drawn without the awareness of digressions, e.g. Schüssler Fiorenza, *Revelation*, 64 (cf. 81–2); Beale, *Revelation*, 390–1, Bauckham, *Climax*, 280–1; Reddish, "Theme of Martyrdom," 149–150; Pattemore, *People of God*, 96. However, the analysis of digressions explains how the argument is effective.

dressed in white – and then discover they have come out of a great persecution.[65] This fear becomes more tangible in Rev 11:1–2 as God's people are described as worshipping around the altar while the nations trample the courtyard. Finally, fear of persecution takes its most concrete form when the beast kills the two witnesses and the inhabitants of the earth celebrate their death.

This progression from ambiguous hint of fear to detailed description slowly reveals John's concern that people will not endure to witness because they are afraid of persecution. This fear is explicitly raised in the message to Symrna:

> Do not fear (φοβοῦ) what you are about to suffer. Beware, the devil is about to throw some of you into prison in order that you may be tested, and for ten days you will have persecution (θλῖψιν). Be faithful until death, and I will give you the crown of life (Rev 2:10).

The risk is that John's audiences will not be willing to "be faithful until death," but instead will love life in the face of death (cf. Rev 12:11). The risk is that Christians will not go through the Great Persecution (τῆς θλίψεως τῆς μεγάλης) but avoid it. The risk is that Christians like the Laodiceans will not want to lose their gold, robes, and ointment to "buy" the luxuries encrusting the New Jerusalem.[66] The risk is that Christians will want to stay in the economic system of Babylon rather than "come out!" (Rev 18:4).[67] In order to convince them to witness, even at the cost of their lives, John must overcome their fear of persecution. This is an emotional issue and requires an emotional solution.

Ethical/emotional digression is one strategy to address emotional issues, and this fact helps us to understand the effect of Rev 7:1–17 and 10:1–11:13. The seal and trumpet series vividly illustrate why God should be feared over any other threat. Fear of God is presented in such cosmic and tragic proportions as to overshadow fear of public persecution. Who could fear the beast or even death when compared to the fear of the cosmic distress after the sixth seal or the cosmic destruction and suffering of the trumpet plagues?

Thus John's argument from emotion represents a three-part strategy: First, present the fear of God as so overwhelming that every other fear is minimized. Second, relieve fear of God by confidence in God's protection

---

[65] Pattemore (*People of God*, 86–88, cf. 143) emphasizes that the white robes connote ethical purity and not martyrdom. The souls under the altar are given robes, but the great crowd washes their own robes and this contrast increases the audience's processing effort to connect the two (Pattemore, *People of God*, 149).

[66] Cf. R. Royalty, *The Streets of Heaven: The Ideology of Wealth in the Apocalypse of John* (Macon, Ga.: Mercer University Press, 1998).

[67] Cf. Friesen, "Satan's Throne."

and promise and by examples of characters for the audience to emulate as a way out of fear. Third, and last for a good reason, introduce fear of public persecution gradually and balance it with confidence in God's ultimate vindication so that the audience will be willing to witness, even up to death.

The digressions are the key to this strategy. The seal and trumpet series present the fear of God. Embedded within this matrix, the digressions relieve fear with confidence, provide examples to emulate, and gradually introduce the audience to examples who witness and are killed and who are vindicated, thus introducing them to the fear of public persecution and addressing that fear. Throughout the rest of Revelation, the people of God will witness, face death, and finally receive vindication (e.g. Rev 12:10–12).[68] The pattern of digressions within the seal and trumpet series prepares the audience to accept this role with minimal fear and maximum confidence.

7. Digressions as Chaos in the Midst of Order

Even as I describe how digressions in Revelation are similar to digressions in other literature and how they persuade the audience to have confidence in God and willingness to witness in the face of persecution, this may be an attempt to manage disorder. Härter argues that every attempt to label a unit as a deviation and to explain its coherence replicates the author's own attempt to manage and control chaos.[69] Rhetoricians also attempted to control disorder by discussing digressions, giving them a name, and circumscribing their use and function.[70]

By calling Rev 7:1–17 and 10:1–11:13 digressions, I am trying to manage the disruption of order. This should not be seen as a totalizing claim, but as an explanation of the details of the text and the diverse responses to these passages. John has already ordered these digressions by placing them between the sixth and seventh elements, which manages the chaos they introduce. The wide variety of terms and interpretations for these two passages confirms their ambiguous status and reflects the attempts by interpreters to manage disorder. Although I have proposed an interpretation for these two passages and their rhetorical impact, it should be clear that the ambiguous nature of these two units leaves them open to a variety of interpretations. However, a keener awareness of the use of digressions in antiq-

[68] Bauckham, *Climax*, 283–337; Pattemore, *People of God*, 90–116.
[69] Härter, 11.
[70] Härter, 12; cf. 18, 40.

uity limits the range of interpretations and leads one to see a coherent strategy to persuade the audience.

Härter emphasizes how digressions contest the validity claims of the order of the surrounding text. This also seems the case in the book of Revelation. The order of seals and trumpets seems relentless: seven seals are opened and an announcement of suffering or death follows each seal. Seven trumpets are blown and a scene of destruction, death, and suffering follows each trumpet. If an audience connects these events to the Exodus narrative and the plagues, the audience will understand them as signs of God's sovereignty over the earth, specifically over Pharaoh and the magicians who support his rule with signs and wonders.[71] The order of plagues is unyielding, or so it seems.

But Rev 7:1–17 and 10:1–11:13 disrupt that expected order with scenes of protection and vindication – and hints of persecution and death. The relentless progression of seals and trumpets is challenged by these digressions, their progression delayed and their inevitability questioned. If the plague narrative in Exodus is in mind, an audience can link the way the Passover narrative interrupts the plague narratives, giving confidence in God's protection and liberation. Revelation 11:3–13 confirms the insight from Exodus 12 that plagues alone will not achieve repentance or liberation, but adds that witness is necessary.

The point is that the digressions in Revelation (and in Exodus) are successful in wresting control from the order of seals and trumpets. As a result Rev 7:1–17 and 10:1–11:13 become more memorable and significant passages than the seal and trumpet series in which they are embedded. This is true for at least four reasons. First, the digressions disrupt the narrative flow with discontinuous signals that require additional processing. Second, the digressions describe the people of God, with whom the audience is encouraged to identify. Third, communication is between God's agents and the people of God, which replicates immediate experience of speech between the reader and the audience. Fourth, the digressions make a unique emotional argument (confidence and emulation) that stands out from the surrounding material (fear of God). As a result the digressions become more significant to the audience than the surrounding material. The scenes of protection, worship, prophecy, and witness stand like islands of mercy in a sea of judgment and destruction.

---

[71] See discussion in chapter 4.8.c, "Exodus 12:1–28."

8. Theological Implications

The use of digressions in Revelation has theological implications. Protection of God's people breaks in and delays the seemingly inexorable progression of God's judgment. Confidence in God's grace overrides fear of God's wrath. The role of the people of God during times of cosmic distress is worship and witness, so that the remnant may give glory to God. I will examine each of these in turn.

Scenes of protection, worship, prophecy, and witness digress from the order of seals and trumpets. From the point of view of an audience eagerly expecting God's judgment, this explains any delay. The digressions give audiences a way to manage the chaos in their own lives by reinterpreting delay in justice as a time for protection, worship, prophecy, and witness. For an audience that fears God's wrath, the digressions suggest that God's judgment is not ultimate, but that God's gracious protection and vindication mitigates and delays judgment. From this point of view, there is time: time for Ephesians to regain their lost love, time for Pergamenes, Thyatirians, and Sardians to repent, and time for Laodiceans to buy robes and gold and ointment from Jesus. The time of persecution is limited: only ten days for Smyrnans and a short time for the Philadelphians before the hour of trial. The digressions represent that God is gracious and gives time. Judgment is not as final or inexorable as it may seem (and some may want).

Theologically speaking, the digressions within the series of seals and trumpets represent confidence in God's grace triumphing over fear of God's wrath. This is perhaps stated too strongly, because John depends on fear of God to motivate people to action. But confidence in God's promises triumphs in the end over God's wrath, even for the kings of the nations who will bring their glory into the New Jerusalem (Rev 21:24–25). The tension between confidence and fear is resolved with emphasis on confidence, perhaps analogously to the way that the portrayal of Jesus as lion and lamb (Rev 5:5–6) is resolved in favor of Jesus as lamb who was slaughtered. The emphasis on confidence in the digression, mitigating both fear of God and fear of public persecution, minimizes the fear aroused by the seal and trumpet series.

Finally, the use of digressions has theological implications for ecclesiology, how the people of God are understood. Systematically, Rev 7:1–17 and 10:1–11:13 characterize John and the people of God as moving from passivity to activity, ignorance to knowledge, and powerlessness to authority. One also should note how the digressions (1) separate the people of God from the inhabitants of the earth, (2) locate them in the midst of and not separate from tragic events on earth, (3) give them the role of worship and witness, and (4) prepare them for persecution.

First, by focusing attention on the people of God the digressions increase the contrast with the seal and trumpets which focus generally on humanity or, as in the case of the fifth (and perhaps sixth) trumpet plague, specifically on those not sealed. Even given the ambiguity, audiences are left with the sense that the plagues apply to the rest of humanity and that they will be protected. The digressions separate them from the rest of humanity just as much as the seal marks them as God's slaves, just as much as the blood of the Lamb bought them out of humanity (cf. Rev 14:1–5), just as much as no one unclean will be allowed to enter the New Jerusalem (Rev 21:27). God's people are a separate people, and digressions are a structural way of expressing that ecclesiology – and persuading the audience to be separate too.[72]

Second, the digressions embed the people of God in the world of tragic historical events. The digressions are not separate from the events following seven seals or seven trumpets, but are embedded within them. The continuous signals that link Rev 7:1–17 to the seal events and Rev 10:1–11:13 to the trumpet plagues likewise locate the people of God in the middle of these tragic events. The 144,000 are sealed in the midst of the cosmic distress following the sixth seal. John receives the little scroll in the midst of one third of the world's population being killed by plague. By embedding the digressions within the sixth element of each series, John insists that the people of God do not escape from responsibility during disasters like earthquakes and plagues but instead are called to be faithful witnesses to Jesus in the midst of those events.

Third, the digressions give the people of God the role of worshipping and witnessing on earth and in heaven, as modeled first by Jesus.[73] They are not explicitly shown around the throne in Rev 5, but are introduced in Rev 7:9 as the Great Crowd in heaven and those worshipping around the altar on earth (Rev 11:1–2). Just as Jesus, John, and Antipas are called witnesses, two anonymous witnesses testify and become paradigmatic for all the people of God who will witness.[74]

Fourth, as argued above, the primary purpose of the digressions is to obliquely persuade the audience to suffer persecution and accept even

---

[72] Pattemore, *People of God*, 218; cf. 86–7, 133, argues this is also an ethical separation. Cf. Bauckham, *Climax*, 226–229.

[73] Pattemore, *People of God*, 114: "The martyr church is modeled on Christ in every dimension of its existence." Blood is shed, death is the result of witness, victory leads to death, reigning means reigning with Christ.

[74] That the two witnesses are paradigmatic, see Aune, *Revelation*, 2:631; Beale, *Revelation*, 573; Pattemore, *People of God*, 161–164; cf. 79–80. Cf. Schüssler Fiorenza, *Revelation*, 78.

death because of their witness. This is a martyr ecclesiology.[75] The development of this theme in digressions indicates that this is not an easy message to accept, but that the audience can face public persecution in confidence of limited protection, the effectiveness of witness, and final vindication. Not all of the people of God will face martyrdom (John, for instance, never suggests he will), but that every witness should be prepared to "not love their life to the point of death" (Rev 12:11).[76]

---

[75] Cf. Bauckham, *Climax*, 228–9, 273–283. Especially see Pattemore, *People of God,* chapter 4: "A Martyr Ecclesiology."

[76] John does not believe that all Christians will be martyred, but that "the church as a whole is defined by a willingness to sacrifice one's own life" (Pattemore, *People of God*, 114). Also, Schüssler Fiorenza, *Revelation,* 64; Beale, *Revelation*, 390.

Chapter 6

Conclusions and Trajectories

1. Conclusions and Contributions

The driving question of this book has been: "How would first century audiences experience the structure of Rev. 7:1–17 and 10:1–11:13?" I have proposed that they likely would identify them with other experiences of παρέκβασις, or 'digression,' as used in a wide variety of speeches and literature and as described by Greco-Roman rhetoricians. Audiences would pay more attention to these passages because they require additional processing effort, they shape the ethos of author and audience, and they excite their emotions. These digressions obliquely develop the case that witnesses will suffer persecution and even death by being faithful witnesses modeled after Jesus. This thesis may be difficult for audiences to accept. The digressions are a potent strategy to persuade them to accept the call to witness and its consequence. To move their emotions and sway their judgment, Revelation 7:1–17 and 10:1–11:13 disrupt the order of the seals and trumpets at the point of maximum emotion and expectation. Protection delays judgment, confidence in God's grace triumphs over judgment, and the people of God become active, knowledgeable, and authorized participants in Jesus' work of witnessing.

The conclusion that John is trying persuade the audience to become faithful witnesses in the face of persecution is not new. What is new about the present investigation is the analysis of digressions and their importance for understanding the rhetorical strategy of Revelation. This chapter summarizes the contributions of this book and sketches trajectories for future research on digressions and Revelation.

First, I described a Greek term and technique, παρέκβασις, that explains deviations in the order of a text. D. Aune, C. Koester, and J. D. Hester suggested the presence of digressions in the New Testament and they have pointed the way towards this more detailed study. Race commented that digressions are common in Greco-Roman literature and literary critics like Sabry and Härter celebrate the rhetorical discussion of digression but many New Testament scholars remain unaware. The term 'digression' may be problematic for some because it suggests that the unit is unrelated to the text. But further awareness of the use of digressions and their subordination to a text's rhetorical goals may relieve interpreters' discomfort.

Second, identifying these passages as digressions explains the divergent interpretations and terms that interpreters have used. Digressions require the audience to work harder to establish the relationship with the surrounding material, and inevitably this leads to different, even divergent, interpretations. If interpreters focus on the immediate literary context, they are likely to emphasize the continuity with the digression and use terms like expansion and enlargement. If interpreters emphasize the text as a whole, they emphasize the discontinuity and use terms like interlude, parenthesis, and delay. These divergent responses replicate an audience's struggle to understand the relevance of a digression. The tension between continuity and discontinuity is exactly the effect of a digression.

Third, this analysis explains the effect of the placement between the sixth and seven element of a series. Revelation's use of digressions is consistent with the advice that the penultimate position is the most emotionally potent. After having built up expectation for the seventh element with a series of fear inspiring events, the emotional pitch is at its height. Awareness of the use of digressions explains that the audience is most receptive at this point to be shaped by visions of confidence.

Fourth, digressions may be used to work together as a system. Authors used them not simply in isolation from one another but as a system in order to obliquely develop an argument. In Revelation, John gradually introduces the threat of persecution and death for witnesses through digressions so that the audience will be willing to "not love life to the point of death" (12:11). The digressions, in this respect, relate more closely to one another than to the seals and trumpets.

Fifth, the argument from emotion is critical to understand the structure. The principal motivation for using digressions was to arouse or curb emotion. In Revelation, the digressions mitigate fear of God with confidence in God's protection and examples to emulate. Fear of persecution is slowly introduced but quickly overshadowed by confidence in God's vindication. Awareness of the emotional aspect of digressions explains how a digression is essential to the rhetorical effect even as it is unessential to the logic of the narrative.

Sixth, the use of digressions has theological implications. Structure does inform meaning. The disruption of the order of seals and trumpets suggests that the orderly, seemingly unstoppable, progress of judgment and eschatological events is delayed for protection of God's people and time to witness so that some may repent. This represents the supremacy of God's grace over judgment. By using digressions, Revelation urges the audience to have confidence that minimizes fear of God and fear of public persecution. The people of God are participants with the rest of humanity during the devastation – they have not been whisked away. They are separated from the inhabitants of the earth by God's seal, their knowledge of God's mystery and their witness. They are subtly urged to leave behind passivity for activity in worship and witness in a hostile world, to leave behind ignorance for knowledge of God's revelation of Jesus, and to leave behind powerlessness in the face of ungodly powers for authority to witness against kings, beasts, and inhabitants of the earth.

2. Trajectories: Other texts marked as deviations

Although a comprehensive analysis of other deviations in Revelation is beyond the scope of this book, this analysis may illuminate other passages. Three questions for future research include: (1) Is there a comparable digression in the bowl series (Rev 16), which is the only other explicitly numbered series? (2) Since the 'orderly' digressions (pardon the irony) of Rev 7:1–17 and 10:1–11:13 occur consistently between sixth and seventh elements, is there a pattern to the deviations in Rev 12–22? (3) Are the other deviations in Rev 12–22 also digressions? I will address these questions in order.

a) From Delayed to Imminent Judgment and Long to Short Digressions

On first glance, it does not appear that there is a digression between the sixth and seventh bowl plagues,[1] although audiences may expect one based on previous experience with the seal and trumpet series. Three options have been proposed. First, Caird and Mounce propose that the mighty angel's announcement, "no more delay" (Rev 10:6) means that that there will be no more interruptions on the way to judgment.[2] This, however, is inaccurate, as there are a number of deviations on the way to judgment.[3] In the bowl series alone, the angel of the waters and altar interrupt with an antiphonal hymn after the third bowl (Rev 16:5–7) and Jesus speaks directly through the Seer in Rev 16:15.

[1] E.g. R. H. Mounce (*The Book of Revelation* [2nd ed; Grand Rapids, Michigan: Eerdmans, 1998], 154) notes that the parenthesis between the sixth and seventh seals and trumpets is not repeated with the bowls.

[2] G. B. Caird, *The Revelation of St. John the Divine* (New York: Harper & Row, 1966), 127–129; Mounce, 205–6; cf. R. Bauckham, *Climax of Prophecy: Studies in the Book of Revelation* (London: T & T Clark, 1993), 263.

[3] See Table 1.

Second, Steinmann proposes that Jesus' interruption in Rev 16:15 is analogous to Rev 7:1–17 and 10:1–11:13.[4] He points out that the focus is again on the people of God and that Rev 16:15 relates to the previous digressions (he calls them expansions) by the motif of clothes. "Behold, I am coming like a thief! Blessed is the one who stays awake, keeping his garments, in order that he may not walk naked and they look at his shamefulness!" (16:15). There is a shift in communication axis, personal references, *dramatis personae*, spatial and temporal signals, and thematic vocabulary. By all these measures, Rev 16:15 is a digression. However, Rev 16:15 is very short (only 21 words), it does not signal a delay, and it lacks the narrative movement of Rev 7:1–17 and 10:1–11:13 which each tell a self-contained story with beginning, middle, and end. Rev. 16:15 is qualitatively different than Rev 7:1–17 and 10:1–11:13.

A third option argues that the brief interjection in Rev 16:15 highlights the absence of a long digression where one was expected. As opposed to delay, this verse emphasizes the speed of the coming Christ: "Behold! I am coming like a thief!" Bauckham says that, "there is *not* in this series of judgments the intercalation which the first two series might have led us to expect."[5] Bauckham observes that Rev 16:15 is (1) in the right position between the sixth and seventh element and (2) it is focused on time, although now imminence rather than delay. With Bauckham, I conclude that Rev 16:15 reverses the expectation of delay with the imminence of Jesus' coming. The immanence of Jesus' coming is stressed in content and structure.

Like the two digressions already analyzed, Rev. 16:15 is embedded in the sixth bowl event in an A-B-A' pattern and can be removed without changing the narrative logic. Rev 16:16 returns to the assembly of the kings of the earth (Rev 16:14), keeping Jesus' interruption in place just as the second woe (Rev 11:14) reminded the audience of the sixth trumpet/second woe structure.

Revelation 16:15 satisfies an audience's expectation of an ethical/emotional digression following the sixth element in a series. It includes all the shifts expected of a digression (communication axis, etc.) and directly addresses the audience in order to construct their ethos. It relates to the Rev 7:1–17 and 10:1–11:13 by the vocabulary of clothing. It recalls

---

[4] A. E. Steinmann, "The tripartite structure of the sixth seal, the sixth trumpet, and the sixth bowl of John's Apocalypse," *Journal of the Evangelical Theological Society* 35 (Oct 1992): 69–79.

[5] Bauckham, *Climax*, 14. His emphasis. He argues that there is no delay because there is no more time for repentance, pointing at the lack of repentance during the bowl series (Rev 16: 9, 11). The lack of repentance in the face of terrible plagues makes the absences of the witnesses more pronounced. Given the response by the remnant of the Great City, one wonders what might have happened if there were witnesses to proclaim in the empire of the beast.

Rev 1–3, including the initial announcement that "the time is near" (Rev 1:3) and the messages to Sardis ("wake up" γρηγορῶν, 3:2, 3; "like a thief" ὡς κλέπτης, 3:3 and "their robes" τὰ ἱμάτια αὐτῶν, 3:4, 5) and Laodicea ("naked" γυμνός, 3:17). By recalling the initial address to the seven congregations, John calls the audience to pay attention to their behavior in the midst of the sixth bowl. Emotionally, the series is at a climax after the sixth event, with the frightening gathering of kings called by the demonic spirits. The voice of Jesus in this context is the voice of confidence in his coming and the blessing on those who are clothed. As in Rev 7:1–17 and 10:1–11:13, the short saying in Rev 16:15 attempts to overshadow fear of worldly forces with fear of God by threatening those who are naked and exposed to shame.

This brief analysis reveals that the form of deviations changes after Rev 11:13. There are still deviations, texts that interpreters use special terms to describe, but they are shorter, delaying the progress of the visions less in structure and content. Charles, Schüssler Fiorenza, Beale, and Pattemore agreed that Rev 12:10–12 and 15:2–4 required special terminology, and at least three of them identified Rev 8:2–5, 14:1–5, 16:15, 17:9, 19:8b, and 20:4–6.[6] These later deviations are also not shaped as independent narratives, but are often short speeches by one or more characters (including John).

Rev 14:1–5 and 20:4–6 are exceptions. They have a narrative arc and are longer (133 and 108 words in Greek respectively), but significantly shorter than Rev 7:1–17 (400 words) and 10:1–11:13 (622 words). These passages are consistent with Cicero and Quintilian's discussion of digressions as figures of thought, so are appropriately called digressions.[7] They are not major parts of the speech, but short digressions that exhibit all the criteria discussed in chapter 3. The key difference is length and complete lack of transition.[8] D. Lee identifies many of these as narrative asides,[9] but both Cicero and Quintilian calls these figures of thought *digressio*.[10]

---

[6] See chapter 1.3, "An Overview of Deviations in the Structure of Revelation."

[7] *De oratore* III.53.205; *Orator* xl.137; *Inst.* IX.2.54–57. See chapter 3.

[8] Consider Quintilian's two examples: "For as Cicero says, the shorter form of digression made effected in a number of different ways. The following passages will, however, suffice as examples: 'Then Gaius Varenus, that is, the Varenus who was killed by the slaves of Ancharius – I beg you, gentlemen, to give careful attention to what I am about to say;' the second is from the pro Milone: 'Then he turned on me that glance, which it was his wont to assume, when he threatened all the world with every kind of violence.'" (IX.2.28; cf. IX.1.28 [Butler, LCL]).

[9] D. Lee, *The Narrative Asides in the Book of Revelation* (Lanham, Maryland: University Press of America, 2002).

[10] Quintilian uses the term *apostrophe* to refer to the change of address from the judge to someone else (e.g. the opponent) (IX.2.38), or a diversion from the question before an

I suggest that the shorter deviations also are digressions. Digressions in the expected order are not so surprising since Rev 7:1–17 and 10:1–11:13 have trained the audience to expect them between the sixth and seventh elements. Rev 16:15 fulfills this expectation but emphasizes that Jesus' coming is imminent rather than delayed. Although further investigation is necessary, shorter digressions support the sense that the pace of narrative is increasing and the end coming sooner.

b) From Orderly to Disorderly: Digressions in Rev 12–22

Although Rev 16:15 fits the pattern of a digression embedded between the sixth and seventh, a number of digressions do not fit this pattern. A victory song (Rev 12:10–12) interrupts the story of the dragon and the woman, the 144,000 gathered with the Lamb (Rev 14:1–5) deviates from the beast and the announcement of judgment, the Song of Moses (Rev 15:2–4) separates the introduction of the seven angels with bowls and their exit from the temple, the song of the Angel of the Waters (Rev 15:5–7) interrupts between the third and fourth bowls. Others include 17:9 (Explanation of the beast); 19:8b (the Bride's fine linen) and 20:4–6 (The thousand year reign). The digressions between the sixth and seventh seals and trumpets, ironically, are orderly compared to the lack of a pattern with other deviations.

This shift from orderly to disorderly digressions suggests that God's judgment is also becoming more disorderly as the end of the book approaches. As discussed in chapter 5, Rev 7:1–17 and 10:1–11:13 challenge the claims of the orderly march to judgment. As digressions later in the book become shorter and less predictable, the audience is given the impression that the end is coming faster and that orderly judgment itself is being dissolved by these interruptions.

Despite the lack of predictable order, the topics of these digressions reliably deal with the people of God.[11] Rev 12:10–12 equates Michael's victory in heaven with those who conquer by the blood of the Lamb and their testimony. Rev 14:1–5 concern the 144,000 and those who follow the lamb. Rev 15:2–4 anticipates all nations worshipping God. Rev 16:3–7 bring the blood of the saints and prophets in parallel with the water becom-

---

assembly (quoting *Aeneid* IV.425). A. Härter (*Digressionen: Studien zum Verhältnis von Ordnung und Abweichung in Rhetorik und Poetik* [Verlag: Wilhem Fink, 2000], 21) argues that this is another term to be associated with the rhetorician's attempts to manage deviation.

[11] Compare Pattemore's list of passages concerning the people of God (*People of God* [MSSNTS 128; Cambridge: Cambridge University Press, 2004], 64–67). They almost exclusively are in texts identified as deviations by Charles, Schüssler Fiorenza, and Beale.

ing blood. Rev 19:8b identifies the fine linen of the bride with the righteous deeds of the saints. Rev 20:4–6 portrays the saints raised to rule with Christ. In the midst of describing the judgment of the enemies of God, these digressions address the ethos of the people of God, as observed in Rev 7:1–17 and 10:1–11:13.

The rapid and unpredictable digressions also heighten their emotional impact. Audiences may be surprised that the dragon's defeat in heaven is paralleled with their activity as witnesses (Rev 12:10–12). Similar to the argument from emotion in Rev 7:1–17 and 10:1–11:13, the fear of persecution is overshadowed by confidence in God. Only after a celebratory hymn is fear of the dragon addressed ("Woe to the earth and sea...").

Digressions in Rev 12–22 continue to shape the ethos of the people of God by their activity, knowledge, and authority to witness. The people of God are not removed from conflict with God's enemies, but embedded just as the digressions are embedded in the surrounding narrative. Even as the threat from the dragon and its minions becomes more clear, the argument from emotion moves the people of God to confidence in God's help and vindication.

c) Questions for future research

I identified Rev 7:1–17 and 10:1–11 as digressions comparable to those in speeches and other literature, and suggested that shorter units in Rev. 12–22 are digressions as a figure of thought. At least three questions remain for understanding these shorter passages.

The first question relates to macrostructural terms. What is the relationship between a digression and other techniques, such as ring composition? One of the basic criteria for identifying a digression was the A-B-A' pattern, which is also the pattern for observing ring composition. Not all ring compositions are digressions, however, because not all involve shifts in communication axis, personal references, *dramatis personae*. temporal and spatial signals, and thematic vocabulary. Not all ring compositions can be removed without loss to the logic of the narrative. Gaisser and Austin identify ring compositions as digressions in the *Iliad*. Wendland and Aune argue that Rev 12:10–12 and 20:4–6 are ring compositions.[12]

A second question is: how are short digressions and other microstructures (e.g. figures of thought and speech) to be distinguished? It is not clear how rhetoricians distinguish between a digression as a figure of thought and what D. Lee calls a narrative aside. Quintilian (*Inst.* IX.2.54–

[12] E. Wendland, "7 x 7 (x7): A Structural and Thematic Outline of John's Apocalypse," *OPTAT* 4 (1990), 371–87; D. Aune, *Revelation* (3 vols; WBC; Waco, Texas: Word, 1997–8), 2:663–4; 3:1079.

57) discusses the digression as a figure of thought as distinct from *aposiopesis* because not all digressions involve breaking off mid-sentence. *Aposiopesis* is one way to transition into a digression.[13] He and the author of *Rhetorica ad Herennium* discuss *apostrophe* as a separate figure of thought.[14] *Anacoluthon*[15] and *parenthesis*[16] are two other figures of speech to be considered. Further precision is needed to analyze the shorter deviations in Revelation.[17] One common denominator among all these figures is the concern for the emotional impact on the audience.[18]

Third: Do authors use longer digressions and shorter figures of thought to work together as a system? After longer digressions, in *Or.* 36 Dio of Prusa uses shorter figures that refer back to the Dio's supremacy over both poet and philosopher as a source of knowledge of the divine.[19] The shorter digressions in Revelation also feature the people of God, which suggests that long and short digressions do work together to shape the ethos of the audience.

In order that others may evaluate how ancient authors used digressions, I present a list of digressions in ancient literature in the Appendix. A detailed search for and analysis of digressions in the Hebrew Bible and early Jewish and Christian literature remains a goal for scholarship. By becoming immersed in ancient communication patterns, we will come to better detect and appreciate digressions as a strategy to persuade.

---

[13] Quintilian quotes his favorite speech by Cicero, *Pro Milone*.

[14] Quintilian, *Inst.* IX.2.38–39; *Rhet. Her.* IV.15.22.

[15] E.g. Xenophon, *Anabasis*, I.8.13, III.1.20.

[16] Quintilian, IX.3.23

[17] Another possible figure of speech is ἄφοδος (Quintilian, *Inst.* IX.3.87).

[18] *Rhet. Her.* IV.15.22 (Caplan, LCL) identifies *apostrophe* as the figure "which expresses grief or indication by means of an address to some man or city or place or object….If we use Apostrophe in its proper place, sparingly, and when the importance of the subject seems to demand it, we shall instill in the hearer as much indignation as we desire." Quintilian cites Cicero's *Pro Leg.* turning to ask a rhetorical question of his opponent: "What was that sword of yours doing, Tubero, in the field of Pharsalus?" The purpose is to inflame the audience's hatred towards the Tubero (IX.2.38; cf. Cicero, *Pro Leg.* 3.9).

[19] For example, *Or.* 36.39c–h, 43a–e. See Appendix.

Appendix

A List of Digressions in Ancient Literature

This list is provided as a basis for future research. Many passages need additional analysis in light of the theory and practice discussed in chapters 3 and 4. In general, I used the Loeb editions; other editions are listed in the Bibliography. Scholars who identify and discuss these digressions are noted in parenthesis. The digressions I alone suggest are marked with a plus sign (+).

Aeschines (May 1979, 244 n. 11)		
In Timarchus	170–176	Ethical/Emotional Digression
Anonymous Seguerianus	II.61–67	Contrasting παρέκβασις and παραδιήγησις
Antiphon (Martin, 56; May 1979, 244)		
Murder of Herodes	64–73	Ethical/Emotional Digression
Apthonius (Lausberg; Martin)		
Progymnasmata	Rabe 17–20	Use παρέκβασις to attack opponent's past life and reject pity
Apuleius (Poser, 16)		
Metamorphoses	2.8f	
	4.2	
	10.33	
Aristeas ad Philocrates (Shutt in OTP 2:10; Honigman; Wasserstein and Wasserstein)		
	51–82	Details of the gifts from the king
	83–120	High Priest's vestments
	128-171	Digression on the Law in Judaism
	187–300	Wisdom Symposia: "If I have dwelt at length on these matters, Philocrates, I beg your pardon," §295
Aristotle (Sabry, 171; May 1979)		
Rhetorica	I.1.1–3	λέγειν ἔχω τοῦ πράγματος only to arouse emotion
	III.13.16–18	ἐπιπίστωσις ("supplementary proof") and ἐπεχέλεγξος ("supplementary refutation") by Theodorus of Byzantium;

		and ἀποπλάνησις ("wandering") by Licymnius
Politica	V.7.5	Deviation of forms of government (Sabry, 171)
Aristides, Aelius (Race 1980)		
Orationes	2.66–74	"carried away" (73–74).
	+21.14–15	"I have added to my song these remarks concerning the Meles" because of the river Nymphs' influence
Bacchylides (Race 1980)		
	10.51–52	ἔκτος ὁδοῦ
Cicero (see esp. Canter, who cites 55 examples; see also Härter and Sabry)		
Brutus	(See Kennedy, *New History*, 155)	
	70–76	Comparing oratory to Art
	82	Servius Galba used digression as embellishment (Canter, 351)
	183–200	How to Judge Oratory
	292–300	Ridiculing that Cato is new Lysias
	322	Skill in pleasing digressions (Canter, 351)
De domo	3–31	Defense of Cicero's political conduct
De har. resp.	18–19	Authority and influence of religion
	28–29	Desecration of Pessinus, seat of Cybele
	41	Honorable foes of the state
De inventione	I.51.97	Quoting Hermagoras that digression placed after refutation before conclusion
De lege agr.	I.18–22	Capua as a source of peril to the Roman State
	I.87–97	Wise policy of early Rome in dealing with Carthage, Corinth, Capua
Pro lege Manila	57–58	Appointment of Gabinius as Pompey's lieutenant
De oratore	II.80–82, 311	Digression as means for moving audience
In Pisonem	68–72	Philodemus the Epicurean
In Verrem	III.2–10	In praise of the Sicilians (digressions help break the monotonous recital of Verres' crimes; cf. Canter 357)
	III.28–30	Character necessary in praetor's cohort
	III.51–52	A festival in honor of Verres
	III.110–114	Eulogy of Sthenius
	IV.159–162	Depravity of Verres' son
	V.33–34	Verres as a judge of silver plate
	V.56–57	Degeneracy of manners; Verres contrast with L. Piso
	V.72–74	Segesta and the statue of Diana
	V.79–81	An appeal to Scipio Nasica
	V.106–108	Worship of Ceres and Libera in Sicily
	V.117–119	Description of Syracuse

	V.129–130	Honor paid to Jupiter Imperator at Syracuse
	V.132–135	Value set upon works of art by the Greeks
	VI.25–37	The self-indulgent Verres
	VI.57–58	Praise of Verres by the Mamertines
Orationes Phil.	II.116	Julius Caesar's gifts and accomplishments
	V.39	Caesar and the Civil War
	VI.12–15	Statues in honor of L. Antonius
Orator	ii.7–iii.12	Comparing oratory to sculpture philosophical, "leaving well-trodden paths" (iii.11)
Part. Orat.	v.15	Digressions weaken or bury proofs on which prosecution relies
	xv.52	Uses materials of explanatory, illustrative, enforcing character
	xxxvi.128	Digressions to excite pity or hatred
Pro Archia	12–30	In praise of poetry and learned men (digression is more than half!)
Pro Balbo	13	Eulogy of Cn. Pompey
Pro Caecina	70–75	In praise of civil law
Pro Caelio	59–60	Eulogy of Q. Metellus
Pro Cluentio	15	Denunciation of Sassia (Martin 1974:91)
	109–112	The tribune L. Quinctius
Pro Milone	33	A figure of thought (Quintilian, *Inst.* IX.2.56; cf. Martin, 91)
	47	Cicero's part in Clodius' murder
	72–91	(Quintilian, *Inst.* IV.3.12–17; May 1979)
Pro Murena	3–10	Apologia for Cicero's defense of Murena (Martin 1974, 91)
	43–53	Sulpicius ill-conducted contest for consulship
	55–56	Peril of reversal of fortune incident
	61–66	Stoic precepts and paradoxes
Pro Plancio	64–67	Ignorance of provincial affairs at Rome
Pro Rab. Post.	29–30	Eulogy of C. Marius
Pro rege Deiotaro	28–32	Denunciation of Castor
Pro Rosc. Am.	33–34	Prosecution of Quintus Scaevola
	55–57	Roles of accusers in the state
	59–61	Frivolity of accuser Erucius
	61–73	Crime of parricide
	136–142	Political creed and supremacy of the Optimates
Pro Sestio	36–52	Cicero's political principles and conduct
	60–63	Cato's part in the dethronement of Ptolemaeus
	91	Society's development from savagery to civilization
	96m–131	The Optimates
	132–135	Denunciation of Vatinius

	136–143	Eulogy of the Optimates: virtues, sacrifices, and fame
Pro Sulla	2–10	Apologia for Cicero's defense of Sulla
	21–35	Cicero the third king of Rome
	46–50	A warning to Torquatus
Demosthenes		
Aristocrates	196–214	Ethical Digression (May 1979, 244 n. 11)
De Corona	18	ἐκτροπή (identified by Anon. Seg. II.140)
	199–211	(Race 1980)
De Falsa Leg.	177–78	(Anon. Seg. IV.239: "recapitulated in the middle and scattered the amplified material in each of the headings")
Dio of Prusa		
Orationes	7.81	Apology for the long story of the hunter. Thesis: "The poor are not at disadvantage in words, deeds or social intercourse"
	7.102	Defense that the "present procedure" is the usual one (cf. 7.103 on length; Russell 1992, 188)
	7.127–132	ἐκτροπή; has not abandoned the theme of the whole; hunter who leaves trail to bag chance game (Race 1980, 4 n. 11). Fair to call orator to task whose remarks have no bearing on the matter in hand (Russell 1992, 148–150)
	12.38	ἔκβας; attack on Epicureans (Aune 2004, 133; Race 1980; Russell 1992, 17, 188)
	12.43b	Getting argument from bypath to the straight way; concern for length of speech
	30.20–24	Wandering philosopher explains the nature of the chain "But first it is right to say…" (see Moles 2000, 191ff) "…but this is not right, and does not befit the gods" (see §25)
	36.7	Description of Borysthenes has interrupted action, so Dio resumes, "Well as I was saying…"
	+36.33–35	Poets inferior to mystagogues
	+36.39c–h	Poets ignorant/Magi know
	+36.43a–e	Poets graceful and Greek/Magi inconsistent and barbaric
	+36.48	Poets inaccurate/Magi accurate
	+36.50	Humanity misunderstands/Magi understands
Diodorus (Aune 2004, 134)		
	20.2.1	Provide variety

Dionysius of Halicarnassus		
Isocrates	4	Isocrates relieves "monotony by varying the treatment of the different elements of the subject itself and by introducing changes in the same material itself and foreign episodes" (τὸ διαλαμβάνεσθαι τὴν ὁμοείδειαν ἰδίαις μεταβολαῖς καὶ ξένοις ἐπεισοδίοις)
Thucydides	7	"[L]ocal historians were obliged to embellish their accounts with mythical episodes" (μυθώδεσιν ἐπεισοδίοις)
Fortunatus (Lausberg; Martin; Sabry, 17)		
	113.15	διέξοδος used synonymously with παρέκβασις
Gorgias (May 1979, 244)		
Palamedes	28–32	Ethos of speaker
Hebrew Bible		
Genesis	2:8–15	Description of Eden (Bullinger, 906–7)
	36	Esau's Descendants (Bullinger)
	38	Judah and Tamar (Bullinger)
Exodus	+12:1–28	Passover Narrative
Zechariah	+2:6–13	Exhortation to flee "Babylon" and return
	3:8–10	"supplementary oracle" (Meyers and Meyers)
	4:6b–10a	"Zerubbabel insertion" (Meyers and Meyers)
	6:9–15	"oracular insertion" (Meyers and Meyers)
Herodotus (Aune 2004, 189: Herodotus includes more than 200 digressions)		
	2	On Egypt
	1.5	ταῦτα of dismissal (Race 1980, 7)
Hesiod (Race 1980, 7 n.23)		
Theogonia	22–36	Steps out of his song "But why am I concerned…"
Himerius (Race 1980)		
Orationes	1.11 = 9.11	Colonna
Eclogae	36.14 = Or 36.17	Colonna on emotion imparting spontaneous dimension
Homer (Austin; Gaisser; cf. Kirk; Hainsworth; Richardson; Louden)		
		** denotes not discussed by Gaisser*
Iliad	1.69–72	Kalchas' introduction*
	1.247–53	Nestor's introduction*
	1.260–73	Nestor's prowess*
	1.396–406	Thetis' petition to Briareus*

	1.423–25	Zeus' 12 day rest with the Ethiopians*
	1.590–94	Hephaistos reminds Hera of Zeus' anger*
	2.100–109	The Descent of Agamemnon's Scepter
	2.299–332	The Portent at Aulia
	2.494–759	The Catalogue of Ships
	2.816–877	Trojan Catalogue
	3.204–224	Menelaus and Odysseus in Troy
	4.370–400	Agamemnon Tells Diomedes about Tydeus
	4.405–10	Sthenelos tells another story about Tydeus*
	5.381–404	Dione's Catalogue
	6.119–236	The Encounter of Glacus and Diomedes
	6.407–432	The Sack of Andromache's City
	7.123–160	How Nestor Slew Ereuthalion
	7.327–337	Nestor during feast (Louden, 47–48)
	9.434–605	Phoenix' Speech to Achilles
	10.1–579	The *Doloneia* (Hainsworth; Richardson)
	10.254–272	The Descent of Meriones' Helmet
	11.655–803	Nestor's Appeal to Patroclus
	14.110–127	The Geneology of Diomedes
	14.313–328	Zeus' Catalogue
	15.14–33	How Zeus bound Hera
	18.37–50	Catalogue of Nereids
	18.117–20	Allusion to Heracles' death*
	18.393–409	Hephaestus' Debt to Thetis
	18.478–608	Achilles' Shield
	19.86–136	Agamemnon's Allegory
	20.213–241	The Geneology of Aeneas
	23.624–650	Nestor's Youthful Prowess
	23.740–749	The Silver Mixing Bowl
	24.599–620	The Legend of Niobe
Odyssey	2.85–112	Antinous' Story of the Web
	3.102–200	Nestor's Account of the Greek Sufferings
	3.253–312	Orestes' Revenge
	4.240–264	Helen's Story of Odysseus
	4.265–289	Menelaus' Story of Odysseus
	4.347–592	Menelaus' Story of Proteus
	5.118–129	Calypso's Catalogue
	7.241–297	How Odysseus Came to Scheria
	8.72–82	The Quarrel of Odysseus and Achilles
	8.266–369	The Loves of Ares and Aphrodite
	8.499–520	The Wooden Horse
	11.225–329	The Catalogue of Heroines
	13.256–286	Odysseus' Story to Athena
	14.199–359	Odysseus' Story to Eumaeus
	15.223–257	The Geneology of Theoclymenus
	15.403–484	Eumaeus' Story
	17.415–444	Odyseus' Story to Antinous
	19.123–163	Penelope's Story of the Web

	19.165–202	Odysseus' First Story to Penelope
	19.221–248	Odysseus' Second Story to Penelope
	19.262–307	Odysseus' Third Story to Penelope
	19.386–470	The Scar of Odysseus
	21.8–42	The Story of the Bow
	24.120–190	Amphimedon's Story of the Web
	24.266–279	Odysseus' First Story to Laertes
	24.304–314	Odysseus' Second Story to Laertes
Homeric (Race 1980, 7–8)		
Hymn to Apollo	140–178	"Carried away" Steps out personally.
Isocrates (Race 1978, 175; Laugaa)		
Ad Philip.	109–112	Ethical Digression on Heracles
Antidosis	107–39	Ethical Digression on Timotheus
	311	One thing leading to another
Helen	29–37	Ethical Digression on Theseus
Panathenaicus	74–90	Ethical Digression on Agamemnon
John of Sardis		
Progymnasmata	Rabe 21–22	To be concise, do not use παρέκβασις (for parallel language see Anon. Seg. II.64–68)
Josephus		
Antiq. Jud.	+13.171–73	On philosophies of the Jews
	+18.1.2–6	On philosophies of Jews (in between discussion of Judas and Saddok in 6 CE; Quirinius census)
Bellum Judaicum	1.9	(Rajak, 79)
	+2.10.2	Description of Ptolemais in between Petronius landing and Jews assembly
	3.70–100	Efficiency of Roman army (Rajak, 160, 180)
	7.259	Invective (Rajak, 81)
Contra Apionem	1.46–56	παρέκβασις (1.57) (Mason 1992; Aune 2004, 189)
	+2.145–286	Encomium on Jewish constitution (compare 2.119–166, called παρέκβασις in Greek mss)
Vita	24–27	Helpful background information (Cohen 1979, 103 n. 9)
	36–42	(Mason 2000, xxv; Cohen, 114–116; cf. 103 n. 9)
	336–367	The 'Great Digression' articulated with παρέκβασις (367) (Rajak; Cohen 1979, 114–121; Mason 2000, xxv, 135 n. 1367–1368) An apologia against rival historian Justus of Tiberias (Whitmarsh 2005, 80).

Jubilees (Wintermute in OTP 2:35, 46–48; Crawford, 79; Segal, 319–22)		
	1.7–18	Future prediction of faithlessness
	6.32–38	Future failure to observe 365 calendar
	7.34–38	Future establishment of cities and agriculture
	15.33–34	Prediction of future faithlessness regarding circumcision
	23.9–32	Future generation's wickedness, punishment, repentance, and reward
Julius Victor (Lausberg; Martin)		
	Halm 429.2	
Justin Martyr (Blunt, 94)		
First Apology	63	It was really Christ who spoke to Moses. "Justin is anxious to avoid anthropomorphism"
Longinus		
De sublimitate	12.5	Cicero uses παρέκβασις; cf. 20.2 on disorder and order
	13.2	Carried away by prophecy
	33–35	(D. Russell, 151; cf. Wilamowitz: *Regel und Genie*)
Lycurgus		
Against Lelocrates	75–148	Ethical Digression (May 1979, 244 n. 11)
Lysias ("ethical digressions" discussed in Kennedy 1994, 67).		
Against Erat. (Or 12)	37	"Not strictly relevant, but helps" (Kennedy 1994, 67)
Against Agoratus	33, 43	Systematic
2 Maccabees (Doran, 52–55, 95–96)		
	2:19–32	Preface to the book (esp note apology for length in 2:32)
	6:12–17	Exhortation not to be depressed but trust God (Aune 2004)
	+7:20–29	Speeches between sixth and seventh deaths of Eleazar's sons
Martianus Capella (Lausberg; Martin)		
	Halm 487.6	
Menander Rhetor (Race 1980)		
Rhet. Gr.	3.440.26–28	

New Testament (Aune 2003, 134; Bullinger, 906–7)		
Romans	1:2–6	The Gospel (Bullinger, 906–7)
1 Corinthians	2:6–16	God's Hidden Wisdom
	6:1–11	Lawsuits against Believers
	9:1–27	Rights of an Apostle
	10:1–13	Example of Israel's Idolatry
	13:1–13	Love
2 Corinthians	5:14–6:2	A New Creation
	6:13–7:1	We are a temple of the living God
Galatians	2:11–14	Antioch Incident (Hester)
Ephesians	3:2–13	Paul's experience as example of God's Triumph (Gombis)
Hebrews	5:11–6:12	Exhortation (Koester 2002)
Philo of Alexandria (Runia, 187–196, 260–308)		
De opificio mundi	45–52	On the number four
	89–128	On the number seven
Philostratus		
Vita Apollonii	+1.16.1–2	Myth of Daphne (inserting tales διαμυθολογῶν)
	+1.25.1–2	A secret tunnel under the river in Babylon/Ekphrasis of Babylon
	+2.20.2–3	The moral of pictures in Taxila is pleasing
	+3.6.2–8.3	Snake Hunt – cannot omit even though Apollonius is not a character in it
Pindar (Race 1980)		
Nemean	8.23–24	
Olympian	1.36–89	
Olympian	2.56–83	on afterlife
Pythian	10.1–6	10.4 "what are these untimely words?"
	11.38–44	Narrative digression. Scholiasts called this an "irrelevant digression" (ἀκαίρος παρέκβασις). Contrast with present celebration
Plato		
Apologia	28a2–34b5	Ethical Digression (May 1979, 244) Socrates on character and divine mission
Lysis	211e	ταῦτα of dismissal (Race 1980, 7 n. 23)
Theaetetus	172c–177c	πάρεργα (177b8); λόγος ἐκ λόγου Philosophical life (Campbell; Barker; Race 1980). "[D]igression only in the sense it develops ideas for their own sake beyond the needs of the general argument in which it is imbedded" (Barker 1976, 457). Philosopher can lead speech wherever, lawyer is slave to rules.

Pliny the Younger (Sabry)		
Epistulae	I.2.4	"[L]avish coloring" as Cicero: "whenever I felt like making a pleasant deviation from my main path, for I did not want the force of my argument to lack all light relief" (see Cicero, *Ep. ad Att.* I.14.5)
	V.6.41–44	Compares his digression to Homer's
Polemo (W. W. Reader, 42–44)		
Cynegirus	12	Euphorion's Thesis appended
	34–35	Exclamations praising Cynegirus' hands
Callimachus	12	Excursus of exclamations praising corpse
	52–55	Long series of exclamations
Polybius (Sabry, 17; Aune 2004, 189)		
	II.35.2–36.1	"We have digressed (παρεξέβημεν) away from the affairs of Spain…" (II.36.1)
	III.2.7	"Simultaneously in a digression (παρέκβασιν) I shall narrate how the dominion of Hiero of Syracuse fell…"
	IV.8.1–9.1	Concluding, "it was at this point that we digressed (παρεξέβημεν)…" (IV.9.1)
	IV.31	Peace with Justice and Honor
	IV.74	Peace and defense of way of life
	XXXVIII.5–6	"…some people will fault this work on the ground that the narrative is imperfect and disconnected" (XXXVIII.5.1)
	XXXVIII.6.1–2	This "is why the most thoughtful of ancient writers were in the habit of giving their readers a rest in the way I say, some of them employing digressions (παρεκβάσεσι) dealing with myth or narratives and others on matters of fact"
Quintilian		
Institutio Oratoria	IV.3	Digressions as a part of speech
	IX.2.55	Digression as a figure of thought
	XI.2.11	Simonides refused payment because he used a digression ("following the common practice of the poets"); cf. Cicero *de Orat.* II.86.352
Sibylline Oracles		
	+I.125–282	Noah the moral preacher and the Flood
Tacitus		
Agricola	10–12	Ethnography of Britain (Cohen, 103 n. 12)
	13–17	Previous History of Roman Britain

Theon, Aelius (Lausberg; Martin)		
Progymnasmata	Spengel 2.80–81	Avoid long παρέκβασις, but use to give hearers a rest
Theopompus (Shrimpton, 72–101; Connor; Klaus Meister, OCD, 1505)		
Philippica	8–9	On Marvels (ff. 64–84)
	10	On the Demagogues (ff. 85–100)
	32–33	On early Spartan history (ff. 171–8)
	35	On Euxine geography and history (f. 179)
	39–40	On Sicilian history (ff. 184–8, 189–91, 194–5)
	42–43	On western geography (ff. 199–207)
Thucydides (Aune 2004, 188)		
	1.126.3–12	Biographical digression on Kylon
	1.128–34	On Pausanias
	1.138	On Themistocles
Troilos (Lausberg; Martin; Hinks)		
	Walz VI.49	Corax was the first to use παρέκβασις as a part of speech
Xenophon (Aune 2004, 188)		
Anabasis	I.9	On Cyrus

Bibliography

1. Primary Sources

Aelius Aristides. *The Complete Works of Aelius Aristides*. Trans. Charles A. Behr. Leiden: Brill, 1981.

___. *P. Aelii Aristidis Opera quae exstant omnia*. Ed. Frederick W. Lenz and Charles A. Behr. Leiden: Brill, 1976.

Anaximenes of Lampsacus. "Rhetorica ad Alexandrum" in *Problemata physica*. Trans. W. S. Hett. LCL 317. Cambridge, Mass.: Harvard, 1953.

Anonymous Seguerianus. *Anonyme de Séguier: Art du Discours Politique*. Trans. and Ed. Michel Patillon. Paris: Les Belles Lettres, 2003.

___. *Two Greek Rhetorical Treatises: Introduction, Text, and Translation of the Arts of Rhetoric Attributed to Anonymous Seguerianus and to Apsines of Gadara*. Trans. and Ed. Mervin R. Dilts and George A. Kennedy. Leiden: Brill, 1997.

Apthonius. Pages 17–20 in *Apthonii Progymnasmata*. Ed. H. Rabe. Leipzig: Teubner, 1926.

___. Pages 89–127 in *Progymnasmata: Greek Textbooks of Prose Composition and Rhetoric*. Trans. George A.Kennedy. Atlanta: SBL, 2003.

Aristeas. "Letter of Aristeas." Trans. R. J. H. Shutt. Pages 8–34 in vol 2 of *Old Testament Pseudepigrapha*. Ed. James H. Charlesworth. 2 vols. New York: Doubleday, 1985.

___. *Lettre d'Aristée a Philocrate*. Ed. and Trans. A. Pelletier. Paris: Les Éditions du Cerf, 1962.

Aristotle. *Aristotle* On Rhetoric: *A Theory of Civic Discourse*. Trans. George A. Kennedy, New York: Oxford University, 1991.

___. *Art of Rhetoric*. Trans. J. H. Freese. LCL 193. Cambridge, Mass.: Harvard, 1926.

___. *Poetics*. Trans. Stephen Halliwell. LCL 199. Cambridge, Mass.: Harvard, 1995.

Cicero. *Brutus, Orator*. Trans. G. L. Hendrickson and H. M. Hubbell. LCL 342. Cambridge, Mass.: Harvard, 1962.

___. *De Inventione*. Trans. H. M. Hubbell. LCL 386. Cambridge, Mass.: Harvard, 1949.

___. *De Oratore*. Trans. E. W. Sutton and H. Rackham. 2 vols. LCL 348–349. Cambridge, Mass.: Harvard, 1948, 1942.

___. *De Partitione Oratoria*. In *De Oratore book III, De Fato, Paradoxa Stoicorum, De Partitione Oratoria.* Trans. H. Rackham. LCL 349. Cambridge, Mass.: Harvard, 1942.

___. *Pro Milone*. Trans. N. H. Watts. LCL 252. Cambridge, Mass.: Harvard, 1953.

___. *Rhetorica ad Herennium.* Trans. Harry Caplan. LCL 403. Cambridge, Mass.: Harvard, 1954.

Dio Chrysostom. *Orations VII, XII, XXXVI*. Ed. D. A. Russell. Cambridge: Cambridge University, 1992.

___. Trans. J. W. Cohoon and H. L. Crosby. LCL. Cambridge, Mass.: Harvard, 1932–1951.

Dionysius of Halicarnassus. *Critical Essays*. Trans. Stephen Usher. LCL 465. Cambridge, Mass.: Harvard, 1974.

Fortunatus. *Rhetores Latini Minores*. Ed. Carolus Halm. Leipzig: Teubner, 1863.

John of Sardis. Pages 21–22 in *Apthonii Progymnasmata*. Ed. H. Rabe. Leipzig: Teubner, 1926.

Josephus. *Flavius Josephus: Translation and Commentary, Volume 10: Against Apion*. Trans. John M. G. Barclay. Leiden: Brill, 2007.

___. *Flavius Josephus: Contra Apionem Buch I: Einleitung, Text, Textkritischer Apparat, Übersetzung und Kommentar von Dagmar Labow*. Stuttgart: W. Kohlhammer, 2005.

___. *Des Flavius Josephus Schrift gegen den Apion. Text und Erklärung aus dem Nachlass von J. G. Müller*. Eds. C. J. Riggenback and C. von Orelli. Basel: Bahnmeier, 1877.

___. *Flavius Josephus: Translation and Commentary, Volume 9:Life of Josephus*. Trans. Steve Mason. Leiden: Brill, 2001.

___. *Vita*. Eds. and Trans. Folker Siegert, Heinz Schreckenberg, Manuel Vogel. Tübingen: Mohr Siebeck, 2001.

Jubilees. *The Book of Jubilees: A Critical Text*. Ed. and Trans. James C. VanderKam. Leuven: Peeters, 1989.

___. Trans. O. S. Wintermute. Pages 36–142 in vol 2 of *Old Testament Pseudepigrapha*. Ed. James H. Charlesworth. 2 vols. New York: Doubleday, 1985.

Julius Victor. *Rhetores Latini Minores*. Ed. Carolus Halm. Leipzig: Teubner, 1863.

Justin Martyr. *The Apologies of Justin Martyr*. Ed. A. W. F. Blunt. Eugene, Oregon: Wipf & Stock, 2006.

Longinus. "On the Sublime." Trans. W. H. Fyfe, D. Russell. LCL 199. 2nd Ed. Cambridge, Mass.: Harvard, 1995.

___. *Longinus On the Sublime*. Trans. W. Rhys Roberts. New York: Garland, 1987.

Lucian. "Anacharsis." Pages 1–69 in *Lucian Volume IV*. Trans. A. M. Harmon. LCL 162. Cambridge, Mass.: Harvard, 1925.

Lycurgus. *Oratio in Leocratem*. Eds. C. Scheibe and F. Blass. Leipzig: Teubner: 1970.

Lysias, *Contra Eratosthenem*. Ed. Alfieri Sinelli. Milan: Società editrice Dante Alighieri, 1968.

Martianus Capella. *Rhetores Latini Minores*. Ed. Carolus Halm. Leipzig: Teubner, 1863.

Menander Rhetor. *Menander Rhetor*. Eds. and Trans. D. A. Russell and N. G. Wilson. Oxford: Clarendon Press, 1981.

Oecumenius. *The Complete Commentary of Oecumenius on the Apocalypse*. Ed. and Trans. H. C. Hoskier. Ann Arbor, Michigan: University of Michigan, 1928.

___. *Oecumenii commentaries in Apocalypsin*. Ed. and Trans. M. de Groote. Traditio exegetica Graeca 8. Leuven: Peeters, 1999.

___. *Oecumenius: Commentary on the Apocalypse*. Trans. John N. Suggit. Fathers of the Church 112. Washington D. C.: Catholic University of America, 2006.

Philo of Alexandria. *On the Creation of the Cosmos according to Moses*. Ed. and Trans. David T. Runia. Leiden: Brill, 2001.

___. *Philonis Alexandrini Libellus de Opificio Mundi*. Ed. Leopold Cohn. Hildesheim: Georg Olms, 1967.

Philostratus. *Lives of the Sophists*. Trans. W. C. Wright. LCL 134. Cambridge: Harvard, 1921.

Plato. *Gorgias*. Trans. E. R. Dodds. Oxford: Clarendon Press, 1959.

___. *Phaedrus*. Trans. H. N. Fowler. LCL 36. Cambridge, Mass.: Harvard, 1914.

___. *Republic*. Trans. Benjamin Jewett. Oxford: Clarendon Press, 1894.

___. *The Theaetetus of Plato: A Revised Text and English Notes*. Ed. and Trans. Lewis Campbell. 2nd Ed. New York: Garland, 1980.

Polemo. *The Severed Hand and the Upright Corpse: The Declamations of Marcus Antonius Polemo*. Trans. W. W. Reader with A. J. Chvala-Smith. Atlanta: Scholars, 1996.

Quintilian. *Institutes of Oratory*. Trans. H. E. Butler. 5 vols. Cambridge, Mass.: Harvard, 1920–2.

Sibylline Oracles. *Book III of the Sibylline Oracles and its Social Setting: With an Introduction, Translation, and Commentary*. Ed. and Trans. R. Buitenwerf. Leiden: Brill, 2003.

___. "Sibylline Oracles." Trans. J. J. Collins. Pages 317–472 in vol. 1 of *Old Testament Pseudepigrapha*. Ed. James H. Charlesworth. 2 vols. New York: Doubleday, 1985.

___. *The Sibylline Oracles: With Introduction, Translation and Commentary on the First and Second Books*. Ed. and Trans. J. L. Lightfoot. Oxford: Oxford University, 2007.

Theon, Aelius. Pages 80–81 in vol 2 of *Rhetores Graeci*. Ed. L. Spengel. 3 vols. Leipzig: Teubner, 1854–56.

___. "Progymnasmata." Pages 1–72 in *Progymnasmata: Greek Textbooks of Prose Composition and Rhetoric*. Trans. George A. Kennedy. Atlanta: SBL, 2003.

Troilos. Vol 6 of *Rhetores Graeci*. Ed. Christian Walz. 9 vols. Osnabruck: Otto Zeller, 1968 [1832–1836].

2. Secondary Literature

Anderson, Graham. "Some Uses of Storytelling in Dio." Pages 143–160 in *Dio Chrysostom: Politics, Letters and Philosophy*. Ed. Simon Swain. New York: Oxford University Press, 2000.

Attridge, Harold W. *The Epistle to the Hebrews*. Hermeneia. Philadelphia: Fortress, 1989.

Aune, David E. "Following the Lamb: Discipleship in the Apocalypse." Pages 66–78 in *Apocalypticism, Prophecy and Magic in Early Christianity*. Tübingen: Mohr Siebeck, 2006.

___. "The Influence of Roman Imperial Court Ceremonial on the Apocalypse of John." *Biblical Research* 18 (1983): 5–26.

___. *The New Testament in Its Literary Environment*. LEC 8. Philadelphia: Westminster, 1987.

___. *Prophecy in Early Christianity and the Ancient Mediterranean World*. Grand Rapids, Michigan: Eerdmans, 1983.

___. *Revelation*. 3 vols. WBC. Nashville: Thomas Nelson, 1997–8.

___. *The Westminster Dictionary of New Testament and Early Christian Literature and Rhetoric*. Louisville, Kentucky: Westminster/John Knox, 2003.

Austin, Norman. "The Function of Digressions in the *Iliad*." *Greek, Roman, and Byzantine Studies* 7:4 (Winter 1966): 295–311.

Bäbler, Balbina. "'Long-haired Greeks in Trousers': Olbia and Dio Chrysostom (Or 36, 'Borystheniticus')." *Ancient Civilizations* 8.3–4 (2002): 311–327.

Balch, David. "Two Apologetic Encomia: Dionysius on Rome and Josephus on the Jews." *JSJ* 13 (1982): 102–122.

Barclay, John M. G., Ed. and Trans. *Flavius Josephus: Translation and Commentary, Volume 10: Against Apion*. Leiden: Brill, 2007.

Barker, A. "The Digression in the 'Theaetetus'." *Journal of the History of Philosophy* 14:4 (Oct 1976): 457–462.

Barr, David L. "The Apocalypse as a Symbolic Transformation of the World: A Literary Analysis." *Interpretation* 38 (1981): 39–50.

___. "The Apocalypse of John as Oral Enactment." *Interpretation* 40.3 (1984): 243–256.

___. *Tales of the End: A Narrative Commentary on the Book of Revelation.* Santa Rosa, California: Polebridge, 1998.

___, ed. *The Reality of Apocalypse: Rhetoric and Politics in the Book of Revelation.* SBLSS 39. Atlanta: SBL, 2006.

Bartlett, John R. *The First and Second Books of the Maccabees.* CBC. Cambridge: Cambridge University, 1973.

Barton, John. *Reading the Old Testament: Method in Biblical Study.* Rev. ed. Louisville, KY: Westminster John Knox, 1996.

Bauckham, Richard. *Climax of Prophecy: Studies in the Book of Revelation.* New Testament Theology. London: T & T Clark, 1993.

___. "The List of the Tribes in Revelation 7 Again." *JSNT* 42 (1991): 99–115.

___. *The Theology of the Book of Revelation.* Cambridge: Cambridge University, 1993.

Beale, Gregory K. *The Book of Revelation.* NIGTC. Grand Rapids, Mich: Eerdmans, 1999.

___. "The influence of Daniel upon the structure and theology of John's Apocalypse." *Journal of the Evangelical Theological Society* 27 (1984): 413–423.

___. "Solecisms in the Apocalypse as signals for the presence of Old Testament allusions." Pages 421–466 in *Early Christian Interpretation of the Scripture of Israel.* Eds. C. Evans and J. Sanders. Sheffield: Sheffield Press, 1997.

Bergant, Dianne. "An Anthropological Approach to Biblical Interpretation: The Passover Supper in Exodus 12:1–20 as a Case Study." *Semeia* 67 (1994): 43–62.

Black, C. Clifton. "Keeping up with Recent Studies, pt. 16: Rhetorical Criticism and Biblical Interpretation." *Expository Times* 100.7 (1989): 252–258.

Blevins, James L. *Revelation as Drama.* Nashville: Broadman Press, 1984.

Blount, Brian K. *Can I Get A Witness: Reading Revelation through African American Culture.* Louisville, KY: Westminster, 2005.

Blunt, A. W. F., Ed. *The Apologies of Justin Martyr.* Eugene, Oregon: Wipf & Stock, 2006.

Boring, M. Eugene. *Revelation.* Interpretation. Louisville, Kentucky: John Knox Press, 1989.

Bousset, Wilhelm. *Die Offenbarung Johannis.* KEK 16. Göttingen: Vandenhoeck and Ruprecht, 1896.

Bowman, John W. *The Drama of the Book of Revelation.* Philadelphia: Westminster, 1955.

___. "The Revelation to John: Its Dramatic Structure and Message." *Interpretation* 9.4 (1955): 436–53.

Boxall, Ian. *The Revelation of St. John.* BNTC. Peabody, Mass.: Hendrickson, 2006.

Brewer, Raymond R. "The Influence of Greek Drama on the Apocalypse of John." *Anglican Theological Review* 18 (1936): 74–92.

Brown, Jeannine K. *Scripture as Communication: Introducing Biblical Hermeneutics.* Grand Rapids, Mich.: Baker, 2007.

Brueggemann, Walter. "Passion and perspective: Two dimensions of education in the Bible." *Theology Today* 42.2 (July 1985): 172–180.

Buitenwerf, Rieuwerd. *Book III of the Sibylline Oracles and its Social Setting: With an Introduction, Translation, and Commentary.* SVTP 17. Leiden: Brill, 2003.

Bullinger, E. W. *Figures of Speech used in the Bible.* Grand Rapids, Michigan: Baker, 1968 [1898].

Butterworth, Mike. *Structure and the Book of Zechariah.* JSOTss 130. Sheffield: Sheffield Academic, 1992.

Caird, George B. *The Revelation of St. John the Divine.* HNTC. New York: Harper & Row, 1966.

Campbell, Antony F. "Psalm 78: A Contribution to the Theology of Tenth Century Israel." *CBQ* 41.1 (1979): 51–79.

Canter, H. V. "Digressio in the Orations of Cicero." *The American Journal of Philology* 52.4 (1931): 351–361.

Carey, Greg. *Elusive Apocalypse: Reading Authority in the Revelation to John.* StABH 15. Macon, Ga.: Mercer University, 1999.

Carrell, Peter R. *Jesus and the Angels: Angelology and the Christology of the Apocalypse of John.* SNTSMS 95. Cambridge: Cambridge University, 1997.

Cassuto, Umberto. *A Commentary on the Book of Exodus.* Sidrat sefarim. Trans. I. Abrahams. Jerusalem: Magnes, 1967.

Charles, R. H. *The Revelation of St. John.* 2 vols. ICC. Edinburgh: T & T Clark, 1920.

Childs, Brevard S. *Exodus: A Commentary.* OTL. London: SCM Press, 1974.

Coats, George W. *Exodus 1–18.* FOTL 2a. Grand Rapids, Mich.: Eerdmans, 1998.

Cockroft, Robert. "Fine-Tuning Quintilian's Doctrine of Rhetorical Emotion: Seven Types of *Enargeia.*" Pages 503–510 in vol. 2 of *Quintiliano: Historia y Actualidad de la Retórica.* Ed. T. Albadejo, et. al. 2 vols. Calahorra, Spain: Ayuntamiento de Calahorra, 1998.

Cohen, Shaye J. D. *Josephus in Galilee and Rome: His Vita and Development as a Historian.* Columbia studies in the classical tradition 8. Leiden: Brill, 1979.

Collins, Adela Yarbro. *The Combat Myth in the Book of Revelation.* HDR 9. Missoula, Mont.: Scholars Press, 1976.

___. *Crisis and Catharsis: The Power of the Apocalypse.* Philadelphia: Westminster, 1984.

Collins, John J. *Daniel: A Commentary on the Book of Daniel.* Hermeneia. Minneapolis: Fortress, 1993.

___. "Sibylline Oracles." Pages 317–472 in vol. 1 of *Old Testament Pseudepigrapha.* Ed. James H. Charlesworth. 2 vols. New York: Doubleday, 1985.

___. *The Sibylline Oracles of Egyptian Judaism.* SBLDS 13. Missoula, Mont: SBL, 1974.

Connor, W. R. *Theopompus and Fifth-Century Athens.* Washington: Center for Hellenic Studies, 1968.

Conrad, Edgar W. *Zechariah.* Readings. Sheffield: Sheffield Academic, 1999.

Conzelmann, Hans and A. Lindemann. *Arbeitsbuch zum Neuen Testament.* Tübingen: J. C. B. Mohr (Paul Siebeck), 1995.

Cooper, John M. "An Aristotelian Theory of the Emotions." Pages 238–257 in *Essays on Aristotle's* Rhetoric. Ed. Amélie Oksenberg Rorty. Berkeley, California: University of California, 1996.

Cousin, Jean. *Études sur Quintilien.* Paris: Boivin, 1935.

Crawford, Sidnie W. *Rewriting Scripture in Second Temple Times.* Studies in the Dead Sea scrolls and related literature. Grand Rapids, Mich: Eerdmans, 2008.

Cruz, María Elena Arenas. "Un Acercamiento a la Forma del Ensayo a la Luz del Concepto Retórico Quintilianesco de *Digressio.*" Pages 463–472 in vol. 2 of *Quintiliano: Historia y Actualidad de la Retórica.* Ed. T. Albadejo, et. al. 2 vols. Calahorra, Spain: Ayuntamiento de Calahorra, 1998.

Cuadrado, J. F. T. *Apocalipsis: Estética y Teología*. Rome: Editrice Pontificio Istituto Biblico, 2007.

deSilva, David A. "Honor Discourse and the Rhetorical Strategy of the Apocalypse of John." *JSNT* 71 (1998): 79–110.

___. "Out of our Minds? Appeals to Reason (Logos) in the Seven Oracles of Revelation 2–3." *JSNT* 31.2 (2008): 123–155.

___. *Perseverance in Gratitude: A Socio-Rhetorical Commentary on the Epistle "to the Hebrews."* Grand Rapids, Michigan: Eerdmans, 2000.

___. "The persuasive strategy of the Apocalypse: a socio-rhetorical investigation of Revelation 14:6–13." *Society of Biblical Literature Seminar Papers* 37.2 (1998): 785–806.

___. "The Strategic Arousal of Emotions in the Apocalypse of John: A Rhetorical-Critical Investigation of the Oracles to the Seven Churches." *NTS* 54 (2008): 90–114.

___. "What has Athens to Do with Patmos? Rhetorical Criticism of the Revelation of John (1980–2005)." *Currents in Biblical Research* 6.2 (2008): 256–289.

Doran, Robert. *Temple Propaganda: The Purpose and Character of 2 Maccabees*. Washington D.C.: Catholic Biblical Association, 1981.

Downing, F. Gerald. "Markan Intercalation in Cultural Context." Pages 105–117 in *Narrativity in Biblical and Related Texts*. Eds. G. J. Burke and J.-D. Kaestli. BETL 149. Leuven: University Press, 2000.

Duff, Paul B. *Who Rides the Beast? Prophetic Rivalry and the Rhetoric of Crisis in the Churches of the Apocalypse*. New York: Oxford, 2003.

___. "Wolves in Sheep's Clothing." Pages 65–79 in *Reading the Book of Revelation: A Resource for Students*. SBLRBS 44. Ed. David L. Barr. Atlanta: SBL, 2003.

Durham, John I. *Exodus*. WBC 3. Waco, Texas: Word, 1987.

Eichhorn, Johann G. *Einleitung in das Neue Testament*. 2 vols. Leipzig: Weidmannische Buchhandlung, 1810.

Farrer, Austin. *A Rebirth of Images: The Making of St. John's Apocalypse*. Westminster: Dacre, 1949.

___. *The Revelation of St. John the Divine*. Oxford: Clarendon, 1964.

Filho, José Adriano. "The Apocalypse of John as an Account of a Visionary Experience: Notes on the Book's Structure." *JSNT* 25.2 (2002): 213–234.

Foley, John M. *Homer's Traditional Art*. University Park: Pennsylvania State University, 1999.

___. *How to Read an Oral Poem*. Chicago: University of Illinois, 2002.

Ford, J. Massyngberde. *Revelation: Introduction, Translation, and Commentary*. AB 38. Garden City, New York: Doubleday, 1975.

Frede, Dorothea. "Mixed Feelings in Aristotle's Rhetoric." Pages 258–285 in *Essays on Aristotle's* Rhetoric. Ed. Amélie Oksenberg Rorty. Berkeley, California: University of California, 1996.

Fretheim, Terence E. *Exodus*. Interpretation. Louisville: John Knox, 1991.

Friesen, Steven J. *Imperial Cults and the Apocalypse of John*. New York: Oxford, 2001.

___. "Satan's Throne, Imperial Cults and the Social Settings of Revelation." *Journal for the Study of the New Testament* 27.3 (2005): 351–373.

___. *Twice Neokoros: Ephesus, Asia and the Cult of the Flavian Imperial Family*. Leiden: Brill, 1993.

Furley, William D. and Jan Maarten Bremer. *Greek Hymns: Selected Cult Songs from the Archaic to the Hellenistic Period*. 2 vols. Studien und Texte zu Antike und Christentum 9, 10. Tübingen: Mohr Siebeck, 2001.

Gaechter, Paul. "The Role of Memory in the Making of the Apocalypse." *Theological Studies* 9 (1948): 419–452.

Gaisser, Julia Haig. "A Structural Analysis of the Digressions in the Iliad and the Odyssey." *Harvard Studies in Classical Philology* 73 (1969): 1–43.

Gamble, Harry Y. *Books and Readers in the Early Church: A History of Early Christian Texts*. New Haven, Conn.: Yale University Press, 1995.

Gelardini, Gabriella. *"Verhärtet eure Herzen nicht": Der Hebräer, eine Synagogenhomilie zu* Tischa be-Aw. Leiden: Brill, 2007.

Gerber, Christine. *Ein Bild des Judentums für Nichtjuden von Flavius Josephus: Untersuchungen zu seiner Schrift* Contra Apionem. AGJU 40. Leiden: Brill, 1997.

Giblin, Charles H. *The Book of Revelation: The Open Book of Prophecy*. GNS 34. Collegeville, MN: Liturgical Press, 1991.

___. "Revelation 11:1–13: Its form, function and Contextual Integration." *NTS* 30 (1984): 433–459.

___. "Structural and Thematic Correlations in the Theology of Revelation 16–22." *Biblica* 55 (1974): 487–504.

Gitay, Yehoshua. "Rhetorical Criticism." Pages 135–149 in *To Each Its Own Meaning: An Introduction to Biblical Criticisms and Their Application*. Ed. S. L. McKenzie and Stephen R. Haynes. Louisville: Westminster John Knox, 1993.

Goldstein, John. *II Maccabees*. AB 41A. Garden City, New York: Doubleday, 1983.

Gombis, Timothy. "Ephesians 3:2–13: Pointless Digression, or Epitome of the Triumph of God in Christ?" *Westminster Theological Journal* 66 (2004): 313–23.

Greenberg, Moshe. "The Redaction of the Plague Narrative in Exodus." Pages 243–252 in *Near Eastern Studies in Honor of William Foxwell Albright*. Ed. Hans Goedicke. Baltimore: Johns Hopkins, 1971.

Groote, Marc de, Ed. and Trans. *Oecumenii commentaries in Apocalypsin*. Traditio exegetica Graeca 8. Leuven: Peeters, 1999.

Guthrie, George H. *The Structure of Hebrews: A Text-Linguistic Analysis*. Grand Rapids: Baker, 1994.

Hahn, Ferdinand. "Zum Aufbau der Johannesoffenbarung." Pages 145–154 in *Kirche und Bibel. Festgabe für Bischof Eduard Schick*. Paderborn: Schöningh, 1979.

Hainsworth, Bryan. *The Iliad: A Commentary: Volume III: books 9–12*. Cambridge: Cambridge University, 1993.

Hall, Mark S. "The hook interlocking structure of Revelation." *Novum Testamentum* 44.3 (2002): 278–296.

Hall, Robert G. "Josephus, *Contra Apionem* and Historical Inquiry in the Roman Rhetorical Schools." Pages 229–249 in *Josephus'* Contra Apionem: *Studies in its Character and Context with a Latin Concordance to the Portion missing in Greek*. Eds. Louis H. Feldman and John R. Levison. AGJU 34. Leiden: Brill, 1996.

Halm, Carolus, Ed. *Rhetores Latini Minores*. Leipzig: Teubner, 1863.

Harrington, Wilfrid J. *Revelation*. SP 16. Collegeville, Minnesota: Liturgical Press, 1993.

Harris, B. F. "Dio of Prusa: A Survey of Recent Work." *ANRW* II.33.5 (1991): 3853–81.

___. "The Olympian Oration of Dio Chrysostom." *Historical Studies* 10.38 (1962): 85–97.

Harris, Michael A. *The Literary Function of Hymns in the Apocalypse of John*. Unpublished PhD diss. Southern Baptist Theological Seminary, 1988.

Härter, Andreas. *Digressionen: Studien zum Verhältnis von Ordnung und Abweichung in Rhetorik und Poetik*. Verlag: Wilhelm Fink, 2000.

Havelock, Eric A. *The Muse Learns to Write: Reflections on Orality and Literacy from Antiquity to the Present*. New Haven, Conn.: Yale University Press, 1986.

Hay, David M. "What is Proof? – Rhetorical Verification in Philo, Josephus and Quintilian." Pages 87–100 in vol. 2 of *Society of Biblical Literature 1979 Seminar Papers*. Ed. P. J. Achtemeier. 2 vols. Missoula, Montana: SBL, 1979.

Heath, Malcolm. "Theon and the History of the Progymnasmata." *Greek, Roman and Byzantine Studies* 43.2 (2002/3): 129–160.

Hellholm, David. "The Problem of Apocalyptic Genre and the Apocalypse of John." *Semeia* 36 (1986): 13–64.

___. "The Visions He Saw or: To Encode the Future in Writing: An Analysis of the Prologue of John's Apocalyptic Letter." Pages 109–46 in *Text and Logos: The Humanistic Interpretation of the New Testament. Essays in Honor of Hendrikus W. Boers*. Ed. T. W. Jennings. Atlanta: Scholars, 1990.

Hemer, Colin J. *The Letters to the Seven Churches of Asia in their Local Settings*. JSNTsup 11. Sheffield: JSOT, 1986.

Hester, James D. "The Rhetorical Structure of Galatians 1:11–2:14." *JBL* 103.2 (1984): 223–233.

Hinks, D. A. G. "Tisias and Corax and the Invention of Rhetoric." *Classical Quarterly* 34 (1940): 67–69.

Hoffmann, Matthias Reinhard. *The Destroyer and the Lamb: the Relationship between Angelomorphic and Lamb Christology in the Book of Revelation*. WUNT 2.203. Tübingen: Mohr Siebeck, 2005.

Honigman, Sylvie. *The Septuagint and Homeric Scholarship in Alexandria: A study in the narrative of the* Letter of Aristeas. London: Routledge, 2003.

Hoskier, H. C., Ed. and Trans. *The Complete Commentary of Oecumenius on the Apocalypse*. Ann Arbor, Michigan: University of Michigan, 1928.

Houtman, Cornelis. *Exodus*. Trans. J. Rebel and S. Woudstra. 4 vols. Kampen: Kok, 1993–2002.

Howard, David M. "Rhetorical Criticism in Old Testament studies." *Bulletin for Biblical Research* 4 (1994): 87–104.

Jauhiainen, Marko. *The Use of Zechariah in Revelation*. WUNT 2.199. Tübingen: Mohr Siebeck, 2005.

Johnstone, W. "The Two Theological Versions of the Passover Pericope in Exodus." Pages 160–178 in *Text as Pretext: Essays in Honour of Robert Davidson*. Ed. R. P. Carroll. JSOTss 138. Sheffield: Sheffield Academic, 1992.

Jones, Christopher P. *The Roman World of Dio Chrysostom*. Cambridge, Mass.: Cambridge Unversity Press, 1978.

Jong, Irene J. F. de. *Narrators and Focalizers: The Presentation of the Story in the Iliad*. Amsterdam: B. R. Grüner, 1987.

Keene, Charles H. *The Electra of Euripides*. London: George Bell & Sons, 1893.

Kelber, Werner. *The Oral and the Written Gospel*. Philadelphia: Fortress, 1983.

Kennedy, George A. *The Art of Persuasion in Greece*. Princeton: Princeton University, 1963.

___. *Classical Rhetoric and Its Christian and Secular Tradition From Ancient to Modern Times*. Chapel Hill: University of North Carolina, 1980.

___. *Comparative Rhetoric*. New York: Oxford University, 1998.

___. *A New History of Classical Rhetoric*. Princeton, New Jersey: Princeton University, 1994.

___. *Progymnasmata: Greek Textbooks of Prose Composition and Rhetoric*. SBLWAW 10. Atlanta: SBL, 2003.

Kirby, John T. "The rhetorical situation of Revelation 1–3." *New Testament Studies* 34.2 (1988): 197–207.

Kirk, G. S. *The Iliad: A Commentary: Volume I: books 1–4*. Cambridge: Cambridge University, 1985.

___. *The Iliad: A Commentary: Volume II: books 5–8*. Cambridge: Cambridge University, 1990.

Klauck, Hans-Josef. *Ancient Letters and the New Testament: A Guide to Context and Exegesis*. Trans. and Ed. D. P. Bailey. Waco, Texas: Baylor, 2006.

___. *The Religious Context of Early Christianity*. Trans. Brian McNeil. Edinburgh: T&T Clark, 2000.

___. "Das Sendschreiben nach Pergamon und der Kaiserkult in der Johannesoffenbarung." *Biblica* 73 (1992): 153–182.

Klauck, Hans-Josef and Balbina Bäbler. *Dion von Prusa: Olympische Rede*. 2nd ed. Darmstadt: Wissenschaftliche Buchgesellschaft, 2002.

Koch, Klaus. *The Growth of the Biblical Tradition*. Trans. S. M. Cupitt. New York: Macmillan, 1988.

Koester, Craig R. *Hebrews*. AB 36. New York: Doubleday, 2001.

___. "Hebrews, Rhetoric, and the Future of Humanity." *Catholic Biblical Quarterly* 64 (2002): 103–123.

___. *Revelation and the End of All Things*. Grand Rapids, Michigan: Eerdmans, 2001.

Kooten, George H. van. "The Year of the Four Emperors and the Revelation of John: The 'pro-Neronian' Emperors Otho and Vitellius and the images and colossus of Nero in Rome." *JSNT* 30.2 (2007): 205–248.

Korner, Ralph J. "'And I Saw…' An Apocalyptic Literary Convention for Structural Identification in the Apocalypse." *Novum Testamentum* 42 (2000): 160–183.

Kovacs, Judith L. and Christopher Rowland. *Revelation: The Apocalypse of Jesus Christ*. Blackwell Bible Commentaries. Malden, Mass.: Blackwell, 2004.

Kraft, Heinrich. *Die Offenbarung des Johannes*. HNT 16a. Tübingen: Mohr Siebeck, 1974.

Kraybill, J. Nelson. *Imperial Cult and Commerce in John's Apocalypse*. JSNTss 132. Sheffield: Sheffield Academic, 1996.

Jebb, Richard. *Sophocles: The Plays and Fragments – Part III: The Antigone*. Amsterdam: A. M. Hakkert, 1971.

Labow, Dagmar. *Flavius Josephus: Contra Apionem Buch I: Einleitung, Text, Textkritischer Apparat, Übersetzung und Kommentar von Dagmar Labow*. Stuttgart: W. Kohlhammer, 2005.

Ladd, George Eldon. *A Commentary on the Revelation of John*. Grand Rapids, Michigan: Eerdmans, 1972.

Lambrecht, Jan. "A Structuration of Revelation 4,1–22,5." Pages 77–104 in *L'Apocalypse johannique et l'Apocalyptique dans le Nouveau Testament*. Ed. J. Lambrecht. Leuven: University Press, 1980.

Landgraf, Paul David. "The Structure of Hebrews: A Word of Exhortation in Light of the Day of Atonement." Pages 19–27 in *A Cloud of Witnesses: The Theology of Hebrews in its Ancient Contexts*. Eds. R. Bauckham, D. Driver, T. Hart, N. MacDonald. LNTS 387. London: T & T Clark, 2008.

Laugaa, Maurice. "La Théâtre de la Digression dans le discours classique." Pages 97–126 in *Semiotica IV*. The Hague: Mouton, 1971.

Lausberg, Heinrich. *Handbuch der Literarischen Rhetorik*. München: Max Hueber Verlag, 1960. [English translation: *Handbook of Literary Rhetoric: A Foundation for Literary Study*. Trans. Matthew T. Bliss, et.al. Ed. David E. Orton and R. Dean Anderson. Leiden: Brill, 1998.]

Laymon, Charles M. *The Book of Revelation: its message and meaning*. New York: Abingdon, 1960.

Lee, Dal. *The Narrative Asides in the Book of Revelation*. Lanham, Maryland: University Press of America, 2002.

Leighton, Stephen R. "Aristotle and the Emotions." Pages 206–237 in *Essays on Aristotle's* Rhetoric. Ed. Amélie Oksenberg Rorty. Berkeley, California: University of California, 1996.

Lemmelijn, Bénédicte. "Setting and Function of Exod 11, 1–10 in the Exodus Narrative." Pages 443–460 in *Studies in the Book of Exodus: Redaction – Reception – Interpretation*. Ed. M. Vervenne. BETL 126. Leuven: Leuven University, 1996.

Leonard, J. M. "Identifying Inner-Biblical Allusions: Psalm 78 as a Test Case." *JBL* 127.2 (2008): 241–265.

Lightfoot, J. L. *The Sibylline Oracles: With Introduction, Translation and Commentary on the First and Second Books*. Oxford: Oxford University, 2007.

Lipson, Carol S. and Roberta A. Binkley. *Rhetoric before and beyond the Greeks*. Albany, NY: State University of New York, 2004.

Loenertz, Raymon-Joseph. *The Apocalypse of Saint John*. Trans. H. J. Carpenter. New York: Sheed & Ward, 1947.

Lohmeyer, Ernst. *Die Offenbarung des Johannes*. HNT 16. Tübingen: Mohr Siebeck, 1953.

Lohse, Eduard. *Die Offenbarung des Johannes*. TNT 11. Göttingen: Vandenhoeck & Ruprecht, 1966.

Loisy, Alfred F. *L'apocalypse de Jean*. Paris: Nourry, 1923.

Longenecker, Bruce W. "'Linked like a Chain': Rev 22:6–9 in Light of Ancient Transition Technique." *New Testament Studies* 47 (2001): 105–117.

___. *Rhetoric at the Boundaries: The Art and Theology of the New Testament Chain-Link Transitions*. Waco, Texas: Baylor University, 2005.

Louden, Bruce. *The Iliad: Structure, Myth, and Meaning*. Baltimore: Johns Hopkins, 2006.

Lupieri, Edmondo. *A Commentary on the Apocalypse of John*. Trans. Maria Poggi Johnson and Adam Kamesar. Grand Rapids, MI: Eerdmans, 2006.

Ma, John. "Public Speech and Community in the *Euboicus*." Pages 108–124 in *Dio Chrysostom: Politics, Letters and Philosophy*. Ed. Simon Swain. New York: Oxford University Press, 2000.

Maier, Harry O. *Apocalypse Recalled: The Book of Revelation after Christendom*. Minneapolis: Fortress, 2002.

Martin, Josef. *Antike Rhetorik: Technik und Rhetorik*. München: Beck, 1974.

Mason, Steve. "The *Contra Apionem* in Social and Literary Context: An Invitation to Judean Philosophy." Pages 187–228 in *Josephus'* Contra Apionem. Eds. L. H. Feldman and J. R. Levison. AGJU 34. Leiden: Brill, 1996.

___, Ed. and Trans. *Flavius Josephus: Translation and Commentary, Volume 9: Life of Josephus*. Leiden: Brill, 2001.

May, James M. "The Ethica Digressio and Cicero's Pro Milone: A Progression of Intensity from Logos to Ethos to Pathos." *The Classical Journal* 74.3 (Feb–Mar 1979): 240–246.

___. *Trials of Character: the Eloquence of Ciceronian Ethics*. Chapel Hill: University of North Carolina, 1988.

Mazzaferri, Frederick D. *The Genre of the Book of Revelation from a Source-Critical Perspective*. BZNW 54. Berlin: Walter de Gruyter, 1989.

Meyers, Carol L. and Eric M. Meyers. *Haggai, Zechariah 1–8*. AB 25B. Garden City, NJ: Doubleday, 1987.

Minear, Paul. *I Saw a New Earth: An Introduction to the Visions of the Apocalypse*. Washington: Corpus, 1968.

Mitchell, Margaret M. *Paul and the Rhetoric of Reconciliation*. Louisville, Kentucky: Westminster/John Knox, 1991.

___. "Rhetorical and New Literary Criticism." Pages 615–633 in *Oxford Handbook of Biblical Studies*. Eds. Rogerson and Lieu. New York: Oxford University Press, 2006.

Moffatt, James. *An Introduction to the Literature of the New Testament*. New York: Scribner, 1915.

Moles, J. L. "The Dionian *Charidemus*." Pages 187–212 in *Dio Chrysostom: Politics, Letters and Philosophy*. Ed. Simon Swain. New York: Oxford University Press, 2000.

Möller, Karl. *A Prophet in Debate: The Rhetoric of Persuasion in the Book of Amos*. JSOTss 372. London: Sheffield, 2003.

Morton, Russell. *One Upon the Throne and the Lamb: A Tradition Historical/ Theological Analysis of Revelation 4–5*. StBL 110. New York: Peter Lang, 2007.

Mounce, Robert H. *The Book of Revelation*. 2nd Ed. NICNT. Grand Rapids, Michigan: Eerdmans, 1998.

Müller, Ekkehardt. *A Microstructural Analysis of Revelation 4–11*. AUSdds 21. Berrien Springs, Michigan: Andrews University Press, 1996.

Müller, J. G. *Des Flavius Josephus Schrift gegen den Apion. Text und Erklärung aus dem Nachlass von J. G. Müller*. Eds. C. J. Riggenback and C. von Orelli. Basel: Bahnmeier, 1877.

Murphy, Frederick J. *Structure and Meaning of Second Baruch*. SBLDS 78, Atlanta: Scholars, 1985.

Navarre, Octave. *Rhétorique Grecque avant Aristote*. Paris: Librairie Hachette, 1900.

Nickelsburg, George. *1 Enoch 1: A Commentary on the Book of 1 Enoch, Chapters 1–36, 81–108*. Hermeneia, Minneapolis: Fortress, 2001.

Nikolakopoulos, Konstantin. "Rhetorische Auslegungsaspekte der Theologie in der Johannesoffenbarung." Pages 166–180 in "*...Was ihr auf dem Weg verhandelt habt": Beiträge zur Exegese und Theologie des Neuen Testaments: Festschrift für Ferdinand Hahn zum 75. Geburtstag*. Eds. P. Müller, C. Gerber, T. Knöppler and P. Muller. Neukirchen-Vluyn: Neukirchener Verlag, 2001.

Noth, Martin. *Exodus: A Commentary*. OTL. Trans. John Bowden. London: SCM Press, 1962.

Ong, Walter. *Orality and Literacy: The Technologizing of the Word*. London: Methuen, 1982.

Osborne, Grant R. *Revelation*. BECNT. Grand Rapids, Michigan: Baker, 2002.

Patrick, Dale and Allen Scult. *Rhetoric and Biblical Interpretation*. JSOTSup 82. Sheffield: Almond, 1990.

Pattemore, Stephen. *The People of God in the Apocalypse: Discourse, Structure and Exegesis*. MSSNTS 128. Cambridge: Cambridge University, 2004.

___. *Souls under the Altar: Relevance Theory and the Discourse Structure of Revelation*. UBS 9. New York: UBS, 2003.

Perry, Peter S. "Critiquing the Excess of Empire: A *Synkrisis* of John of Patmos and Dio of Prusa." *JSNT* 29.4 (2007): 473–496.

___. "Making Fear Personal: Hebrews 5.11–6.12 and the Argument from Shame." *JSNT* 32.1 (2009): 1–27.

Poser, Michael von. *Der abschweifende Erzähler: Rhetorische Tradition und deutscher Roman im achtzehnten Jahrhundert*. Berlin: Verlag Gehlen, 1969.

Prigent, Pierre. *L'Apocalypse de saint Jean*. CNT 14. Lausanne: Delachaux et Niestlé, 1981.

Propp, William H. C. *Exodus 1–18*. AB 2. New York: Doubleday, 1998.

Rabe, Hugo., Ed. *Apthonii Progymnasmata*. Leipzig: Teubner, 1926.

Race, William. "Aspects of Rhetoric and Form in Greek Hymns." *Greek, Roman, and Byzantine Studies* 23 (1982): 5–14.

___. "*Panathenaicus* 74–90: The Rhetoric of Isocrates' Digression on Agamemnon." *Transactions of the American Philological Association* 108 (1978): 175–185.

___. "Some Digressions and Returns in Greek Authors." *The Classical Journal* 76.1 (Oct–Nov 1980): 1–8.

Rajak, Tessa. *Josephus*. 2nd ed. London: Duckworth, 2002.

Reader, William W. *The Severed Hand and the Upright Corpse: The Declamations of Marcus Antonius Polemo*. With A. J. Chvala-Smith. SBLTT 42. Atlanta: Scholars, 1996.

Richard, Pablo. *Apocalypse: A People's Commentary on the Book of Revelation*. Trans. Phillip Berryman. Maryknoll, New York: Orbis, 1995.

Richardson, Nicholas. *The Iliad: A Commentary: Volume VI: books 21–24*. Cambridge: Cambridge University, 1993.

Rissi, Mathias. *Time and History: A Study on the Revelation*. Trans. Gordon C. Winsor. Richmond, Virginia: John Knox, 1966.

Roloff, Jürgen *The Revelation of John*. Trans. John E. Alsup. CC. Minneapolis: Fortress, 1993.

Rossing, Barbara R. *The Choice Between Two Cities: Whore, Bride, and Empire in the Apocalypse*. Harrisburg, Penn.: Trinity Press International, 1999.

Rowland, Christopher. *Revelation*. London: Epworth Press, 1993.

Royalty, Robert M. "The rhetoric of Revelation." Pages 596–617 in *Society of Biblical Literature Seminar Papers* 36 (1997).

___. *The Streets of Heaven: The Ideology of Wealth in the Apocalypse of John*. Macon, Ga.: Mercer University Press, 1998.

Ruiz, Jean-Pierre. "Hearing and Seeing but Not Saying: A Rhetoric of Authority in Revelation 10:4 and 2 Corinthians 12:4." Pages 91–112 in *The Reality of Apocalypse: Rhetoric and Politics in the Book of Revelation*. Ed. D. L. Barr. SBLss 39. Atlanta: SBL, 2006.

Runia, David T., Ed. and Trans. *Philo of Alexandria: On the Creation of the Cosmos according to Moses*. Leiden: Brill, 2001.

Russell, Donald A., Ed. *Dio Chrysostom: Orations VII, XII, XXXVI*. Cambridge: Cambridge University, 1992.

Sabry, Randa. *Stratégies Discursives: digression, transition, suspens*. Paris: Les Éditions de L'École des Hautes Études en Sciences Sociales, 1992.

Salmeri, Giovanni. "Dio, Rome and the Civic Life of Asia Minor." Pages 53–92 in *Dio Chrysostom: Politics, Letters and Philosophy*. Ed. Simon Swain. New York: Oxford University Press, 2000.

Schüssler Fiorenza, Elisabeth. *The Book of Revelation: Justice and Judgment*. 2nd ed. Minneapolis: Fortress, 1998.

___. *Revelation: Vision of a Just World*. Minneapolis: Fortress, 1991.

Schmidt, Werner H. "Die Intention der beiden Plagenerzählungen (Exodus 7–10) in ihrem Kontext." Pages 225–244 in *Studies in the Book of Exodus: Redaction – Reception – Interpretation*. Ed. Marc Vervenne. BETL 126. Leuven: University Press, 1996.

Segal, Michael. *The Book of Jubilees: Rewritten Bible, Redaction, Ideology and Theology*. JSJSup 117. Leiden: Brill, 2007.

Shea, William H. "Further Literary Structures in Daniel 2–7: An Analysis of Daniel 5, and the Broader Relationships Within Chapters 2–7." *Andrews University Seminary Studies* 23.3 (Autumn 1985): 277–295.

Shutt, R. J. H. "Letter of Aristeas." Pages 9–11 in vol. 2 of *Old Testament Pseudepigrapha*. Ed. James H. Charlesworth. 2 vols. New York: Doubleday, 1985.

Shrimpton, Gordon S. *Theopompus the Historian*. Montreal: McGill's-Queen University Press, 1991.

Siew, Antoninus King Wai. *The War Between the Two Beasts and the Two Witnesses: A Chiastic Reading of Revelation 11.1–14.5*. London: T & T Clark, 2005.

Smalley, Stephen S. *The Revelation to John*. Downers Grove, Illinois: InterVarsity Press, 2005.

Smith, Christopher R. "The Structure of the Book of Revelation in Light of Apocalyptic Literary Conventions." *Novum Testamentum* 36.3 (1994): 373–393.

Spengel, Leonard, Ed. *Rhetores Graeci*. 3 vols. Leipzig: Teubner, 1854–56.

Sperber, Dan and Deirdre Wilson. *Relevance: Communication and Cognition*. 2nd ed. Oxford: Blackwell, 1995.

Steck, Odil Hannes. *Old Testament Exegesis: A Guide to the Methodology*. Trans. J. D. Nogalski. SBLRBS 33. Atlanta: Scholars, 1995.

Steinmann, Andrew E. "The tripartite structure of the sixth seal, the sixth trumpet, and the sixth bowl of John's Apocalypse." *Journal of the Evangelical Theological Society* 35 (Oct 1992): 69–79.

Suggit, John N., Trans. *Oecumenius: Commentary on the Apocalypse*. Fathers of the Church 112. Washington D. C.: Catholic University of America, 2006.

Swete, Henry Barclay. *The Apocalypse of St. John*. 2nd ed. New York: Macmillan, 1907.

Tanner, J. Paul. "The Literary Structure of the Book of Daniel." *Bibliotheca Sacra* 160 (July–Sept 2003): 269–82.

Tavo, Felise. "The Structure of the Apocalypse: re-examining a perennial problem." *Novum Testamentum* 47.1 (2005): 47–68.

Tenney, Merril C. *Interpreting Revelation*. Grand Rapids, Michigan: Eerdmans, 1957.

Thiele, Georg. *Hermagoras: Ein Beitrag zur Geschichte der Rhetorik*. Strassburg: Verlag von Karl J. Trübner, 1893.

Thompson, Leonard L. *The Book of Revelation: Apocalypse and Empire*. New York: Oxford University Press, 1990.

Trapp, Michael B. "Plato's *Phaedrus* in Second-Century Greek Literature." Pages 141–174 in *Antonine Literature*. Ed. D. A. Russell. Oxford: Clarendon Press, 1990.

Trebilco, Paul R. *The Early Christians in Ephesus from Paul to Ignatius*. Tübingen: Mohr Siebeck, 2004.

___. *Jewish Communities in Asia Minor*. New York: Cambridge, 1991.

Ulfgard, Håkan. *Feast and Future: Revelation 7:9–17 and the Feast of Tabernacles*. Stockholm: Almqvist & Wiksell, 1989.

VanderKam, James C. *The Book of Jubilees*. Sheffield: Sheffield Academic, 2001.

___. *The Book of Jubilees: A Critical Text*. Leuven: Peeters, 1989.

___. *Introduction to Early Judaism*. Grand Rapids, Mich: Eerdmans, 2000.

Vanni, Ugo. *La Struttura Letteraria dell'Apocalisse*. 2nd ed. Brescia: Morcelliana, 1980.

Wainwright, Arthur W. *Mysterious Apocalypse: Interpreting the Book of Revelation*. Nashville: Abingdon Press, 1993.

Walz, Christian, Ed. *Rhetores Graeci*. 9 vols. Osnabruck: Otto Zeller, 1968 [1832–1836].

Wasserstein, Abraham and David J. Wasserstein. *The Legend of the Septuagint: From*

Classical Antiquity to Today. Cambridge: Cambridge University, 2006.

Watson, Duane F. and Alan J. Hauser. *Rhetorical Criticism of the Bible: A Comprehensive Bibliography with Notes on History and Method.* Leiden: Brill, 1994.

Wendland, Ernst. "7 x 7 (x7): A Structural and Thematic Outline of John's Apocalypse." *OPTAT* 4 (1990): 371–87.

Westfall, Cynthia Long. *A Discourse Analysis of the Letter to the Hebrews: The Relationship between Form and Meaning*. LNTS 297. London: T & T Clark, 2005.

Whitmarsh, Timothy. *The Second Sophistic*. Greece and Rome 35. New York: Oxford University Press, 2005.

Willett, Tom W. *Eschatology in the Theodicies of 2 Baruch and 4 Ezra*. JSPSup 4. Sheffield: JSOT, 1989.

Wintermute, O. S. "Jubilees." Pages 36–142 in vol. 2 of *Old Testament Pseudepigrapha*. Ed. James H. Charlesworth. 2 vols. New York: Doubleday, 1985.

Wise, Jennifer. *Dionysius Writes: The Invention of Theatre in Ancient Greece*. Ithaca: Cornell University, 1998.

Wisse, Jacob. *Ethos and Pathos: From Aristotle to Cicero*. Amsterdam: Adolf M. Hakkert, 1989.

Witherington III, Ben. *Revelation*. NCBC. Cambridge: Cambridge University, 2003.

Witulski, Thomas. *Die Johannesoffenbarung und Kaiser Hadrian: Studien zur Datierung der neutestamentlichen Apokalypse*. Göttingen: Vandenhoeck & Ruprecht, 2007.

Wright, Jacob C. "Warfare and Wanton Destruction: A Reexamination of Deuteronomy 20:19–20 in Relation to Ancient Siegcraft." *JBL* 127.3 (2008): 423–458.

Zeitlin, Solomon. *The Second Book of Maccabees*. JAL. Trans. S. Tedesche. New York: Harper, 1954.

Index of Ancient Sources

A. Hebrew Scriptures and Septuagint

B. New Testament

C. Josephus

D. Early Jewish Literature

E. Patristic Sources

F. Other Greek and Latin Literary Sources

Index of Modern Authors

Index of Subjects

Select Greek Words and Phrases